SHIPS
VERSUS
SHORE

Civil War Engagements along Southern Shores and Rivers

T0371381

SHIPS
VERSUS
SHORE

Civil War Engagements along
Southern Shores and Rivers

DAVE PAGE

Rutledge Hill Press
Nashville, Tennessee

Published by Rutledge Hill Press, a Thomas Nelson Company, P. O. Box 141000, Nashville, Tennessee 37214.

Typography by D&T/Bailey Typesetting Inc., Nashville, Tennessee. Design by Harriette Bateman.

Library of Congress Cataloging-in-Publication Data

Page, Dave, 1954–
    Ships versus shore : Civil War engagements along southern shores and rivers / Dave Page.
      p. cm.
    Includes bibliographical references and index.
    ISBN 1-55853-892-5 (pbk)
    1. United States—History—Civil War, 1861–1865—Naval operations. I. Title.
    E591.P25 1994
    973.7'5—dc20
                                                   94-15005
                                                          CIP

Printed in the United States of America

To my folks

Contents

Preface

When I was a young boy, my parents took me, my brother, and my sister to see the Castillo de San Marcos in Saint Augustine, Florida. From that day on I have harbored a passion for fortifications. Every chance I get, I venture to the masonry forts, presidios, replicas of stockades, earthworks, or historical plaques just *marking* their former locations. I collect literature and snap pictures. Over the past decade I have wanted to shape my research into a book, but I was not sure how to make everything fit.

Eventually I decided to focus on the Civil War and on the reason most of the forts in the South were built: to protect some port or river from incursion by enemy ships or ship-borne troops. To give the reader an idea how successful these defenses were, I decided to provide some historical background. In case my readers wanted to follow my footsteps, I undertook to combine this historical perspective with travel tips.

Although I have tried my best to include every site around which a ship-to-shore confrontation took place during the Civil War, there is no doubt I overlooked many skirmishes and missed some sites on my various trips.

Regarding the historical information, my particular approach was to read as much about an engagement by as many authors as I could find, then synthesize the material into what seemed to me an accurate and balanced portrait. I understand that some scholars cited are more careful than others when it comes to research. In any event, I have made an effort to reveal my sources and explain discrepancies. Even so, the danger of being seduced by a lost-cause mentality is great. In writing about the Northern technological juggernaut crushing Southern defenders, I found myself sympathizing with the underdog on several occasions—not because I agree with the Confederacy in principle but for the same reason I rooted for the Trojans against the Greeks even though Paris's abduction of Helen cannot be rationalized. Sometimes it is nice to see the little guys win even if they have questionable motives and you already know the outcome. Although I tried to avoid bias, I am sure one develops from time to time.

Regarding the travel information, phone numbers change, names change, hours change, places close, and prices rise. That's about as clear a warning as I can give.

By doing a state-by-state guide, I think I have created a unique approach to understanding amphibious operations during the Civil War and, in retrospect, the war as a whole. This method of organization obviously sacrifices historical continuity. Still, I hope the context of the local engagements in the broader strategy of the war is evident. Also, because each section is meant to stand on its own, there are times when some repetition of background information is necessary. I hope I have managed to keep such echoes to a minimum.

Finally, it would be impossible to thank everyone who answered a question or did me a favor during the five years I've been working on this project, so a general, heartfelt thank you will have to suffice. Specifically, I would like to thank Inver Hills Community College for technical and emotional support. Thanks also to Sharon Kjellberg for directing me to most of the sites mentioned in the book without getting me lost more than just a few times.

Introduction

Writing specifically about Ulysses Grant's all-important campaigns in central Tennessee during early 1862 but casting a wider net, historian Benjamin Cooling suggested that the "flow of the inland river . . . provides a theme for the understanding of this chapter in American history."[1] Cooling's vision may seem too restrictive to apply to the entire four years of the Civil War. Upon closer examination, however, the eventual control of the water routes in and around the Southern states by Federal squadrons brought about the failure of the South's struggle for autonomy as much as, and probably more than, any other strategic event.

The movement of goods along the nation's waterways to and from America's hinterland held immense importance during the Civil War, especially below the Mason-Dixon Line. The South possessed few railroads; paved or macadam byways were nonexistent. Even Richmond had cobblestones only in its business district.[2] The lifeblood of the Confederacy, literally and figuratively, streamed through its system of inland rivers and intracoastal passageways. Cut those arteries and the South would die, a slow death perhaps (as it turned out), but an inevitable one.

In this respect, Union General in Chief Winfield Scott understood how to win a relatively bloodless war. His Anaconda Plan, named for the South American snake that crushes its prey, was designed to strangle the Southern states by blockading their ocean ports and controlling the navigable channels of the vital Mississippi Valley. As early as May 1861 Scott defended the advantages of this approach by stating the obvious: "the transportation of men and supplies by water is about a fifth of the land cost, besides the immense saving of time."[3] Additionally, suffocating the Southern states by such means "could bring them to terms with less bloodshed than by any other plan."[4] Many Northerners lusted for quick retribution, however, and Scott realized that the "impatience of our patri-otic and loyal Union friends"[5] would not allow enough time for his rela-tively undramatic policy to run its course. Only a drive on Richmond—costly both in terms of men and materiel—would satisfy that portion of the Northern population incensed at the traitorous secession-ists. Southerners countered by putting up a struggle around their capital worthy of Hector—valiant but doomed. Rather than providing a quick fix for either side, this myopic focus on Virginia guaranteed a long and ruinous war. With their eyes only on one prize, strategists on both sides failed to foresee the significant role riverine and blue-water naval forces could (and eventually did) play in the coming struggle.

Hampered by the added pressures of forming a new government, Confederate officials appeared to have many more economic and political hurdles to overcome in order to put together a naval strategy. High on the list of limitations under which incoming Southern bureaucrats worked were problems of infrastructure. Throughout their thirty-five hundred miles of combined coastlines, Southern states boasted 180 harbors and navigable inlets,[6] but only about a dozen seaports had railroad service to the interior. Of greater significance, just six ocean ports possessed inter-state rail connections. Furthermore, only Norfolk could handle deep-draft (more than twenty feet) ships.

An even greater hindrance to the South was its lack of facilities for building and repairing warships. There were only three shipyards in the Confederacy at the beginning of the war: Norfolk, the Pensacola repair yard, and private shipbuilding facilities in New Orleans. Given these restrictions alone, even had the South desired to take an offensive naval posture, it lacked the resources to construct a fleet to counter the North's deep-water threat that could—and did—keep Southern land forces away from almost all areas warships could reach.[7] For all practical purposes, this meant every industrial center in the North was off-limits to Rebel pene-tration.

The Richmond government's weak fiscal condition, a reflection of the South's limited industrial base, prevented a quick fix for infrastructure problems even if time were available. The worldwide market for cotton was too soft to support a substantial war effort, but Confederate leaders kept hoping for the best.[8] In some cases, their schemes took on almost comical proportions. Confederate Vice President Alexander H. Stephens, for instance, proposed issuing $100 million in government bonds to pay for several million bales of cotton and fifty ironclad steamers. The ships could safely transport the cotton to Europe, where it would be sold once the price rose to fifty cents a bale, providing a tidy profit of $800 million. Gen. Joseph E. Johnston, for one, thought it a good plan.[9] Although there sim-ply was not that much cotton available for sale or that many ironclads waiting to be purchased, had the Confederate government pursued a more vigorous export policy, its purse might not have been so empty. But the very notion of a centralized policy for anything, from conducting rail transportation to selling cotton, was anathema to Southern states revolting against just that type of central government interference in their internal affairs.[10] Trying to remain solvent without raising taxes, Confederate leaders printed more money and paved the way for almost triple-digit inflation. Attempts by government agents to purchase supplies at less-than-inflated prices caused merchants to withhold goods and concentrate on importing luxuries for vast profits rather than necessities for the war effort.

Considering all that he was up against, Confederate Secretary of the Navy Stephen Mallory did a remarkable job.[11] The former U.S. congressman from Florida had been chairman of the Senate Naval Affairs Committee and, therefore, understood the requirements of his new job. In his favor, approximately 125 captains, commanders, and lieutenants resigned from the Union navy to join the Confederacy. The problem was there were not enough vessels to go around since officers going south "relinquished their ships, an act they considered honorable and for which they have never been given proper credit."[12] If Confederate forts occasionally held off Federal naval attacks, much of the credit can be given to Rebel naval officers who had no other option than to direct land batteries. This is not to say it was always easy to find crews for the available warships. An abundance of brass did not mean a supply of ordinary seamen. Unlike New England, for instance, most Southern states did not have a naval tradition. Officers in charge of ironclads knocked together in the bayous of the lower-Mississippi often found themselves collecting crews any way they could.

Despite his best efforts, Mallory failed to give the Confederacy what it really needed: protection from Union blue- and brown-water naval threats. Through the use of ironclads, Mallory hoped to overcome a disparity in numbers, but the obstacles arrayed against him were too great.[13] A major hindrance was Confederate President Jefferson Davis. A West Point graduate, Davis saw the navy as a mere auxiliary for the army and assumed the war would be won on land.[14]

Even after agreeing with Davis and other Confederate leaders that "the Rebels should have concentrated in the Old Dominion to make there the supreme effort to achieve their independence,"[15] historian Richard McMurry later admitted, "the really decisive area—the theater where the outcome of the war was decided—was the West. The great Virginia battles and campaigns on which historians have lavished so much time and attention had, in fact, almost no influence on the outcome of the war. They led, at most, to a stalemate while the western armies fought the war of secession to an issue."[16]

Stephen Mallory

How did the North win the war in the West? By eventually adopting a strategy remarkably like Scott's: controlling the vital inland rivers while at the same time attempting to put the squeeze on Southern ports. "Naval operations, *especially on the western rivers,* contributed directly and greatly to the destruction of Confederate military power" (emphasis added).[17] Specifically, McMurry noted, "The Mississippi, the Cumberland, and especially the Tennessee were mighty streams that were dominated by Yankee gunboats from early in the war. They provided the Northerners with safe, convenient avenues to move easily and quickly deep into the geographical heartland of the Confederacy."[18] As indispensable as railways were, an earlier historian similarly concluded that they were "far inferior to rivers in respect of security. Aided by gunboats, the Federal armies could advance to any distance along the banks of a navigable river, obtaining their supplies with promptness and regularity."[19] Whatever advantages the South may have held by moving men and materiel along interior lines to threatened sectors, once the "Yankees controlled many of the important western rivers, there were no interior lines in the West for the Confederates to use."[20]

Given the economic and political problems in the South and the material wealth of the North, several students of the Civil War, such as historian Richard Current, have pointed out that the real question is not why the South lost, but how it managed to hold on for so long.[21] Part of an answer lies in the North's poor utilization of its overwhelming naval advantages.

To be fair, the U.S. Navy in the 1850s was a peacetime navy, doing a fine job of protecting Americans abroad, conveying scientists and diplomats on important journeys, and opening trade to distant places. This is not meant to suggest the sea dogs were lax—far from it. The "Navy's record for twenty years before 1861 shows that it was active, progressive and possessed of much initiative."[22] Still, it was basically a deep-water navy, ill-trained and unprepared for inland fighting.[23] Southern legislators, perhaps prescient, made sure of that. For five years beginning in 1854, thirty new ships were added to the fleet. Deep South senators insisted that the draft of these new ships, which included the *Hartford* and *Merrimack,* was too great to enter Southern harbors before they voted to approve them.[24]

By 1861, there were ninety ships on the navy's list, but only forty-two were in commission. Of those, twenty-seven were on foreign station. President Franklin Buchanan's secretary of the navy, Isaac Toucey of Connecticut, did not call them home as the crisis brewed. Had he done so, they might have prevented the Confederates from erecting or strengthening fortifications at important ports, undoubtedly shortening the war.

Once the conflict began in earnest, the misinformed and parochial views of the Federal Naval Advisory Committee—created to help provide an overall naval strategy—restricted the navy's mission. Initially, the board failed to recognize that the balance of power had shifted to the offense in ship-versus-shore confrontations. In 1855, during the Crimean War, the French had attacked the Russians at Fort Kinburn near the mouth of the Dnieper River with three crude ironclad floating batteries. The rafts squared off only eight hundred yards from shore and demolished the fort. They sustained no fatal damage despite being hit at least two hundred times. With steam power, ship captains could deliver a decisive barrage at any point they chose. In the estimation of historian William Trotter, "The strategic prospects for employing this newly expanded naval force were striking. Fortunately for the Confederacy, they were but dimly and erratically perceived at the highest levels of the Federal command."[25]

Even after a few early successes (notably at Cape Hatteras, North Carolina, and Port Royal, South Carolina), the recommendations of committee members remained "dominated by initiating, maintaining and strengthening the blockade."[26] Although several advisers warned Lincoln that his insistence upon a blockade could be regarded as a de facto recognition of the Confederate States of America, Lincoln's view prevailed and every effort was made to put some punch behind the paper blockade. Ironically, the technological advance of steam power that enabled Federal ships to subdue Confederate shore defenses worked against the blockader for at least two reasons. Underway blockade runners could run past a line of blockading ships before the latter could raise steam and anchors.[27] Even more serious, patrol ships were bound by short leashes to coaling ports. "By 1863 the four [Federal] squadrons required more than 3,000 tons of anthracite coal a week."[28]

Quite soon the advantages of seizing Southern ports over blockading them became apparent, but even then the committee did not recommend exploitation of enclaves established by naval landings. Board members felt any inland movements would have required army cooperation and were, therefore, out of their jurisdiction.[29] Consequently, the "North failed to take full advantage of the great strategic assets"[30] it possessed for attacking where and when its commanders desired. In other words, the "failure to have a sizable effective Marine Corps to send in conjunction with fleet operations reduced considerably the effectiveness of the Navy and may have lengthened the war."[31]

If success in the western theater provided the impetus for the North's eventual victory, I hope to show in the following chapters that the flotillas of the gulf and inland waters deserve much of the credit for making those successes possible. Fleet commanders such as Andrew Hull Foote, David Glasgow Farragut, and David Dixon Porter persevered despite handicaps in the command system (initially the brown-water fleet reported to the Army Department) and limitations in the availability and design of fighting ships. The combination of the army's Grant and the navy's Porter in the West had no comparable team in the East. "Along the saltwater coasts," the authors of *Why the South Lost the Civil War* noted, "cooperation was minimal; the army typically proved less than enthusiastic."[32] Eventually, Grant headed east to assume overall command of the war effort and personally oversee the activities of the most prestigious fighting force, the Army of the Potomac. Foote would travel east, too, but would succumb to injuries before taking command of the impressive squadron off Charleston. Secretary of the Navy Gideon Welles next tried to force Farragut to assume command of the North Atlantic Blockading Squadron, but the hero of Mobile Bay excused himself on account of his health. Porter was then given command.

One man in the South with some insight into the potential threat posed by the Federal navy was Robert E. Lee. Even before Union gunboats helped decimate his attacks at Malvern Hill during the seven days' campaign, Lee understood the potency and mobility of Northern sea power. Sent by Davis in the summer of 1861 to organize coastal defenses in Florida, Georgia, and South Carolina, Lee—although erroneously assuming fixed batteries could counter a landing—wisely chose not to defend coastal areas outside the range of guns in fortified positions. His plan was to draw Federal troops away from the protection of their supporting ships and use mobile forces to destroy them far from their base of supplies.[33]

Gideon Welles

Lee continued to utilize a similar strategy after his appointment to command the Army of Northern Virginia. All the battles of importance during the next two years fell west of a line from the falls on the Potomac above Washington, D.C., to Drewry's Bluff on the James River below Richmond—a line over which Union gunboats could not easily pass. "Lee's military genius, with help from the geography of Virginia, gave Southern political leaders two years in which to save something for the Confederacy"; in fact, during the Gettysburg campaign "had he reached the Susquehanna and Delaware Rivers he would have cut the entire supply of anthracite coal to the Union Navy whose blockading squadron required over a thousand tons a day."[34] Lee tried to hold the right while attempting to force the issue on his left one last time in 1864. He sent Jubal Early with the remnants of Stonewall Jackson's Second Corps to push up the Shenandoah Valley "to relieve the pressure which sea power again was putting on his right"[35] at City Point on the James River. But Grant was able to send his Sixth Corps by water overnight to counter the threat to Washington by Early's footsore foot soldiers.

Although it did not prevail in the long run, an "adherence to the place-oriented strategy of [French general and military critic] Antoine Henri Jomini"[36] pretty much describes the shoreline defenses used by the South throughout most of the war. Except for a few ocean raiders—which did a great job chasing Federal transports from the high seas but drew very few blockading ships from their stations—the Confederacy tended to rely on coastal and riverbank fortifications. These were bolstered where possible by armored floating batteries, rather than large mobile reserves, to guard vital waterborne supply lines.[37]

Not everyone in the South accepted such a strategy. Capt. William Nugent, writing his wife from Mobile during the summer of 1863, complained: "Our force added to Bragg's would enable [us] to whip the Army of the Cumberland, and this would accomplish more for our cause than the retention of Mobile. Jeff. Davis, tho', I fear will continue his old policy of endeavoring to hold fortified places and seabord [sic] cities to the great detriment of our cause. We need *concentration*. Charleston ought to have been left to take care of itself and Beauregard should have been sent to Lee's assistance. Johnston ought to have sent all possible reinforcements to Bragg and beat the life out of [Grant] while Grant was driving away at V.Burg; why it is our Generals can't see through a campaign I cannot discover."[38]

As the ship-versus-shore duels developed, they usually followed a set pattern: Union ships, sometimes supported by land forces, slugged it out at close range with Confederate forts, occasionally supported by naval forces and mobile reserves. As often as not, the reserves played no role in the subsequent contests, especially when led by officers who feared Union naval supremacy.

The shoreline defenses faced by the Federal navy during the Civil War varied from last-minute emplacements constructed of whatever was available to state-of-the-art masonry fortifications. The development of these permanent harbor defenses in the United States began in a haphazard fashion. Attempts to guard ports had previously been made only under the immediate threat of war, first during the American Revolution (called first-system fortifications) and then the War of 1812 (called second-system fortifications). The ease with which the invading British army had torched Washington, D.C., clearly indicated the weakness of America's coastal defenses. The public's traditional fear of a large standing army, however, led military planners to conclude that the United States needed an economical defense system, not "in the dollar sense, but rather in terms of personnel requirements."[39]

Although during America's earlier wars dirt-and-log breastworks had served as the primary port defenses, these were constantly subjected to the erosive actions of storms and waves and required significant numbers of workers to maintain them. Consequently, given the lessons learned at Fort McHenry during the War of 1812, a special board of officers was organized in 1816 and headed by French military engineer Simon Bernard to create a permanent and genuine system of coast defenses. These fixed defenses, called the third system, would require small garrisons in times of *both* war and peace. Furthermore, they were patently inoffensive in nature and would not offend Europe as much as a large navy.[40]

As a member of the Bernard Board, Bvt. Lt. Col. Joseph G. Totten worked to make America's fortifications second to none by refining the protected casemate, a covered enclosure for guns. According to fortifications scholar Emanuel Lewis, "By utilizing certain embrasure configurations he succeeded in bringing the openings down to an area of less than ten square feet, one-fourth or one-fifth the size of those in many European forts as late as 1855. [Small embrasures meant smaller targets for ships.] Moreover, his design allowed guns to swivel laterally through sixty degrees while those in Europe were generally limited to about forty despite the greater dimensions of their embrasures."[41] Finally, Totten was the first to introduce several inches of iron plating to his embrasures, some of which had iron shutters that opened and closed with the firing of the cannon.

Although the board had been created to oversee construction of coastal defenses, by the 1820s it was extensively engaged in projects along the country's waterways in what was the national government's first efforts to upgrade harbors and rivers. The rationale behind the move was that the protection of the major ports ultimately depended on secure interior communication so troops and supplies could arrive unmolested in case of attack. "Greater trade, better transportation, and increased military defense were thus integral elements of a general plan for improving national security,"[42] observed transportation historian Forest Hill. Among the rivers receiving major expenditures were the Mississippi (below Saint Louis), Ohio, Red, Arkansas, Missouri, Cumberland, Hudson, Cape Fear, and Savannah. Five of these projects served only slave states, two passed through border states, and only one—the Hudson—ran exclusively through a free state.

Ironically, as secretary of war under Franklin Pierce, Jefferson Davis had helped ease the federal government out of the civil engineering business. He demanded that army engineers plan river and harbor works so as not to depend on later appropriations for completion or maintenance and refused to submit bids for works that he thought of little value. River and harbor bills passed the legislature very infrequently from then until the Civil War, and those projects already completed were transferred to the control of the Topographical Bureau. The Bernard Board returned to the business of building forts.

Millions of dollars and bricks after the board first met, several of the principal harbor defensive works planned by Bernard and his team stood complete or nearly so. Because only caretaker complements or construction crews manned most of the positions, it was usually not difficult for the militias of seceding states to seize these posts. Rather than collecting unconquerable defensive structures, however, Confederate officials found themselves burdened with masonry white elephants made obsolete by rifled cannon and steam-powered warships. Sand and soil quickly replaced brick and mortar as the preferred materials for defense. Earthworks absorbed punishment much better and could be repaired more quickly. As World War II general and historian Bernard Montgomery pointed out, the "spade and axe became necessary articles"[43] during the Civil War.

Since there were relatively few permanent forts on inland rivers and engineers on either side could not count on having years to complete defensive positions, almost all the fortifications the Federal brown-water navy confronted consisted of earthworks, occasionally fronted by wood or railroad iron. Some withstood tremendous punishment; others were surrendered without much of a fight. As always, leadership and the determination of the men involved played roles as important to the outcome of any ship-versus-shore confrontation as the thickness of the walls and the number of guns.

The American Civil War is rightly considered one of the first modern wars, but more often than not, military engineers on both sides borrowed existing technologies or relied on old systems. Trenches around Atlanta and Petersburg provided vivid glimpses into the future horrors of World War I, but with few exceptions land engagements during the Civil War mimicked the Napoleonic principles of massed concentrations of troops that gave victory to the side with the heaviest battalions. Rifled artillery, heavy mortars, repeating rifles, and Gatling guns almost changed that philosophy by the end of the war; nevertheless, in most battles—right up until the spring of 1865—distances between combatants were often measured in inches.

It was on the oceans and rivers that the industrial age really had a tremendous impact. Plans for self-propelled vessels armed with iron date back at least to the eighteenth century, but none of the major powers were ready to promote their use until France launched *La Gloire* in 1859; Britain followed suit with HMS *Warrior* the following year. These were true ironclads in the sense that iron plate had been mounted on the hulls of traditional sailing vessels. With the launch of the USS *Monitor* in 1862, a revolutionary advance took place in warship construction. The revolving armored turret as the centerpiece of fighting vessels lasted until the development of aircraft carriers and missiles.

The introduction of iron-sheathed vessels brought a change in the role of seamen. Aboard Federal and Confederate ironclads, men were confined to not much more than iron boxes. In the lightless confines of these floating coffins, crew members easily became disoriented. To alleviate the problem partially, the *Monitor*'s officers painted white lines inside the turret so their tars could tell port from starboard. In the engine rooms, conditions were even worse. The "black gang" could respond to orders but knew virtually nothing about what was happening topside. Temperatures ranged up to 120 degrees, steam hissed, and the occasional thud of solid shot ricocheting off iron plates mixed with the clank of ventilators, turret machinery, and propeller shafts. From the Civil War forward, sailors "would be more and more cogs in an industrial machine gone to sea," concluded historian William Fowler Jr.[44] The successful sinking of Union and Confederate warships by underwater mines, torpedo boats, and a submarine are further examples of technological achievements in naval warfare during the Civil War.

Not every naval undertaking could be considered revolutionary, however. On the western rivers, for instance, the first gunboats were converted freight-passenger steamers to which oak bulwarks five inches thick were added. These timberclads provided protection against musket balls but little else. Other conversions included a thin layer of iron, perhaps a quarter-inch thick, and were called tinclads. Bales of cotton were sometimes piled around a ship's deck, giving rise to the term cottonclad. Not all boats on the western rivers were conversions, however. The seven ironclad gunboats built by James B. Eads in late 1861 for the U.S. government were designed specifically for river fighting. These flat-bottomed boats presented two and a half inches of iron and twenty inches of oak to the enemy, yet drew only six feet of water.

There are two final observations about technology. While the Union navy under ordnance chief John Dahlgren operated primarily with large smoothbore guns, the Confederates—led by Dahlgren's counterpart, John M. Brooke—took the high-tech path to rifled guns.[45] Even as late as December 1865, Dahlgren wrote that "naval smoothbore ordnance will not be superseded by Rifles."[46] Ironically, the Union army placed its faith in rifled guns designed by Robert P. Parrott, president of the West Point Foundry. The Parrott guns proved their accuracy, particularly at Fort Pulaski in Georgia. Smoothbores, however, tended to burst less frequently and, with their greater initial velocity, packed a bigger punch at the shorter ranges expected in naval battles. Consequently, commanders of ships armed primarily with smoothbores had to risk closing with shoreline fortifications if they wanted to inflict as much damage as possible. As improvements in casting techniques, ballistics, and slower-burning explosive charges led to greater muzzle velocities, rifled guns became the standard.[47]

Another nineteenth-century ordnance development was the explosive shell. Had the Union navy been limited to attacking Southern ports with sailing ships only, explosive shells could easily have given the advantage in any engagements to the Confederates. However, steam power—frequently enhanced with armor—allowed attacking Federal vessels to bring a preponderance of ordnance to bear on most occasions.

Finally, before the Civil War, the highest rank in the U.S. Navy was that of captain. Squadron commanders were designated as flag officers and could fly personal pennants from their flagships. Unofficially they were called commodores. Several important naval officers in this book advanced to flag rank during the war. As much as possible, I tried to use the rank held during the particular campaign under discussion at the time.

As defense analyst Colin Gray has pointed out in *The Leverage of Sea Power*, the American Civil War, along with a few other conflicts such as the Crimean War, "registered epochal shifts in military-naval technology."[48] Superior forces at sea, Colin argued, has been the catalyst of victory in the great wars in history. In fact, with sea power serving as the great enabling agent in conflicts on land and water, no superior sea power has been defeated in any great military struggle of modern time. The American Civil War was no exception.

CHAPTER 1

VIRGINIA

NAT TURNER'S slave insurrection in Southampton County, Virginia, during the summer of 1831 led to "one of the most searching debates on slavery ever held by the elected representatives of a slaveholding people."[1] In the aftermath of the uprising, despite—or perhaps because of—the intense fear sweeping the entire South, more than half of Virginia's House of Delegates spoke out against slavery, even though three-quarters of the members held slaves. These were not just empty words. One historian concluded that 60 of the 134 delegates consistently worked to pass laws prohibiting slavery in the state. Another twelve, although antislavery in their attitudes, would not vote for emancipation for various reasons.[2]

Had those dozen key votes gone the other way, the history of the United States would have been greatly altered. As it was, three decades later the Virginia legislature called for a convention to decide if the commonwealth would join into a confederation with the seven slave states that had already left the Union. Mirroring the state's earlier position on slavery, her populace remained split on secession. Ironically, at the same time Virginia was preparing to vote on joining the Confederacy, her citizens were arranging a peace conference to forestall a permanent rupture in the Union. Three weeks of debate at the conference accomplished little of consequence, and the suggested modification to the Crittenden Compromise that emerged was defeated in the U.S. Congress.[3] Although conference delegates proved unable to find a compromise solution to the widening chasm between the North and the South, on 4 April 1861, voters in Virginia decided by a two-to-one margin to remain in the Union.

Pro-Union or not, with more than 1,047,000 residents (the largest population in the South) and an industrial capacity nearly as great as the entire Deep South combined, Virginia was viewed as an essential addition to the Confederate States by the delegates meeting in Montgomery, Alabama.

These secessionists did everything they could to woo their reluctant sister state. The Confederacy's new constitution, very similar to the U.S. Constitution, forbade the importation of slaves from abroad, partly as a concession to Great Britain but also as bait to the states of the upper South, whose economies benefited greatly from their monopoly on slave exports to the lower South. Furthermore, when rumors reached Montgomery that Virginia's prosecession senators—James Mason and Robert Hunter—favored Jefferson Davis for president, that was enough to get the moderate former secretary of war appointed to the new nation's highest office. Even Davis's eventual decision to fire on Fort Sumter may have been made with Virginia in mind. Louis Wigfall of Texas "urged a prompt attack on Sumter to bring that commonwealth [Virginia] into the fold."[4]

Wigfall proved to be correct in his assessment of the climate in Virginia. When news of Sumter's fall reached Richmond on 13 April, a jubilant procession marched on the state capitol where a battery fired a hundred-gun salute in honor of the victory. The crowd lowered the American flag from the capitol building and ran up the Confederate Stars and Bars. Everyone "seemed to be perfectly frantic with delight, I never in my life witnessed such excitement," wrote a participant. "Everyone is in favor of secession."[5]

Predictably, the governor of Virginia responded to Lincoln's 15 April call for troops to subdue the insurrection by stating he would send none. Two days later, former governor of Virginia Henry Wise, speaking before another secession convention, reported that Virginia militiamen were seizing the federal armory at Harpers Ferry and the Gosport Navy Yard near Norfolk. Drugged by the certainty of success, the convention passed an ordinance of secession by a vote of eighty-eight to fifty-five. Eager to cement its alliance with Virginia, the Confederate Congress voted on 21 May to accept Virginia's invitation to move its capital to Richmond.

A majority of the delegates voting against secession came from the - thirty-five counties west of the Shenandoah Valley and north of the Kanawha River. Containing one-fourth of the state's white population, western Virginia was home to few slave owners. Citing long-standing grievances against tidewater aristocrats, the voters in these counties decided to detach themselves from eastern Virginia. On 20 June 1863 West Virginia was admitted to the Union, thus making Virginia the only state to lose territory because of the Civil War.

That was not all Virginia lost. Around 60 percent of all military engagements during the Civil War were fought in Virginia,[6] some twenty-six major battles and more than four hundred skirmishes.[7] These confrontations destroyed large sections of northern Virginia and the Shenandoah Valley, not to mention the towns of Fredericksburg, Petersburg, Richmond, Norfolk, and hundreds of smaller hamlets. Eighteen Virginia generals added their names to the seventeen thousand sons of the Old Dominion who died from wounds or disease during the war.

This list of devastation and death was not foreseen in those first euphoric months of war when everyone on both sides felt the fighting would end quickly and gloriously. Once the first blush of patriotism faded and the months passed with no end in sight to the conflict, it did not take a scholar to realize that a mere 106 miles separated the capitals of the adversaries, and that those miles would be hotly contested. The Potomac River on Virginia's northern border could provide only a slight barrier to the Union, which had an extant—albeit small—navy. Virginia's eastern coast was just as vulnerable, and on 27 April 1861, Lincoln extended his proclaimed blockade to Virginia's shores.

Less than a month later, a regiment of Zouaves embarked aboard the makeshift Potomac Flotilla at the Washington Navy Yard and sailed across the river to Alexandria, the first landing of Northern troops on Virginia soil. The Confederates evacuated the city upon the demand of Stephen C. Rowan, commander of the *Pawnee*, a 1,533-ton screw-steamer armed with ten guns. The seizure of Alexandria exemplified the flotilla's major responsibility: neutralization of any Confederate attempts to interdict traffic on the Potomac. At Aquia Creek, Virginia, the terminus of a railroad to Richmond, the Rebels tried to do just that by emplacing cannon on the river. On 29 May, the Potomac Flotilla moved down the river from Washington, D.C., to engage these batteries. The operation was carried out "with no expectation . . . of any great success," according to Adm. David Porter, since it was not thought at the time that warships could defeat land batteries.[8] In two days of bombardment, however, the Federal navy convinced the defenders to abandon the position and withdraw their guns. The *Freeborn*, a paddle-wheel steamer of 250 tons, had to put up for repairs at the Washington Navy Yard, but there were no human casualties on the Federal side. It would take several more naval victories against shore emplacements before strategic thinking about such confrontations changed.

Through the summer and fall of 1861, Confederate batteries, including those reintroduced at Aquia Creek Landing, continued to shell shipping on the Potomac. The navy finally convinced Gen. George B. McClellan to cooperate in a joint venture on 30 September against Mathias Point, Virginia, to halt the harassment. On the appointed night, the supporting warships and landing barges waited at the rendezvous, but no troops appeared. Lincoln himself went to the general's headquarters for an explanation, and McClellan agreed to send 4,000 men the following night. Once again the navy was stood up. Asked why, McClellan said that he wished to avoid a major engagement. Ironically, his scheme for "destroying the Confederate batteries along the lower Potomac . . . involved . . . employing no fewer than 118,000 men."[9] The general in chief's lack of temerity allowed the

Confederates to close the Potomac to all but warships for much of the first year of the war.

With pressure building up for action, McClellan forwarded a plan to land a powerful invasion force at Urbanna, Virginia, near the mouth of the Rappahannock River, and rapidly march the fifty miles to Richmond before Gen. Joseph E. Johnston could reach the capital from his fortifications at Centreville and Manassas Junction. When Johnston pulled back to the Rappahannock, the young Napoleon was forced to switch landing sites. By the spring of 1862, just as McClellan had predicted, the Potomac River was fairly well cleared of Rebel batteries to Chesapeake Bay, as gray-clad troops withdrew to contest a Federal naval flanking maneuver toward the Virginia Peninsula. The last major stronghold on the Potomac, Cockpit Point, was captured in March 1862.

As tensions along the Potomac lessened, the flotilla expanded its area of operations into the Rappahannock and Piankatank rivers. Since moving up-river on the former took Federals away from Richmond and the latter was relatively small, neither received much attention. Washington's strategy for the two waterways involved blockade and naval patrols designed to hamper Rebel communications across and along the rivers. Naturally, Richmond hoped to confound these plans. As early as mid-June 1861, Maj. Gen. Robert E. Lee, commander in chief of the military forces of Virginia, reported that a four-gun battery had been erected to protect the Rappahannock. On 14 April 1862, several of the Potomac Flotilla's gunboats ascended the Rappahannock, easily destroying defensive batteries and capturing three vessels.

The next year on 21 February, the USS *Freeborn*, damaged during the Aquia Creek operation in 1861, was hit again while engaging a battery on the Rappahannock below Fort Lowry near the town of Tappahannock. The greatest single disaster to befall the flotilla, however, occurred in August 1863 when Confederate naval officer John Taylor Wood led a raiding party to the Piankatank and Rappahannock rivers. At the mouth of the latter on the night of 22 August, Wood's men captured the *Satellite* and *Reliance* in a ten-minute fight. The next day, after dropping off prisoners and wounded at Urbanna, he took the 217-ton *Satellite*, armed with a 32-pound smoothbore and a 12-pound howitzer, into Chesapeake Bay expecting to find the USS *Currituck*. Instead he chased the schooner *Golden Rod* nearly to the Piankatank where he overtook and captured the Union commercial vessel loaded with coal. On his way back to Urbanna, he seized two more schooners filled with anchors and chains worth $26,000.[10] Four days later, hounded by three gunboats from the sea and troops on land, Wood burned his prizes at Port Royal on the Rappahannock.

As the warring armies prepared for the final showdown in northern Virginia in the spring of 1864, the U.S. Navy supported Grant by destroying Rebel camps at Circus Point and Carter's Creek on the Rappahannock. As

Grant's army moved south of the James that summer, the Confederate forces returned to the Rappahannock, and in March 1865, Union warships were once again exchanging fire with field guns near Tappahannock and supporting troops intent on destroying Confederate bases in the area of Mattox Creek.

Although Lee's strategy of keeping his tatterdemalions out of the range of U.S. warships had succeeded for the most part in Virginia, he understood early in the struggle that Northern sea power could still play havoc in the waters of Hampton Roads, Virginia, and its tributaries.

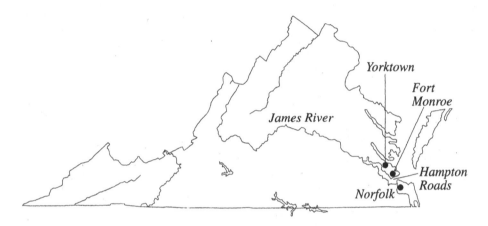

Hampton Roads and Its Tributaries

GIDEON WELLES, the bearded, bewigged former postmaster and newspaper editor, journeyed from Connecticut to Washington, D.C., after the 1860 election expecting to tackle the job of postmaster general. Instead, Lincoln appointed him secretary of the navy. It was not a position to inspire envy. By the time the new administration took over the reins of the failing republic, roughly 20 percent of the U.S. Navy's officers had submitted their resignations, only four active warships were stationed in home waters, and Virginia's Norfolk Navy Yard—the country's largest—was surrounded by a population of questionable loyalty.

Both Lincoln and his counterpart in Montgomery, Alabama, understood the risks and rewards associated with Norfolk. The navy yard, which stretched three-quarters of a mile along the west bank of the Elizabeth River opposite Norfolk at Gosport, contained the navy's largest reserve of guns. Many, if not most, were relics, but three hundred were the latest Dahlgren smoothbores, "fifty-two of them potent, heavy nine-inchers."[11] Like the guns, half of the men-of-war at Norfolk had long since passed their prime. Still, the nucleus of a threatening fleet rested at the yard: the forty-gun *Merrimack,* one of the strongest warships afloat in any navy and the first steam-engine, propeller-driven frigate in the world; the twenty-two-gun sloops *Germantown* and *Plymouth*; and the four-gun brig *Dolphin*. The USS *Cumberland*, a nineteen-year-old frigate with twenty-four guns, had also just arrived from Veracruz, Mexico. Across the river, a relatively new powder magazine with four-and-a-half-foot-thick walls sat within Fort Norfolk, a masonry-and-sod stronghold built a half-century earlier north of the city. A gun-carriage works existed to the southeast of Norfolk proper. The most tempting target, however, was the yard's recently completed granite dry dock. One of only two in the nation, it was stout enough to berth any vessel in the fleet. If the Confederacy hoped to service warships capable of confronting the U.S. Navy, seizing the dry dock intact would be a top priority.

With hindsight, it is easy to blame the North's eventual loss of the yard on its commandant, Charles S. McCauley. Although a staunch unionist, McCauley had seen not enough action and too much of the bottom of a bottle to be able to act with a firm hand in the developing crisis. To be fair, however, much of the responsibility for McCauley's vacillation at Norfolk lay with the Lincoln administration. Rather than risk offending the fence-sitting citizens of the Old Dominion by immediately reinforcing the two hundred or so sailors and marines at the yard, Lincoln chose to counsel caution. The president could have also replaced secessionist yard workers with Republicans loyal to the Union. The political nature of government jobs was such that a complete turnover with every new administration was not unusual. Instead, Lincoln ordered Welles to leave the nearly one thousand civilians employed at the yard. Furthermore, the powder magazine and carriage works were left completely unguarded in deference to the still-wavering Virginians.

As the crisis deepened, Robert Danby, the chief engineer at Norfolk, informed his superiors in Washington that losing the *Merrimack* was a distinct possibility if the laid-up warship was not made seaworthy soon. (After the ship's voyage to the Pacific in 1859, she had been sent to Norfolk for repair of her engines, "which had proved to be somewhat less than a qualified success."[12]) Danby's warning eventually crossed Welles's desk, and the secretary instructed McCauley to prepare the *Merrimack* for removal to Philadelphia, but without taking steps "to give needless alarm" to the locals.[13] As soon as McCauley made arrangements to remount the warship's guns, the citizens and press of Norfolk raised such a clamor that—heeding Welles's caveat—he halted the work. The navy secretary soon realized his mistake and dispatched Comdr. James Alden to Norfolk to make sure the frigate was ready and provisioned for sea. By the time Alden reported to McCauley, another of Lincoln's precautions had backfired: All the civilian yard workers had deserted.

The U.S. Navy's newly appointed engineer in chief, Benjamin Isherwood, arrived at Norfolk on 14 April, the day Federal troops evacuated

Fort Sumter. He and Alden suspected time was short but predicted they could have the *Merrimack*'s engines back in service within four days. One day early, the two exhausted officers asked McCauley for permission to fire the frigate's boilers. He told them to wait a day. The next morning, coal smoke belched from the *Merrimack*'s funnel. Only a skeleton crew was available, but these men could at least get the ship across Hampton Roads to Union-controlled Fort Monroe. As Alden occupied himself with last-minute details, McCauley inexplicably ordered Isherwood to shut down the frigate's boilers.[14] The stunned Alden would have been completely justified had he commandeered the warship and steamed away from Norfolk. Instead, he decided to board the Baltimore packet and leave for Washington, D.C.

Belatedly, Welles put the navy into high gear. He relieved McCauley and ordered Com. Samuel du Pont at Philadelphia to charter a fast steamer and pack it with men and guns bound for Norfolk. He also told Stephen Rowan, captain of the *Pawnee*, to march a hundred marines from the Washington Navy Yard onto his screw sloop for immediate departure. At Norfolk, Capt. John Marston loaded grapeshot into the *Cumberland*'s cannon to prevent any landward approach to the yard. In the meantime, informants told McCauley that secessionists were throwing up earthworks to command the Elizabeth River below Gosport. Lt. Thomas O. Selfridge Jr. of the *Cumberland* parlayed with newly arrived Maj. Gen. William Talliaferro, who had been sent by the Confederate government with orders to secure the navy yard. Selfridge told him that if work continued on the battery, the *Cumberland* would open fire on Norfolk. Outgunned, Talliaferro promised to halt construction, but he moved men into the unguarded Fort Norfolk and confiscated twenty-eight hundred barrels of powder, half of which he sent to Richmond and half of which he prudently moved out of range of Yankee cannon. ·

By Saturday evening, the *Pawnee*, with Com. Hiram Paulding on board, was threading through block ships on the Elizabeth River toward Gosport, her eight 9-inch guns cleared for action. When Paulding reached McCauley's office, the old commander of the Union forces in the area had one more surprise for his replacement: He had already begun the process of scuttling all the vessels but the *Cumberland*. Without divers, Paulding could not save the sinking warships, but with the men and cannon on board the *Cumberland* and *Pawnee*, he could easily have held Gosport until relieved. Instead, he ordered his men to torch the yard. For the dry dock, two thousand pounds of black powder were lowered into the pumping gallery. When Paulding gave the signal, the *Cumberland* and *Pawnee* set off toward Hampton Roads as a great conflagration swept through the yards. Everyone on board expected to hear a mighty roar, but the ton of powder in the dry dock did not explode.

One oft-repeated tale cites a Union petty officer's concern for the nearby homes of his friends. The man, so the story goes, simply cut the fuse.

A Confederate naval history credits a quick-thinking Rebel with opening the dock's gates, thus extinguishing any flames. Whatever the case, Talliaferro had his yard and McCauley soon retired. A senate committee brushed all the disgrace for the debacle out with him.

Several weeks after her sinking, the *Merrimack* lay in the Gosport dry dock awaiting its conversion to become the CSS *Virginia*. The 1,195 guns salvaged by the Confederates were quickly put to use around Hampton Roads at Sewell's Point and Craney Island. Ordnance from the yard would also find its way down the coast to Hatteras Inlet in North Carolina and up the coast to Gloucester Point on the York River. There on 8 May they fired at—appropriately—the USS *Yankee* under Selfridge's command. Railroads would carry the cannon to Forts Henry and Donelson in Tennessee; to Island Number 10, Memphis, Vicksburg, Grand Gulf, and Port Hudson on the Mississippi River; and even to Fort de Russy up the Red River in Louisiana.

As badly as things had gone for the Union at Hampton Roads, Lincoln and his generals still had an arrow pointed straight at the heart of the Confederacy: Fort Monroe at Old Point Comfort.[15] The hexagonal stronghold, the largest ever built in the United States, along with the partly constructed Rip Raps[16] commanded the shipping channel to Hampton Roads and, therefore, cut off the sea approach to five Virginia ports: Norfolk, Suffolk, Portsmouth, Petersburg, and Richmond. Within six weeks of Virginia's secession, the four-hundred-man garrison at Fort Monroe had increased to six thousand officers and men, effectively making the position invulnerable to attack from land as long as its sea supply lines remained secure.

During the same period, Confederates at Sewell's Point, a little over two and a half miles across the channel from Old Point Comfort, had been strengthening the batteries there. From this spot, the Rebels could observe everything in Hampton Roads and part of Chesapeake Bay. The Union navy did not like its activities monitored that closely. So on 18 May, Federal gunboats approached Sewell's Point to convince the defenders to abandon the position. In two consecutive days of action, fire from the shore batteries drove away the warships, a shaky start for the advocates of sea power. A little over a week later, the Sewell's Point batteries tried to disrupt Maj. Gen. Benjamin Butler's naval expedition to Newport News. All the shots fell short, however, and Col. John Wolcott Phelps was able to land on Point Breeze at the mouth of the James River and establish a battery of four 8-inch Columbiads, thus halting water communications between Richmond and Norfolk.

The next year brought one of the most celebrated battles of the Civil War: the sortie of the ironclad *Virginia*. As historic as the occasion was,

The burning of the Gosport Naval Yard and the frigate *Merrimack*

Confederate Secretary of the Navy Stephen Mallory envisioned even greater glory for the armored warship. As early as November 1861, the secretary had suggested that if the *Virginia* could clear the blockading fleet at Hampton Roads, it might steam up the Chesapeake and Potomac to Washington, D.C., where it could destroy the navy yard. On 7 March 1862, Mallory sent a confidential letter to Flag Off. Franklin Buchanan, the *Virginia*'s commander, outlining an even more ambitious project. "I submit for your consideration the attack of New York," he wrote. In a smooth sea, Mallory proposed, the *Virginia* could make the passage and destroy the Brooklyn Navy Yard and its magazines. "Such an event, by a single ship, would do more to achieve our immediate independence than would the results of many campaigns."[17]

Buchanan had little time to entertain such fantasies. He was more worried about getting enough powder for his guns. He had also contacted Confederate Gen. John B. Magruder earlier in the year to see if the Rebel army on the peninsula could move on Newport News in conjunction with the *Virginia*. At first Magruder had agreed to a joint operation, but by late February he had changed his mind.

Finally on 8 March at 11:00 A.M., the hope of the Confederacy slipped her moorings and steamed away from the Gosport Navy Yard. On board, only Buchanan and his executive, Lt. Thomas Catesby ap R. Jones,[18] knew this was not a trial run.

Like a giant sea slug, the *Virginia* crept down the Elizabeth at eight knots and slid into Hampton Roads around noon. The small steamers CSS *Raleigh* and *Beaufort* accompanied her, trying their best to keep to the ram's port side for as much protection from Federal batteries as possible. Off Newport News, Lt. George Morris, executive officer of the USS *Cumberland*, ordered the frigate cleared for action when lookouts sighted smoke across the Roads.

Morris ordered the tug USS *Zouave* toward the Confederate batteries at Pig Point, near the mouth of the Nansemond River, to scout the opposition. Acting Master Henry Reaney made out a Confederate flag and fired his forward gun, a 30-pounder Parrott rifle. After sending five more rounds toward the oncoming ram, Reaney broke off to assist the *Cumberland*.

Buchanan did not answer the *Zouave*, nor did he respond to the batteries at Newport News nor the guns aboard the *Cumberland* and *Congress*. Finally, within easy range of the *Cumberland*, Buchanan directed Lt. Charles Simms to fire the ram's forward Brooke 7-inch rifle. The shell hit the *Cumberland* squarely, wounding some marines. A second shot from Simms's Brooke destroyed one of the frigate's forward guns.

At this point, the *Virginia* was steaming abreast of the *Congress*, whose broadside merely bounced off the ironclad's armor. When the order to retaliate was given, the four guns of the *Virginia*'s starboard broadside—three 9-inch Dahlgren smoothbores and a 6.4-inch rifled Brooke—blasted glowing shot at the *Congress*. Every crew member of gun number 7 aboard the Union warship was either killed or wounded. The hot shot also started two fires, one near the after magazine.

Buchanan ordered his helmsman to ram the enemy ship. The *Virginia*'s two-foot, cast-iron ram stabbed deep into the *Cumberland*. At the same instant, Simms sent another round into the mortally wounded frigate.

As Buchanan had feared earlier, the Union ship immediately listed toward its predator, jamming the *Virginia*'s prow and forcing the ironclad down by the bow. The Confederate ship's engines struggled but could not pull free. The current pushed the ironclad around until it was almost parallel with the *Cumberland*. Then, as the doomed Union ship's gun crews loosed round after round at point-blank range, a wave lifted the two ships, snapping the ironclad's ram and allowing Buchanan to back out. "Like the wasp," Ramsey would write later, "we could sting but once, leaving the sting in the wound."[19] With a loss of 121 men, the *Cumberland* settled upright in fifty-four feet of water, her ensign flying from the top of one of her masts.

As the battle was progressing, the ships of the Confederate James River Fleet arrived. After taking fire from the Federal batteries at Newport News, the CSS *Jamestown* and *Patrick Henry* had gone after the USS *Minnesota*, which had grounded farther down the Roads as she and two other Union frigates had tried to come to the aid of the *Cumberland.* From Sewell's Point, the Confederate batteries added their fire. The batteries at Fort Wool (Rip Raps) retaliated against Sewell's Point.

After dealing with the *Cumberland,* the *Virginia* took a half-hour to turn and stalk the *Congress.* (Aboard was Buchanan's brother McKean, a paymaster in the U.S. Navy.) Within another hour, the Federal ship's captain, Joseph B. Smith, was dead and no guns remained operational. Lieutenant Pendergast took command and raised a white flag. Flag Officer Buchanan ordered signals hoisted to call the *Beaufort* and *Raleigh* to accept the surrender. Confederate Captain Parker was in the process of transferring the wounded to his ship when troops ashore under Gen. K. F. Mansfield, whose headquarters had been smashed by a shell from the *Virginia,* began to shoot at the *Beaufort.* "I know the damned ship has surrendered," Mansfield howled at one captain who questioned his ethics, "but *we* haven't."[20]

Buchanan, who stood exposed in an open hatch, felt a sting as a ball fired from shore went deep into his right thigh. "Plug shot into her [the *Congress*]," Buchanan demanded as he was carried to his cabin, "and don't leave her until she's afire. They must look after their own wounded, since they won't let us."[21] The *Virginia* moved closer to the stricken *Congress* after a crew from the Confederate tug *Teaser* failed to set the frigate on fire. Several red-hot projectiles from the ironclad did the job. The Union ship continued to burn until 2:00 A.M., when she exploded.

Accepting command from the incapacitated Buchanan, Lieutenant Catesby ap R. Jones swung the *Virginia* toward the grounded *Minnesota.* The CSS *Patrick Henry* had been forced to break off its attack when it was damaged by a shell from the *Minnesota*'s 10-inch pivot gun. Disappointingly for the Southerners, the ironclad could get no closer than a mile to the U.S. warship, too far for effective fire. With the tide ebbing, the *Virginia* set off a parting shot and steamed to the protection of the guns at Sewell's Point.

There was no doubt the Confederate navy had won a profound victory. During the five-hour battle, two Union ships had sunk and another had been damaged. Three hundred sailors had lost their lives; another hundred had been wounded. Confederate casualties amounted to fewer than sixty killed and wounded.

The next morning, Lieutenant Catesby ap R. Jones figured to finish off the *Minnesota* and then perhaps bombard some of the shore installations. When the *Virginia* approached the grounded frigate, however, the Federal ironclad *Monitor* intervened. Having expected to fight wooden-hulled vessels, the *Virginia* carried only explosive shells, grape canisters, and smaller balls for hot-shot use. The 68-pound conical, explosive shells of the Brookes were the only ones aboard that could threaten to damage the *Monitor*'s armor plate. The 168-pound solid shot fired by the *Monitor,* however, might have been

The *Virginia* ramming the *Cumberland*

able to destroy the *Virginia,* but Capt. John A. Dahlgren, chief of ordnance, prohibited the gun crews from using more than fifteen pounds of propellant. As the confrontation developed, then, the two iron beasts flailed at each other hoping for a lucky shot.

After two hours the *Monitor* had to break off to replenish her ammunition, an act that required the turret to be precisely aligned with holes in the deck. Seeing the Union ironclad withdraw, Capt. Gershom Van Brunt prepared to scuttle the *Minnesota.* Jones tried to get the *Virginia* closer to the *Minnesota* during this break in the fighting, but the ironclad grounded. Just as the *Monitor* began to approach again, the *Virginia* pulled herself out of the mud. Jones prepared to ram the Union ship but changed his mind at the last minute and ordered the engines reversed. The half-blow on the *Monitor*'s starboard beam knocked down most of its crew but caused no damage. As Jones had feared, the *Virginia* sprung a leak in her prow. Now it was the *Monitor*'s turn. Steering problems caused her to miss the Rebel ram's unprotected stern by a few feet. As she passed, Confederate Lt. John Taylor Wood, gun captain of the stern 7-inch Brooke, fractured a part of the *Monitor*'s observation slit in the turret with a shot at thirty yards.[22] Another shot struck the pilothouse and blinded Capt. John Worden. Helmsman Peter

Williams instinctively turned the Union ironclad away from the Confederate ship. Again, Jones thought to close on the *Minnesota,* but with the tide falling, he opted to steam back to Sewell's Point and renew the fight in the afternoon. As the ship neared the Elizabeth River channel, the *Virginia*'s other officers convinced Jones to put in at Gosport for repairs.[23] With replacements for damaged guns and a new ram, they could surely defeat the Federal ironclad.

The long dominance of wooden warships had ended with a bang.

When it became known that the *Virginia* was in dry dock at Norfolk Navy Yard, the Army of the Potomac began to land at Fort Monroe. By 1 April, close to a hundred thousand men had encamped at the tip of the Virginia Peninsula. To thwart any Federal advance, Confederate Gen. John B. Magruder had established three defense lines. The first ran from the mouth of Deep Creek to the Poquoson River. The second, ten miles farther north, extended from Fort Crafford on Mulberry Island on the James River up the Warwick River to Lee's Mill and on to Yorktown, whose Revolutionary War fortifications had been expanded. Redoubts along the James River at Jamestown anchored the right flank of the third line, which then ran to Fort Magruder below Williamsburg and along Queen's Creek to the York River. Before the first week of April was over, Magruder had retreated to his second line, his "real line of defense."[24]

McClellan hoped that the navy would flank Magruder by passing up the York River between the batteries at Yorktown and those across the river

The engagement between the *Monitor* and the *Virginia*

at Gloucester Point. Commodore Goldsborough, however, sent only a few light gunboats, stating that his primary duty was to contain the *Virginia.* The Confederate ram made an appearance on 11 April, but Flag Off. Joseph Tattnall, the ironclad's new commander, was not looking for a challenge.[25] Refusing to enter the confining and heavily protected waters of the channel leading to Hampton Roads, Tattnall managed to capture three transports in the Roads within view of the *Monitor,* which stood between Fort Monroe and Rip Raps. Five days later, Confederate troops, entrenched behind the swollen Warwick River, threw back the advancing Army of the Potomac at the battle of Lee's Mill (Dam Number 1). By this time, around fifty-six thousand Rebel reinforcements had arrived under the command of Gen. Joseph E. Johnston, who complained that Magruder's line could not withstand a sustained artillery pounding. As the Federal commander settled in for a siege, Johnston wired Richmond, "No one but McClellan could have hesitated to attack."[26] But even McClellan, Johnston realized, would eventually take advantage of Northern sea power to turn the Yorktown position.[27] The Confederate commander had no way of knowing that Goldsborough was not cooperating fully.

The Union naval commander had his own agenda and refused to detach his large vessels to support McClellan. Finally, Capt. J. F. Missroon was given a squadron of four gunboats and ordered to coordinate with the army. His reputation as an aggressive officer notwithstanding, Missroon refused to test the Yorktown and Gloucester batteries. Even as more ships arrived, Missroon continued to claim he would be outgunned against the shore fortifications. His predictions seemed borne out at mid-month when the *Sebago*—a side-wheel steamer armed with one 100-pounder rifle, one 9-inch smoothbore, and four 24-pounders—approached Yorktown's water defenses and was nearly struck by a masked battery. Missroon lied to McClellan and said that the ship had been hit twice. The remainder of Missroon's brief command included a few more attempts to support the land forces. On 25 April, for instance, the *Maratanza,* a side-wheel steamer mounting six guns, began a lone bombardment of Gloucester Point and Yorktown. Had Missroon been more bold, he would have discovered that the Confederate works protecting Yorktown were miserably armed.

Without the expectation of a naval breakthrough, McClellan ordered the Union army to emplace nearly one hundred heavy guns facing Yorktown. Meanwhile, Comdr. William Smith replaced Missroon and immediately took a more pugnacious posture by ordering the *Marblehead* to bombard Yorktown on 1 May. Smith was even willing to run the Yorktown batteries, exactly what McClellan had desired all along. But before McClellan could unleash his full hailstorm of iron as a signal for Smith to race up the York River, Johnston slipped out of the Yorktown line in the rain beginning on 2 May. "The opening of McClellan's right siege battery on the 30th and the aggressive behavior of the Federal squadron on 1 May decided the question."

Union Brig. Gen. Joseph Hooker, impatient at the time it was taking to position the army, independently advanced his division toward the third Rebel line at Fort Magruder. Confederate Maj. Gen. James Longstreet recognized the danger and sent reinforcements from the withdrawing Southern army, including a section of Capt. John Pelham's horse artillery. Hooker's troops began to give ground under the pounding of Pelham's guns, and soon a regrouping turned into a rout, allowing the Confederates to capture 160 prisoners and eight guns. McClellan arrived from Yorktown and ordered Smith to move two gunboats into Queen's Creek to enfilade the Confederate line. The mere appearance of the *Maratanza* and *Marblehead* on his left convinced Longstreet to evacuate. The next day, the Federals found themselves in control of a deserted battlefield. Johnston had disappeared again.

As the Rebel army fell back toward Richmond, the Union navy advanced up the York. On 6–7 May, three gunboats escorted transports up the river to West Point, Virginia, then did a reconnaissance up the Pamunkey River. Across the peninsula at Hampton Roads, Union Commodore Goldsborough was more cagey. Whenever the *Virginia* appeared, his fleet retreated to the protection of Fort Monroe. On 8 May, for example, the *Virginia* chased the *Monitor* and five other vessels bombarding Sewell's Point to within a mile and a half of Old Point Comfort, just short of effective cannon range.

Before a decision could be made by Confederate authorities to attack the Union fleet in a desperate effort,[28] Lincoln arrived at Fort Monroe and directed Maj. Gen. John Wool to land a strong force at Willoughby's Point, across the Roads from Fort Monroe. Soon, men in blue were marching toward Norfolk. Confederate Gen. Benjamin Huger razed the Gosport Navy Yard and began to withdraw without informing Tattnall. On 10 May, the men aboard the *Virginia* discovered that Norfolk was about to fall. Tattnall decided to make for the James River. To enter the channel he would have to cross Harrison's Bar, which carried only eighteen feet of water. To lessen the ship's twenty-foot draft, all coal and ballast were thrown overboard, exposing the ironclad's unprotected deck. The next day, the blowing wind swept too much water off the bar to allow passage. With no other choice, Tattnall decided to destroy the pride of the Confederacy. At 4:30 A.M. on 11 May off Craney Island, where in 1813 as a young midshipman Tattnall had fought his first battle, the ironclad exploded in a bright flash visible from Fort Monroe.

At last, Goldsborough prepared to send his ships up the James River in support of McClellan. Although the Confederates had evacuated their defenses on the east side of the James, they still occupied several forts on the west bank. These positions had little chance of stopping the Federal advance up the James, but they contributed greatly to the defense of Richmond because of Commodore Goldsborough's orders to his naval officers "'to reduce all the works of the enemy as they go along, spike all their guns, [and] blow up all their magazines.' Only then were the Union commanders to approach Richmond and 'shell the city to a surrender.'"[29] Following such orders, the bluejackets gave precious time to the Rebels preparing the defenses for their capital.

The first strongpoint on the south bank of the James River to fall was Fort Boykin. Situated at the lower end of Burwell's Bay directly across the James from Fort Crafford, the site had been selected by Col. Andrew Talcott at the behest of General Lee. The extensive position was armed with eight 32-pounders, three 42-pounders, and two 8-inch guns. Four miles up the James, Fort Huger was constructed to cover the upper end of the bay.

Soon after the *Virginia*'s destruction left the James unguarded, a Confederate soldier stationed at Battery Park, the Pagan River outpost guarding the town of Smithfield, noticed three Union vessels steaming up the James. In the van was the *Galena*, an experimental armored gunboat mounting four 9-inch Dahlgrens and two 200-pounder Parrott rifles. Commanding the expedition was John Rodgers, the first naval officer sent to western rivers. After clashing with Western Department commander John C. Frémont, Rodgers had returned east in time to fight at Port Royal, South Carolina. He was anxious to mimic Com. David Farragut's run up the Mississippi to New Orleans a few weeks earlier. In Rodgers's way stood a scattering of Rebel militia, who rushed to the guns at Fort Boykin and briefly blasted away. The two wooden gunboats accompanying the *Galena* dropped back and allowed the ironclad to silence the shore batteries. Fort Huger received the same treatment an hour later.[30]

Joined by the *Monitor* and the *Naugatuk* (a lightly armored screw steamer with one rifled gun), the *Galena* continued the dash for Richmond. Passing Fort Powhatan, a masonry structure built before the War of 1812 downriver from City Point, the fleet dropped a few shells onto the defenders, "whose answering fire was puny and ineffective. Without pausing, a similar salute was paid to City Point and Appomattox Manor."[31] On 14 May, the Union armada halted a few miles below some river obstructions at Drewry's Bluff, the last obstacle before Richmond. Called Fort Darling by the Union, the army entrenchments already there had been expanded by the former crews of the *Virginia*, *Jamestown* (which had been scuttled in the main channel below the bluff), and *Patrick Henry* and were under the command of Lieutenant Catesby ap R. Jones. Confederate marine sharpshooters under Capt. John Taylor Wood lined both banks of the river.

The following morning at 7:30, Rodgers anchored the *Galena* just eight hundred yards below the two-hundred-foot bluff and opened fire. The *Monitor*, having also arrived at the scene, was forced to drop farther downriver because her guns could not be elevated enough at the shorter range. On the sixteenth round, the *Naugatuck*'s gun burst, forcing her to retire. The two

Drewry's Bluff overlooking the James River *(Eastern National Parks)*

wooden gunboats stayed well back. After three hours, the *Galena* had been holed several times, but Rodgers refused to quit. Finally, Capt. J. R. Tucker in the CSS *Patrick Henry,* anchored unobtrusively among the obstructions, loosed an 8-inch shot that passed through the Union ironclad's bow gun port. Having expended nearly all his ammunition and with his vessel on fire, Rodgers signaled his fleet to discontinue the action. The U.S. Navy had come within eight miles of capturing Richmond. No one knew this better than Lee, who witnessed the mobility of sea power from across the James River at Chaffin's Bluff.

This time shore batteries came out on top, literally. Plunging fire from the Confederate naval battery had found its mark on the *Galena* twenty-eight times. Eighteen shells penetrated its armor, killing thirteen men and wounding eleven. The *Monitor,* hit three times, escaped unharmed. The gunboats USS *Port Royal* and *Aroostook* suffered only slight damage.[32] Passing slowly down the James, Rodgers's ships again came under attack from Fort Powhatan. Once more, the guns at the fort proved as ineffective as gnats. A bothersome insect gets swatted, nonetheless, and the gunboat USS *Sebago* returned soon after and razed the half-century-old fortification.

On the last day of May, General Johnston was wounded and Robert E. Lee took command of the armies defending Richmond. On 25 June, the seven days' campaign began; two days later McClellan's troops began falling back toward the James with Lee hotly pursuing his larger foe. By the last day of the month, McClellan was searching for "a safe haven on the James under the guns of the navy."[33] Lee hoped to end the war with a major push that day but could not coordinate his entire army. Late in the afternoon, as Confederate troops trudged toward Malvern Hill, the *Galena*, with McClellan on board, steamed upriver to shell the advancing Rebels. "The gunboats rendered most efficient aid at this time, and helped drive back the enemy," McClellan wrote later.[34] At Commodore Rodgers's suggestion, McClellan moved his base from Haxall's Landing downriver to Harrison's Landing so Union gunboats could protect both his flanks. In the late afternoon of the first day of July, Lee made one last fateful push against the retreating Army of the Potomac at Malvern Hill. Once again, Rodgers's warships contributed to mowing down the advancing lines of gray:

> About five o'clock in the afternoon the gunboats *Galena, Aroostook,* and *Jacob Bell* opened from Turkey Island Bend, in the James River, with shot and shell from their immense guns. The previous roar of field artillery seemed as faint as the rattle of musketry in comparison with these monsters of ordnance that literally shook the water and strained the air.[35]

A captain aboard one of the army transports was even more generous toward the navy in a statement quoted by Flag Off. Samuel du Pont: "McClellan's army would have been annihilated but for the gunboats." Also at the scene, Col. Garnet J. Wolseley, a British army observer, "noted with some interest the superstitious dread of gunboats that possessed the Southern soldiers. These vessels of war, even when they have been comparatively harmless[,] had several times been the means of saving northern armies."[36]

McClellan braced for another attack, but the only Confederate movement was on the water and in the air. On 4 July, Edward Porter Alexander brought his balloon down the James aboard the CSS *Teaser*. He made several ascents from the deck of the ship to see where the dreaded Federal gunboats lay, then proceeded to City Point where he landed in an attempt to communicate with Lee. After speaking with some cavalry pickets, Alexander returned to the *Teaser* to find it under attack by the *Maratanza* with distant support provided by the *Monitor*. The Confederate crew abandoned ship, thus destroying the first Rebel aircraft carrier. By then, Lee had concluded that "the Federals' position, and their gunboats, were too much for his strained army to overcome."[37] Lee wrote to Davis:

> The great obstacle to operations here is the presence of the enemy's gunboats which protect our approaches to him & should we even force him from his positions on his land front, would prevent us from reaping any of the fruits of victory & expose our men to great destruction.[38]

The might of the U.S. Navy was certainly awe inspiring. The Petersburg *Daily Express* reported the scene from the Prince George County shore in mid-July: "The river is filled with vessels of every size and description, whose masts ascend as numerous as trees in a forest."[39] No less than six hundred warships, supply vessels, and transports were officially reported anchored between Fort Powhatan and City Point. The Confederates tried to interdict some of the traffic, but during a two-day period beginning 6 July, they damaged only the transport *Juniata* despite firing 172 rounds at Union shipping from Weyanoke Point and Willcox Wharf (Buckland plantation), downstream from Harrison's Landing.[40] To counter such raids, the U.S. Navy assigned twenty-three gunboats of the James River Flotilla to escort transports on the James.

On 8 July, Lincoln arrived at Harrison's Landing aboard the *Ariel* and made a weak effort to push McClellan back into the offensive. Little Mac insisted he needed more reinforcements before he could think about another attack. For the next three weeks, the greatest threat to the Union troops came in the form of swarms of flies. At midnight on 31 July the situation became a bit more serious as forty-one Rebel artillery pieces emplaced on the south side of the James at Coggin's Point opened on the thousands of lights swinging from the shipping on the James. Federal land batteries responded. The gunboats, anchored several miles upriver to guard against Confederate naval sorties, joined in. Within an hour, the Southern cannoneers broke off the duel, but they seemed to accomplish their goal of holding McClellan's attention while Lee prepared to move against Union Gen. John Pope's Army of Virginia.[41] When McClellan did nothing in response to Lee's departure, Lincoln ordered the Army of the Potomac back to northern Virginia. By 16 August, the works around Harrison's Landing were abandoned except for some dummy sentries stuffed with straw.

During the last months of 1862, the attention of both sides focused on the fighting in northern Virginia and Maryland, but in February 1863, the transfer of the Ninth Corps of the Army of the Potomac to the peninsula led Richmond to believe another threat might develop from that region. Lt. Gen. James Longstreet was detached from Lee's army to deal with the situation. He tried to get help from the Confederate navy in the shape of the ironclad *Richmond*, fitted out at Rocketts near Richmond. Frightened Rebel congressmen refused to allow a passage to be cut through the river barrier at Drewry's Bluff lest the Federal ironclads attempt another dash up the James.[42]

Longstreet did not give up. On 11 April, he attacked Suffolk at the head of the Nansemond River, southwest of Norfolk. When his initial advance failed to overrun the Union defenses, he laid siege to the town. Confederate shore batteries tried to keep the Union navy at bay, but on 19 April, a combined operations attack captured the Confederate position at Hill's Point on the Nansemond, along with five howitzers. Although Longstreet lingered two more weeks, the gunboats had broken his offensive.

By 1864, the situation looked grim for the South. Aided by ironclad warships, the U.S. Army had opened the Mississippi. Closer to Virginia, Lee had been repulsed at Gettysburg. Still, there was plenty of fight left in the South. In January of that year, a Federal steamer on the James was fired upon in the vicinity of Fort Boykin, and immediately the gunboat *Smith Briggs* was dispatched to Smithfield with 150 men. The Federals had not gone far when they encountered a mixed Confederate force of infantry, cavalry, and artillery. The Union troops retired to Smithfield expecting to be picked up, but the gunboat had left. The next day the Confederates attacked. The *Smith Briggs* returned during the fight, but the Rebels managed to hole her steam chest, putting the warship out of commission. Without naval support, the Union landing force surrendered.

In March 1864, Richmond finally approved cutting a passage through the obstructions at Drewry's Bluff, but the Union army struck before engineers could carry out the proposal. On 1 April 1864, Lt. Gen. Ulysses Grant arrived at Fort Monroe to outline for General Butler his plans for the upcoming campaign. (Butler had replaced Foster as commander of the Department of Virginia and North Carolina.) The newly appointed general in chief of the armies of the United States wanted Butler to capture City Point and move on Richmond as the Army of the Potomac came to grips with Lee in northern Virginia.

On 5 May 1864, as the battle of the Wilderness opened, the thirty-thousand-man Army of the James sailed from Fort Monroe. Butler quickly occupied City Point and Bermuda Hundred. After two days of fighting, Federal troops reached the railroad connecting Petersburg to Richmond. During that time, the Confederate navy had been unable to challenge Acting Rear Adm. S. P. Lee's gunboats protecting the army's right flank on the James. Torpedoes, however, claimed the *Commodore Jones*, and shore batteries destroyed the *Shawsheen*.[43]

Undaunted, Butler's men continued their methodical advance up the railroad toward Richmond. By 16 May, Confederate Gen. P. G. T. Beauregard, in command of the local troops, was ready to take the initiative. His attack did not succeed in separating the Army of the James from its naval support, but it did force Butler to retreat within the Bermuda Hundred peninsula, where the Rebels easily penned them up east of a series of entrenchments called the Howlett Line. Anchoring the north end of the line was a battery that would eventually be named after Col. O. M. Dantzler of the Twenty-second South Carolina, who would die in a skirmish on 2 June. Constructed on a bluff occupied by the Howlett house, the battery kept the Union navy from advancing up the James.

One of a class of twenty-eight double-ended gunboats, the *Mendota* supported Grant's forces along the James River. Reversible engines eliminated having to turn the vessel around in narrow waters. *(U.S. Army Military History Institute)*

After much discussion, Confederate Secretary of the Navy Mallory finally convinced the War Department to keep its promise concerning the opening of the obstructions at Drewry's Bluff. On 24 May 1864, engineers blew a hole through the last of the debris that blocked the channel. That day three Confederate ironclads passed through safely, but by then Mallory's ardor for a river attack had lessened considerably. At Trent's Reach, just below Howlett's property, his armorclads would be forced to engage Federal ironclads, including the captured ram *Atlanta,* not just wooden transports. Confederate General Beauregard correctly surmised that Grant intended to shift his forces to the south side of the James, but with little confidence in the Confederate navy's ironclads, he did not energetically support a combined attack on Federal positions on the upper James to prevent a crossing by Grant's forces. Although Beauregard furnished a battery of heavy guns, by the time it was in position Grant had already bridged the James near Fort Powhatan. To secure his movement against naval attack, Grant ordered Butler to sink block ships at Trent's Reach.

To allow the Union ships to bypass the guns at Battery Dantzler, Butler devised a plan to build a canal across Dutch Gap. Lee ordered an immediate bombardment of the working parties, mostly black soldiers. On 13 August, the Rebel ironclads *Virginia II, Richmond,* and *Fredericksburg,*

The reflagged Confederate ram *Atlanta* on the James River
(*U.S. Army Military History Institute*)

accompanied by the gunboats *Hampton, Nansemond,* and *Drewry,* began an all-day attack in conjunction with shore batteries that damaged two Federal wooden gunboats and killed thirty of Butler's diggers. Three days later, twelve hundred Union soldiers forced their way to within two and a half miles of Chaffin's Bluff across from Fort Darling. The next day Confederates counterattacked and recovered everything but Signal Hill. At 3:00 P.M., Confederate Comdr. Thomas R. Rootes, temporarily in command of the James River Squadron, opened fire on the hill with his ironclads and continued to shell the enemy positions throughout the night. The next day the Confederates advanced to find the hill had been evacuated.

On 28 September, Butler again advanced on the north side of the James, capturing Signal Hill and Fort Harrison. The *Virginia,* guarding a bridge north of Chaffin's Bluff, once more came to the rescue. A signal officer on shore directed the ironclad's fire against the mass of blue approaching Chaffin's Bluff. The naval support succeeded in throwing back Butler's attack, but Fort Harrison remained in Union hands despite all efforts to recapture it.

Federal troops on the south side of the James continually harassed Confederate squadron commander John K. Mitchell's warships, but Lee refused to grant permission for their withdrawal upriver. During November and December the Rebel ironclads regularly slipped downriver from Chaffin's Bluff under cover of darkness to disrupt work at Dutch Gap. By the end of the year the digging parties had moved fifteen thousand cubic yards of soil, but when six tons of gunpowder were exploded on New Year's Day 1865 to open the bulkhead at the western end, the earth fell back into the canal, effectively blocking it.

The month of January 1865 brought the South its best chance to destroy Grant's base at City Point. Observing an unusually heavy flow of ice down the James, Lt. Charles Read, who had served on the *Arkansas* and was then in charge of a naval battery overlooking Trent's Reach, concluded that the Federal obstructions had washed away. A patrol confirmed his suspicions, and the information was forwarded to Mitchell on 16 January. The bulk of the Union's James River Flotilla had been sent south to support the Fort Fisher operation in North Carolina, leaving only the double-turreted monitor *Onondaga* and a handful of wooden gunboats on station. Mitchell balked at his golden opportunity until Navy Secretary Mallory prodded him into action. On 23 January at 6:45 P.M., the ironclads and their consorts slipped their moorings at Chaffin's Bluff.

Union authorities had learned about the operation and warned all shore batteries to be prepared for action. At 8:00 P.M., the Rebel fleet came abreast of Fort Brady, the powerful Union battery three miles downriver from Chaffin's Bluff at Signal Hill. Its two 100-pound and three 30-pound Parrott rifles belched fire in the night. Commanding the Confederate batteries on the opposite shore, Gen. George Pickett of Gettysburg fame smothered Fort Brady, dismounting the 100-pound Parrott nearest the river and cracking the muzzle of the second. The Connecticut artillerists at the fort then accidentally ran two of the 30-pounders off their platforms trying to train the pieces downriver to follow the path of the ironclads. A near miss also knocked the fort's commander senseless. Adding to the Federals' problems, the dark night cloaked the ships so that few of the twenty-five shots fired by the Connecticut veterans found their mark, and none caused any major damage.

The Rebel ironclads had easily passed the first obstacle, but there was more to come. Union engineers had laid out four batteries along the southern and eastern edges of Trent's Reach, where the James curved sharply north at that time. Battery Sawyer, situated twelve hundred yards downriver from the elbow, was armed with a 100-pound Parrott and two 10-inch seacoast mortars. At the elbow's south side, Battery Spofford concealed a 30-pound Parrott. A few hundred yards southeast, Batteries Parsons and Wilcox added another 100-pound Parrott and a 10-inch seacoast mortar respectively.[44] Capt. William A. Parker, the *Onondaga*'s commander, chose to move downstream instead of supporting the batteries.

The *Fredericksburg* and the torpedo launch *Scorpion* approached to within fifty yards of the sunken hulks at Trent's Reach before Union batteries opened fire. At 1:30 A.M., Read worked to break the chains holding a single spar blocking the channel. The *Fredericksburg* finally forced its way through, missing the spar but striking one of the hulks on her port side. The gunboat *Hampton* followed. Anchoring four hundred yards downriver, Mitchell returned for the other ships. After suffering two hours of heavy,

One of Fort Brady's batteries guarding the lower James River *(Eastern National Parks)*

inaccurate fire, Lt. F. E. Sheppard, commander of the *Fredericksburg,* sent the *Hampton* back to check on the rest of the fleet. The *Hampton* returned with bad news. The other two ironclads had grounded along with the *Drewry* and *Scorpion,* and Sheppard had been ordered to return to protect them.

Realizing that the *Drewry* would be destroyed as soon as the sun rose, John Kell, commander of the *Richmond,* ordered the wooden gunboat abandoned. Minutes later, two shots from Battery Parsons blew it to bits. Heavily damaged, the *Scorpion* drifted down to the obstructions where she was captured. Unable to bring its guns to bear, the *Virginia* endured the pounding of the land batteries until 10:15 A.M. when the *Onondaga* finally appeared. At fifteen hundred yards, its broadside of two 15-inch Dahlgren smoothbores and two 150-pound Parrott rifles ripped into the *Virginia,* perhaps helping the rising tide to knock the hapless ram off the mud. Although hit more than seventy times, the ironclad still managed to limp upstream to the protection of Battery Dantzler. A half-hour later the *Richmond,* whose oblique angle to the oncoming shot caused most of the rounds to glance off her armor, pulled free. Mitchell called off the attack and ordered the ironclads to stand by until the wooden gunboats could steam back to Battery Dantzler.

The next night a quickly patched *Virginia* led the squadron back around the Union-controlled bend in the James only to "find the river west of the obstructions engulfed in brilliant light."[45] A bright Drummond light had been placed on the south side of the James, nullifying any advantage darkness might have given the Rebels. Mitchell's pilots lost their nerves, and the decision was made to cancel the operation to reach City Point.

During the return engagement, the garrison at Fort Brady managed to fire some 130 rounds at the retreating Confederates, but other than riddling the *Richmond*'s smokestack, no serious damage hampered the passage of the fleet. Four and a half hours later, the last vessel moored safely at Chaffin's Bluff.

Authorities on both sides chaffed at the handling of the various navies. Commander Parker of the *Onondaga* was court-martialed. Confederate Secretary Mallory replaced Mitchell with Rear Adm. Raphael Semmes, the former commander of the *Alabama*, but there was nothing he could do but sit and wait for the inevitable. By the time he took over, the Federals had strengthened their obstructions and stationed additional monitors on the James. On 3 April, under orders from Mallory, Semmes scuttled the three ironclads at Drewry's Bluff. The next day Lincoln steamed up the James with Rear Adm. David Porter aboard the flagship *Malvern*.

When obstructions blocked the flagship's way, the two embarked in Porter's barge, with three aides and a boat crew of twelve. Thus, in a single small boat under oars, significantly by water, the president reached the Southern capital that for four years had been so near for conquest by the Union armies.[46]

If you go there . . .

For Civil War buffs, Virginia's siren song is hard to resist. Every mile of road brings another battlefield or site associated with the tremendous struggle that flowed red across the countryside. More than 250 official Civil War highway plaques dot every part of the state. From a comfortable distance, it's easy to assume that the preservation of the commonwealth's historic landmarks has been a natural and easy process. On the contrary, the conflict between Virginia's past and future erupts frequently and furiously, pitting those in favor of continuing the legacy against those who favor commercial and financial progress. These battles, fought in courtrooms and on the front pages of newspapers, are in some small way as fierce as those that took place more than 130 years earlier.

Isobel Bryan, for instance, led the fight to preserve Jamestown, the first successful English colony in North America. In the opposite camp, her great-grandson, J. Stewart Bryan III, has proposed building a multi-million-dollar complex on Lockwood, the property at which Robert E. Lee rested before the battle of Cold Harbor.

Interestingly, Isobel's efforts at Jamestown have also benefited Civil War buffs. Within the borders of Jamestown Island, now administered by the **Colonial National Historical Park,** are two Confederate earthen forts. The first sits just to the west of the Old Church Tower, the only surviving seventeenth-century structure of the original town. The other earthwork rises beside the island's three-mile loop drive. The island is open 8:30 A.M. to 6:30 P.M. daily from mid-June through Labor Day and until at least 5:00 P.M. the remainder of the year. The cost for entering is $5.00 per car. The large visitors center houses an impressive gift shop and exhibits, most dealing with the colonial period. Address inquiries to Superintendent, Colonial National Historical Park, Yorktown, VA 23690 (804) 898-3400.

In Williamsburg, a small section of Fort Magruder's earthworks remains behind **Fort Magruder Inn.** Surprisingly, the lobby of the motel contains a nice display of paintings and artifacts dealing with the Civil War battle fought there. For information, contact: Fort Magruder Inn, Route 60 East, Williamsburg, VA 23187 (804) 220-2250.

The right flank of the Confederate second line was anchored at Fort Crafford on the James. Work on a water battery at Mulberry Point began on 14 August 1861. Because the position would be vulnerable to attack from its rear, construction of a fort—named Crafford after the family that owned the farmland—began in February 1862 and was completed by the start of McClellan's campaign. When Gen. Joe Johnston ordered the right side of his Yorktown line evacuated on 21 April, Fort Crafford continued to support the Confederates' James River Squadron. Beginning in May, however, the entire line was withdrawn, including the garrison at Crafford. Union forces occupied the earthwork the remainder of the war.

The fort, named a national historic site in 1973, now sits within the boundaries of Fort Eustis. The **Besson Army Transportation Museum** on the base has a few Civil War exhibits. Admission is free to the museum, which is open from 9:00 A.M. to 4:30 P.M. daily. Officials there can provide information about the current status of the star-shaped fort, which is sometimes off-limits to visitors. For information, contact: U.S. Army Transportation Museum, Building 300, Besson Hall, Fort Eustis, VA 23604 (804) 878-1183.

Across Highway 60 from Fort Eustis sprawls **Newport News City Park,** the largest municipal park east of the Mississippi. A footbridge crosses the site of the original dam to the extensive earthworks where the battle of Dam Number 1 was fought. Artifacts excavated from the battlefield are displayed at an interpretive center, which is open Wednesday through Sunday from 9:00 A.M. to 7:00 P.M. For information, write:

Newport News Park, 13564 Jefferson Avenue, Newport News, VA 23603 (804) 886-7916.

The city park abuts the Colonial National Historic Park at **Yorktown.** Confederate General Magruder utilized Revolutionary War earthworks around the town. Although the focus is, of course, on the American War for Independence, the earthworks are still worth a visit. A small exhibit on the Civil War is on display in the interpretive center, which is open the same hours as the Jamestown Center. For information, call (804) 887-1776.

Within the town itself, **Nelson House** on Main Street was used as a hospital during the Civil War. For information on tours, call (804) 398-3400.

Across the York River, **Tyndall's Point Park** lies immediately north of the Coleman Memorial Bridge on the west side of Highway 17. A few of the worn earthworks constructed by the Confederates in 1861 and occupied by Union troops in 1862 are still visible.

Nothing remains of Magruder's first line of defense, but on Big Bethel Road just before the Big Bethel Reservoir stands a monument to the battle of Big Bethel. The actual battle site is under the reservoir.

The **War Memorial Museum of Virginia** in Newport News contains more than twenty thousand exhibits documenting America's wars from 1775 to the present, including uniforms, accouterments, and artwork from the 1860s. There is a $2.00 admission charge for the museum, but visitors can walk around the terrific outdoor display of weapons for free. The museum is open Monday through Saturday from 9:00 A.M. to 5:00 P.M. and Sunday from 1:00–5:00 P.M. except holidays. For information, contact: War Memorial Museum, 9285 Warwick Boulevard, Newport News, VA 23607 (804) 247-8523.

From exit 6 on I-64, proceed south toward Newport News on Virginia 167 for 4.6 miles. At the second roadside historical marker is the **Monitor-Merrimack Overlook.** Situated near the site of Camp Butler, the overlook provides a good view of Hampton Roads and the approximate area of the famous naval battle that took place two miles west.

The most impressive historic site in the area is without a doubt **Fort Monroe.** Named in honor of President James Monroe, the massive stone fort was designed by the French engineer Simon Bernard and constructed between 1819 and 1834. Engineer Robert E. Lee came to the fort in 1831. His quarters are still standing but make up part of the active military base and are not open to the public.

The **Casemate Museum** opened in 1951 to showcase the cell in which Jefferson Davis was imprisoned after the war. The museum expanded through the years and now occupies a large number of the fort's casemates. Many of the displays and models cover the Civil War years. A

Fort Monroe, the largest stone fort on the American continent, never fell to the Confederacy

The Lincoln Gun atop the rampart of Front Number 4 at Fort Monroe, overlooking the Chesapeake Bay and denying the Confederates access to the ports of Hampton Roads and the James River

walking-tour guide available at the museum highlights sites inside and outside the fort's walls, such as the first 15-inch Rodman gun cast in the United States. The massive cannon, called the Lincoln gun, helped bombard Confederate batteries near Norfolk. Quarters Number One, the oldest residence on the post, hosted Lincoln during his visit. The gift shop in the museum sells a packet of articles that tell everything about the post from its role in the Civil War to its association with poet Edgar Allan Poe, who was stationed at the post three years before the arrival of Lee. He rose to the rank of sergeant major of artillery before paying to get out of the service in 1829 in order to attend West Point.

The museum is free and open from 10:30 A.M. to 5:00 P.M. daily except holidays. For information, contact: Casemate Museum, P.O. Box 341, Fort Monroe, VA 23561 (804) 727-3391.

Trips to **Fort Wool** leave from the Hampton Visitors Center in downtown Hampton at 10:00 A.M. during May and September and 10:00 A.M. and 2:00 P.M. from June to August. The three-hour cruises let visitors off for a guided tour of Fort Wool, built on an artificial fifteen-acre island. Lee reluctantly left Fort Monroe for this pile of rocks in 1834, but the fort was still not finished by the time of the Civil War. It was modified in 1901–8, but fortunately some of the pre – Civil War casemates are still visible. The $10.00 cruises also pass the two-mile waterfront of the world's largest naval installation. For information, contact: Hampton Visitors Center, 710 Settlers Landing Road, Hampton, VA 23669 (804) 727-1102.

Within the Pennsylvania Building of the Norfolk Base, across Hampton Roads from Fort Monroe, is the **Hampton Roads Naval Museum.** To enter the base and visit the museum, you must obtain a pass at the tour office on Hampton Boulevard just outside the base gates. Displays at the museum depict the naval history of the Hampton Roads area. An entire wing is devoted to the Civil War. Open free to the public daily from 9:00 A.M. to 4:00 P.M., the museum is closed Thanksgiving, Christmas, and New Year's. For information, call (804) 444-2243.

In an industrial park west of the city of Norfolk, **Fort Norfolk** waits to be renovated into the headquarters of the Norfolk Historical Society. The society has already hosted Civil War living-history programs at the fort and hopes to have displays open soon. During the Civil War, fifteen guns were mounted at the fort as part of the defenses of the city. When Union General Wool captured Norfolk, the U.S. Navy immediately demanded full control of the city, navy yard, hospital, and Fort Norfolk. Wool refused. Finally on 24 May 1862, he gave everything up except the fort, which General Butler turned over to the navy in March 1863. Prisoners kept at the fort during the Civil War covered their cell walls with graffiti, some of which can still be read today.

An aerial view of Fort Norfolk, c. 1930s (*Norfolk Public Library*)

Fort Norfolk's importance is more architectural than historical since the only time shots were fired in anger inside its walls occurred during the War of 1812 when a three-time deserter was executed.[47] Structurally, the post is the only harbor defense with a semicircular face built prior to the War of 1812 still standing in the United States.

Across the Elizabeth River in Portsmouth at High and Water streets is the **Naval Shipyard Museum.** The museum displays models of the USS *Hartford,* which sank in the Elizabeth River on 20 November 1956, and the CSS *Virginia* and artifacts from both ships, including armor plate and a gun carriage possibly from the latter ship. The museum costs $1.50 and is open Tuesday through Saturday from 10:00 A.M. to 5:00 P.M. and on Sunday from 1:00–5:00 P.M. For information, contact: Portsmouth Naval Shipyard Museum, P.O. Box 248, Portsmouth, VA 23705 (804) 393-8591.

On the west end of Portsmouth along State 337, markers denote the site of **Fort Nelson,** a companion to Fort Norfolk; it was razed during the expansion of the naval hospital. The area was fortified during the Civil War. A couple of miles farther out, a marker indicates the site of **Craney Island** (now no longer an island) where the *Virginia* was destroyed in 1862. Before its evacuation, the Confederates had emplaced forty-two guns there.

Up Virginia Route 10 from Portsmouth is Smithfield and **Fort Boykin.** The junglelike atmosphere around the mounds of dirt outlining the massive fort was increased by the eerie calls of peacocks during my visit. The brightly colored birds strolled around the grounds where, during the Civil War, Alabama poet Sidney Lanier penned a poem eulogizing a comrade killed in battle.

The fort grounds, four miles north of Smithfield, offer picnic tables and grills to the traveler but little else. The area is open 9:00 A.M. to dusk Wednesday through Sunday.

Farther up Route 10 spreads **Brandon Plantation.** With forty-five thousand acres, it is one of the largest working farms in the United States and one of the oldest. During the Civil War the property was fired upon by Federal warships and the damage to the south side of the main house, designed by Thomas Jefferson, has been preserved. Federal soldiers also occupied the structure and used a portion of the paneling in the living room for firewood.

Those who stop by can stroll through the gardens surrounding the main house from 9:00 A.M. to 5:00 P.M. daily for $3.00. The house itself is open during Garden Week and by appointment. For information, contact: Brandon, 23500 Brandon Road, Spring Grove, VA 23881 (804) 866-8486.

A few bricks from **Fort Powhatan** (Fort Hood), built in a similar design and at the same time as Fort Norfolk, are said to be still visible within the Prince George Hunt Club, on Route 10 south of Hopewell. Unfortunately, visitors cannot enter the private club.

Just inside the town of Hopewell along Route 10 stands the local tourism office, phone (804) 541-2206. A walking-tour map of Hopewell and City Point is available there. Just off Cedar Lane on the way to City Point, **Fort Abbott,** one of ten small forts built between 1864–65 to protect the supply depot from Confederate raiders, is preserved in a city park. The **City Point Unit** of the Petersburg National Battlefield manages the actual site of the massive Union supply base for Union soldiers fighting at Petersburg. The cabin that served as Grant's headquarters during the winter of 1864–65 and a small earthwork still stand on the property. Appomattox Manor, which was repeatedly shelled during the Civil War, now serves as a visitors center. It offers a brief audiovisual explanation of the area's history, a few displays of relics, and a small gift shop. Be sure to pick up "The Bermuda Hundred Campaign in Chesterfield County, Virginia." The brochure outlines a driving tour through eight of the important sites associated with Butler's campaign, including his headquarters at **Half Way House, Dutch Gap Canal** (Henricus Park), and **Forts Carpenter** and **Drake** of the Union army's Bermuda Hundred defense line. Other positions associated with the January 1865 attack by the Confederate ironclads, such as Batteries Wilcox and Dantzler, are not open to the public at this time.

Two other sites on the tour that are open to the public are **Fort Stevens** and **Drewry's Bluff**. Fort Stevens was a main bastion of the Confederate inner-defense line built in 1862 to defend Richmond. From this position on 16 May 1864, Confederates launched a counterattack that drove back General Butler's Army of the James.

National Park Service signs along I-95 and U.S. Route 1/301 indicate the turnoffs for Drewry's Bluff (the Willis Road exit). The earthworks are a brisk walk from the parking lot. Exhibits and markers line the self-guided trail. At its end, a reconstructed battery overlooks the James River. One look down the steep slope provides ample evidence of what Captain Rodgers was up against during his May 1862 attack. Soon after the battle, the Confederate Marine Corps Camp of Instruction and the Confederate Naval Academy were established at Drewry's Bluff. The fort also served as General Beauregard's headquarters during his successful defense against General Butler's attack in May 1864. Today, reenactors with the James River Squadron put on occasional living-history programs here. Recently, the Confederate Naval Historical Society led a fight to protect the three Rebel ironclads scuttled adjacent to Fort Darling *Richmond, Fredericksburg,* and *Virginia II.* Along with other preservation groups, the society convinced the Virginia Marine Resources Commission not to grant the Army Corps of Engineers a permit to dump dredging refuse in the area. For information about the group's other activities, contact: The Confederate Naval Historical Society, 710 Ocran Road, White Stone, Virginia 22578 (804) 435-0014.

Seven miles north of Drewry's Bluff, I-95 crosses the James into Richmond. As might be expected, the capital of the Confederacy offers dozens of museums and sites associated with the Civil War. Contact the Virginia Division of Tourism, 202 N. Ninth Street, Richmond, VA 23219 (804) 786-4484, for more information. The following is only a partial list:

Outside the **Museum of the Confederacy** lie the propeller shaft and anchor from the *Virginia* and the anchor chain from one of its victims, the *Cumberland.* The museum boasts the largest extant collection of Confederate artifacts, including a dented piece of the *Virginia's* armor plate and the field uniforms of Generals Lee, Jackson, Stuart, and Johnston. Admission to the museum is $4.00. For $7.00, you can also walk next door and tour the **Confederate White House,** the 1818 Brockenbrough mansion, which served as the official residence for Jefferson Davis. The museum is open Monday through Saturday from 10:00 A.M. to 5:00 P.M. and Sunday from 1:00–5:00 P.M. For information, contact: The Museum of the Confederacy, 1201 East Clay Street, Richmond, VA 23219 (804) 649-1861.

At the south end of Sixth Street, near the James River, the **Tredegar Ironworks** is being renovated. The plant furnished munitions for the Confederacy and rolled armor plates for the *Virginia.* At 428 N. Boulevard, four blocks south of Broad Street, stands **Battle Abbey.** Inside, the Virginia Historical Society maintains one of the best research libraries on the Civil War in the state.

At the east end of town at 3315 Broad Street is the **Chimborazo Visitors Center** of the Richmond National Battlefield Park. It sits in the middle of what used to be the Chimborazo Hospital, which treated more than seventy-six thousand sick and wounded Confederates during the four years of the conflict. The visitors center, free and open daily from 9:00 A.M. to 5:00 P.M., houses exhibits and an audiovisual program. Be sure to pick up the tour guide to the battlefields surrounding Richmond. For more information, call (804) 226-1981.

Eight miles southeast of Richmond off State Route 5 on Battlefield Park Road past **Forts Gilmer, Gregg,** and **Johnson** are the remains of **Fort Harrison.** Here another visitors center, free and open from 9:30 A.M. to 5:30 P.M., June through August, relates the drama of the struggles in the vicinity. There are also restrooms and a picnic area. Farther south, the Hoke-Brady Road leads to **Fort Brady,** where Union gunners fired on Mitchell's ironclads in January 1865. The fort is one of the best preserved in the entire hundred-mile loop comprising the Richmond battlefield tour.

Eventually State Route 5 intersects with Route 156. A short way up the latter rises **Malvern Hill.** A parking area allows travelers to leave their cars and walk the fields where more than five thousand Confederates lost their lives in a futile effort to keep McClellan from reaching the safety of his gunboats on the James River. Unfortunately, in early 1993 a lawsuit by preservationists failed, and a gravel company gained permission to excavate part of the hill.

Back on Route 5 heading east, visitors should stop at **Berkeley,** one of Virginia's most historic plantations and site of Harrison's Landing. Benjamin Harrison, son of the builder, was a signer of the Declaration of Independence and three times governor of Virginia. His son, William Henry, led the American forces at the battle of Tippecanoe. Although born at Berkeley, William claimed to be born in a log cabin during his successful run for the presidency in 1841. William's grandson, Benjamin, was elected the country's twenty-third president. One marker on the plantation claims that on 4 December 1619 the first official Thanksgiving was celebrated there, although most texts credit the governor of Plymouth Colony, William Bradford, with issuing the first Thanksgiving proclamation in 1621. In any event, a national holiday was not established until the Civil War, when Lincoln designated the last Thursday in November as Thanksgiving Day.

For forty-five days in the summer of 1862, Berkeley Plantation was home to more than a hundred thousand soldiers of the Army of the Potomac. On 8 July of that year, Lincoln arrived at Harrison's Landing aboard the *Ariel* to politely prod the popular McClellan into action. When nothing came of the president's visit, General in Chief Henry Halleck ordered McClellan to march his army to Fort Monroe where it would board transports for Aquia harbor on the Potomac. As the army prepared to leave, Gen. Daniel Butterfield summoned bugler Oliver W. Norton to his tent and "whistled to him the few notes that would become known as 'Taps.'"[48] A monument on the property commemorates the event.

Berkeley is open daily for tours of the house and gardens from 8:00 A.M. to 5:00 P.M. There is a charge. For information, contact: Berkeley Plantation, Charles City, VA 23030 (804) 829-6018.

Route 5 heading east leads back to Jamestown.

CHAPTER 2

NORTH CAROLINA

MOST NORTH CAROLINIANS looked upon Abraham Lincoln's election in November 1860 as scant reason to dissolve their state's bonds with the Union. Poor soil limited the number of large cotton and rice plantations, and the nonslaveholding majority adopted a neutral posture in sectional disputes over slavery. Even those with an interest in slavery understood that revolution posed more of a threat to slaveholders than abolitionists. As North Carolina's *Daily Conservative* reminded its readers in 1865, "Unionists had warned southern politicians in 1861 that leaving the Union 'jeoparded [*sic*] the institution of slavery a thousand-fold more by secession, than by carrying on the contest under the old government."[1] Nevertheless, the state's cultural ties to the rural, export-oriented South were much stronger than to the industrialized, protectionist North. Expressing the feelings of many, one Tar Heel noted: "I am a Union man but when they send men South it will change my notions. I can do nothing against my own people."[2]

Predictably, the first overt action intending to disrupt the status quo in North Carolina occurred near the border with its more contentious sister state, South Carolina, which had seceded 20 December 1860. On the last day of that year, a group of Wilmington citizens wired Gov. John Ellis for permission to seize Forts Caswell and Johnston at the mouth of the Cape Fear River. Ellis refused.

The next day a commission traveled to Raleigh to meet with the governor. He continued to counsel inaction. A week later, a dispatch arrived in Wilmington inaccurately suggesting that the revenue cutter *Harriet Lane* was steaming toward Fort Caswell with guns and men. The following day, 9 January, a group of men from Wilmington, who had been training in case of such an event, loaded provisions aboard a transport, plied downstream to the federal barracks at Smithville (now Southport), roused the caretaker out of bed, and forced him to surrender his custodianship. Fifteen of the militia remained to guard the newly acquired property, called Fort Johnston, and the rest of the Cape Fear Minute Men sailed on to Fort Caswell. Once again, a single ordnance sergeant kept watch. He was easily convinced to relinquish his duties.

Once these niceties were accomplished, Maj. John Hedrick, in charge of the expedition, found himself in command of a skeleton of a fort. Just two cannon were mounted in the pentagonal brick structure, and these could not be fired for fear their carriages would disintegrate.

Meanwhile, when Governor Ellis learned of Hedrick's action, he wired President James Buchanan, both to deny any complicity and to ask the president's intentions. When Buchanan assured Ellis he had no plans to reinforce the Cape Fear forts, the governor ordered Col. John Cantwell, the only person in the area who outranked Hedrick, to recall the Minute Men. When the order to retire reached the men at Fort Caswell, they were already bored and beset with mosquitoes. The would-be Rebels grumbled but headed home after returning the keys to the two ordnance sergeants. North Carolinians living near the barracks at Smithville could not believe the war had ended so quickly.[3]

Although the occupation and evacuation of the forts and the secession of four more states by mid-January 1861 had sparked growing interest in the radical movement within North Carolina, a popular vote on the last day of February resulted in a victory for the conservatives who desired to continue with the Union. No one accepted the decision as a done deal, however. When on 15 April Lincoln called for seventy-five thousand troops to suppress the southern insurrection, Ellis penned his famous reply to the secretary of war: "You can get no troops from North Carolina."[4] He followed that with another order to Cantwell, this time to garrison the forts at the mouth of the Cape Fear River and Fort Macon on the Outer Banks outside Beaufort.

On 20 May, North Carolina voters formalized these preemptive moves by ratifying the Provisional Constitution of the Confederate States of America. The message from the voting population was loud and clear: Even though North Carolina was strongly unionist with few proslavery sentiments, her people felt the federal government, which threatened to become more dominated by the business-oriented Northeast, had no right to impose its will on the separate states.

Despite its late entrance into the Confederacy, North Carolina uniformed 125,000 of its sons, a larger number than registered voters. Nearly 20,000 North Carolinians died in battle, almost one-fourth the total Confederate combat losses.[5] An equal number succumbed to disease or other noncombat causes, giving the state the dubious distinction of suffering more losses than any other state in the Confederacy.

Unfortunately for the Tar Heels, Governor Ellis died as the state was making preparations to leave the Union. Henry T. Clark replaced him, but the former speaker of the state senate did not share his predecessor's clout with the power brokers in Richmond. Twenty 13-pounder field pieces were transferred to North Carolina during the last days of Ellis's term to protect the land approaches to the coastal forts. Incapable of holding off a determined seaborne attack, these few weapons, nevertheless, proved to be the last such delivery until it was too late.[6] When the Federals finally stirred themselves to attack the coast of North Carolina, the largest weapons they would initially have to face were 32-pounders dating back to the War of 1812. They had an effective range of a mere two thousand yards and could be pointed but not truly aimed. This performance just about summed up the Confederate government's policy in North Carolina.

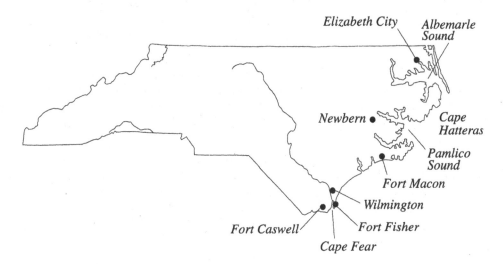

Hatteras Inlet

HAD CONFEDERATE privateers left well enough alone, the Union high command would certainly have postponed any interest in the "sterile and half-drowned shores of North Carolina."[7] As it was, however, seaborne raiders insisted on slipping through passes in the Outer Banks to seize merchant ships. A week's catch in July 1861 included four schooners, a brig, six hundred bushels of salt, and tons of sugar.[8] One ship, the *Winslow*, took sixteen prizes in six weeks.[9] In consequence, marine insurance rates in the North climbed, and traders in Boston, New York, and Philadelphia clamored for action. On 9 August, six of the largest maritime insurance companies in the United States addressed a joint petition to Gideon Welles, secretary of the navy, demanding the "pirates" at Hatteras be cleaned out.[10]

Maj. Gen. Benjamin F. Butler, in command of some of the troops at Fort Monroe, had submitted a plan for attacking Hatteras Inlet, one of only six deep-water channels along the coast leading into the state's interior. A political favorite of the Lincoln administration, Butler had led one of the first regiments to relieve beleaguered Washington after the president's election. The army ignored Butler, but after its defeat at Manassas, the Federal government turned to the navy for a needed victory.

Confidential orders were dispatched to Flag Off. Silas Stringham, in charge of the Atlantic Blockading Squadron, to level the forts guarding Hatteras Inlet, the gate to Pamlico Sound, and to sink block ships in the channel. Despite his poor showing at the battle of Big Bethel in Virginia, Butler was selected to lead the 880 army troops. Stringham commanded the largest fleet yet assembled by the North: the steam frigates *Minnesota* and *Wabash*, the sloop *Cumberland*, three gunboats (the former revenue cutter *Harriet Lane*, the *Monticello*, and *Pawnee*), a side-wheel steamer (*Susquehana*), two transports, and a canal tug (the *Fanny Cadwalader*). The warships mounted a total of 149 guns.

Stringham's first objective was to destroy the two forts guarding the inlet. Confederate Brig. Gen. Walter Gwynn, in charge of the northern portion of North Carolina's coast, had done his best to protect the most strategically important point in his department. Fort Clark, a square redoubt, was raised at the seaward mouth of the inlet. Mounted within its walls were seven guns, five 32-pounders, one rifled, and two smaller field pieces. On the other side of a shallow bay jutting in Hatteras Island stood Fort Hatteras. Its walls were twenty-five feet thick, six feet high, and made of sand covered by wooden stakes and transplanted marsh grass. Ten 32-pounder smoothbores provided close-range punch. A 10-inch weapon was available, but there was no ammunition.

As Col. William F. Martin, in command of the Hatteras forts, counted masts, he knew his 350 men would be no match for a determined Federal landing and looked for a steamer to carry a message to the 230 men stationed at Portsmouth near Fort Ocracoke (or Fort Morgan). No vessels happened by and Martin had to send a man in an open launch, a trip that took twenty-four hours. Stringham was not willing to give the Confederate commander that much time. By 10:00 A.M. on 28 August, landing craft rested alongside the transports, and the warships were ready to test the heavy metal of Fort Clark. Rather than anchor and trade volleys with the forts, Stringham ordered his ships to cruise in a large circle, "the first recorded use of such a tactic by the U.S. Navy."[11]

Within a short while, the tars realized the Rebel guns were no match for the 8-, 9-, and 10-inch weapons on the vessels. The one rifled gun in Fort Clark hit the *Wabash* and *Cumberland* four times, but the shells only embedded themselves in the ships' sides. In the meantime, Butler was having trouble getting his troops ashore. A heavy surf disrupted operations, and by noon only 318 men under Col. Max Weber had reached shore. The *Pawnee,*

Monticello, and *Harriet Lane* blasted the surrounding countryside to make sure no Confederates interfered, but a second wave attempting to reach the beach aboard two dismasted schooners (brought along to serve as block ships) had to be pulled to safety by the tug *Fanny.* Weber's men, along with their powder, were soaked. Within twenty-five minutes, however, the Union navy had convinced Fort Clark's defenders to abandon the sand pile. Capt. John Lamb, in charge of the eighty-five men within Clark, spiked the guns and made for Fort Hatteras "under the heaviest shelling any man ever saw."[12] When a group of Federals entered the fort a little over an hour later, the captains aboard the *Pawnee* and *Monticello* assumed the enemy had returned and soon two shells burst among the Yankees. They fled just as the Rebels had done but returned after a U.S. flag brought the friendly fire to an end.

At 4:00 P.M., when no activity had been observed from the Confederates for two hours, Butler ordered the *Monticello* to enter the inlet and scout Fort Hatteras. The careful approach of the thin-skinned steamer was what the gray-clad defenders had been anticipating. When Comdr. John Gillis brought his ship within range of the fort's 32-pounders, they belched a small measure of revenge. The aim of the untested gunners proved erratic, and in the fifty minutes it took Gillis to back the *Monticello* once more into open water, the steamer was hulled only four times. After pouring two more hours' worth of lead into Fort Hatteras, Stringham ordered his larger ships to find safe anchorage in deeper water. Squalls forced the smaller ships away.

Weber took stock of the dismal situation. His men were wet, hungry, and thirsty. The Confederates could easily overwhelm his small force if they chose to attack during the night. He posted a few pickets toward Fort Hatteras, left a few men in Fort Clark, and retired with the bulk of his command toward the initial landing site.

On the sound side of the island, a small Confederate flotilla worked to bring over reinforcements and ammunition and carry away the wounded. One of the boats carried Com. Samuel Barron, who only a few months earlier had been captain of the USS *Wabash.* A frazzled Martin gladly relinquished responsibility for the defense of the fort to Barron, commander in chief of the coastal defenses for the district of upper North Carolina and lower Virginia. Barron planned to attack Fort Clark after the arrival of reinforcements from Newbern (the name of the town was spelled Newbern until the 1880s when it was spelled New Bern). In the meantime, he wished the weather would win the battle for him or that he had ammunition for the 10-inch gun. As the hours passed, the expected troops did not appear and the weather moderated.

At 5:30 A.M., Stringham ordered his fleet to engage the enemy batteries. Since there was little chance of being hit, Stringham put his ships into an anchored line two miles from Fort Hatteras. By 8:00 A.M. the smaller vessels opened the attack. Twenty minutes later the two larger steam warships

View of Forts Hatteras and Clark *(Leslie's)*

followed suit, and an hour later the sailors and soldiers witnessed the passing of an era as the *Cumberland* joined the fray, "one of the last times a sailing ship would move into battle under full canvas."[13]

Weber's men ended Barron's hopes when they set up a battery facing Pamlico Sound and chased away the *Winslow,* which was trying to bring reinforcements to the embattled Rebels. Although fire from their own fleet once again forced the Federals on land to retire, by then it was all over except for some face-saving posturing by Barron. In retrospect, the Confederate commander had only himself to blame. Had he taken more initiative the previous night, he would have certainly captured a sizable Federal force and perhaps dissuaded Butler and Stringham from continuing the operation.

Once the warships found the fort's range, Confederate Capt. Thomas Sparrow counted twenty-eight shells landing within the earthwork during one sixty-second period. When smoke floated out of the ventilator within the bombproof next to the magazine, Barron decided to surrender rather than risk the annihilation of his men.

Weber and his Federals raced for the walls as Butler steamed toward the fort aboard the *Fanny.* Observing the *Winslow* preparing to pick up small craft pulling away from the island, Butler ordered the tug's bow gun to discourage any more Rebels from seeking safety in that direction.

Barron agreed to relinquish the forts, weapons, and ammunition, but desired that the men be allowed to return to their homes. Butler would have none of that and sent Barron a terse message: "The terms offered are these:

Full capitulation; the officers and men to be treated as prisoners of war. No other terms admissible [*sic*]." Ulysses Grant was thus beaten to the "Unconditional Surrender" title by almost six months. While Butler waited for Barron's reply, two of Stringham's ships ran aground within range of Fort Hatteras. The Union general feared that Barron would take advantage of the situation by refusing his terms and opening fire, but Barron had no such devious mind. The Confederate officer accepted Butler's terms but refused to surrender to the army since it had taken little part in the engagement. Butler insisted that Barron surrender to both Stringham and him, and Barron finally agreed.

At a cost of three slightly wounded men, the Federal forces had captured 678 prisoners, two forts, thirty cannon, a brig, a sloop, whiskey, coffee, and onions.[14] They would also relight the Cape Hatteras lighthouse and securely plug one of the outlets for blockade running and privateer activity. That night Butler and Stringham came to the conclusion that simply blocking the channel was at best a short-term solution. Why not garrison the forts permanently? The next day Butler began a fast trip to Washington via Fort Monroe and convinced Lincoln's cabinet to hold the captured forts. Once it became clear the Federals were intent on staying, the Rebels abandoned Forts Ocracoke and Oregon without a fight.

Writing later about the victory at Hatteras, Adm. David D. Porter noted: "It was a death-blow to blockade running in that vicinity, and ultimately proved one of the most important events of the war."[15]

If you go there . . .

A new lighthouse was built at Cape Hatteras in 1870, the tallest brick lighthouse in the United States. Fearing the old lighthouse would collapse, engineers destroyed it. Erosion threatened the new lighthouse, so a skeleton tower was built in 1936 and the **Cape Hatteras Lighthouse** was turned over to the National Park Service for inclusion in the Cape Hatteras National Seashore. The double keepers' dwelling has been converted into a bookstore and museum detailing the history of the lighthouse.

Farther down Highway 12, a forty-minute, free ferry ride takes cars to Ocracoke Island, frequent headquarters of Edward "Blackbeard" Teach and the site of his death in 1718. At the end of the highway sits the town of Ocracoke and the **Ocracoke Lighthouse.** Built in 1854, it still guides ships through the Ocracoke Inlet. The Confederates damaged the lens in 1861, so the Lighthouse Board installed another in 1864.

For information about lighthouses and public campgrounds, contact: Cape Hatteras National Seashore, Route 1, Box 675, Manteo, NC 27954 (919) 473-2111.

Pamlico and Albemarle Sounds

ALTHOUGH EVENTUALLY overshadowed by his tactical and political bumbling, George B. McClellan's strategic insights were, for the most part, quite sound. As part of the American commission sent to study the Crimean War, he realized that the bayonet charge had outlived its usefulness in an age of longer-range weapons. After returning home and observing his own country's turmoil, he reasoned that the technological advances of the telegraph and railroad, and not superior fighting ability, had allowed the Confederates to concentrate forces and defeat the Federals at First Manassas. If one side could seize and control another's transportation and supply centers, he concluded, it would no longer be necessary for field armies to engage in butchery.

Taking over the role of army commander in November 1861, Little Mac decided to incorporate his ideas into an overall strategy for the conquest of the Confederacy. As part of his plan, he intended to take advantage of the North's overwhelming naval superiority to launch a series of combined operations ultimately aimed at capturing crucial locations along Southern railways. Such expeditions would not only choke off the flow of essential supplies to Rebel armies, but they would also siphon away the South's limited supply of men and materiel from what most Northern military leaders saw as the critical front in Virginia.

As one part of this grand strategy, McClellan planned to send an amphibious force into coastal North Carolina to establish a base, then march inland to cut the Wilmington and Weldon Railroad at Goldsboro, North Carolina, one of only a dozen or so places in the entire Confederacy where a major north-south rail line connected with an east-west line. As the flow of goods from the Deep South trickled to a halt, McClellan assumed, Confederate commanders in Virginia would be forced to transfer troops to reestablish the rail link, thus weakening or abandoning their position around Richmond.

The man chosen to raise the Coast Division for the North Carolina invasion was thirty-seven-year-old Ambrose E. Burnside, a friend of McClellan whose performance as a brigade commander at First Manassas "left much to be desired."[16]

Because Gens. Benjamin Butler and Thomas Sherman were also recruiting troops for their own expeditions, Burnside took far longer than expected to assemble his fifteen-thousand-man division. To carry his diverse regiments, he gathered a motley assortment of transports, including steamers, schooners, barks, former slave ships, tugs, and even a couple of garbage scows. The man with the mutton-chop whiskers also put together a force of nine steam gunboats, ranging in size from two hundred to four hundred tons, each mounting — on the average — three guns. Five canal boats, converted to floating batteries, would also be towed into battle. Including the guns of Flag Off. Louis M. Goldsborough's North Atlantic Blockading Squadron, Burnside would be able to bring the combined firepower of 108 cannon, including 15 new 9-inch rifles, on any coastal defenses.

Burnside's objectives were ambitious. He was to capture and fortify Roanoke Island, seize Newbern, invest Fort Macon, move inland to cut the railroad at Goldsboro, then, if feasible, move on Wilmington. Burnside's three brigadiers had less grandiose goals on their minds. They had their hands full teaching their commands the rudiments of drill without considering the fine art of amphibious operations.

During the second week of January 1862, the Coast Division embarked at Annapolis, Maryland, and sailed for Fort Monroe, where the ships took on coal and fresh water. On 11 January, the fleet moved out from Hampton Roads. As the vanguard rounded Cape Henry, a series of storms lashed at the armada, forcing the battered ships to seek shelter outside Hatteras Inlet until the end of the month. By then the Confederates had ascertained that Roanoke was the fleet's destination, but forewarned was not forearmed.

Gov. Henry Clark of North Carolina refused to send reinforcements to Roanoke, contending that responsibility for the island's defense should rest with Maj. Gen. Benjamin Huger's Department of Norfolk. The Third Georgia under Huger's command had been sent south in mid-1861, but it was withdrawn in January, right before it was needed the most. Gen. D. H. Hill, in charge of the defense of Pamlico and Albemarle sounds, sensing the futility of the situation, resigned his command and reported to Virginia.[17]

Hoping to rectify the situation, the Confederate War Department gave former governor of Virginia Henry A. Wise the job of defending Roanoke and attached him to Huger's command. Although he was "no general,"[18] even the inexperienced Wise could tell that the defenses on Roanoke were a joke. Though the water passage from Pamlico Sound through Croatan Sound into Albemarle Sound was the narrowest at the southern tip of Roanoke, and the enemy would undoubtedly come from that direction, the Rebel defenses were concentrated on the northern tip of the island. Thirty-four cannon, mostly 32-pounder smoothbores, were emplaced in five separate locations, but they could not provide supporting fire to any of the other batteries. Fort Huger, a twelve-gun sand-and-turf fort, faced Croatan Sound from Weir's Point on Roanoke. Fort Blanchard, brandishing four guns, lay twelve hundred yards farther down the sound. Fort Bartow, nine guns, stood more than a thousand yards farther south on Park Point. Across Croatan Sound, two canal boats had been beached to form Fort Forrest, armed with seven 32-pounders. A two-gun lunette at Ballast Point guarded shallow Roanoke Sound on the eastern side of the island. Wise's fourteen hundred men had to rely on three field pieces, including an 18-pounder Mexican War souvenir, for tactical support.

Against orders, Wise journeyed to Richmond to do what he thought he could do best: lobby for more men and supplies. Even a few exploding shells might make a difference, he argued. Eventually elements of two infantry regiments and six artillery pieces were dispatched from Virginia, but Burnside struck before most of them arrived.

Perhaps weighed down by the helplessness of the situation, Wise became bedridden with an illness that had incapacitated him the previous year. He left orders for Col. Henry M. Shaw, commander of the Eighth North Carolina, to have his men drive piles and sink ships to obstruct the channel beside Fort Forrest. Wise also suggested that Shaw meet the Federal assault at the beach, then — only if forced — retreat to prepared breastworks bisecting the main north-south road on the island. If Shaw's men could keep the Federal troops away from the rear of the forts long enough, then perhaps Capt. William F. Lynch's "mosquito fleet" could draw the Federal ships northward within range of the majority of the Rebel batteries.

At 11:30 A.M. on 7 February, Goldsborough's warships of the North Atlantic Blockading Squadron made contact with Fort Bartow. Only four of the fort's nine 32-pounders could traverse far enough to engage the fleet's forty guns. Solid shot from Lynch's gunboats and the other forts had no effect. Still, Maj. Gabriel H. Hill's gunners inside Bartow managed to fire 205 rounds and obtain 27 hits. When the *Commodore Perry* grounded near the fort, eight shots in rapid succession smashed into the vessel, including three that passed through the hull below the waterline. Explosive shells would most likely have destroyed the *Perry* and inflicted greater damage on the fleet. As it was, the most serious damage occurred aboard the *Hetzel* when an 80-pounder rifle burst, sending a half-ton chunk of hot metal through the deck into the powder magazine; a quick-thinking officer managed to douse the flames. Despite the terrific cannonade, losses on both sides were slight. Bartow's garrison lost two killed and three wounded. The navy suffered fourteen casualties, including three killed.

Twice Lynch moved his ships forward in an attempt to divert attention from Fort Bartow. Both times he lost a vessel. Running low on ammunition and realizing his squadron could do nothing at Roanoke, Lynch retreated. From Elizabeth City he dispatched one steamer through the Dismal Swamp Canal, the back door to Norfolk, for more ammunition.

Federal troops began disembarking in the area of Ashby's Harbor on Roanoke Island around 3:00 P.M. Hidden in bushes along the shoreline crouched two hundred Confederates and two cannon under the command of Col. J. V. Jordan. After a taste of grapeshot from the Union gunboats, he ordered his gray-clad defenders to head inland without firing a shot. More than four thousand men in blue under Sr. Brig. John G. Foster came ashore in the first wave. The balance of the division and a naval battery of six guns followed as a light rain fell. By midnight, approximately ten thousand Federals were forming up on the southern end of the island.

Some of the promised reinforcements from Virginia reached Roanoke just in time to join the Carolinians at the three-gun redoubt covering the road north. Belatedly, Shaw realized no one knew how to fire the artillery. A captain arrived from Wise's headquarters at Nag's Head, but he was still giving lessons when the Yankees slogged into the clearing in front of the breastworks around 7:30 the next morning. Union Col. Edwin Upton's Twenty-fifth Massachusetts, however, faced waist-deep muck stretched out from either side of the road, making it impossible to deploy in line of battle. Heavy fire raked the road.

Foster ordered the Bay Staters to push through the morass to the Confederate left. As the New Englanders struggled through the slime, Jesse L. Reno arrived with the first regiments of his Second Brigade and personally led the initial elements on a flanking movement toward the enemy right. By 10:30 A.M., Reno's men had reached the breastwork and rushed upon the Confederates. Surprised by an attack from the supposedly impenetrable swamp, the defenders raced north along the road, sped along by Foster's men and a fresh assault on their center from elements of John G. Parke's Third Brigade.

Once the position folded, Shaw ordered the Croatan Sound forts destroyed and the garrisons withdrawn. While most of the Rebels were making their way north, more Confederate reinforcements arrived. After a brief skirmish with an advancing Massachusetts regiment, they too found themselves with nowhere left to run. As Foster's men prepared to pounce on the cornered men in gray, Shaw asked for terms. Perhaps taking a cue from Benjamin Butler at Hatteras, Foster replied, "Nothing but immediate and unconditional surrender."[19]

The men stationed at Fort Forrest torched the grounded barges and the fort's magazine, then straggled back to Virginia. Several hundred other Rebels managed to remove themselves from Roanoke, including Wise's wounded son, Capt. Jennings Wise. He was hit a second time as his men rowed him to Nag's Head, however, and he died that night. More than 2,500 others laid down their arms on the north end of the island. Total Confederate casualties were 24 killed and 68 wounded. The Union lost 41 killed, 227 wounded, and 15 missing.

Burnside had easily accomplished the first of his many objectives, and Foster's men began to repair the forts and improve communications on Roanoke by adding a telegraph, expanding wharf facilities, and fixing the road.

Lynch knew Goldsborough would not allow the Confederate fleet to remain up the Pasquotank River forever, so he set about to strengthen his position. The six artillery pieces intended to follow the Virginians to Roanoke Island still sat in Elizabeth City. Two miles below the town four 32-pounders commanded Cobb's Point from a small earthen fort. Lynch coerced local officials to call out the militia, but before any substantial body of men could be organized, Lynch's scouts reported Federal warships steaming north across Albemarle Sound.

Com. Stephen C. Rowan, sent by Goldsborough with fourteen warships to destroy Lynch, spotted the Confederates around 8:30 A.M. on 10 February. Low on ammunition, Rowan decided to ram and board the opposing vessels. The eight militiamen inside the Cobb's Point fort, some of them mere boys, fled as soon as they spotted the fleet. Lynch, who had spread his half-dozen ships across the river opposite the fort, ordered Capt. William H. Parker to abandon the *Beaufort* and man the weapons at Cobb's Point, the linchpin of his defense. By the time Parker and Lynch managed to load the artillery pieces, the Union vessels were engaging the mosquito fleet. As Parker's men spiked the now useless guns of the fort, the two Confederate officers inside watched the destruction of the Rebel warships.

The lost colonists from Roanoke left only a one-word clue to the disaster that befell them in the sixteenth century. Wise lashed out against Secretary of War Judah Benjamin and General Huger with 143 pages of poison-pen testimony. Benjamin managed to stay in the cabinet, but his days as secretary of war were numbered. Huger never again held an important command.

The Federals now enjoyed uncontested control of Albemarle Sound and most of its tributaries. Taking advantage of the situation, Goldsborough dispatched Rowan and eight gunboats to burn the Seaboard and Roanoke Railroad bridges over the Nottoway and Blackwater rivers in Virginia. Providing infantry support was Rush Hawkins's Ninth New York Zouaves.

On 18 February the force approached Winton, North Carolina, a small town on a bluff overlooking the Chowan River. Lt. Col. William W. Williams and the First North Carolina Battalion, supported by four cannon, had laid a trap for the unsuspecting marauders. The bait was a mulatto woman who agreed to urge the Federals to land at the wharf. Even though reports that "500 Union sympathizers . . . had taken over the town"[20] had reached Union lines, thirty-year-old Hawkins was skeptical. From a perch on the mainmast of the USS *Delaware,* he spied slivers of sunlight reflecting from bayonets in the woods. He warned the pilot to pull away. The Tar Heels plastered the side-wheeler as it scraped by the dock but only managed to sever Hawkins's perch and send him tumbling to the deck.

Incensed, Rowan conned his ship upriver out of rifle range, then tore into the bluff with his Dahlgren and Parrott guns, scattering the Rebels along the bluff. The *Delaware* then returned downstream to join the rest of the flotilla, setting off a premature celebration in Winton. The next morning Rowan reappeared with eight ships. A few shells convinced Williams's men and most of the townspeople to show their backs. The Confederate soldiers retreated to earthworks at Mount Tabor Church and did not emerge even when, at Hawkins's command, the Zouaves torched and pillaged the community. Figuring surprise was lost, Hawkins and Rowan returned to Roanoke; Williams headed for Virginia. Locals complained of Williams's lack of courage, and in 1863 he resigned from the Confederate army in disgrace.

Brig. Gen. Richard Gatlin, in overall charge of North Carolina's defenses, assumed correctly that Burnside would next move on Newbern, the second largest coastal city in the state. He ordered all but five artillery companies from Fort Macon and contingents from several other areas to converge on the city, situated at the confluence of the Neuse and Trent rivers.

Gen. Lawrence O'Brien Branch, the local commander, felt confident that he could hold the town with his four thousand men. A true defense in depth began ten miles south of the city at Otter Creek. A mile-long breastwork, called the Croatan Line, ran behind the creek between the Neuse and a swamp. Five miles upriver, four guns could sweep the Neuse from earthen Fort Dixie on Johnson's Point. A mile north, Fort Thompson mounted thirteen cannon and anchored another mile-long breastwork, whose flanks were guarded on one side by sunken hulks in the Neuse and on the other by a series of redans fronted by Bullen's Branch. The redans stretched to the wider Brice's Creek. Several more earthen batteries lined the Neuse farther back toward Newbern.

Burnside sailed from Roanoke on 12 March, and scouts informed Branch the moment Union ships entered the Neuse. Before the Rebels could break camp and trudge to their first line of defense, units of Reno's brigade had already landed at Slocum's Creek under protection of a naval bombardment and scampered to the unmanned Croatan Line. Branch pulled his troops back to the Fort Thompson line.

The Confederate commander hoped Burnside would delay his attack long enough for reinforcements to arrive by train from Wilmington and South Carolina, but Foster's brigade was already sloshing its way forward along the muddy Beaufort-Newbern Road as Reno's men advanced along the Atlantic and North Carolina Railroad. Rain fell throughout the night, and the morning of 14 March was obscured by fog and rain. Nevertheless, Foster quickly had his regiments deployed to attack the hidden enemy's left flank. Rowan heard the firing and brought his naval ordnance into the fray. Because the battlefield was shrouded in smoke and low clouds, Foster's Federals found themselves in a crossfire between three of the enemy's guns in

Fort Thompson and several of their own aboard Rowan's gunboats, which inadvertently helped pummel the Union right to a standstill.

In the meantime, Reno's skirmishers, advancing toward the middle of the Rebel line, discovered unprotected artillerists trying to finish a two-gun lunette meant to cover the railroad. Reno's lead companies of the Twenty-first Massachusetts swept over the lunette, then turned on the relatively raw North Carolina militia anchoring the center of Branch's dispositions.

Becoming aware of the seriousness of the situation, Branch ordered his reserves to close the gap, then attempted to halt the militia himself. The day was almost saved when portions of the Seventh and Thirty-seventh North Carolina regiments pushed the outnumbered companies of the Twenty-first Massachusetts back across the earthworks as the Thirty-third North Carolina arrived to stitch the rip in the middle of the Confederate position. At that point, however, Col. Isaac P. Rodman of the Fourth Rhode Island, the lead element of Brig. Gen. John G. Parke's reserve brigade, took the initiative to smash into the newly reformed Confederate line. Having just defeated one attack, the Tar Heels were not ready for another and fell back to regroup. Misinterpreting the movement, Branch assumed all was lost and ordered his entire command to move behind the Trent River while the Twenty-eighth North Carolina, fresh off the train, covered the withdrawal. Branch's orders did not reach the Confederate far right, and the Thirty-third and Twenty-sixth North Carolina regiments — under the command of Harry Burgwyn and the future governor of North Carolina, Zebulon Vance — held on for more than three hours under the full onslaught of two Federal brigades before they too fell back, making their way across Brice's Creek.

As the gray infantry retreated, the garrisons of the river batteries spiked their guns and blew up their magazines. Sighting the flames, Commodore Rowan urged his warships to plow through the river obstructions and speed for Newbern. When Branch saw the Union flotilla barreling down upon the city, he realized Newbern had to be abandoned. After making sure military supplies and bridges over the Trent were destroyed, Branch led his remaining troops thirty miles farther upriver to Kinston.

Burnside's Coast Division had suffered almost twice as many casualties as the Rebels, but it had captured forty-one heavy cannon, nineteen field pieces, six unmounted guns, and a base from which to launch further raids.

Before a week was out, Parke's brigade began the trip south aboard transports toward Beaufort Harbor and Fort Macon, the third of Burnside's objectives. Col. Moses J. White, a twenty-seven-year-old graduate of West Point, commanded the pentagonal brick fortress situated on the east end of Bogue Banks. His 450 officers and men served a relatively large number of cannon, forty-five, but only twelve were rifled: two 10-inch and five 8-inch

Columbiads, four 32-pounders, and one 24-pounder.[21] Also, many of the guns intended to guard the land approaches had been lost at Newbern.

To delay the inevitable overland assault, the Confederates burned the 180-foot railroad bridge over the Newport River and ripped up a large section of track. For some reason, however, the road bridge was not touched. Parke's vanguard entered Carolina City by the evening of 22 March and demanded White's surrender. When the Confederate commander declined, Parke garrisoned the surrounding towns and waited for the rail lines to be repaired.

Parke's men quietly seized Morehead City, the terminus of the railroad, but Beaufort, the main port, lay across a wide bay within range of Fort Macon's guns. During the night of 25 March, Maj. John A. Allen took two companies across the bay and occupied the town. Colonel White did not fire on Beaufort as he had threatened, but he did toss a few shells at any passing Federals.

On 29 March the railroad bridge over the Newport River was reopened, and Parke sent twenty men of Company K, Fourth Rhode Island, to Bogue Banks. They landed at Hoop Pole Creek under the protection of a boat howitzer (brought from the Neuse River via Clubfoot Canal) and the *State of Georgia*. When no resistance was offered by the Confederates, the remainder of the company rowed across. On the same day, sailors from the gunboats *Albatross* and *State of Georgia* landed on Shackleford Banks to establish a permanent Federal garrison. In response, the small detachment of Confederate pickets on the island returned to Fort Macon.

That night on Fort Macon's ramparts, Colonel White turned to Capt. Stephen D. Pool, commander of Company H of the Tenth North Carolina Artillery Regiment, and pointed out the lights at Bogue Banks, Carolina City, Morehead City, Beaufort, Shackleford Banks, and on the blockading squadron. "What . . . does it mean?" White asked.

"It is the Federal anaconda of which we have read," the former teacher replied. "Its folds encircle Fort Macon, and they must be broken or they will crush it."[22]

On 8 April, men from the three companies of the Fourth Rhode Island on Bogue Banks drove back Confederate pickets from the immediate landing area. The next night, a boat carrying several men from the fort's garrison managed to evade the blockaders and get out a message requesting a relief operation. Their concerns were forwarded to Maj. Gen. Theophilus H. Holmes, now in command of the Department of North Carolina, who in turn wrote a letter to Robert E. Lee, military adviser to President Jefferson Davis. Lee suggested withdrawing the garrison, which by that time was impossible.

By 11 April, Parke was ready to make a reconnaissance in force toward the fort to choose sites for his siege weapons. Pool's men fell back slowly.

The advancing Rhode Islanders called on the *State of Georgia* and *Albatross* to hurry along the Rebels. Once the Federal officers selected battery sites, the Yankees withdrew and Pool's men resumed their picket duty outside the fort. The next day the Eighth Connecticut threw back the Rebel pickets. Once more the two Federal warships slammed shells into the dunes in front of the advancing companies dressed in blue. When the Connecticut men came within a mile of the fort, Colonel White's North Carolinians opened up. The two gunboats moved up to take some pressure off the foot soldiers, and White, reluctant to reveal the limited range of his weapons, fired only eleven rounds at the ships. That night, Federal troops dug a line of rifle pits in the sand less than a half-mile from the fort.

While Parke's men began erecting siege battery positions behind the sand dunes, White watched with mounting frustration. He did not command enough men to counterattack and did not have any mortars, which were the only weapons capable of disrupting the Federals by lobbing shells behind the dunes. Desperate, White sought to improvise by rigging makeshift mounts for his 32-pound carronades. Test shots from these weapons landed more than a mile from their intended targets. Had there been enough powder and shot, the fort's artillerists probably could have done more than just slightly harass the Federals' work.

In Newbern, Burnside's remaining troops were digging entrenchments around the entire town. Fort Totten, mounting twenty-eight guns within its seven acres, guarded the middle of the line. Supported by some of Rowan's gunboats, the fortifications around the city were all but impregnable to Confederate assault. Yet all this defensive work was almost certainly counterproductive. While it is true Burnside had no cavalry to speak of and desperately needed draft animals and wagons, there:

> seemed to be no good reason why Burnside would not . . . boldly thrust inland, severing the important Wilmington & Weldon Railroad. He might even drive on to Raleigh, and possibly even knife lengthwise through the Piedmont region of the state. That would allow him to link up with the Unionists in eastern Tennessee, effectively cutting Virginia off from the rest of the Confederacy. For a period of time after [the fall of Newbern], there was virtually nothing to stop him.[23]

This opportunity, however, did not last long. Besides shuffling the high command within the state, by the end of March the Davis administration sent more than twenty thousand men to augment the three thousand to four thousand men already on hand. Had even half as many men been available earlier, Burnside would have been outnumbered and his forces easily defeated.[24] By the beginning of May, however, most of the new arrivals had returned to Virginia to help halt McClellan's sweep up the peninsula toward Richmond.

Had Burnside kept up the pressure toward Goldsboro, McClellan's plan to split the Confederacy might have worked. Instead, on 18 April, as Burnside and his staff inspected General Parke's progress, General Reno and three thousand men, including three regiments under Col. Rush C. Hawkins, were moving across Albemarle Sound toward Elizabeth City. After the success of the ironclad ram *Virginia* in Hampton Roads in early March, Commodore Rowan feared that the Rebels might send a smaller ironclad from Norfolk down the Dismal Swamp Canal into Albemarle Sound. To prevent such a possibility, Burnside dispatched Reno to destroy the canal locks north of South Mills, but Reno's force was repulsed.

On 22 April, Burnside returned to Fort Macon towing two floating batteries. He sent a last surrender demand to the beleaguered Colonel White. The adversaries met two days later, and although White once again refused to vacate the fort, he promised not to bombard Beaufort or Morehead City. For his part, Burnside agreed to allow a load of mail from the fort to be delivered to Beaufort; any replies would be returned to the fort at ten o'clock the next morning.

Burnside had wished for Parke to open fire immediately after the cessation of the surrender negotiations, but adjustments to the siege batteries postponed any bombardments until the morning of 25 April. For the first couple of hours little damage was inflicted by either side as smoke hanging over the fort hampered the view.

At 8:40 A.M. Union Comdr. Samuel Lockwood led his naval squadron of four ships mounting twenty-three cannon into the fray, but rough seas prevented the naval gunners from taking aim. Three of the ships steamed an elliptical course roughly one and a quarter miles from the fort; the fourth anchored about a mile away. At 9:25 the fort scored the first hit, an 8-inch shot passing through the chief engineer's cabin and missing the *Daylight*'s machinery by inches. Another shell smashed the *Gemsbok*'s main forward topmast backstay and slashed away a good deal of rigging. Lockwood had had enough. If a projectile found a vital spot, the unfortunate victim would be at the mercy of the Confederates and the pounding sea. At 9:45 A.M. he hoisted signals for the fleet to retire.

The Confederate gunners cheered their achievement. Their fort had been designed specifically for ship-versus-shore encounters and had won this contest. Yet no sooner had they chased away one seaborne antagonist when another appeared from the opposite direction. Federal naval officers were making efforts to bring the armed canal barges into action, but once again the high seas kept their participation to a minimum. At the same time, the boat bringing mail to the garrison tried to enter the harbor under a flag of truce. The truce was ignored, so the boat returned to Beaufort.

In the meantime, without orders, U.S. Signal Corps personnel stationed in Beaufort began to communicate elevation corrections to the sand

The bombardment of Fort Macon *(Harper's)*

batteries. Soon the tide of battle began to turn against the Confederates. As the afternoon wore on, a twelve-foot crack appeared near one of the fort's batteries. Seventeen of the fort's guns were also put out of action. Late in the afternoon, White ordered one last salvo. When that failed, he sent a flag of truce to ask for terms. Burnside held to his earlier demand, that the fort be surrendered in its present condition. If so, the garrison would be allowed to return home on parole. Colonel White finally agreed, and the following morning at nine o'clock the Rebels marched out of Fort Macon.

Despite the severe damage inflicted on the fort, there were only seven casualties. Another twenty were wounded. Parke lost one killed and six wounded during the bombardment. Coming two weeks after a similar feat at Fort Pulaski in Georgia, the fall of Fort Macon did not receive as many headlines. Its capture, however, gave Burnside a major supply port for his army.

Before Burnside could complete arrangements to advance on Goldsboro, however, Lincoln ordered him to reinforce McClellan, who was having troubles outside Richmond.[25] Foster remained behind at Newbern. Having complete control of the inland waterways, Foster encouraged his energetic naval commander to patrol the numerous inlets. On 9 July 1862, Lt. C. W. Flusser led three Union gunboats into the Roanoke River to threaten the vital railroad bridges at Weldon. Confederate cavalry Lt. Alexander B. Andrews heard about the flotilla as soon as it entered the river and rode with forty-one men to Rainbow Bend (where Confederate engineers were constructing a fort) to set up an ambush. When Flusser's vessels rounded a turn in the river below the hidden dismounted cavalry, the Confederates opened fire, killing two sailors and wounding nine before the warships could scare them off by literally blowing the bluff into the river with a few well-placed shots.

One hundred men and one gun landed at nearby Hamilton, but withdrew after causing only slight damage.[26]

Fearing more such river raids, "the Confederate Congress passed a resolution calling for the defense and obstruction of southern and western rivers."[27] A cordon defense of this type was thought by Lee, President Davis's military adviser in early 1862, to be impossible given the limited resources of the South. Lee felt railroads could concentrate men and materiel faster than the enemy could advance. Confederate Gen. G. W. Smith disagreed and wrote Lee that in North Carolina he had "no confidence in the ability of our railroads to transfer troops with promptness and regularity."[28]

Lee proved to be partially correct when in early November a landing party from the USS *Seymour* blew up the magazine of the fort at Rainbow Bend that left the works only partially destroyed. Before Foster could reach his objective at Tarboro, however, trains had managed to transport enough Confederates to threaten Foster's line of communications, so the attack was halted.

The following month Foster marched out of Newbern with eleven thousand men to cut the railroad at Goldsboro while his former commander, Burnside, now in command of the Army of the Potomac, approached Fredericksburg. Due to falling water, supporting Union gunboats on the Neuse retreated downriver. On 14 December Foster learned of the trouncing Burnside suffered at Fredericksburg. Hoping to beat Confederate reinforcements to Goldsboro, he set off the next day. That night his scouts discovered an unfinished Rebel ironclad, the first incarnation of the CSS *Neuse*, at Whitehall, and attempted to destroy it. Confederates were firmly entrenched on the other side of the river, however, and managed to protect the unfinished warship.

Foster once again set his army on the road to Goldsboro. The following day his men were close enough to strike toward their main objective: the railroad bridge at Goldsboro. Just as a couple of volunteers set the span on fire, a cheer went up from the Rebel side of the river. The first reinforcements from Gen. James J. Pettigrew's brigade had arrived from Fredericksburg. Confederate work crews had the trains running again in a fortnight.

On 13 February 1863, Yankee gunboats steamed up the Roanoke again to complete the destruction of Williamston. By then, Confederates had finished constructing the fort just above the town at Rainbow Bend, although only a few guns had been mounted. Named after Gen. Lawrence O'Brien Branch, the former adjutant general of North Carolina who had been killed at Sharpsburg the previous September, the earthworks rose seventy feet above the twisting river. Despite continued reports of a Rebel ironclad taking shape at Edward's Ferry (above Hamilton), the U.S. Navy indicated it could not pass the defenses at Rainbow Bend without help from the army.

Early in 1864, Lee finally "understood there was much to be gained by even a single success on the North Carolina coast."[29] The Confederate commander demurred from leading any operations himself but did suggest that Robert Hoke, a native North Carolinian, stage an attack against Newbern. President Davis instead selected Gen. George Pickett, who immediately adopted Hoke's plan.

As a critical element of the offensive, John Taylor Wood, a former gunnery officer on the ironclad *Virginia,* would lead a force of fourteen boats loaded with 285 officers and men down the Neuse River to paralyze Union gunboat support for the Newbern's garrison. At 2:20 A.M. on 2 February, Wood's raiders approached the *Underwriter,* the only gunboat on duty. The Rebels were spotted but managed to board the larger ship and capture it after a sharp fight.

On land, the Confederates balked. When Gen. Seth Barton had "a signal failure of nerve,"[30] the three-pronged Rebel attack fizzled.

By April 1864 the strategic situation appeared bleak for the Confederacy, but Confederate troops still managed a measure of success at Plymouth on the Roanoke River.

The initial attack began on 17 April. Despite the sinking of the Union steamer *Bombshell* by Rebel batteries, by 9:00 P.M. that day the advance had sputtered to a halt in the face of supporting fire from the gunboats USS *Southfield* and *Miami.* Two days later at 2:30 A.M., the ironclad ram CSS *Albemarle,* under the command of Capt. James W. Cooke, made its long-anticipated appearance. Cooke reported that the 200-pounder Parrott at Fort Grey and another 200-pounder at Battery Worth both fired upon his ship with no effect.[31] Lieutenant Commander Flusser, U.S.N., hoping to stop the ram, lashed his wooden warships together and brazenly ordered them to advance upriver. Coming downriver, Cooke ordered ramming speed. The Union ships blasted away as the *Albemarle* glanced off the *Miami* and slammed solidly into the *Southfield.* Flusser, commanding one of the guns on board the *Southfield,* died when a shot ricocheted and landed back on his own vessel.[32] With the *Southfield* sinking, the remainder of the Federal fleet withdrew down the Roanoke toward Albemarle Sound.

The Rebel ram now controlled the waters around Plymouth and gave the South "a taste of the priceless advantage Union armies enjoyed in all theaters throughout the war"[33] as Rebel gunners aboard the ram were able to enfilade Union positions. The next day Plymouth surrendered to General Hoke's attackers.

By the spring of 1865, the CSS *Neuse* was once again ready to make another stab at Newbern, but the Confederate army was in no position to offer any support. Gen. Joseph E. Johnston had taken command in North Carolina and pulled troops out of Kinston as part of an effort to consolidate enough strength to meet Gen. William Tecumseh Sherman's army, sweeping north from South Carolina. The withdrawal of the Rebels allowed the unmolested approach of Federals toward Kinston. When the Confederate ironclad's new commander, Joseph H. Price, discovered on 10 March that bluecoated soldiers had advanced within five miles of his position, he realized that any attempt to navigate the sixty miles to Newbern would be futile. He opted for using the *Neuse* as a floating battery to counter the troops of Union Gen. Jacob Cox. After pouring a few rounds of grape into the enemy's ranks, Price ordered the detonation of a scuttling charge in the bow. The resulting explosion ripped a hole in the port side, sinking the unlucky ship and extinguishing fires almost as soon as they started.

By 22 March, Sherman's unstoppable horde had joined Gen. John M. Schofield's army at Goldsboro, well over three years since McClellan first suggested the city held one of the keys to Union victory.

If you go there . . .

Most Civil War sites on Roanoke Island have disappeared as completely as did the Lost Colony. The location of **Fort Defiance,** the three-gun battery that briefly thwarted Burnside's advance up the island, is just south of U.S. 64/264 on Route 345. The few remains of the fort are encircled by a white wooden fence. A brick-and-metal monument at the site contains a detailed color map of the battle. A house used as a hospital by Union forces still stands near the present shoreline at Ashby's Harbor, the Federal landing area.

Along the east side of U.S. 64/264 in Manteo, the major town on the island, two plaques indicate to passersby the location of **Fort Bartow** (of which nothing remains) and the channel obstructions constructed by the Confederates. Also in Manteo, **The Outer Banks History Center** holds an extensive collection of photographs, paintings, and manuscripts, many of which deal with the Civil War period. The reading room and gallery are open 9:00 A.M. to 5:00 P.M. and 10:00 A.M. to 4:00 P.M. respectively on weekdays. For information about the collections or special programs, contact: The Outer Banks History Center, P.O. Box 250, Manteo, NC 27954 (919) 473-2655.

The **Fort Raleigh National Historic Site,** which focuses on the Lost Colony, covers a large portion of the northern end of the island.

Archaeologists fear, however, that much of the Confederate camp on the island — including barracks, wharves, and hospital — and the actual location
of the Lost Colony may fall victim to private development adjacent to the
park. The only confirmed Lost Colony site is Fort Raleigh, which lies within
the boundaries of the park. A reproduction earthwork covers the fort's original borders.

At a pullover west of the Fort Raleigh Historic Site on the south side of
the highway just before the bridge to the mainland, signs point to the remains of **Fort Blanchard** and **Fort Huger.** The remnants of the two forts
are covered by trees and brush. On the mainland another plaque briefly tells
about **Fort Forrest.**

Across Albemarle Sound at Elizabeth City, the **Museum of the Albemarle** houses a small collection of Civil War artifacts. It is free and open
Tuesday through Saturday from 9:00 A.M. to 5:00 P.M. and Sunday from
2:00–5:00 P.M. For more information, contact: Museum of the Albemarle,
1116 U.S. Highway 17 South, Elizabeth City, NC 27909 (919) 335-1453.

At the west end of the sound up the Roanoke River, the town of Plymouth has added a terrific Civil War attraction in the form of the **Port O'
Plymouth Roanoke River Museum.** Situated in the former train station,
the newly opened museum has the best display of Civil War ordnance I have
seen. Also on view are artifacts from the USS *Southfield,* a barrelhead from
the USS *Miami,* and a model of the CSS *Albemarle.* One of the more interesting displays is a series of photographs taken during the filming of "Glory
Hunters," a 1959 CBS production in its series, "The Desperate Years." Documenting the sinking of the *Albemarle,* the film utilized a life-size model of
the Confederate ram. Unfortunately, after previewing in Plymouth, the film
was lost. For information, contact: The Historical Society of Washington
County, P.O. Box 296, Plymouth, NC 27962 (919) 793-1377.

A booklet available for purchase at the museum pinpoints the location
of other sites in the town associated with the Civil War. For example, almost
across the street from the museum, the **Grace Episcopal Church** served
as a hospital during the attack on Plymouth in April 1864. Its pews and
gallery were dismantled to make coffins. At the corner of Washington and
Third Street, the north side of **Ausbon House** still shows the effects of
shelling from Federal gunboats in 1862.

Farther up the Roanoke River at Hamilton, reenactors of the First
North Carolina Volunteers are working to preserve **Fort Branch.** The day
after Lee surrendered at Appomattox Court House, the district commander,
Gen. Laurence S. Baker, ordered the fort to be evacuated and its cannons
thrown into the river. Mud and silt kept the barrels and carriages from dis-
integrating. Consequently, when efforts to raise the ordnance paid off in the
1970s, locals could brag that Fort Branch had become the only Civil War
fort with most of its original armament. Eight of the post's twelve cannon

and carriages are on display in the visitors center, where a free map of the fort is available. The winter headquarters of the reenactors stands outside the fort proper and can also be toured.

Fort Branch remains an excellent example of the Confederate Engineer Bureau's strategy for river defense. Situated on a high bluff, its guns could control three-quarters of a mile of the Roanoke River. River obstructions in the form of a chain and torpedoes kept the Union navy at bay. A floating battery was also under construction at Halifax (where Baker eventually surrendered what was left of his command). The *Albemarle* had priority in armor, however, and the battery was never finished. In April 1865, the battery was cut loose, drifted down to Jamesville, struck a torpedo, and blew up.

The fort is free and open April through November from 10:30 A.M. to 5:30 P.M. on Saturdays and 1:30–5:30 P.M. on Sundays. For information about the fort or reenactments, contact: the Martin County Travel and Tourism Director, 305 East Main Street, P.O. Drawer 1048, Williamston, NC 27892 (919) 792-2044. To contribute to the fort's preservation, contact: Fort Branch Battlefield Commission, P.O. Box 355, Hamilton, NC 27840.

On the Neuse River, your first stop should be New Bern. In that city, Will Georges is a real blue-and-gray blood. Besides acting as curator of the **New Bern Civil War Museum** and operating a Civil War antique store, he is pushing for the creation of a park on the site where Colonel Vance's Twenty-sixth North Carolina Infantry held off a flood of Yankees during the battle of Newbern on 14 March 1862. For those interested in Civil War history in the New Bern area, the obvious hangout is Georges's museum. Although small, the museum holds an award-winning collection of weapons and includes a small gift shop. Admission to the museum, which is open 10:00 A.M. to 6:00 P.M. daily except holidays, is $3.00. For more information, contact: New Bern Civil War Museum, 301 Metcalf Street, New Bern, NC 28560 (919) 633-2818.

Another place to gather information is the **Craven County Visitor Information Center** at 219 Pollock Street. The center offers tourists a good guide booklet to the city. It is open 8:00 A.M. to 5:00 P.M. Monday through Friday, 10:00 A.M. to 5:00 P.M. on Saturdays, and 11:00 A.M. to 4:00 P.M. on Sundays. The booklet includes information on the **Charles Slover House** at 201 Johnson Street. Both General Foster and General Burnside used this house as headquarters. In 1908, C. D. Bradham purchased the property. He invented "Brad's Drink," now known as Pepsi-Cola. Burnside also took advantage of the **John Wright Stanley House,** one of the places where Washington slept during his southern tour in 1791. Moved several times since the war, it now stands at 307 George Street and is open to the public.

Farther up the Neuse River at Kinston hunkers a monument to amateur enthusiasm: the remains of the Rebel ironclad **CSS *Neuse*.**

Fort Macon *(North Carolina Department of Natural Resources)*

Construction of the ram began in the fall of 1862 at Whitehall, but by that time the ore fields of Kentucky and Tennessee had fallen to Union forces. Consequently, construction delays followed. When the ram finally left on its first mission in April 1864, it was still lacking its second layer of iron.

Scuttled in March 1865, the *Neuse* lay forgotten until the Civil War centennial when three locals decided to try to raise the hull. A cofferdam was built in November 1961, and empty steel barrels brought the warship to the surface. However, winter floods that year almost destroyed the remains. Finally, in the spring of 1964, what was left of the hulk was transported to the Richard Caswell Memorial, which honors the first governor of the independent state of North Carolina.

A museum at the site houses artifacts taken from the ship as well as a model of the original ironclad. A slide show details Civil War river operations around Kinston. There is also a small gift shop. Visitors can walk around the 136-foot by 37-foot hull which sits nearby underneath its own awning. The museum, situated three-quarters of a mile off the U.S. 70 bypass on West Vernon Avenue, is free and open seven days a week from April through October and every day but Monday the rest of the year. For information, contact: Richard Caswell Memorial, P.O. Box 3043, Kinston, NC 28501 (919) 522-2091.

Following Burnside's route to Fort Macon, drivers will pass a marker for **Huggins's Island Fort** in Morehead City. The six-gun battery guarded Bogue Inlet. Union troops burned it on 19 August 1862.

The main entrance to the inner citadel of Fort Macon

Fort Macon State Park lies at the northeast end of Highway 58 on Bogue Banks. Because Beaufort was one of the first towns in the colonies to be designated as a port of entry, the defense of Topsail (now Beaufort) Inlet became a priority. Gov. Arthur Dobbs selected a site for the first fort on the southwest point of the inlet in May 1755. The next year the governor visited the almost-completed fort named in his honor and deemed it "in no condition of defense."[34] A half-century later, Fort Hampton, a small brick fortress, took shape on the same site but was soon swallowed by the encroaching sea. Construction on the present fort, named after North Carolina Sen. Nathaniel Macon, was begun in 1826. Robert E. Lee served as the engineering officer during the initial building phases. After its capture by Union forces in 1862, Fort Macon protected a Union coaling station, then served as a Federal prison until 1876. The Civilian Conservation Corps restored the abandoned property during 1934–35, and Fort Macon became North Carolina's first functioning park in 1936.

As you circle past the U.S. Coast Guard base on the way to the fort site, look to your left. The pentagonal brick fortress is barely visible behind its protective hills, certainly a portent of future fortress design. Unlike many of the other Civil War–era coastal forts, no additions were made to Fort Macon during the Spanish-American War or later. Consequently, the fort's appearance remains quite faithful to its Civil War configuration. Visitors can take a guided tour of the fort or follow the printed map available at the sally port entrance. A museum, which includes displays in restored officers' and

The east side of the inner citadel, overlooking the Beaufort Inlet

enlisted men's quarters and a bookstore, is open weekends throughout the year and daily, June through Labor Day, from 9:00 A.M. to 5:30 P.M.

The park itself includes restrooms, picnic facilities, a concession stand, swimming area, bathhouse, and hiking paths.

For further information, contact: Fort Macon State Park, P.O. Box 127, Atlantic Beach, NC 28512 (919) 726-3775.

Wilmington

ON 4 JULY 1862, Col. William Lamb stepped onto Confederate Point, originally named Federal Point, at the mouth of the Cape Fear River and assumed command of Fort Fisher, at that time a modest link in the defenses of the port of Wilmington. The next day the twenty-six-year-old former editor proved himself to be a lion when he confronted his junior officers about a Federal ship lying within range of the post's cannon. It had been policy up to that point, the officers informed Lamb, not to instigate confrontations. Lamb promptly directed his men to fire upon the ship, which just as promptly raised anchor and slipped out of range.

The newly appointed colonel then surveyed the fort on the sandy slip of peninsula between the Atlantic Ocean and the Cape Fear River. Just four batteries faced the sea. Those, along with two adjacent earthworks, mounted a mere seventeen guns. Lamb lamented that "one of the Federal frigates could have cleared it out with a few broadsides," so he determined at once to build "a work of such magnitude that it could withstand the heaviest fire of any guns in the American Navy."[35]

Within two years Lamb gave shape to his dream by keeping upward of a thousand men, both soldiers and slaves, busy shoveling together one of history's greatest sand castles. By 1864, the land face of the L-shaped fortress ran a half-mile from the Atlantic to the Cape Fear. A series of fifteen traverses thirty feet high and twenty-five feet thick protected twenty heavy seacoast guns guarding the landward approach. To their front ran a nine-foot palisade fence. Beyond that, a primitive electronically controlled minefield, composed of two dozen torpedoes filled with a hundred pounds of powder, stretched along the land face between the two bodies of water. At Fort Fisher's elbow, Lamb designed forty-three-foot-high Northeast Bastion from which an 8.5-inch Blakely rifle confronted the entire landscape far out into the ocean. Next to that, crescent-shaped Pulpit Battery contained Lamb's combat headquarters.

The fort's sea face ran south from the Northeast Bastion a mile along the channel leading to the Cape Fear River and contained another twenty-four heavy guns, including a 150-pound Armstrong midway down the line of massive traverses. At the southern end of the sea face, a crew worked for eighteen months to raise the wondrous Mound Battery, a sixty-foot-tall pile of sand fortified with two heavy seacoast artillery pieces. Battery Buchanan covered the rear approaches to the fort. It was a detached bastion at the tip of the peninsula armed with two 11-inch Brooke smoothbores, two 10-inch Columbiads, and one 6-pounder howitzer. With the help of Lamb's masterpiece, by 1864 Wilmington was one of the most heavily protected cities in the world. Fort Caswell, a brick-and-masonry third-system fortification, and more than a half-dozen earthworks in addition to Fort Fisher guarded the water approaches to what was the largest city in North Carolina.

For good reasons the Confederacy turned Wilmington into the "Malakoff Tower of the South."[36] Situated well beyond cannon range up the Cape Fear River, Wilmington could not be reached by deep-draft warships. Its best attribute as a haven for blockade runners, however, had to do with the Cape Fear estuary. The river split at the Atlantic on Smith's Island into two inlets ten miles apart. Adding the necessity of skirting Frying Pan Shoals, Federal men-of-war had to patrol a fifty-mile arc to police the sea approaches to Wilmington with any effectiveness. In July 1861, this seemed an impossible task for the overtaxed U.S. Navy. At that time, the USS *Daylight*, a 682-ton screw steamer armed with four 32-pounders, took up blockade duties and raised more derision than fear. By December 1864, however, with every other major port in the Confederacy east of the Mississippi captured or sealed against European traffic, thirty-three Federal warships maintained a constant watch on Wilmington's inlets, a number approximating the entire strength of the U.S. Navy at the beginning of the war.[37]

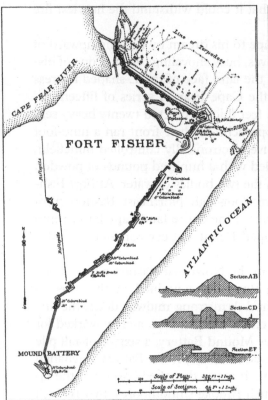

The plan and sections of Fort Fisher (*left*) and the plan of attack on January 15, 1865, showing the placement of naval vessels and their approximate firing angles on the fort (*right*)

Lamb had arrived in Wilmington with virtually no military experience. As an elected captain of a Norfolk militia company, he had assisted Confederate batteries at Sewall's Point along Hampton Roads in a skirmish with the USS *Monticello* soon after the Civil War began. That was the total extent of his exposure to combat when he came to Wilmington in 1861 to serve as quartermaster for the District of Cape Fear. When it was evident that the fighting would last longer than first anticipated, Major Lamb was given command of Fort Saint Philip, an earthen battery along the west bank of Cape Fear, south of Wilmington. He sent his wife north to Providence, Rhode Island, to live with her folks while he studied engineering. Then he proceeded to turn his post into the formidable Fort Anderson. This demonstration of Lamb's ability as an engineer convinced his superiors to make him a colonel and give him command of Fort Fisher, named after North Carolinian Col. Charles F. Fisher, who had died at First Manassas.

In August 1863, Colonel Lamb got a taste of what was to come when the blockade runner *Hebe* ran aground nine miles north of Fort Fisher after being chased by the USS *Niphon*. Confederate cavalry captured the sailors from the *Niphon* who were attempting to refloat or destroy the *Hebe*. Another Federal ship appeared and its tars tried to rescue the prize crew. Lamb sent more cavalry, which precipitated a standoff of sorts. From behind some dunes, a flying battery of Whitworths kept the blockaders at bay while the Rebels worked to offload the stranded ship's cargo. Several days later, on the morning of 23 August, five Federal warships mounting sixty-eight guns moved into position and savaged the sand hills around the *Hebe*. The Confederates fled, leaving their Whitworths behind. Sailors from the victorious fleet came ashore to claim them for the Union.[38]

Confederate Gen. W. H. C. Whiting had felt Wilmington's defenses to be inadequate since taking command of the District of Cape Fear in November 1862. The incident with the *Hebe* confirmed his fears; his requests for additional troops and artillery became more shrill. Unfortunately for Whiting, he was not in good standing with either Jefferson Davis or North Carolina Gov. Zebulon Vance. Given the chance to redeem himself at Drewry's Bluff, Virginia, in May 1864, Whiting had failed to rise to the occasion. Although he tried to defend his actions during the battle, no one in power was willing to listen. Forced to return to Wilmington, Whiting remained as out of favor with President Davis as ever. Vance then petitioned for Whiting's removal and asked that he be replaced with D. H. Hill. In the fall of 1864, Davis partially fulfilled Vance's request by assigning his longtime friend Braxton Bragg as district commander. Demoting Whiting, Colonel Lamb's friend and mentor, was bad enough, but assigning Bragg to Wilmington was adding insult to injury as far as many in the South were concerned. "Bragg has been sent to Wilmington," editorialized the *Richmond Examiner*. "Goodbye Wilmington!"[39] The loss of the harbor was not to be taken lightly. "Hold Fort Fisher," pleaded General Lee in the waning days of 1864, "or I cannot subsist my army."[40]

For their part, Northern strategists were trying to make sure the headlines came true by finalizing plans to capture Wilmington and Fort Fisher. Adm. David Porter, although young and known to be ambitious, was assigned to lead the naval portion of the operation. U.S. Secretary of the Navy Gideon Welles had little choice. The secretary needed Gen. Ulysses Grant's support, and Grant wanted the man who had served him so well around Vicksburg. Porter was also Assistant Navy Secretary Gustavus Fox's brother-in-law. To command the army troops, Grant appointed Gen. Godfrey Weitzel, chief engineer for the Army of the James. Much to everyone's chagrin, Benjamin Butler, commander of the Army of the James, pulled rank and took field command of the expedition.

Like many others, Porter could not tolerate Butler and was surprised when the general invited him shortly before the Fort Fisher operation for a cruise down the James River aboard the *Greyhound*, Butler's headquarters ship. Skeptical about security aboard the former blockade runner, Porter was on his way to the bridge to report some suspicious-looking characters when an explosion ripped through the vessel, which sank in five minutes. Porter and Butler barely escaped. The incident cemented Porter's negative feelings toward Butler. As the expedition sailed out of Hampton Roads on 13 December 1864 toward Fort Fisher, the admiral fully intended to capture the great bastion without any help from the bumbling army commander.

As one of his first acts as district commander, Bragg led half of Lamb's garrison south to Augusta, Georgia, to help stem the blue tide following William Tecumseh Sherman from Atlanta to the sea. The Tar Heels did not arrive in time to save Savannah. By 17 December, Bragg was back in Wilmington, but without his troops. Taking a risk to save his last supply base, Lee ordered Gen. Robert Hoke's division of 6,155 men south to reinforce the port's garrison. Had Butler followed Grant's orders to attack immediately, he probably could have walked into Fort Fisher long before Hoke arrived. Instead, he invested his time in rigging a flat-bottomed steamer, the *Louisiana,* with 250 tons of powder. He and Fox had concocted a plan in November to run the ship close to Fort Fisher and blow down its walls. Most of Butler's futuristic schemes met with skepticism.[41] But with the backing of Fox, Butler was determined to carry through the powder-boat brainstorm. By the time the *Louisiana* was ready and the fleet had arrived off Wilmington in mid-December, Butler's transports had begun to run out of supplies. Rather than push forward, the general elected to return his ships eighty miles to reprovision at Union-controlled Beaufort, South Carolina.

Porter waited until the night of 23 December and then decided to proceed with the powder-boat plan without Butler. The admiral withdrew all but one vessel of his fleet far out to sea and ordered the steam to be released from all boilers just in case shock waves broke any fittings. Comdr. Alexander Rhind slipped the *Louisiana* behind a blockade runner and brought it as near Fort Fisher as he dared, but he was three hundred yards farther away than he thought. He ignited various fuses, triggered clockwork mechanisms, lit a box of candles, started a slow-burning wick, and for good measure set fire to some resinous pine stacked on the deck. Afterward, Rhind and two volunteers rowed to the USS *Wilderness,* which raced to the distant line of anchored warships.

At 1:30 A.M. on Christmas Eve, the powder ignited, providing a spectacular show to those lining the decks of the Union ships. Many sailors, perhaps through wishful thinking, agreed the explosion must have destroyed a large portion of the fort's defensive power. Rhind, however, was skeptical. "There's a fizzle," he muttered, then excused himself to get some rest.[42] Inside Fort Fisher most of the garrison assumed a boiler had exploded on an enemy ship and went back to sleep.

When the sun rose, Porter realized Rhind was correct. The stronghold would have to be reduced from the sea. Thus, on the day before

Christmas, the monumental task of getting his armada into a battle line began. The "deep blue sea was calm as a lake, and broke lazily on the bar and beach," wrote Colonel Lamb as he watched the mile-wide arc of warships take position. "A grander sight than the approach of Porter's formidable armada towards the fort was never witnessed on our coast."[43] With an average of seventy to eighty rounds per gun, Lamb ordered no weapon to be discharged more than once every half-hour. His prized 150-pound Armstrong, with a mere thirteen rounds, was to be fired only under his direct supervision.[44]

At 12:45 P.M., a flash and a puff of smoke leapt from the forward starboard gun of the *New Ironsides*. A deep boom followed as an 11-inch shell zipped over the heads of the defenders and exploded harmlessly past the fort's flagstaff. Lamb responded with the 10-inch Columbiad near the Pulpit. Its solid shot ricocheted off the flat surface of the ocean and punched a hole in the *Susquehanna*'s stack. The remainder of Fisher's guns bellowed, hitting the *Minnesota* four times on the first salvo. Since the bulk of Porter's ships were anchored, Lamb's gunners had no difficulty finding a mark. But with such a severe shortage of ammunition, crippling one of the men-of-war would be difficult. On the Union side, three lines of broadsides from almost five dozen warships began throwing a hailstorm of iron toward the fort, sometimes as many as 115 shells per minute.

Ironically, but not unusually, the first damage on both sides had nothing to do with enemy exertions. One of the fort's 8-inch Columbiads tore loose from its mounting and tumbled backward, scattering the frightened crew. Aboard the warships, one of the 100-pounder Parrott guns, which already had reputations as widow-makers, exploded aboard the USS *Juanita* shortly after 2:00 P.M., "disemboweling one gunner, decapitating another, killing two more with shrapnel, and wounding eight other men."[45] The captain pulled his ship out of line but returned sheepishly when Porter, weaving in and out of the fleet aboard the *Malvern*, strongly suggested he utilize his other weapons. Two other warships, the side-wheel steamer *Mackinaw* and its sister ship *Osceola*, both suffered serious damage when struck by shore batteries, but they managed to stay in formation.[46]

Lamb noticed that much of the fleet's malice was directed toward the garrison flag hanging in the middle of the parade ground in an area where no threat could be posed to the fort or its garrison by exploding shells. When the flagstaff became so splintered it could no longer support the colors, Lamb "went to the left salient and planted a company battle-flag . . . where it would do the most good by causing the least harm."[47]

After several hours, despite few casualties, Rebel fire grew erratic as noise-deafened gunners grew weak from smoke inhalation. In addition, five artillery carriages had been smashed and two cannon dismounted within the fort. Porter's sailors were equally disoriented by the constant concussion and drifting smoke. Adding to the strain, Parrotts had exploded on four more ships, killing or wounding thirty-seven.

At 4:30 P.M., Colonel Lamb learned that his Brooke battery had taken a direct hit. Just then, the disheartened commander looked up to see General Whiting. After landing at the wharf near Battery Buchanan and discovering that all the post's horses had been killed, he and three staff officers walked over a mile through the shower of hot lead to the Northeast Bastion. Lamb offered to turn over command, but Whiting insisted he had only come to see things for himself and bring some good news: two companies were on their way from Fort Caswell and the first elements of Hoke's division under the command of Gen. William Kirkland had reached Wilmington. Actually, Kirkland was already on the scene near Battery Anderson, five miles north of Fort Fisher. Kirkland immediately familiarized himself with the topography, then deployed his men to repel a landing or support Lamb.

General Butler had also finally arrived from Beaufort. Angry that his project had been exploded without him, and even angrier that it had failed, he requested to see Porter, who excused himself on the grounds he was too tired after the long day of fighting. General Weitzel, in tactical command of the ground forces, suggested that Porter run his lightest warships over the New Inlet bar and bombard Fort Fisher from behind. Porter refused. Butler accused him of having "torpedoes on the brain," and the admiral repaid the compliment by insisting Butler was "an ignorant liar."[48] Cyrus Comstock, one of Butler's subordinates, sarcastically noted the "fine cooperation" between the two services, but convinced Butler and Weitzel — both of whom were ready to return to Fort Monroe — not to quit without a fight.[49]

By 7:00 A.M. Christmas Day, Porter's ships were back in line, pounding Lamb's sand pile. A little before noon, Capt. Oliver Glisson, commanding the *Santiago de Cuba*, steamed north with seventeen vessels to confront the Confederate batteries covering the prospective beachhead. Confederate Lt. Col. John Read tried to convince his gunners to stand and fight, but when his arm was ripped away, the frightened crews hid among the dunes. Read's replacement concentrated on preparing for the landing he knew would come soon.

At 10:00 A.M. firing commenced from the full procession of naval boats, "fully six miles long, including those which were shelling the water-batteries along the sea beach to effect a landing for infantry," wrote one of the participants. "From that time until night did the lurid flame flash and the grim roar mutter while everything trembled as if it were rocked in the cradle of consternation."[50] Around 2:00 P.M., 450 men from two New York regiments landed less than a quarter-mile from Battery Anderson and began to advance through the sand. The battered Rebels raised a white flag, but before the New Yorkers could reach them, crew members from the USS *Britannia* rowed ashore and captured the Rebel colors. Pleased at the alacrity with which his men had taken their first objective, Butler ordered the bulk of his troops ashore and threw out a picket line. Kirkland's veterans moved forward and made contact, but they withdrew when Kirkland realized his men were outnumbered.

Meanwhile, Porter had second thoughts about the proposed attempt to enfilade the fort. He sent William Cushing — a man who thrived on suicide missions — to sound the channel. After a moment of stunned silence, Lamb gave the officer in charge of the two 7-inch Brookes discretion to fire at will on this threat to Fort Fisher's rear. The Confederates began to bang away at Cushing's small boats, but the lieutenant's incredible good fortune continued when both guns in the Brooke battery burst trying to swamp the Federal volunteers. Remarkably, the plucky naval officer made it back to Porter with only one casualty. His news, however, was not good: He felt the channel was too crooked to navigate with warships.

When Lamb learned that both his Brookes had exploded, he decided it was time to unleash the 150-pound Armstrong. He personally directed its fire and cheered with his troops when its fourth round ripped through a frigate, causing it to leave the line. His pleasure was short-lived when he was told that Battery Anderson had capitulated. All through the fight so far, Lamb had worried about the fort's detachments of junior reserves, boys too young to serve in regular units. He tried to send some to Fort Holmes on Smith's Island, but their transport never arrived. Several hundred others were trapped north of the fort near Battery Anderson. They were the only troops between the Union forces and Fort Fisher. Lamb's fears for their safety proved premature as their commander surrendered the boys to the advancing 117th New York.

Soon afterward, Bvt. Brig. Gen. Newton M. Curtis, in charge of the initial landing, and General Weitzel moved to within eight hundred yards of Fort Fisher's land face. Weitzel, who had witnessed the assault on Battery Wagner near Charleston, South Carolina, balked, but Curtis and his men inched forward and captured a detached redoubt and field piece without suffering a single casualty. When one of the brigadier's men sprinted through a gap in the log palisade to seize an enemy banner at the foot of the main Rebel ramparts without drawing any fire, Curtis insisted he could overrun the fort with only a few regiments. Instead, Butler ordered him to evacuate. Curtis refused, but by then it was too late. The naval bombardment had stopped. As he had on the previous day, Lamb discharged the last gun in the duel at 5:30 P.M. "to let our naval visitors know that we had another shot in the locker."[51] The empty parapets of Fort Fisher filled with seven hundred cheering Confederates, who fired joyously, but without much effect, at the Yankees beyond the palisade fence. Following several abortive attempts to convince Butler to change his mind, Curtis finally ordered his men back to the beach at 7:30 P.M.

The next morning seven hundred of the New Yorkers remained hunkered in the sand. No doubt Curtis's men felt abandoned, especially when Butler ordered his flagship to weigh anchor and return to Fort Monroe. Hoke arrived the next day to find the New Yorkers still stranded on the beach, their transports unable to get through the rough surf. Unreliable information about their numbers kept both Lamb and Hoke, whose troops were tired from their long journey south from Petersburg, from attacking. That afternoon, a disgusted Porter finally brought the men off the beach. Low on ammunition, his warships returned to Beaufort. Porter had expended 20,271 rounds on a lost cause, but he took heart in the fact that the army's poor showing meant "the end of Butler's national political aspirations."[52]

In his history of the naval war, Porter was kinder to Butler, writing that all the blame being put on the army commander "was unfair to General Butler." He was less kind to General Weitzel, suggesting that his "course at Fort Fisher was quite in keeping with his previous record at Sabine Pass [Texas], where, with a force greatly outnumbering the enemy, he ignominiously retired, leaving two frail gunboats to attack the Confederate works and be cut to pieces."[53]

Lamb could take pride in what his men had accomplished. Although seven guns had been damaged, his ordnance experts assured him that three or four could be repaired. His greatest reward came on 28 December when two blockade runners slipped into Wilmington and one slipped out. For his part, Bragg prematurely announced that "the superiority of land batteries over ships of war has been reestablished by the genius of the engineer."[54] Remarkably, Bragg considered the entire matter settled and made plans to release Hoke's division. Whiting and Lamb could not believe Bragg's complacency. The two of them worked furiously to repair damage to the fort as Bragg planned a parade of Hoke's men through Wilmington. On 8 January 1865, the Confederates learned through a deserter that another fleet had left Hampton Roads to have a second round with Fort Fisher.

This time there would be no interservice bickering. Picking Brig. Gen. Alfred Terry to be the army commander for the expedition, Grant made it clear to the former law clerk and volunteer soldier that cooperation with Admiral Porter was essential. When Terry and Porter met for the first time on 8 January at Beaufort, the admiral was not immediately taken with the formal Terry, but soon the two officers warmed to each other. Four days later, after ensuring the campaign would be "a model of army-navy cooperation,"[55] the invasion force sailed south. Two long lines of warships flanked the 21 transports carrying 8,897 officers and men. The 59 men-of-war, 3 more than the first expedition, carried 627 guns. Grant even had 4,000 reinforcements standing by in Baltimore should Terry need them.

The fleet reached its anchorage five miles above Fort Fisher at 10:00 P.M. As an act of indifference to the enemy's ability to repel them, Porter allowed his warships to display their normal lights. These red, white, and green lamps signaled a second Christmas-season ordeal for Colonel Lamb. His warning to Bragg reached Wilmington at midnight. The district commander ordered Hoke back to Confederate Point.

The next morning all but the ironclads took up a temporary anchorage near the point where Terry's troops would push ashore. They bombarded the woods to keep Hoke's forces from attacking the landing site. By 8:45 A.M. the first men waded through the breakers. Soon the immediate area was black with wet uniforms. Hoke's pickets watched from a safe distance; they had no orders to pick off any Northerners. A few wondered, however, why Hoke did not advance. The landing site had taken on the air of a circus and appeared ripe for attack. A group of Federals had slaughtered some cattle they found and were grilling steaks. Others fished for oysters in Myrtle Sound. The regimental bands struck up snappy tunes. By 3:00 P.M., however, almost all the Yankees were ashore. The moment for an easy Confederate victory had passed.

Back in Wilmington, Whiting asked to take command of Hoke's division and throw it against the beachhead. Bragg did nothing, so Whiting attempted to go over his head to Confederate Secretary of War James Seddon, who responded by confirming Bragg's authority. When Bragg began to map out a line of defense to be used in case Fort Fisher fell, Whiting could no longer stomach what he considered to be Bragg's defeatism and left for Fort Fisher without orders.

As the Federal launches spilled their human cargoes onto the beaches, Lamb ordered the fort's gunners to begin their duel with the five Federal ironclads anchored off Northeast Bastion. This time Porter had given specific orders that no rounds were to be wasted on Rebel flagstaffs. He intended the barrage to be accurate and punishing. All day the two sides jousted evenly, but by 4:00 P.M. the remainder of Porter's fleet joined the ironclads, and their salvos began to take a toll, especially on the fort's land face. Through the iron storm, Whiting strolled about offering encouragement. He requested reinforcements from the forts across the river and sent a telegram to Bragg via Smithville asking why Hoke had not assailed the landing site.

By this time Bragg had taken a steamer downriver to Sugar Loaf, his headquarters on the Cape Fear River above Fort Fisher. That night he cautioned Hoke to stay in position between the Yankees and Wilmington. Terry was not so irresolute. The Union commander pushed his troops down the beach. At 2:00 A.M. they began to dig in two miles above the fort. The next day Bragg realized the Federals had slipped through a cavalry picket and managed to install themselves between him and the fort. He immediately ordered Hoke to rush the mile-long entrenchments. When Bragg surveyed the Federal line, however, he canceled the attack.

Lamb, studying the same enemy troops through a telescope, was shocked to see a Confederate supply ship moving toward the wharf at Craig's Landing above the fort. The only conclusion Lamb could reach was that Bragg, who had made arrangements for the supplies, had no idea of the true situation if he thought the dock was still in Confederate hands. Lamb ordered one of the land-face guns to fire a warning shot, but it went unheeded. The *Isaac Wells,* loaded with much-needed ammunition, glided alongside the wharf and immediately was swarmed by a jubilant blue horde. The converted blockade runner CSS *Chickamauga* propitiously hove into view, fired a broadside into the *Wells,* and the steamer settled into the mud. The satisfaction of seeing the provisions kept out of enemy hands did little to satisfy Lamb, who for the first time became convinced that Whiting was correct when he said, "You and your garrison are to be sacrificed."[56]

That night Terry traveled to the *Malvern* for a conference with Porter, who was pleased with the day's work. Although Parrotts had exploded on three more ships, casualties were light. Terry asked if Porter's warships could knock out the remaining artillery on Fisher's land face and rip apart the palisade fence. Porter believed it would be no problem. Signal corpsmen with the army would direct the fleet's gunnery once the assault on the land face began.

Porter did not intend to let Terry get all the credit, however. Determined that the navy would gain as much glory as the army, the admiral asked for volunteers to form a naval "boarding party." The response among the tars was enthusiastic. More than four hundred marines equipped with Sharps rifles and carbines would provide covering fire for sixteen hundred sailors armed with cutlasses and revolvers. As one segment of the overall assault force, the naval party's assignment was to scramble down the beach toward the Northeast Bastion.

In the fort that night Lamb convinced Whiting to ask Bragg once again to pounce upon the Federal rear. The 11- and 15-inch projectiles bouncing around on the darkened sand provided a show for the nine companies Lamb ordered to remain awake all night. They were to move out once Hoke's division made its move. With another company, Lamb ventured out of the fort to skirmish with the nearest Federal pickets. After compelling them to fall back, he waited on the beach for a Confederate counterstroke that never came. Just before dawn, a discouraged Lamb brought his bone-weary company back through the land-face traverses. Once inside, he learned that only a small portion of the one thousand reinforcements that Bragg finally promised to send had arrived. These few men from Gen. Johnson C. Hagood's brigade barely made up for the previous day's

Interior of Fort Fisher during the bombardment *(Illustrated London News)*

casualties. Furthermore, no more than four of the land-face guns were still serviceable. There was also little left to eat. Despite the appalling conditions, Lamb determined to go down fighting.

By noon only a single land-face cannon remained fully serviceable, a Columbiad near the Northeast Bastion. Wide gaps yawned in the palisade fence. Although Porter could not be certain of the destruction that his armada had inflicted, he decided it was time to send in the naval landing force. Lt. Comdr. K. Randolph Breese, in charge of the 2,261 officers and men, worked diligently to prepare for the assault on the fort's sea face. His men dug rifle pits and formed into four attack divisions. One was under the command of Breese's superior, James Parker, and another was under Thomas O. Selfridge Jr., former captain of the ill-fated USS *Cairo*, the first warship to be sunk by a torpedo. Breese shouted instructions at the assembled troops over the din of the surf and crashing shells. The men were to wait for a signal that the army had begun its sweep toward the river side of the land face.

While the Federals formed their columns, Whiting continued to forward Lamb's pleas to Bragg but received no reply. Finally, at 1:00 P.M. a message got through from Bragg. He ordered Whiting to return to headquarters in Wilmington and announced that Brig. Gen. Alfred H. Colquitt, one of Hoke's brigade commanders, would come down the river that night to take command of the fort. Although Lamb understood the insult was not directed against him, he felt that replacing the "gifted, brilliant" Whiting would demoralize the garrison.[57]

As Lamb and Whiting sought to discover a way to replay the Christmas defense, another shipload of Hagood's South Carolinians sailed up to the wharf by Battery Buchanan. The transport had braved Federal shot and shell only because some of Hagood's men held their rifles on the crew. Of the 350 toughened veterans — many of whom had fought at Fort Sumter, Cold Harbor, and Petersburg — only 100 finished the mad dash through the worst cannonade they had ever experienced. The others died or hid in bombproofs along the sea face.

To discourage the naval party forming for its attack, Lamb directed two field pieces to open fire with grape and canister from the sally-port redoubt. The single Columbiad near the Northeast Bastion and the two heavy coastal guns in the Mound Battery added harassing fire. Their combined efforts kept the marines at bay but also brought down the wrath of the fleet upon the Confederate sharpshooters lining the fort's walls. Watching the unfolding drama, Whiting ignored Bragg's orders to return to Wilmington and sent another desperate dispatch to his superior: "Attack! Attack! It is all I can say, and all you can do."[58]

At 3:25 P.M., General Terry's signal corpsmen finally indicated to Porter that the army's move was imminent. Porter ordered the *Malvern* to blow its whistle, the signal for the fleet to shift their firing from the land face to the lower sea face. Breese, perhaps impatient or desirous of glory or both, decided not to wait for Terry's troops to reach Fisher's land face and urged his men to charge immediately. Ignoring prearranged plans, a wedge of sailors darted forward, carrying with it the marine sharpshooters who were supposed to remain behind and provide covering fire.

When the signal whistle sounded, five hundred selected Rebel troops disgorged from the bombproofs, joining sharpshooters already lined along the sandbag parapets around the Northeast Bastion. Hagood's South Carolinians moved to reinforce the western land-face wall near the river. The lone Columbiad and field pieces continued to snipe at the advancing naval party. Lamb ordered his men to hold their fire. As the unorganized mass of seamen raced to within six hundred yards of the fort, Confederate sharpshooters began to pick off the unlucky ones. Until then it had been a challenge to see who could reach the fort's walls first, but glory was not the only reward that awaited the brave. Death bided its time by the Northeast Bastion.

Whiting could sense the uneasiness in the outnumbered defenders as the sailors continued to sprint forward. He jumped atop the parapet, shouted a few words to stiffen his men's resolve, then turned to face the foe. It was the right gesture at the right time. The Confederate line steadied. At 150 yards, Lamb shouted a command, and the front line of blue dropped like a falling wave. But like the ocean, the men rose again as Breese, Parker, and Selfridge shouted for them to continue. They had barely covered fifty more yards when a second sheet of flame flashed from the muskets on the parapets. Again the Union officers rallied the shaken sailors, who once more stumbled forward over their fallen comrades. There would be no more volleys from the fort. The defenders simply fired as quickly as weapons could be reloaded.

Within fifty yards of the traverses, the naval attack finally spluttered to a halt. Fewer than two hundred sailors remained on their feet as their officers strove to goad them on. Eventually, almost everyone, including the daredevil Lt. William Cushing, took cover behind the palisade fence. A few slipped through the logs and continued a personal quest toward the heights above them. Only one sailor made it all the way to the top of the parapet, but he tumbled dead inside the fort.

The naval contingent, though badly shaken, still outnumbered the Rebels on the Northeast Bastion. Breese made a final attempt to form up his command. "Charge!" he yelled. "Charge! Don't retreat!"[59] As could be expected among the din and death, most of the sailors only heard the word "retreat," and soon their withdrawal became a stampede. The Tar Heels had shellacked the tars.

Before Lamb and Whiting could savor their triumph, the colonel noticed something wrong at the far end of the land face. Battle flags fluttered atop the parapet, enemy flags! The army's plan, like the navy's, had called for a line of sharpshooters to rush forward, dig in, and provide covering fire. Unlike the navy, however, the army sharpshooters carried out their orders with precision. Behind them, pioneer troops waited with axes to knock down the palisade.

Inside the fort, Confederate Capt. Kinchen Braddy commanded Shepherd's Battery, the westernmost emplacement on the land face of the fort. The battery's two heavy guns had been knocked out, but a Parrott field piece still covered the Wilmington road bridge and a Napoleon loomed behind a nearby wall of sandbags at the river gate. Braddy had given permission to Lt. Charles Latham, detached from the artillery section at the fort's main land-face sally port, to take his gun crews inside the bombproofs during the worst of the cannonade. Now the Yankees were forming for a charge, and only one of Latham's men, a corporal, had come out to work the all-important field pieces. Even worse, the fort electrician could not detonate the minefield; the naval bombardment had cut the wires. Only Braddy and his thin line of butternuts faced General Curtis's New Yorkers, anxious to make up for the Christmas debacle.

While the 117th New York tore gaps in the palisade and began their scramble up Shepherd's Battery, the lone Confederate corporal managed to fire one round from a field piece before being killed. Curtis's troops swept forward to take advantage of the situation, but thirty of Braddy's men reached the guns before they did. Finally, units of the First North Carolina Heavy Artillery arrived and discharged a round of canister from the Napoleon, clearing the Wilmington road. They also loosed an explosive round from the Parrott, hitting the bridge and leaving behind a pile of Federal dead among the flame and splinters. Down the land face, Zachariah Adams's gun crews in the sally-port redoubt poured canister into the left flank of the Federal line.

Although inflicting heavy casualties on these men from Galusha Pennypacker's Pennsylvania brigade, Adams inadvertently pushed the Federal formation to its right. As this new surge of blue uniforms crushed against the men already on the right flank, the Pennsylvanians wheeled farther right and swept toward the riverside gate. It was more than the handful of Confederate survivors at the field pieces could handle. Soon Pennypacker's men were mingling with Curtis's troops as they swarmed around the river gate and up the slopes of Shepherd's Battery. The Federals bounded into the gun chamber and were beginning to climb the next traverse when a bullet ripped through Pennypacker's hip. The mortally wounded brigade commander was carried to the rear among the hundred or so Rebel prisoners he had helped capture.

Finally at 4:00 P.M. Bragg gave in to Lamb's requests and ordered Hoke to advance on the Federal rear. Charles J. Paine's division of U.S. Colored Troops held firm long enough for Federal warships to open fire, smashing the pine and scrub oak occupied by Hoke's men. The North Carolinians were eager to fight and expected to set upon the Federals any moment. Instead, convinced of the power of the Union navy, Bragg once more reined in his dogs of war.

Upon realizing that the repulse of the naval party may have cost them the battle, Lamb and Whiting rushed to confront the enemy on the land face. Maj. William Saunders, chief of artillery at the fort, ordered the lone surviving land-face gun — the Columbiad next to the Northeast Bastion — to swivel toward the enemy and open fire. Down the peninsula at Battery Buchanan, Capt. Robert T. Chapman — upon first sighting the enemy flags planted on the land face — told his men to evacuate their post. After they waded into the icy waters of the Cape Fear River, he called them back and directed them to open fire with the two guns that could bear on the invaders.

Whiting meanwhile managed to round up about five hundred Confederates and sped off toward the developing struggle. They slammed into the Federals at the fourth gun chamber and threw them back over the third traverse. At the head of the counterattack, Whiting was severely wounded in the

The interior of the sea face after the fall of Fort Fisher. Note the unexploded ordnance in the foreground. *(North Carolina State Archives)*

thigh. Captain Braddy, still in search of reinforcements for the riverside battery, helped pull the general from the melee. Finding no support to return with him, Braddy ran back alone, only to discover that his position had already been overrun.

Lamb was also alone. He strode through the sally port and stood outside the fort trying to gain an accurate picture of the threat. Two U.S. marines, pretending to be dead, could not resist the high-ranking target, but as one sat up to aim, he was shot dead. Unaware of his close brush with death, Lamb made sure the sally-port artillery crews continued their deadly work, then hurried back into the fort. Bad news greeted him. The erratic fire of naval gunners at Battery Buchanan was killing just as many of their own men as Yankees and many of the South Carolinians were refusing to leave the bombproofs to fight. Despite these handicaps, Lamb felt he could save the fort. The Rebels on the third traverse appeared to be holding their own, and rifle fire from the troops assembled near Lamb in the rear earthworks had begun to rip into the Federals massing around Shepherd's Battery.

Before Lamb could give action to his thoughts, a flock of artillery shells screeched out of the sky onto the land face. The Union army signal corpsmen had made contact with the navy and with unheard-of precision were walking naval shells down the land face to within yards of the hand-to-hand bloodbath on the third traverse. Rebels lining the oceanside of the land-face parapet jumped for shelter or were killed. For the first time, even the battery at the sally port took a beating. Lamb sprinted to the sea face and found four heavy artillery pieces that could be traversed far enough to strike the Federals at Shepherd's Battery. He also rounded up nearly a hundred men to reinforce his intended counterattack and sent a message to Battery Buchanan to ensure that its guns would fall silent the minute the Confederates went over the top. Lamb had never led a bayonet charge, but he was prepared to do so. He sprang over the inner breastworks, his men and officers following. Only a hundred yards away, a Federal volley tore into the gray line. Most of the bullets went high, but one fractured Lamb's hip. Immediately, the Rebel rush sputtered, then died.

In the Pulpit hospital, Lamb realized he would not be able to return to the fight. Neither would General Whiting, who lay next to him. Lamb's second-in-command, Maj. James Stevenson, had also been wounded, so the responsibility for the defense of the fort fell to land-face commander Maj. James Reilly, the man Lamb held responsible for letting the Federals into the fort in the first place. Reilly had no better luck getting the attackers out than his predecessors. With 150 men, he advanced against the blue swarm buzzing around Shepherd's Battery. Fewer than sixty made it back to the starting point.

Curtis kept the pressure turned up for the Union side. He prowled near the swirling front, issuing orders and leading a charmed life. Once his troops had forced their way over the fourth traverse, he ordered a sailor to deliver a message to General Terry. Curtis wanted the navy to drop another avalanche of iron. Soon the explosive march of shells began to pound westward along the land face, slaughtering the Confederates trying to staunch the blue flood. An errant shell killed all but four of the Union troops atop the fifth traverse, but Curtis and four others stood fast until more men could fill the gap.

Once the naval barrage lifted, two more traverses quickly came under Federal control. The Yankees on the parade ground also finally moved forward to support the fighting on the parapet. The remaining Rebel troops in the sally-port tunnel surrendered, and Federal sharpshooters silenced the Columbiad next to the Northeast Bastion, the only working artillery piece

Battery Buchanan was completed just weeks before the Federal attack and guarded the Cape Fear River behind Fort Fisher. *(North Carolina State Archives)*

remaining in Rebel hands on the land face. Curtis sent another messenger requesting that a separate column advance along the outside of the now nearly deserted land-face traverses. Instead, the courier returned with an order from the division commander, Brig. Gen. Adelbert Ames, requesting that Curtis dig in for the night.

Shocked, Curtis went under Ames to subordinate officers for more troops but came up empty-handed. He then tried to go over Ames to Terry, but decided he could not wait for a reply. The angry brigade commander retraced his steps to the riverside gate and lost another fight in a long-standing feud with Ames. No more troops would be sent forward. Curtis returned to find his men over the ninth traverse but pinned. Before he could decide what to do, a shell exploded overhead, destroying his left eye and knocking him out of the battle.

General Terry had a tough decision to make. His three brigade commanders all appeared mortally wounded. The divisional commander was digging in. He turned for advice to Col. Cyrus Comstock, who urged him to send in a fourth brigade. Comstock had been in almost exactly the same position during the Christmas assault and was now suggesting the same course he had proposed the previous month. Terry, worried about a possible attack on his rear by Hoke's troops, eventually gave in to Comstock's arguments and sent Joseph Abbott's fresh brigade into the breach. Having watched enough of the day's bloody work, the red sun dipped below the horizon.

Terry waited for the new brigade to have an effect, but nothing seemed to be happening in the gathering twilight. The general finally crossed into the fort himself to discover that Abbott's troops had been dispersed by Ames, therefore adding little weight to the desperate slugging match along the land face. Comstock advised reorganizing Abbott's men and renewing the drive to capture the land face. Terry readily assented. The Third New Hampshire of the regrouped brigade quickly helped overwhelm two more traverses. Two more of Abbott's regiments, led by Lt. Col. Augustus W. Rollins, double-quicked toward the Northeast Bastion between the palisade and the fort wall, at last carrying out the plan Curtis had developed three hours earlier. Rollins stopped his troops just below the prize that had eluded the sailors and marines in the initial assault. He then led the right wing up the fort wall, overrunning from the ocean side the three land-face traverses remaining in Confederate hands. Simultaneously, his left wing scampered up the Northeast Bastion. The time was 10:00 P.M. The battle for the land face was over.

Confederate Major Reilly, who had assured Lamb he would not give up the fort, decided to make a stand at Battery Buchanan. He ordered Lamb and Whiting to be carried down the peninsula to the battery. Unknown to Reilly, however, chief of artillery Maj. William Saunders — sent earlier by Lamb to Battery Buchanan to see if any reinforcements had arrived —

ordered the evacuation of the battery when he saw the Northeast Bastion fall. The bearers and escorts who reached the battery with Lamb, Whiting, and Reilly found themselves stranded with no ammunition and no way to cross the Cape Fear River.

It took the victors a few minutes of quiet to realize the fighting had ended. The noise of the cheering on shore reached Admiral Porter's flagship before a torch could blink the official notice of Fort Fisher's fall. Signal rockets of all colors immediately burst over the fleet. "The sight was magnificent," wrote Seaman Robert Watson, who had stopped briefly with the rest of his mates at Battery Lamb on his retreat from Battery Buchanan to Wilmington.[60]

Major Reilly understood the helplessness of the situation and started back up the peninsula with two other officers to await the Federals. He wished to avoid any accidental slaughter of his unarmed men in the dark. Left behind, Lamb looked up from his litter to see General Colquitt of Hoke's division. Bragg had made no serious effort to attack the Federal rear and had not insisted that the rest of Hagood's brigade reinforce the fort. He did make sure, however, that Colquitt arrived to relieve Whiting. Lamb wished to remain with his men but asked Colquitt to take Whiting with him when he reported back to Bragg. Colquitt was in no mood to listen. His aides — who had been guarding the rowboat that brought them from Sugar Loaf — told the general the Yankees were close by. Colquitt disappeared in the dark and made good his escape. Whiting died two months later in a Northern prison.

That night General Ames ordered Col. Samuel Zent of the Thirteenth Indiana to post men at all the bombproofs to prevent looting. Early the next morning, Zent began making the rounds to ensure that guards were properly posted. The colonel had erred, however. He had failed to establish a watch at the entrance to the main magazine, which contained thirteen thousand pounds of black powder. With no one to keep them out, soldiers went inside with torches to see if any valuables had been left behind. At 7:30 A.M. the powder ignited, instantly killing most of those sleeping nearby. Sand buried and suffocated others who survived the initial blast. It was Butler's plan in reverse. Between 130 to 265 Northerners were killed or wounded.[61] Zent blamed himself for the catastrophe and was haunted by the memory until his own death.

Total casualty figures for the two Fort Fisher operations are sketchy. Estimates on the Union side — including those lost in the magazine explosion and aboard ships — ran as high as seventeen hundred men, almost one for every defender inside the fort. This deadly statistic serves as a macabre tribute to Lamb's engineering and tactical success. Confederate dead and wounded reached approximately six hundred men, with another fourteen hundred to fifteen hundred captured.

The Mound Battery, the product of eighteen months labor to raise a sixty-foot sand pile that would accommodate two heavy seacoast guns. *(North Carolina State Archives)*

The first three gun emplacements on the land face of Fort Fisher, the river side. Shepherd's Battery is at the far left. *(North Carolina State Archives)*

The news of Fisher's capitulation raced up the coast to Grant's headquarters at City Point, Virginia, where a series of hundred-gun salutes commemorated the victory. The *New York Tribune* called "the storming of Fort Fisher . . . the most brilliant, as it surely is the most remarkable, victory of the war."[62]

Publicly, Bragg accepted blame for the defeat. Privately, he continued to find fault with Whiting and others. The closing of Wilmington meant the end of the war, and everyone knew it from the lowliest private to Jefferson Davis. The Confederate president reluctantly sent a peace commission to Hampton Roads, but the offer of an armistice was rejected by Lincoln. Davis's negotiations with Europe also suffered irreparable harm. Confederate Congressman Duncan F. Kenner, a major slaveholder who favored emancipation, had been waiting in Wilmington to board a blockade runner to Europe. He had the authority to offer freedom for the South's slaves if either France or England would recognize the Confederacy. Fort Fisher's fall forced him to find an alternate route. By the time he reached the continent, his plea fell on deaf ears.

On 16 January at 7:00 A.M., under Bragg's orders, the Confederates blew up Forts Caswell and Campbell protecting Old Inlet. They also abandoned and destroyed works on Smith's Island and those at Fort Johnston in Smithville and Fort Lamb, across the Cape Fear River from Fort Fisher. Some troops retreated upriver to Fort Anderson, while others were sent to strengthen forts closer to Wilmington.

On 22 February, word went out to the men in the trenches around Wilmington to pack what they could carry and retire toward Goldsboro, North Carolina. Gen. John M. Schofield's troops were close behind. In fact, as some of the Southerners marched out of one end of Wilmington, Northern troops were marching in at the other. General Terry rode into Wilmington at the head of a column at 10:00 A.M. to accept the surrender of the town from Mayor John Dawson. When Terry took off his hat and extended his hand, Dawson felt relieved. He had feared that his beloved city might be burned, but Terry acted more like an old friend than a conquering hero.

If you go there . . .

In 1909, the Fort Fisher Survivors Association tried to convince the House Committee on Military Affairs to support legislation to turn Fort Fisher into a national park. A snowstorm kept Colonel Lamb and many of the other old veterans from making the trip to Washington. The bill died in committee and by the next year, Lamb — who had served three terms as Norfolk's mayor after the war — was dead. So was General Curtis. With them passed the last best chance for preserving Lamb's sand pile; it had already started to slip into the sea.

The gradual erosion of the beach had begun in 1881 when the U.S. Army Corps of Engineers closed New Inlet to improve navigation of the Cape Fear River. The ocean swallowed more than four hundred feet of beach before the process reversed itself. Then in 1928, the New Hanover County Board of Commissioners decided to dredge up tons of coquina rock to build a road to improve access to the fort, a popular tourist destination for those staying at beach resorts popping up along the coast. The removal of this natural sea wall doomed the old fort. By the mid-1930s the Northeast Bastion had collapsed into the encroaching sea. During World War II, the government bulldozed part of the land face to build a runway for a reactivated base on Federal Point. It was not until 1958 that the state of North Carolina acquired the few sand hills remaining on the land face to form the **Fort Fisher State Historic Site.** Today, the same U.S. Army Corps of Engineers that began the destruction of the fort is designing plans for a revetment to prevent coastal erosion, estimated at five to fifteen feet a year. Unfortunately, in August 1992, the North Carolina Coastal Resources Commission denied a variance to permit construction of the protective sea wall amidst a political squabble concerning the loosening of rules that prohibit development along the state's coastline. "Meanwhile, the waves continue to break, and one hurricane is all that it will take to entirely eradicate the Confederacy's largest fort."[63] If you wish to become involved in the preservation of the fort, contact: Paul M. Laird, Committee to Save Fort Fisher, Box 330, Wilmington, NC 28402 (919) 762-2611.

The historic site offers a reconstructed palisade fence and gun chamber at Shepherd's Battery, which also holds a 32-pounder from the USS *Peterhoff.* The czar of Russia's former yacht had been a blockade runner. As such, it was captured off Matamoras, Mexico, in 1863 and pressed into service with the U.S. Navy. On 6 March 1864, the eight-hundred-ton side-wheeler sank off Wilmington following a collision with the *Monticello.*

Just north of the land face, a visitors center contains exhibits and an audiovisual presentation relating the story of Fort Fisher. The staff also provides packets of information to educators about the fort and the Civil War in general. Admission is free. The center is open April through October, Monday through Saturday, from 9:00 A.M. to 5:00 P.M. and on Sunday from 1:00–5:00 P.M. From November through March, it is closed an hour earlier each day and all day on Mondays. A building housing exhibits from underwater archaeological finds stands at the north end of the visitors center parking lot. It is open Monday through Friday from 9:00 A.M. to 4:30 P.M. For information, contact: Fort Fisher, P.O. Box 68, Kure Beach, NC 28449 (919) 458-5538.

An aerial view of Fort Fisher from 1931, before the ocean washed away the sea face. Northeast Bastion and Pulpit Battery are just above the "y" in the road at the center. *(North Carolina State Archives)*

A monument to the battle of Fort Fisher raised by the Daughters of the Confederacy stands along the ocean just south of the fort. Farther down the peninsula, past the loading point for the Southport-Fort Fisher Ferry, rises a mound of sand — the remains of Battery Buchanan.

A thirty-minute ferry ride across the mouth of the Cape Fear River takes you to Southport. The recently opened **Southport Maritime Museum** includes exhibits dealing with blockade running. Heading west on Highway 211 will bring you to Highway 133. Turn south toward Oak Island. On the eastern tip of Caswell Beach Road slumps the skeleton of **Fort Caswell.** Later works of reinforced concrete now dominate the post, but the old fort's name can still be read above one of its sally ports. The entire installation is now part of a church camp, but you might be able to obtain permission to take a look and walk around the brick walls.

Almost to the South Carolina border, one of the many North Carolina barrier islands, Ocean Isle, offers the **Museum of Coastal Carolina** to visitors who take the time to find their way through the labyrinth of highways. Closed during the winter months, the museum is known for its natural history exhibits, but it has a few Civil War artifacts.

Back up Highway 133 toward Wilmington lies **Brunswick Town-Fort Anderson State Historic Site.** Brunswick Town was founded in 1726 and burned by the British or Tories in 1776. The foundations of several of the homes and businesses can still be seen adjacent to the fort. The massive earthen walls of Fort Anderson have been well preserved and perhaps provide a better understanding of Lamb's engineering skills than the few traverses left standing at the more famous Fort Fisher. One warning: Instead of one of those Smokey Bear gauges indicating the relative danger of a forest fire, the visitors center has a mosquito gauge. When the arrow points to maximum infestation, you had better have some repellent. The site is open free to the public the same hours as Fort Fisher. For information, contact: Brunswick Town-Fort Anderson State Historic Site, Route 1, Box 55, Winnabow, NC 28479 (919) 371-6613.

The city of Wilmington has a wonderfully restored and updated waterfront from which visitors can view the stern of the USS *North Carolina*. The former World War II battleship is now a floating museum. For those interested in the Civil War, the ironclad CSS *North Carolina* was built at Berry and Brothers Shipyard, just downriver from the present-day battleship memorial. The six-hundred-ton ironclad was completed in 1863. Unreliable engines taken from the tug *Uncle Ben,* the first ship confiscated by the Confederate government, forced the leaky ship to serve as a floating battery near Smithville. Marine worms bored so many holes into her unsheathed hull that the *North Carolina* sank at her moorings on 27 September 1864.

Her sister ship, the CSS *Raleigh,* built at J. L. Cassidy and Sons Shipyard, situated across the river at the foot of Church Street, had a more illustrious career. In the spring of 1864, Com. W. F. Lynch decided to make an attempt to disperse the blockading squadron, which — as far as Lynch could tell — consisted of seven ships. At 8:00 P.M. on 6 May the *Raleigh* and two wooden gunboats crossed the New Inlet bar and engaged the Federal squadron. The wooden ships of the U.S. Navy fled into the darkness, and the next morning the Confederate trio returned to the protection of Fort Fisher. As the *Raleigh* steamed back upstream, she ran aground near Smithville. The strain of the dropping river broke the ironclad's back. Crewmen removed the guns and armor and set her afire.

No matter how long you linger beside the Cape Fear River, be sure you find your way up Market Street to the **Cape Fear Museum** (formerly the New Hanover County Museum). The $4.2 million expansion of the museum, completed in early 1992, has as one of its major attractions an impressive, room-size model of Wilmington's waterfront during the Civil War. In other display cases are models of the blockade runner *Dare* and the ironclad CSS *Raleigh*. The museum's Civil War centerpiece, however, is a forty-foot diorama depicting the January 1865 combined operations attack on Fort Fisher. The sound and light show surpasses any other exhibit of its type I've seen. Other articles in the museum's collection include a bell from the *Flora,* a British blockade runner sunk off Fort Moultrie near Charleston on

22 October 1864. The museum is open 9:00 A.M. to 5:00 P.M., Tuesday through Saturday, and 2:00–5:00 P.M. on Sunday. It is closed Mondays and national holidays. There is a suggested donation of $2.00 for adults. For information, contact: Cape Fear Museum, 814 Market Street, Wilmington, NC 28401 (919) 341-4350.

Walking maps of Historic Wilmington are available at the **Cape Fear Coast Convention and Visitors Bureau** on the southeast corner of Third and Princess streets. It is open 8:30 A.M. to 5:00 P.M., Monday through Friday, 9:00 A.M. to 4:00 P.M. on Saturday, and 1:00–4:00 P.M. on Sunday.

The **deRosset House** at the northwest corner of Second and Dock streets served as the Confederacy's District of Cape Fear headquarters. The Greek Revival and Italianate monstrosity provided the Confederate commanders with great views of the river. It now serves as headquarters of the Historic Wilmington Foundation. Elsewhere in the city, Judah P. Benjamin, one of Davis's cabinet members, lived for a time at 308 South Third Street.

One warning about Wilmington: Twice I have visited the city when there were no rooms at any of the town's many inns. Plan your visit accordingly. Don't be afraid to try some of the wonderful bed and breakfasts on South Third Street, such as the **Worth House,** a large Victorian with five rooms. For reservations, call (919) 762-8562.

CHAPTER 3

SOUTH CAROLINA

IN THE LATE 1980s, I made my first trip to Charleston, South Carolina. Excited about visiting what I considered to be the cradle of the secession, I called the local visitors bureau to make sure I did not miss anything. The woman who answered promised to track down some of the more obscure Civil War sites and report back to me. When I spoke with her again, she said, "You know, the people around here really aren't that interested in the Civil War."

You could have knocked me over with a palmetto frond.

I am not sure what I expected, but certainly it was not indifference. Without the firebrands and fireworks provided by South Carolina, it is hard to imagine the American Civil War. In his bicentennial history of the state, Louis B. Wright even went so far as to claim — almost proudly — that in "the long sweep of history, South Carolina has been one of the most contentious states in the union."[1] Anyone with even a slight interest in history cannot dismiss such a statement lightly, especially when almost every high school American history text runs a picture of Congressman Preston Brooks of South Carolina beating Charles Sumner of Massachusetts with a cane in the Senate chambers in 1856.[2] The hero's welcome Brooks received back in his home state provides support for Wright's observation. But when Wright later suggested that "only those owning the largest number of slaves [in South Carolina] were eager for an immediate break with the union,"[3] I began to suspect his scholarship was too simplistic.

Even had I not read several authors who argued quite persuasively that many, if not most, of the large planters in the South had no interest in secession, common sense would indicate that men of wealth, even if that wealth comes from ownership of slaves, tend to be conservative. Such men usually do not want to rock the ship of state, especially when they have the most to lose overboard. Although South Carolina had "the only state legislature in which a majority of representatives were planters,"[4] I suspect South Carolina's antebellum plantation aristocracy behaved no differently. Evidence for such a conclusion abounds,[5] even in Wright's book.

James L. Petigru, a respected Charleston jurist, has been called a solitary Carolina unionist, but he was not quite alone. John C. Calhoun, the state's premier orator, was not in favor of secession.[6] Neither was South Carolinian Wade Hampton, grandson of the "richest planter in all North America."[7] (Nevertheless, Hampton rose to the rank of general in the Confederate armies after the Union dissolved.) James L. Orr, a South Carolinian who became Speaker of the U.S. House in 1857, counseled moderation and desired to hold his state within the Union. The antislavery Republican presidential candidate in 1856, John C. Frémont, was born in South Carolina, confirmed in Saint Philip's Episcopal Church in Charleston, and attended Charleston College. Charlestonian Joel Poinsett, the first American minister to Mexico and mentor to Frémont, "was a strong Union man, opposed to nullification and secession."[8] Even Francis Pickens — a kinsman of Calhoun's, owner of several hundred slaves, and South Carolina's wartime governor—"thought his fellow citizens were being foolishly precipitous,"[9] that is, until he sensed a shift in the political winds and changed his pronouncements to woo secessionist-minded voters. After tough talk turned to action, a popular legend has Petigru expanding on Pickens's initial observation by stating, "South Carolina is too small for a republic and too large for an insane asylum."[10]

From these examples it is easy to see that the unionist label did not necessarily imply an antislavery sentiment. Oftentimes with the plantation aristocracy, it was quite the opposite. South Carolina planter James Chesnut Sr., whose daughter-in-law Mary Boykin Chesnut kept one of the most famous wartime diaries, indicated, "Without the aid and countenance of the whole United States, we could not have kept slavery. I always knew that the world was against us. That was one reason why I was a Union man. I wanted all the power the United States gave me to hold my own."[11]

The premier exception to the lineup of South Carolina moderates presented by Wright and others appears to be Robert Barnwell Rhett, master of 190 slaves. For three decades he campaigned against the Union from the pages of his Charleston newspaper so vehemently that "even most of his colleagues thought him a hot-headed crank."[12] Rhett's wish-come-true, the creation of the Confederacy, led to his greatest disappointment when he was not selected to be president of the fledgling southern confederation. Instead, delegates in Montgomery chose the moderate Jefferson Davis as president and Alexander Stephens, a "conditional unionist,"[13] as vice president.

Nevertheless, antisecessionists like Calhoun, who contrived with the help of the clergy to promote slavery as a "positive good,"[14] ended up laying the groundwork for the destruction of the Union, even though such a reaction to their polemics may not have been the objective. "And because the ground had long since been plowed and planted," James McPherson noted in *Battle Cry of Freedom*, "the harvest of disunion came quickly after the thunderstorm of Lincoln's election."[15] "The prudent and conservative men in the South," wrote Louisiana Sen. Judah P. Benjamin, a conditional unionist like Stephens and later a member of Davis's cabinet despite having once challenged him to a duel, were not "able to stem the wild torrent of passion which is carrying everything before it."[16]

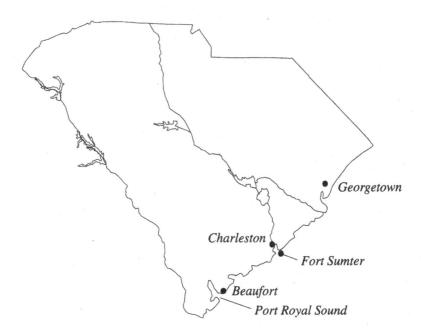

Once the groundswell in late 1860 swept South Carolina out of the Union as the first state to declare itself a sovereign nation, its citizens did not shirk from what they saw as their duty. Of the sixty-three thousand men from South Carolina who fought for the Confederacy,[17] nearly one-fourth did not live to see the Palmetto State defeated. Even William Tecumseh Sherman, who along with Ulysses S. Grant is credited with the development of the total-war concept, felt some pity toward the cradle of secession. As his bummers crossed from Savannah into South Carolina, he wrote: "The whole army is burning with an insatiable desire to wreak violence upon South Carolina. I almost tremble for her fate."[18]

Port Royal

AFTER INEXCUSABLE communication foul-ups surrounding the dispatch of a relief force to Fort Sumter and the subsequent surrender of the post, the U.S. Navy was understandably embarrassed. Even the reduction of the enemy earthworks at Hatteras Inlet, North Carolina, late the following August appeared to be — in retrospect — more an indication of the tactical abilities of the attacking fleet's commander, Flag Off. Silas H. Stringham, than the strategic insights of the Navy Department. Despite the fact that the Hatteras operation was "poorly planned and executed"[19] and that less than half of the 860 untrained troops comprising the landing force managed to reach shore, the superior range of Stringham's naval weapons smothered the defenses.

Union Secretary of the Navy Gideon Welles had not intended to hold the captured forts, but Stringham, commander of the Atlantic Squadron, convinced him otherwise. Welles then persuaded Lincoln, but neither the Federal army nor navy saw fit to exploit the victory by moving forcefully into Pamlico Sound. Stringham further tarnished his and the navy's newly brightened image when he sailed his flagship, the *Minnesota*, back to New York Harbor instead of remaining closer to the action by anchoring at Hampton Roads.

A former journalist, Welles understood that it took only a few critical stories in the nation's papers to negate any positive publicity the Hatteras operation had earned. So even though the board in charge of naval strategy had discouraged an attack on Port Royal, South Carolina, as being too risky, Welles saw a victory in the state that had initiated secession as a sure way to gain front-page headlines.

Besides the obvious public relations benefits, the capture of Port Royal Sound — or another like it — was necessary if the navy hoped to fulfill Lincoln's blockade orders. Not only could its deep, protected anchorage accommodate the entire Union navy, its location halfway between Charleston and Savannah made Port Royal a convenient base for operations against either city and a perfect location for naval repair and coaling facilities. Furthermore, the Broad River, one of two major tributaries that fed the roadstead, provided a route to the interior as far as the town of Coosawhatchie, which sat astride the Charleston and Savannah Railroad, a vital lifeline for the Confederacy. Cut the rail line, and the national government could "destroy the inland communications between Charleston and Savannah and blockade Savannah completely."[20] As a bonus, Lincoln's attorney general, Edward Bates, had heard about "the great Sea-Island cotton crop and wanted to know why the government should not seize [South Carolina's offshore] islands and take the cotton," which could provide cash for the Federal treasury.[21]

To make certain that nothing untoward happened to imperil the anticipated attack, the navy secretary proceeded with extreme caution and secrecy to unfold his plan. First, Welles's assistant secretary, Gustavus Fox, wrote a critical letter to the aged Stringham, who — as expected — offered

Samuel F. du Pont

his resignation. Stringham's Atlantic command could then be divided, with one of the nation's most talented officers, Samuel F. du Pont, put in charge of the southern section. Welles made it clear to du Pont that he was expected to capture Port Royal, although for the sake of confusing the enemy or any spies in the Navy Department, the flag officer's orders read that his destination was to be determined only after he had sailed.[22]

Du Pont began to gather supplies in New York in early October, having raised his flag aboard the *Wabash*, a forty-four-gun steam frigate commanded by C. R. P. Rodgers. Secrecy even at this early point in the campaign proved elusive, and English correspondent Howard Russell wrote soon after du Pont's arrival in New York about the "new expedition which I have been hearing for some time is about to sail for Port Royal."[23]

The apparent breach of security did not deter continued attempts by Welles and du Pont to mask the fleet's objective. On 28 October, ten days after removing his fleet to Hampton Roads, the flag officer dispatched twenty-five coal-laden schooners to Tybee Bar off Savannah as part of a series of planned deceptions. The ruse fooled few on either side. B. S. Osbon, a correspondent for the *New York Times*, asked during an interview with Welles to be introduced to the commander of the Port Royal expedition. When Welles indignantly asked the reporter who had given him the information, Osbon replied: "You did, Mr. Secretary, just now."[24]

To be fair, "the most formidable armada ever assembled under the American flag"[25] was hard to keep under wraps. If the 18 men-of-war carrying 148 guns, some as large as 11 inches, and escorting 36 transports crowded with almost 13,000 soldiers under Brig. Gen. Thomas W. Sherman that sailed from Hampton Roads on 29 October had as many water leaks as information leaks, the expedition never would have made it past Fort Monroe. Still, the pretense was preserved. All naval commanders carried sealed orders to be opened only in case of separation from the flagship.

The next night the bulk of the ships' captains were ripping through sealing wax after a violent wind hauled to westward, "and phosphorescent animalculae lit up the sheet of foam that covered the rough sea."[26] A gale on 1 November threatened to destroy the scattered ships, some of which were nothing more than New York ferry boats, but du Pont remained on a course toward Bull's Bay, South Carolina, an anchorage north of Charleston, in the continued hope that the enemy might be deceived about the armada's ultimate destination. On that same day, however, acting Confederate Secretary of War Judah P. Benjamin sent a telegram to Gov. Francis Pickens of South Carolina indicating his belief that Port Royal was the fleet's target.[27]

By the morning of 2 November, du Pont, who had shifted his direction toward Charleston, had graver concerns than fooling Confederates. Only one other sail could be seen from his flagship. The next night, du Pont's small command blockaded Charleston, then proceeded to Port Royal. Miraculously, only two ships of the motley assemblage had been lost in the storms, and in groups of one and two the bulk of the Union attacking force appeared off the bar at Port Royal.

Commodore du Pont immediately ordered a coast survey officer and six shallow-draft gunboats to mark the channel since the defenders had destroyed all the navigational buoys. At this moment, Josiah Tatnall, who had rushed his Rebel "mosquito fleet" through the backwaters from Savannah, sortied from the bay with three small river steamers and a tug, each mounting two 32-pounder smoothbores. After a few long-range greetings, the Confederates retreated to the earthen forts protecting the harbor.

However admirable, the navy's unsophisticated attempts at disinformation had been totally unnecessary: The Confederates did not have the wherewithal to contest the colossal force the North could throw at any point along the South's long eastern coastline. As early as May 1861, five months before du Pont brought his men-of-war to Port Royal, Gen. P. G. T. Beauregard had recommended to Governor Pickens that the two-and-five-eighths-mile-wide harbor mouth at Port Royal be protected by "strong works on Bay Point and Hilton Head, on either side of the entrance, and [a] steel-clad floating battery moored halfway between the two, all armed with the heaviest rifled guns that can be made."[28] Beauregard did not get his floating battery nor heavy guns. Instead, the smaller of the earthworks, erected at Bay Point on Saint Phillips Island, bore his name. Its four faces frowned over the water approaches to the Broad and Beaufort rivers with thirteen cannon: five

32-pounders, one rifled 6-inch, five 42-pounders, and one 10-inch and one 8-inch Columbiad. Flanking outerworks held five more pieces: two 24-pounders and three 32-pounders. Two 6-pounder Spanish field pieces rounded out Bay Point's armament.[29]

Across the bay entrance, Fort Walker occupied the northern tip of Hilton Head Island. Protected by a deep trench and strong ramparts covered with a thick layer of sod, it could have been a formidable deterrent. Seven heavy guns for its sea face never arrived, however, so thirteen lighter weapons were mounted instead. The crowding together of these weapons prevented the construction of traverses against enfilading fire, a fatal mistake. Furthermore, two guns intended to cover the beach approaches lacked carriages. They were buried in the sand, but once fired would be worthless.

The morning following Tatnall's first foray, the Confederate fleet brazenly steamed toward the Union host again. This time when the plucky Rebels turned back, they managed to draw the pursuing Federal gunships within range of the earthworks. The Confederate plan backfired when a random shot from a Union warship hit a caisson in Fort Beauregard. That same morning, Commodore du Pont brought his deep-draft vessels over the bar, which at Port Royal forms ten miles outside the opening to the bay. This fact meant his fleet could anchor inside the bar but remain outside the range of the shore defenses.

Because there was no convenient place to land Sherman's troops, du Pont decided to subdue Fort Walker with naval gunfire, then have the accompanying soldiers put ashore immediately in front of the earthworks on Hilton Head.

The naval bombardment was scheduled to begin that afternoon. The *Wabash* would lead one column into the bay about halfway between the two forts at a point out of range of most of the defenders' guns. Once inside the bay, this force would turn to port and pass slowly by Fort Walker, then continue to circle between the two forts until the question was decided. A second line of warships would flank the main group but remain to the northwest of Fort Walker once inside the bay, both to prevent the enterprising Tatnall from slipping out amongst the transports and to smother Fort Walker with enfilading fire.

As a sailor was about to run up the signal to commence the operation, the flagship grounded on Fishing Rip Shoals. When the *Wabash* jerked free, du Pont decided to postpone the attack. The next day a gale forced another delay, but the morning of the following day, 7 November, dawned clear and bright, a flat sea surface offering perfect conditions for accurate shooting from the naval platforms. Drums beat the sailors to quarters and the Union tars smartly stood at their stations, anxious to prove themselves in front of the army spectators.

The squadrons got underway at 9:00 A.M. Within a half-hour the larger guns from Fort Walker screamed an angry warning. Another half-hour

passed during which most of the ships took hits and suffered a few casualties. By 10:00 A.M. the main column swung to port, then unleashed its starboard guns on the enemy at a range of a mere eight hundred yards. Just three
ships — the *Wabash, Susquehanna,* and *Bienville* — began the second loop,
but that was enough. For twenty-five minutes, the fifty heavy guns aboard
the men-of-war bearing on Fort Walker remained almost stationary in front
of the earthworks as the warships maneuvered against the flood tide.

Comdr. John Rodgers, the officer in charge of the earlier survey party,
wrote later to a friend that shells plowed into the fortress "not 28 per minute
[as at Hatteras Inlet] but as fast as a horse's feet beat the ground in a gal-
lop."[30] Another source put the figure at one shell a second, ranging in size
from eight to eleven inches.[31] The adversarial thunder could be heard as far
away as Saint Augustine, Florida — a distance of 150 miles![32]

Understandably, the relatively untrained gunners in Fort Walker were
beset with problems, but the most telling had little to do with the Union onslaught. The Rebels' two best guns, rifled 6-inchers, stood idle because of
faulty ammunition. Several other pieces bounced off their carriages after
only one shot. When a 32-pounder was disabled by a direct hit early in the
brawl, almost half the bastion's effective firepower was incapacitated.

Still, the Fort Walker garrison fought back, even when later in the
morning a bursting shell stunned Col. John A. Wagener, the fort's commanding officer. Maj. Arthur M. Huger continued the hopeless struggle,
more as a point of honor than anything else.

Honor was on the mind of a Northern ship captain that morning as
well. Comdr. Percival Drayton of the USS *Pocahontas* had hove into Port
Royal late due to damage his ship had sustained during the earlier storms.
His brother, Thomas Drayton, owned a plantation on Hilton Head and was
in charge of the Confederate shore defenses. Commander Drayton, U.S.N.,
feared his tardiness might be mistakenly considered by his fellow naval officers as an indication of his desire not to risk harming his brother. To allay
any doubts about his loyalty, he brought his steamer immediately below Fort
Walker and blasted away, getting off seventy shots from his five guns in just
over an hour.[33]

The Confederates battled back, hitting the *Wabash* twenty-five times,
but by the time du Pont finished his second circuit of the bay, General Drayton, C.S.A., had decided to abandon the two fortresses. A mile of open land
separated Fort Walker from a protective forest, and the retreat became a rout
as the defenders bolted from the earthworks, discarding anything heavier
than their clothes. Soldiers on board the transports cheered the footraces,
but no one doubted that the defeated Rebels had "stood to their guns like
men."[34] The fleeing Confederates knew that the shelter of the trees did not
get them totally out of the woods, for du Pont's shallow-draft steamers could
still cut off their escape from Hilton Head by blocking the ferry to the main-

land. Nevertheless, most of them managed to make the six-mile hike and board steamers and flats that carried them across Skull Creek to safety.

When Fort Walker no longer returned fire, Comdr. John Rodgers of du Pont's staff was rowed ashore, and around 2:00 P.M. he and Lt. John S. Barnes became the first Yankee officers to enter the deserted fort. Barnes recorded that near each dismounted gun "one or two dead, horribly mangled, were lying, crushed out of all semblance to the human form divine, a mere miserable dusty heap of gory clothes and flesh."[35] Despite the gruesome scene, officers visiting Fort Walker after the battle expressed surprise that a mere ten defenders had lost their lives and only twenty were wounded. "Looking from the direction of the enfilading fire from the north . . . , the wonder was that the ammunition at the guns had not been exploded, and that many more of the men who served the guns were not killed."[36]

In contrast, the lack of attention the attackers paid to Fort Beauregard was evident by the fact that no lives were lost and only thirteen were wounded at Bay Point. Ignored through most of the morning, the garrison at Fort Beauregard did what it could, but its best gun had exploded on the thirty-second discharge and the remaining weapons lacked the range to have much effect on events unfolding across the bay. When cheers were heard from the fleet, the officers on Bay Point assumed the worst. The fort's gunners touched off the last round at 3:35 P.M., then retreated off Saint Phillips Island.

At dusk, the jubilant Union army began to land outside Fort Walker, and Comdr. C. R. P. Rodgers relinquished the fort to Brig. Gen. H. G. Wright. A few miles up the Broad River, a newly appointed general in the Confederate army under personal orders from President Davis to organize the defenses of Georgia and South Carolina pulled into the train depot at Coosawhatchie. He was too late to save Port Royal, but Robert E. Lee learned a lesson about the power of ships' batteries that he would not soon forget, "and his later offensive campaigns were made in regions where the Union Navy was unable to support the Army."[37]

Overall, even considering the Keystone Cops' quality of the disinformation efforts, du Pont's plan to capture the forts had been executed with textbook perfection. The human cost was small when compared to the engagements yet to come, only eight seamen killed and twenty-three wounded. Nevertheless, the operation suffered the same lack of inertia that had occurred at Hatteras Inlet. Both Daniel Ammen, a participant in the attack on Port Royal, and David Porter, a U.S. naval officer at the time of the operation, questioned the decision not to dispatch a squadron into Skull Creek to cut off the Confederate garrison stampeding from Fort Walker. The two officers admitted there were good reasons for not doing so: darkness was coming on, the channel was intricate, and the Confederates might have fortified strategic points along the creek bank. With hindsight, both suggested that

The bombardment of Port Royal

the retreating Tatnall, whose fleet helped bring off the Fort Walker garrison from Hilton Head, "should have been followed by our gunboats."[38]

An even greater prize lay within reach of the Federals. Had Sherman pushed inland, he could have cut the vital rail link between Charleston and Savannah and forced the Confederates to fight a multifront war. Fearing that, Confederate Brig. Gen. James H. Trapier wired acting Secretary of War Benjamin for a declaration of martial law in the area. Benjamin left the decision to Lee, but when Sherman remained on Hilton Head, even the small number of Rebel forces in the area (approximately seven thousand scattered along the coasts of South Carolina and Georgia) were deemed sufficient for the time, and martial law was not enforced.

George B. McClellan had accepted command of the Army of the Potomac after Irvin McDowell had managed to snatch defeat from the jaws of victory at Manassas the previous July. Now he proposed to Lincoln that an inland campaign be conducted from a captured Southern harbor, but no evidence exists that a major operation was ever seriously considered using Port Royal as a base.[39]

Writing home on the evening of his victory, du Pont correctly assessed the mood of the enemy: "It is not my temper to rejoice over fallen foes, but this is a gloomy night in Charleston."[40] Citizens there indeed feared their city was du Pont's actual objective, and rumors of slave revolts and blue troopers on the march quickly spread. Similar stories found their way north, as

New Yorkers cried, "On to Charleston! On to Charleston!" Still, du Pont and Sherman waited for reinforcements, and, as one officer lamented, "The golden opportunity . . . passed."[41]

As du Pont's ships fanned farther north and south from Port Royal, his sailors discovered the entire coast from Charleston to Tybee Island outside Savannah had been abandoned under orders from Lee, who struggled to set up a defensive line beyond the range of Federal gunships. Lee remained in charge until the following March, but no serious fighting took place during that time since Federal troops at Port Royal "showed a strong inclination to follow rather than get in front of Du Pont's gunboats."[42]

The expeditionary force spent most of its time securing the area immediately surrounding the sound. Toward that purpose, on the last day of 1861, Comdr. C. R. P. Rodgers guided three gunboats and three armed boats through the Coosaw River to Confederate positions at Port Royal Ferry, Beaufort's main connection to the mainland. Fire from the warships and guns that had been landed as artillery support disrupted Confederate efforts to construct batteries at the position in an attempt to cut off Port Royal Island. Confederate Brig. Gen. John C. Pemberton, the future defender of Vicksburg, noted that at "no time during [its] occupation of the river bank" did the enemy force leave the protection of the accompanying gunboats, and that "by far the larger proportion of the [Confederate] casualties" resulted from the "shells of the fleet."[43]

Had the battles at Hatteras Inlet not already disproved the prevailing notion that ships were no match for shore defenses, du Pont's precision attack at Port Royal forever changed the dynamics of ship-versus-shore confrontations. From that moment on, lengthy sieges became the exception rather than the rule. Even more important to the Northern military who were looking for something to offset the aura of Southern invincibility on land, the U.S. Navy had established itself as a force to be reckoned with on both sides of the shoreline.

If you go there . . .

Hilton Head Island is not what you would call a hotbed of historic preservation. The average traveler cannot even turn off Highway 278 since the majority of the island is privately owned, complete with guard shacks and polite people who tell visitors they must turn around.

Apparently this was not always the case. A 1965 article in the *News and Courier* documented the opening of a three-mile state road. Known as Fort Walker Parkway, the road reportedly "affords easy access to a view of [Fort

Walker's] miles of earthworks, gun batteries and powder magazines."[44] The article continued by detailing the history of Fort Sherman, built to defend the eight-hundred-acre Union military and naval base that sprang up around Fort Welles, the name the Yankees gave to Fort Walker. The base on Hilton Head established by General Sherman eventually contained a hospital, warehouses, shops, administrative buildings, and barracks for fifty thousand troops. Near the base, a town sprang up, complete with a 120-room hotel, theater, two newspapers, several stores, restaurants, and, of course, saloons lining the appropriately named Robbers Row. All traces of these hundreds of buildings had disappeared by the centennial of the Civil War, but apparently a gun emplacement erected during the Spanish-American War was visible when the article was written.

There is still a Robbers Row on the north end of Hilton Head, along with Fort Walker Drive, Sherman Drive, Gunpowder Place, Tattnall Place, Drayton Place, and other streets that suggest that a developer had a head for history.

I think a person not arriving on a Sunday, when the visitors center adjacent to the Wilton Graves Memorial Bridge is closed, would have an easier time than I did. All those private drives can become a bit daunting, but all is not without hope. Barbara Brundage, assistant director of the under-construction **Museum of Hilton Head Island,** will provide information about areas on the island related to the Civil War if you contact: The Museum of Hilton Head Island, P.O. Box 5836, Hilton Head Island, SC 29938 (803) 842-9197.

A map of a self-guided walk through the **Stoney-Baynard Ruins** is available at Sea Pines Plantation on the southern end of the island. In 1776 Capt. John Stoney purchased the one thousand acres known as Braddock's Point Plantation from a Beaufort merchant. Before the turn of the century the tabby house was constructed. Stoney's grandson lost the house, according to legend, in an all-night poker game to William Baynard, who moved to the big house and planted Sea Island cotton. When Union forces occupied Hilton Head in 1861, the Baynards evacuated the house and Federal troops moved in. Local lore suggests that Confederate raiders burned the mansion. It took the Baynards fifteen years after the war to regain Braddock's Point by paying $500 in back taxes; however, they never lived at the property again.

Union **Fort Mitchel** on Hilton Head Plantation offers interpretive signs to explain its role in the Civil War. Access to the site is gained simply by asking the guard at the Hilton Head Plantation gate, situated near Skull Creek Marina. According to Brundage at the Hilton Head Museum, Canadian tourists brought public attention to another earthwork off Highway 17 near Shelton, South Carolina, that was threatened by highway widening.

Until the museum on Hilton Head is completed, a good place for tracking down information on Port Royal during the Civil War is the **Parris**

Island Museum. Through its displays the museum depicts the history of Parris Island from the landing of the French Huguenots in 1562 to the capture of Port Royal by the Federal navy in November 1861 to its selection as a site for a navy yard in 1885. Stephen Wise, the museum director, pointed out that while Forts Walker and Beauregard no longer exist, the Confederate fort on Sam's Point, northeast of Beaufort near the town of Wilkins, still stands. According to Wise, another area fort in "unusually good condition" remains on Otter Island. The Nature Conservancy recently purchased the island and the fort, which still has parts of its wooden palisade, unusual for a Civil War–era earthwork. Because no bridge goes to the island, the fort has not been plundered as thoroughly as other sites more accessible to artifact seekers.[45]

Parris Island still serves as an active training site for marines, but the museum is open free to the public from 10:00 A.M. to 4:30 P.M. every day except Thanksgiving, Christmas, and New Year's. For information about tours, contact: Marine Corps Recruit Depot, Parris Island, SC 29905 (803) 525-2951.

The town of Beaufort served as a leave center for Federal soldiers in the Department of the South during the Civil War. Consequently, it seems that almost every other house in the older part of the town was used as a hospital or barracks for Union troops. The Historic Beaufort Foundation puts out a booklet called "A Guide to Historic Beaufort," which can be purchased at the Foundation Headquarters at 801 Bay Street or the chamber of commerce offices at the intersection of Charles and Bay streets. The booklet provides pictures and short, insightful histories of the structures in antebellum Beaufort.

Several homes are particularly interesting. The **Elizabeth Barnwell Gough House,** circa 1789, was built at 705 Washington Street for Elizabeth Barnwell Gough, whose only daughter, Marianna, married James Harvey Smith in 1791. The Smiths' six sons changed their name to Rhett. One son, Robert Barnwell Rhett, who may have been born in the house, grew up to be called "the Father of the Secession." The Smiths had sixteen other children, many of whom lived in grand homes in Beaufort. Edmund Rhett, for example, rebuilt the **Milton Maxcy House** at 1113 Craven Street. Because the Beaufort County delegation met in the east room of the house to support South Carolina's secession, the home is still called "Secession House." During the Federal occupation of Beaufort the dwelling was used as headquarters for Gen. Rufus Saxton, as a billet for officers, as a hospital, and as an office for the paymaster.

Edward Barnwell, a nephew of Elizabeth Barnwell Gough, not only supervised the construction of her home but his as well. During the Civil War, Federal officers used the **Edward Barnwell House** at 1505 Bay Street for their quarters. They flattened one of the chimneys to erect a signal platform.

The **Henry McKee House,** built in 1834, possesses a singular history. In a cabin in back of the house, Robert Smalls was born in 1839. As a slave, he captured a Confederate steamer at Charleston, and with the prize money he earned after delivering the ship to Federal forces at Beaufort, he bought the house at a tax sale in 1863. The DeTrevilles, who had purchased the dwelling in 1855, sued to regain their property. The U.S. Supreme Court held Small's title valid, thus upholding all wartime tax-title cases in favor of the government. When Mrs. McKee returned to Beaufort after the war, she confusedly wandered into her old home. Smalls is said to have established the elderly McKee in her former room and taken care of her until she died.

Smalls (1839–1915) is buried at the **Tabernacle Baptist Church,** 907 Craven Street. A bust next to the church outlines the former slave's accomplishments, which included serving as a U.S. congressman and collector of the Port of Beaufort.

The **Arsenal** at 713 Craven Street was originally established on its present site in 1795 and rebuilt in 1852. The castellated, pseudomilitary structure has Gothic windows and a massive, pointed-arch gateway. Two brass guns captured from the British in 1779 and seized by Union troops in 1861 were returned in 1880. The building now houses a museum that is fascinating or dull depending upon how you feel about strolling through other people's attic leftovers. For information, contact: Beaufort Museum, 713 Craven Street, Beaufort, SC 29902 (803) 525-7471.

Charleston

CAPT. ABNER DOUBLEDAY disliked anything disorderly. A few years before arriving in Charleston, he took an informal children's game played with bats and balls and gave it some organization by introducing a diamond field and a scoring system. True to form, as second-in-command at Fort Moultrie in the late summer of 1860, the forty-one-year-old West Pointer cringed at what he considered laxity on the part of the post commandant, septuagenarian Lt. Col. John Lane Gardner.

Beach sand rose in waves almost to the top of Moultrie's sixteen-foot brick walls. No sentries paraded on the parapet. Even if they had, any hothead in the upper stories of nearby summer homes could neatly pick them off. Worse yet, some Carolinians had intimated doing just that. When the captain suggested to Gardner that the garrison be more energetic in making the post defensible, the colonel replied that any movement in that direction would be an insult to their neighbors.

Gardner, a native of Massachusetts, was not totally unconscious of his duty. Although his sympathies lay with the South, he had warned Washington of his exposed situation. Eventually the Buchanan administration reacted by sending a thirty-seven-year-old engineer from New Hampshire,

Capt. John Gray Foster, to oversee the upgrading of Charleston's harbor defenses.

The largest of these was Fort Sumter, which hunkered on a shoal a mile across the harbor entrance from Moultrie. Work on Sumter had started more than thirty years earlier in 1829. A decade passed before an artificial island made of granite "leavings" from New England quarries poked above the sea. A score of years later, there was still much to be done to the pentagonal brick fortress before the first gun could be mounted. West of Fort Sumter on the south side of Charleston Bay, a small Revolutionary War work on James Island called Fort Johnson had been abandoned and was a virtual ruin. Castle Pinckney, erected between 1804 and 1811, stood on Shute's Folly Island just three-quarters of a mile east of the Charleston docks. The small half-moon-shaped fortress was one of the first casemated defensive structures raised in the United States.[46] Four 42-pounders, fourteen 24-pounders, four 8-inch howitzers, one 10-inch mortar, one 8-inch mortar, and four lighter artillery pieces made Pinckney a potential threat to the city in any sectional conflict, but only an ordnance sergeant, his wife, and their fifteen-year-old daughter were available to handle the weapons.

Captain Foster began work immediately. He heard grumblings from locals wondering about the motivation behind the sudden burst of activity after such a long period of glacial progress, but he paid them no mind. "It seemed to him that he had heard and read of nothing but growls from South Carolina as long as he could remember, and he took the opinion that growling must be the nature of the beast."[47]

Unlike Foster, Doubleday did not underestimate the potential for violence in the Deep South's smallest state. And like sixty-year-old Robert Barnwell Rhett (the rabid prosecessionist owner of the Charleston *Mercury*), Doubleday was not one to compromise his beliefs. He declared publicly that he planned to vote for Lincoln in the fall. From that moment on, his civilian acquaintances in the area treated him as though he carried the plague.

When Lincoln was elected, Captain Foster wired his superiors asking that some of his 109 workers be armed. Washington yielded to Gardner's judgment, who refused Foster's request. He reasoned that at least half of the workers were known secessionists, and he hesitated to do anything that might upset his uneasy relationship with the work parties.

When Moultrie's ammunition stocks dwindled, Doubleday convinced Gardner to replenish them from the U.S. Arsenal in Charleston. On the night of 8 November, despite being dressed in civilian clothes, soldiers carrying cartridge boxes out of the arsenal were spotted. An angry crowd surged to the docks, and the expedition returned to Moultrie empty-handed. The next day Mayor Charles Macbeth apologized and informed Gardner that he could, of course, take whatever he wanted from the arsenal. The colonel feigned indignation and refused to accept Macbeth's offer. In reality, he feared the consequences of sending his troops back into the smoldering atmosphere of the city.

In the meantime, lame-duck U.S. Secretary of War John Floyd, "despite the fact that he was even then arranging to sell thousands of government muskets to the state of South Carolina through an intermediary,"[48] informed Gardner indirectly that he was not to perform the routine task of restocking Moultrie's ammunition. Floyd's answer to the developing tensions was to send not reinforcements, but a new commander. The man he chose was Kentuckian Robert Anderson.

The fifty-five-year-old major had no idea when he arrived at Moultrie in mid-December 1860 that his new assignment would strain his health to the breaking point.[49] The new commandant of Charleston's harbor forts had, coincidentally, sworn into the army during the Black Hawk War a man from Illinois named Abraham Lincoln. Yet Anderson's ties to the South appeared stronger than his support for his future commander in chief. Anderson was a former slaveholder who supported the institution on biblical grounds. His wife came from Georgia, and Anderson was a respected acquaintance of Jefferson Davis, a West Point classmate. His father, Virginia-born Maj. Richard Clough Anderson, had fought the British from old Fort Moultrie in 1779 and spent nine months in prison there after Charleston fell to the Redcoats.

When the new Fort Moultrie was built on Sullivan's Island near the site of the Revolutionary War fortress of palmetto logs, it served as a prison for Osceola, the Seminole chieftain whose grave still lies just outside the main gate. Anderson, who had served a tour of duty at Moultrie in 1845, had no desire to find himself in a situation similar to that of his father or the great Indian leader.[50]

Much to everyone's surprise (except perhaps the future president of the Confederacy, who had called Anderson a "man of the finest sense of honor"[51]), the major began daily gun drills and posted sentries day and night around the fort's fifteen-hundred-foot perimeter. Doubleday, although skeptical of his new commander's loyalty, energetically assumed the new tasks. He loaded an 8-inch howitzer with double canister from time to time and fired it into the water to startle the watching crowds with a great shower of iron balls. He also planted a few torpedoes around gaps in the walls created by new construction. No one knew they were powderless duds.[52]

On 20 December 1860 South Carolina voted to secede from the Union. Six days later in a well-executed plan, Anderson managed to sneak his entire command from Moultrie to Sumter past Rebel picket boats. Doubleday was the first to arrive. He ordered his men to fix bayonets and round up the workmen, many of whom sported the blue cockade of secession.

Upon hearing of Anderson's peremptory movement, Gov. Francis Pickens quickly dispatched his aide, Col. J. Johnston Pettigrew, to Sumter. Anderson took sole responsibility for his actions. "In this controversy between the North and South," Anderson told Pettigrew, "my sympathies are entirely with the South." But, he added, his duty as commander came first.[53] Pettigrew tried to convince Anderson that an agreement not to alter the status quo existed between the lame-duck Buchanan administration and former Gov. William Gist. Anderson denied any knowledge of such a pact and refused to retreat.

Fearing that Anderson's rebuff would hurt his reputation, the recently elected Pickens directed Pettigrew to occupy Castle Pinckney. Around 4:00 P.M. on 27 December, Pettigrew carried out his orders. U.S. Army Lt. R. K. Meade, a Virginian, was in charge at the fort. Ironically, delegates from his home state were at that moment trying to convince South Carolina to join a peace conference. Meade made it clear to the militiamen scaling the walls that, with only one soldier under his command, he had no means of resistance but verbal protest. The lieutenant also refused to give his parole since he did not consider a state of war to exist. After making sure Ordnance Sergeant Skillen and his family would be treated fairly, he and four of the thirty-four workmen at Pinckney left for Fort Sumter. The bloodless capture of Castle Pinckney by the Southerners became "the first overt act of war."[54]

Later that night, Lt. Col. William G. deSaussure dispatched 225 state troops to Sullivan's Island to occupy Fort Moultrie. Fearing mines, they waited until the next day to enter the fortification. Although Foster had managed to spike the weapons facing the channel and burn many of the gun carriages, Colonel deSaussure's men captured sixteen 24-pounders, nineteen 32-pounders, ten 8-inch Columbiads, one 10-inch seacoast mortar, four 6-pounders, two 12-pounders, and four 24-pounder howitzers. The U.S. Arsenal in Charleston, seized two days later, added another 22,430 pieces of ordnance, from artillery to pistols. Caretaker F. C. Humphreys, another ordnance sergeant, was allowed to fire a salute of thirty-two guns, one for every state remaining in the Union, as the U.S. flag was lowered.

The thunder at the Charleston arsenal was nothing like the explosion in Washington, D.C. Both Buchanan and Floyd denied giving Anderson permission to abandon Moultrie, but Maj. Don Carlos Buell of the adjutant general's staff, who visited Moultrie on 7 December, had handed Anderson written instructions authorizing him to occupy any fort "you may deem most proper."[55]

Buchanan was prepared to order Anderson back to Moultrie until he heard that South Carolina troops had taken possession of Castle Pinckney, Fort Moultrie, the arsenal, the custom house, and the post office. Still, Buchanan did nothing to relieve the Sumter garrison. His administration also failed to give Anderson further instructions, although Major Anderson's wife, brother, brother-in-law, and Peter Hart, his old Mexican War orderly, were given permission to visit Fort Sumter by Charleston authorities. They arrived 6 January and could have easily carried a message to the beleaguered garrison commander. Any news that reached the fort came from Charleston newspapers, and rumor had it that a merchantman, the *Star of the West,* was bringing men and materiel to Anderson.

On 9 January, an incredulous Anderson discovered the *Mercury* had told the truth as the *Star of the West* crossed the Charleston Harbor bar and steamed abreast Morris Island toward Fort Sumter.[56] At 7:15 A.M., Maj. P. F. Stevens, in command of cadets from The Citadel at Morris Island Battery, ordered Cadet George Haynesworth to fire on the side-wheeler. Although eventually hit twice, the *Star* suffered little from the 24-pounders hidden in the dunes. But Fort Moultrie, which would soon be within range, was another matter. When its guns opened fire, the ship's captain, John McGowan, turned about.

Tempers within Sumter flared as the Virginia-born wife of Pvt. John H. Davis "seized a friction tube, sprang to a gun, and vowed she would fire it herself" to defend the *Star.*[57] Doubleday dissuaded her, and the final break was postponed.

Negotiations continued. As Anderson agonized over his situation, South Carolina erected a ring of iron around his post. Fort Johnson was occupied, work commenced on a floating ironclad battery, and guns were emplaced on the northern tip of Morris Island. The men and women within Sumter were likewise busy making the unfinished fort defensible, including the placement of mines atop the paved walkway along the south wall. In the North, reporters assured the public that Anderson and his men were in no danger. From "a defensive point of view, [Sumter] is regarded as impregnable. . . . [T]here's no artillery in the possession of South Carolina which, even if undisturbed, could make anything like a breach in its massive walls."[58]

With tensions increasing by the minute, wives and children were evacuated from Sumter on 3 February. Later that month, a fledgling Confederate government ordered P. G. T. Beauregard to take over command of Charleston's defenses. In 1837 when Anderson was artillery instructor at West Point, one of his students had been Cadet Beauregard. The plebe from Louisiana had shown such promise that Anderson requested he be named assistant instructor of artillery upon his graduation.

On 3 March 1861, Lincoln was inaugurated as president of the United States — what remained of them. Postmaster General Montgomery Blair, the only one in Lincoln's cabinet with military experience, feared the new president was being overly influenced in military matters by his ambitious secretary of state, William Seward. Blair telegraphed his brother-in-law, former navy Capt. Gustavus Fox, and requested he come to Washington with the outline of a plan for relieving Fort Sumter. Before the end of the month, Fox had managed to visit Sumter and then convince the Lincoln government to reinforce the post, despite General in Chief Winfield Scott's recommendation to evacuate. The president, also hoping to strengthen Fort Pickens in

Pensacola, Florida, allowed Seward to send the *Powhatan*, a heavily armed side-wheel steamer, to the Gulf of Mexico without informing the Navy Department. Both Fox and Secretary of the Navy Gideon Welles assumed the *Powhatan*, one of only a handful of warships in the Atlantic, would provide the necessary punch for the Sumter expedition.

In the meantime, Anderson heard nothing directly from the newly installed Lincoln administration. The soldiers in the fort, already on short rations, assumed the garrison would be evacuated within a matter of days. As they packed their belongings on 3 April, the Morris Island batteries fired on another vessel flying the Stars and Stripes. Anderson again refused to answer the insult. The ship turned out to be a merchantman lost in the fog. Governor Pickens immediately apologized for the apparent dereliction of duty of the patrolling picket boat and promised to punish the officer in charge.

On the evening of 8 April, emissaries from Washington arrived in Charleston and surprised Governor Pickens by notifying him that Sumter would be reprovisioned. Anderson learned of the decision from U.S. Secretary of War Simon Cameron through regular mail delivery, which had been resumed in mid-February via Fort Johnson. The orders to hold the fort were Anderson's "first instructions from the Lincoln government."[59]

Anderson was as stunned as Pickens. He had allowed his flag to be insulted twice in the hope that his personal humiliation could purchase peace. Now his worst fears were realized. War was inevitable. The others inside the fort, on the other hand, were thrilled with the news. They set about cutting up surplus blankets and woolen shirts to sew into cartridge bags with the half-dozen needles inside the post.

Meeting in Montgomery, Alabama, the Confederate government mulled over the tidings from Charleston. Seward's counterpart, former Sen. Robert Toombs of Georgia, warned that "firing on the fort will inaugurate a civil war greater than any the world has yet seen."[60] Despite the Confederate secretary of state's prescient vision, Davis and his other advisers decided to instruct Secretary of War Leroy Pope Walker to order Beauregard to "demand its [Sumter's] evacuation, and if this is refused proceed, in such manner as you may determine, to reduce it."[61] The message reached Beauregard on 10 April, and he immediately dispatched last-minute orders. A rifled Blakely gun just in from Liverpool was shipped to Cummings Point. The floating battery was towed to the west end of Sullivan's Island, adding its two 42-pounders and two 32-pounders to the weapons covering the spot where any relief boat would have to anchor.

On the afternoon of 11 April, Beauregard again asked his former West Point instructor to vacate the fort. All the officers in Sumter voted to refuse, including the young Virginian, Meade, who would later offer his services to the armies of the Confederacy.[62] Early on the following morning, Beauregard sent yet another negotiating team. Anderson proposed to move out in three days if he did not receive supplies or further instructions. It was 3:30 A.M. when Beauregard's representatives let Anderson know that his offer contained too many conditions. Therefore, in one hour's time, Col. James Chesnut informed Anderson, the bombardment would begin.

The departing Confederates rowed toward Fort Johnson and ordered Capt. George S. James, commander of the mortar battery there, to open fire at 4:30 A.M. James offered to allow Roger Pryor, one of the men in the boat with Chesnut, the honor of pulling the lanyard that would signal the crews servicing the forty-seven other guns surrounding Sumter. Only thirty hours earlier Pryor had given a fiery speech from a balcony on the Charleston Hotel demanding that Charlestonians "strike a blow!"[63] Now given the chance himself, he had second thoughts. With a heavy heart, Pryor, Chesnut, and two other aides returned to their boat and began to row toward Fort Moultrie. Before they reached their destination, they saw the spluttering arc of a mortar shell that detonated almost directly over Sumter.

Hearing the explosion, troops on Morris Island rushed to their guns. The first to go into action were three 10-inch mortars of the King's Trapier Battery, followed by the Cummings Point Battery and finally by Stevens's Iron Battery, three 8-inch Columbiads poking through a wood and railroad iron embrasure. Among the men serving the Iron Battery was Edmund Ruffin, the sixty-six-year-old Virginian who had been a one-man secession society. He had been made an honorary member of the Palmetto Guard, part of Stevens's command. Capt. G. B. Cuthbert gave him the honor of pulling the first lanyard at the Iron Battery. The shell from Columbiad number 1 "burst directly upon the parapet of the southwest angle of the fort."[64] Soon the entire harbor was ablaze as Confederate artillerists, including one of Major Anderson's brothers-in-law, worked their guns under the scudding clouds. Not until the sun rose did Sumter reply. Doubleday was given the honor of firing the first shot, and he blasted one right back at Ruffin.

Navy Captain Fox arrived off Charleston bar just in time to see the opening fireworks. Each of the ships in his rescue fleet had sailed separately and secretly to avoid detection, but of the half-dozen or so vessels he expected to meet off Charleston, only one waited, the revenue cutter *Harriet Lane*. Missing were the crucial tugs, which were to race into the harbor under cover of darkness, and the *Powhatan*, which would provide covering fire or, if necessary, her own large boats in case the tugs failed to make the rendezvous. Fox was unaware that bad weather had stopped the tugs and that the *Powhatan* had been commandeered by Seward. Last-minute attempts by Lincoln and Welles to recall her did not succeed. All that Fox and his two hundred men aboard the transport *Baltic* could do was watch the deadly pyrotechnics. Even the arrival of the *Pawnee,* a second-class screw sloop, did not alter the situation.

All that day the men in and surrounding Fort Sumter expected the vessels anchored off the bar to send help as iron rain fell upon its defenders. Certainly under cover of darkness an attempt would be made, the South Carolinians reckoned, so fire barges were kept burning throughout the night. When the sun broke through on Saturday, 13 April, even the Confederates expressed contempt for the "timorous inaction" of the fleet.[65]

A fire broke out in the fort soon after 8:00 A.M. and by noon the fort was enveloped in black smoke split by orange flames. The garrison choked back the smoke and fought on. At 1:00 P.M. the flag staff toppled, and Brig. Gen. James Simons, in command at Morris Island, sent Col. Louis Wigfall, a former senator from Texas, to see if Anderson would now surrender. Surprised gunners in Sumter saw Wigfall appear at an embrasure and at first refused to let him enter. Eventually, Anderson was sent for, and Wigfall convinced him to surrender despite the fact that the garrison flag had been heroically raised again.

Wigfall triumphantly returned to Morris Island about the same time Beauregard's aides arrived at Sumter. When Anderson learned that Wigfall had no authority, he indicated he would recommence the fight, but the aides convinced him that Beauregard would agree to any terms Wigfall had offered, and the fighting ceased. Around four thousand shells had been exchanged between the adversaries, yet there were no casualties on either side, "a comparatively bloodless beginning," Horace Greeley later observed, "for the bloodiest war America ever knew."[66] Despite the lack of bloodshed, the demise of the masonry stronghold was chiseled into Fort Sumter's walls. Observers noted near "the top [of the wall opposite the Cummings Point Iron Battery] a breach as large as a cart."[67]

The time for embarkation of the Sumter garrison was set for 11:00 A.M. Sunday. The Confederate steamer *Isabel* would take Anderson and his men to the three ships still standing off the bar. However, it was not until 1:00 P.M. that the first discharge of a hundred-gun salute for the lowered Stars and Stripes boomed over the harbor from Sumter. On the seventeenth round, either a pile of cartridges ignited or there was a premature explosion. In any case, Pvt. Daniel Hough died instantly and another soldier, Sgt. James Galway, expired soon afterward in a Charleston hospital. The salute was reduced to fifty guns. Still, it was not until 4:00 P.M. that Anderson took the garrison flag aboard the *Isabel.* Due to the lateness of the hour, the *Isabel* missed the tide and the Sumter garrison watched as the Stars and Bars fluttered over the still-burning fort.

All Fox could do for the tired and hungry men who reached his ship early the next morning was to give them food, some rest, and take them back to a hero's welcome in New York City.

The week following the surrender of Fort Sumter, Lincoln ordered a blockade of all Southern ports. The screw frigate USS *Niagara* took her station off Charleston on 11 May, but the effect of one ship was negligible. With a population of forty thousand, half of whom were black, Charleston was the South's second largest city and certainly one of the most important, both economically and psychologically. To humiliate and subdue this cradle of secession was certainly a high priority for Northern strategists. Fox, anxious to make up for the debacle of the Sumter relief expedition, suggested that two dozen old sailing ships be sunk across the channel leading to Charleston Harbor to bottle up the port. Welles gave his blessing, and the first "stone fleet" (so-called because the holds of the various ships were filled with rocks) assembled at Port Royal, the anchorage south of Charleston captured 7 November by Flag Off. Samuel du Pont. Before the plan to close "at least one cursed rathole"[68] could be put into effect, disaster struck Charleston. On the night of 11–12 December 1861, almost a year after the Ordinance of Secession had been signed, a fire rampaged through the town, leaving little but a forest of chimneys in a 540-acre area. Six miles out to sea, the crew aboard the transport *Illinois* bound from Port Royal to New York thought the entire city was aflame. Their observation only slightly missed the truth. Five churches, hundreds of private residences, and many commercial buildings, including Institute Hall, where the secession ordinance had been signed, collapsed.[69]

As Charleston's residents struggled with what Northerners were calling divine retribution, Yankee sailors scuttled sixteen hulks across the main shipping channel. Gen. Robert E. Lee, in charge of the Department of South Carolina, Georgia, and East Florida, indicated to Secretary of War Judah P. Benjamin that Maffitt's Channel remained open. Early in 1862, fourteen more ships were sunk to block that route into the harbor. The British foreign office called the sinkings a "cruel plan,"[70] and the French posted similar misgivings. A backtracking Seward tried to claim the scuttled ships were not meant to injure Charleston Harbor permanently. Whether or not his statement was diplomatic double talk or a sincere intention, it proved to be true. Within a short time, the entire stone fleet disappeared into the mud.

In March 1862 Jefferson Davis called Lee to Richmond and replaced him with Maj. Gen. John C. Pemberton. The future commander at Vicksburg immediately showed his knack for doing the wrong thing by ordering the withdrawal of guns from Cole's Island, which lay at the mouth of the Stono River, the back door into Charleston. Pemberton feared — with good reason — that outlying forts could not defend themselves against the U.S. Navy, but his decision was very unpopular among the locals, including Governor Pickens. To make matters worse, the *Planter*, the steamer that transported the guns back to Charleston, was hijacked 12 May by several of its black crew members led by a slave named Robert Smalls, who immediately

Interior views of Fort Sumter after the surrender

let Com. Samuel du Pont know that the entrance to the Stono River was undefended.

Wasting little time, Maj. Gen. David Hunter, in command of Union forces on Hilton Head, sailed most of his men to Stono Inlet. On 2 June, the troops splashed ashore on the southwesternmost tip of James Island. Col. Johnson Hagood, one of the local Confederate commanders, commented later about the "rapid fire of gunboat shells"[71] that allowed the advance guard of the Union forces to push inland about a mile. Pemberton ordered Hagood to set up a battery of heavy guns and drive away the pesky Union gunboats. But under enemy naval gunfire, the Rebel counterattack spluttered to a halt.

Yankee troops now stood within eight miles of Charleston. In between stood some breastworks at a cluster of cabins called Secessionville, named long before the present confrontation swept through their midst. In the early morning hours of 16 June, almost seven thousand Federal soldiers crept toward the five hundred sleeping Confederates protecting the hamlet. Col. Thomas G. Lamar woke in time to pull the lanyard of a Columbiad loaded with grapeshot, blasting a hole in the blue line and arousing his command. Attacking a fortified 125-yard-wide strip of land snug between two marshes, the Union troopers were not able to take advantage of their superiority in numbers. Brig. Gen. Henry Benham, in command of the Federal columns, hoped to call down naval supporting fire to alter the odds, but the gunboats *Ellen* and *E. B. Hale* could steam no closer than a mile from the Confederate works. Since a large forest covered the intervening ground, the naval shells frequently hit friendly forces. After two and a half hours of grueling combat, Confederate reinforcements began to shift the balance of power. Benham ordered a retreat.

The Federals suffered almost seven hundred casualties; the Confederates, slightly more than two hundred, including Colonel Lamar, wounded in the neck. He died the following year of fever but left his name behind on the battery he and his men had stiffly defended. The loser, Union General Benham, was placed under arrest. Hunter then turned the James Island forces over to Brig. Gen. Horatio G. Wright and instructed the new commander not to advance. With Union gunboats playing backstop in the Stono River, the victorious Confederates were not eager to repeat their earlier abortive strike against the bridgehead. Union General Hunter, not wishing to be stalemated on the unhealthy coast, pulled all troops from James Island by 9 July.

A Confederate officer present at the battle of Secessionville told a young Charleston woman the reason he had not retreated was that he had no doubts the women of the city would have beaten them back into the fray with their broomsticks.[72] He probably had gained part of his healthy respect for the women of Charleston earlier in the year when at the end of February

1862 someone asked in the *Courier:* "Cannot the women of Charleston give an order for a gunboat?"[73] Money poured in from all over the state, and when the Confederate government picked up the cost of one ironclad, the citizens of Charleston decided to use the donated money for another.

Pickens wanted cannon emplaced back on Cole's Island, but Pemberton argued that until the completion of the ironclads, enemy gunboats could always prevent any movement of weapons in that direction. By the end of August, the Confederate ironclads were launched and Beauregard was back in command of the Department of South Carolina and Georgia. Three months later, du Pont's fleet left Hilton Head and Beauregard prepared to meet the enemy anywhere between Wilmington, North Carolina, and Savannah, Georgia. The Federal ships sailed for North Carolina, and Beauregard was able to transfer units from his district via the untouched Charleston and Savannah Railroad toward the threatened sector.

Whether or not Governor Pickens's grumblings about Pemberton's retreat from the mouth of the Stono influenced Beauregard, at the end of January 1863 a plan was put into effect to capture the *Isaac P. Smith,* a converted river steamer that patrolled the Stono River and was heavily armed with eight 8-inch smoothbores and one rifled 30-pounder. Confederates hauled heavy cannon to an abandoned post at Battery Island and to Thomas Grimball's place farther up the river on James Island. Across the river at Paul Grimball's plantation on Johns Island, four guns of the Palmetto Light Artillery guarded the river. The next day, the *Smith* steamed into this gauntlet. Despite a stubborn fight, the crew surrendered when the ship's boilers were hit.

With two new ironclads riding in the harbor, Beauregard began to think about more offensive operations. From a practical point of view, there were good reasons why the two warships, the *Chicora* and *Palmetto State,* should never have raised their anchors: They were poorly designed, inadequately armed and armored, and underpowered, even by Southern standards. On the plus side, each armored ship had a well-trained crew. When Beauregard suggested to Com. D. N. Ingraham that naval pressure be brought to bear on the blockade, the Confederate captain proved cooperative.

Near midnight on 30 January 1863, the two steam rams raised anchor. Four hours later they crossed the haze-covered bar and surprised the USS *Mercedita* before its crew could take action. The *Palmetto State* stove in the wooden ship's side and one of the ram's shells passed through the hapless enemy's port boiler. Although Union Capt. H. S. Stellwagon pledged to parole his ship and crew, when the Confederate ram moved off to join the *Chicora,* the *Mercedita* limped away to Port Royal under its own power.

After exchanging broadsides with several ships, the *Chicora* engaged the converted merchant steamer *Keystone State.* With the help of the *Palmetto*

State, the *Chicora* had been able to force this Union warship to strike its colors. But before the ram's decrepit engines could bring the ironclad within boarding range, one of the Federal vessel's paddle wheels began turning. That allowed her to escape far enough to be brought under tow by the USS *Memphis.* The two Confederate rams limped after more prey, but the nine ships of the blockading squadron had suffered enough. Although almost within their grasp, the prizes the Confederates coveted escaped.

This was not the first, nor would it be the last, time that Union vessels that had struck their colors avoided capture. Even so, the Confederates hoped to make political hay from their empty victory. Officials declared the blockade had been lifted. Furthermore, Southern lawyers argued, proper notice would have to be given once again before more Federal warships could take up station. All this politicking might consume weeks, during which time merchant ships could run in and out of the port unmolested.

Foreign emissaries on hand in Charleston were escorted past the bar to see for themselves. While the Spanish, French, and English consuls agreed among themselves that the blockade had indeed been raised, their respective governments did not. Within a short time, an even tighter Union vise was clamped around Charleston. In addition, a force of nine Federal monitors was even then forming at Port Royal for an attack on Charleston's defenses.

As is so often the case, the losers at Port Royal had gained more from the battle than the victors. What the Confederates learned at Fort Walker was that thick traverses must separate the guns in a battery. Applying those lessons, they developed Fort McAllister, part of the defenses of Savannah, into an earthen stronghold of such proportions that du Pont's four warmup duels with the fort during the first three months of 1863 depressed the usually enthusiastic naval commander. He began to convey his doubts not only to friends but also to the Navy Department, to which he confided that his monitors' "offensive powers [were] found to be feeble in dealing with forts."[74]

In the meantime, Beauregard plunged into his work. He sowed torpedoes (mines) throughout Charleston's inner harbor and hastened development of semisubmersible torpedo craft. The currents at the harbor entrance proved no less a problem for Confederates than for the Yankees. Log booms erected between Moultrie and Sumter were carried away like the stone fleet. Beauregard had to settle for a feeble rope barrier supported by empty barrels, hardly enough to stop a determined naval advance.

But du Pont insisted there were torpedo fields in the channel and made his plans accordingly. On 7 April at 2:30 P.M., Capt. John Rodgers in the *Weehawken* led eight other ironclads toward Fort Sumter. The fleet carried a total of twenty-two 11-inch guns, seven 15-inch guns, and three 8-inch rifled Parrott cannon. Although the Confederates would be able to bring seventy-six pieces to bear, none of them carried the weight of the fleet weapons. The day was clear; the water calm.

Already under considerable stress because a clumsy mine-clearing device was making his ship difficult to handle, Rodgers balked when he saw the barrels holding the rope obstructions. The only egress for those below decks was by means of an opening in the deck that had to be aligned with a hole in the turret floor, and just one man could pass through at a time. With these thoughts in his mind, Rodgers thought he felt his ship shudder from an underwater explosion. He stopped his engines, then backed away. The rest of the column lost formation. Du Pont, sheltered behind the armored walls of the *New Ironsides* halfway back in the line, could not effectively signal his other commanders. To make matters worse, the flagship became unmanageable in the shoal water, collided with the *Catskill* and the *Nantucket*, then finally anchored over a large mine. Ashore, Assistant Engineer Langdon Cheves tried to detonate the mine, but nothing happened.

Any organization within the fleet broke down completely, and the battle developed into a slugging match as one ironclad after another stepped up for a round or two. Following the *Weehawken,* which was hit fifty times, came the *Passaic,* under the command of Percival Drayton. After getting off only four shots from its 11-inch gun, the ironclad was hit twice in quick succession in the lower part of the turret, jamming it. Her 15-inch gun was brought to bear, but then the turret failed again after the ship took thirty-five hits in as many minutes.

The *Montauk* sheered away from the battle line after being on the receiving end of fourteen Confederate shells. Her captain reported that he was unable to maneuver "in the narrow and uncertain channel, with the limited means of observation afforded from the pilothouse under rapid and concentrated fire from the forts, the vessels of the fleet close around . . . and neither compass nor buoys to guide him."[75]

The *Nantucket* and *New Ironsides* each absorbed fifty or so hits, although the latter suffered little damage. The *Nahant* was not as fortunate. Early in the action, a well-aimed shot knocked an eighty-pound chunk from the pilothouse, killing the quartermaster. The *Keokuk,* trying to avoid a collision, was forced to spend a half-hour under a crossfire between Forts Sumter and Moultrie at a range of six hundred yards from the latter. Only calm weather kept the ship afloat as it crawled back down the ship channel. The next day a roughened sea washed over the deck, sinking the warship off Morris Island.

By 5:00 P.M. du Pont recalled his battered command. He planned to renew the fight the next day, but the damage to the ironclads proved too great. Fox and Welles let du Pont know they thought he had given up too early. The hero of Port Royal sent back word that if they felt someone else could have done better under the circumstances, they should replace him. Perhaps waiting for the invitation, the Navy Department promoted Andrew H. Foote, the hero of the western waters, to rear admiral and ordered him to take command of the South Atlantic Blockading Squadron. On his way to relieve du Pont, however, Foote died in New York from complications of a wound suffered during the attack on Fort Donelson, Tennessee, more than a year earlier. John A. Dahlgren, chief of the Bureau of Ordnance, was assigned to combat duty to prove he could handle things at sea as well as he had on land.

In the meantime, a Confederate ordnance officer, Adolphus LaCoste, was called to Charleston to salvage the guns of the *Keokuk*. He put together a makeshift group of men and vessels for the monumental task. Working at night without lights, drenched by waves, his crew dismantled the tops of the ironclad's turrets. The next part of the operation required men to hold their breath, dive into the turret, and loosen the brass trunnion caps. Finally the 15,700-pound guns were free. The steamer *Etiwan* towed an old lightship rigged with a block and tackle to the wreck. The *Palmetto State* and *Chicora* stood guard in case any of the blockading squadron, just two miles away, should choose to investigate.

Workers attached the tackle and strained at the ropes. When the breech broke the surface with the tube still inside the turret, the blocks of the tackle met. The gun could be raised no more. The sun lay just under the horizon when LaCoste ordered the men to shift fifteen hundred sandbags farther aft on the *Etiwan*. When the last sandbag and last man moved to the rear, the barrel rose, but not enough. Just then a slightly larger wave lifted the lightship. When it fell, the cannon muzzle was clanking against the turret, but this time on the outside.

Three nights later, the expedition removed the second gun without a hitch. By early May, both guns, the largest in the South at the time, had been transported to the city.[76] One eventually went to Fort Sumter where for a time it was the only serviceable cannon in the fort. By September it was returned to the city and mounted at Battery Ramsey in White Point Garden. The other Dahlgren was sent to Battery Bee on Sullivan's Island where it remained throughout the war.

In June the argumentative Union Major General Hunter lost his command to Brig. Gen. Quincy A. Gillmore, the engineering hero who had made short work of Fort Pulaski in Savannah, Georgia. Cooperating closely with Dahlgren's monitors, Gillmore planned to attack Morris Island and reduce Sumter from Cummings Point on the island's north end. In his way stood Fort Wagner and Battery Gregg.

The first part of the operation went like clockwork. On 10 July, Brig. Gen. George C. Strong launched a surprise amphibious landing on the southern end of Morris Island. His men swept up 150 prisoners and a dozen guns before Gillmore reined him in. The next day the Seventh Connecticut rushed Fort Wagner, named for slain South Carolina Lt. Col. Thomas M. Wagner, but by then the defenders were prepared. Despite the inspired leadership of Strong, the Union forces fell back, leaving behind 330 men. Confederate casualties totaled 12 killed or wounded. Had Gillmore succeeded, the capture of Morris Island, added to the victories at Vicksburg and Gettysburg the previous week, would have put the entire Confederacy in a tailspin from which it may not have recovered.

Gillmore studied the fort as he pondered his next move. The work spanned 250 yards from the Atlantic on the east to an impassible swamp on the west. Sand and earth, strengthened with palmetto logs and sandbags, reached skyward thirty feet. Fourteen cannon, including a 10-inch Columbiad that fired a 128-pound shot, gaped over the parapets fronted by a water-filled trench ten feet wide and five feet deep. Land mines and sharpened stakes compounded the menace. To reduce such an obstacle, Gillmore decided to crush the position from four land batteries and the guns of eleven ships in Dahlgren's fleet.

To Brig. Gen. William B. Taliaferro, the forty-year-old commander of the Confederate garrison, the ironclads that closed to within three hundred yards of the shore on 18 July, seemed "like huge water dogs, their black sides glistening in the sun."[77] These canines had an exceptionally fierce bite, sending four-hundred-pound shells into the defenders with a terrific howl. Most of the seventeen hundred defenders were sheltered in the fort's bombproof, but Lt. Col. P. C. Gaillard's Charleston Battalion had to man the ramparts in case of a land attack. As Taliaferro offered encouragement to Gaillard's sentries, he was buried to his waist by a near miss.

Following an unprecedented eleven-hour smothering, the fort seemed ripe for a determined infantry assault, or so Gillmore thought. His confidence was bolstered by Brig. Gen. Truman Seymour, in command of the actual attack. As a captain, Seymour had been forced by Beauregard to surrender at Sumter. He was anxious to return.

Strong's brigade would once again spearhead the charge, and as the sun set, twenty-five-year-old Col. Robert Gould Shaw formed the Fifty-fourth Massachusetts on the beach. At 7:45 P.M., Shaw raised his sword and his 624 men advanced northward, bayonets fixed. By necessity the fleet terminated its crushing bombardment, but apparently not in time. Cpl. James Gooding wrote that he and his companions in the Fifty-fourth "were exposed to a murderous fire from the batteries of the fort, from our Monitors and our land batteries, as they did not cease firing soon enough."[78]

Taliaferro's Confederates rushed out of the bombproof to prepare the dozen surviving cannon within Fort Wagner for the human onslaught. With Shaw's men still 150 yards away, the gray-clad defenders ripped into the blue ranks. Shaw's adjutant, Garth Wilkinson James, and his second in command, Lt. Col. Edward N. Hallowell, both fell wounded. Undaunted, Shaw scrambled up the steep slope, waved his sword, shouted, "Forward, Fifty-fourth!" then tumbled to the ground, dead from three fatal wounds.[79]

The night assault on Fort Wagner *(Illustrated London News)*

Color Sgt. Gustave De Bonge managed to plant the regimental flag of the Sixth Connecticut, the next regiment in line, on Wagner's crest. The Forty-eighth New York followed close behind, but by then Taliaferro had several howitzers pouring grape into the flanks of the three regiments bunched together in the southeast corner of the fort. Others raked the remaining Union regiments strung along the beach, effectively stifling their advance. Strong tried to revive the attack, but several iron balls ripped through his thigh, wounds from which he would not recover. In pain, he reluctantly ordered his men to retreat.

Furious that his second brigade had not advanced to support Strong, Seymour sent his chief of staff to order the four regiments of the brigade forward. By the time they reached the moat, a rising tide had begun to cover the dead piled three to four deep in front of Wagner's hellish rise. In the dark, the One Hundredth New York fired on the Forty-eighth New York still fighting inside the fort. By the time Col. Haldimand Putnam arrived to take charge of his brigade, the situation was desperate. Seymour had been wounded, Gillmore was out of touch, and when Putnam tried to organize a retreat from the Federal stronghold atop the bombproof, the back of his head exploded under the impact of a bullet.

At this point, Brigadier General Hagood threw his Thirty-second Georgia into the fray and swamped the Northerners who still clung to their toehold inside Wagner. Pvt. Joseph Hibson, his arm broken in two places and his scalp bleeding from shell fragments, managed to save the flag of his regiment, the Forty-eighth New York, thus earning a Medal of Honor. Sgt. William Carney was also awarded a Medal of Honor for bringing back the colors of the Fifty-fourth Massachusetts.

Brig. Gen. Thomas Stevenson's third brigade finally arrived at 10:30 P.M., but Stevenson did not attempt to fulfill his belated attack orders; the flow of bloodied refugees from the fort prevented any coordinated rush along the narrow beach.

The next day, Taliaferro totaled his losses: 36 killed, 145 wounded or missing. On the Union side, the Fifty-fourth Massachusetts alone had lost 281 men, 54 of those killed and another 48 never accounted for. The Seventh New Hampshire lost 11 officers among its 77 killed or mortally wounded. Total Federal losses approximated 1,500.

After such a setback, Gillmore determined to reduce Wagner as he had Pulaski. He amassed forty-one pieces of heavy artillery, including several 200- and 300-pound Parrott guns. These would be supported by the 11- and 15-inch guns of the fleet. The sailors could not directly hit the parade of Wagner, so they devised an ingenious method of skipping shells inside the fort by bouncing them off the sea on calm days. One day navy gunners blew a mullet almost into the cap of Confederate Capt. Robert Pringle, who thanked them for sending him breakfast. "Shortly afterward, a shell ricocheted into the battery and killed him instantly."[80] On the seaward side of Wagner, only one gun faced the entire Union fleet, a 10-inch Columbiad. With so many targets, it managed a remarkable record. Admiral Dahlgren, reporting the actions of his fleet off Morris Island, stated that his ships had fired 8,026 rounds and received 882 hits, none of them in any way serious.[81]

By late July, some of Gillmore's batteries were within range of the gorge wall of Fort Sumter, and they began firing at the infamous symbol of secession. Sumter's garrison had been making preparations for such a bombardment from the day of the successful landing on Morris Island. Sand, cotton bales, and twenty thousand sandbags had been placed in the fort's casemates. In addition, more than twenty guns were removed to other batteries surrounding the harbor.

The Union iron orchestra had tuned up and by 17 August was ready for its first full concert. At daylight, Battery Brown on Morris Island boomed out with her two 8-inch Parrott rifles, followed by the deep percussion of the other batteries, including a naval battery manned by sailors and including two 8-inch Parrotts and two 80-pounder Whitworth rifles. By mid-morning the monitors *Passaic* and *Patapsco* joined in with their basso profundo. The deadly music continued throughout the night. During the first twenty-four-hour period nearly a thousand shells whistled toward Sumter, disabling seven guns in the fort and turning its brickwork into dust.

The second day the monitors did not participate, but other voices joined the Morris Island chorus, tossing another 876 shells against the fort. For two more days, there was no letup. Late on 21 July, Gillmore demanded Beauregard evacuate Morris Island and Fort Sumter. If not, he would bombard Charleston. At 1:30 A.M. on 22 July, two hours after Beauregard received Gillmore's demands, the first shell from the "Swamp Angel" battery constructed in a marsh off Morris Island exploded into the city, nearly five miles away.

To carry out this feat, Gillmore's men had spent the previous month dragging some 307 tons of timber and 812 tons of sand over two and a half miles of mud to the battery site. Since no target could be discerned from the firing position, several bearings were taken with a pocket compass. "Though a very crude method of calculating data, this was probably the first instance on record in which a gun was aimed by compass at an invisible object and at such a great distance."[82] Although the heavy gun exploded after three dozen rounds, a precedent had been set. Eventually two-thirds of the city fell within range of Union batteries.

Convinced by Gillmore that Sumter was nothing more than a pile of rubble, Dahlgren made arrangements to have another go at it with his ironclads. On the night of 1–2 September, four monitors and the *New Ironsides* approached the misshapen mass of Sumter and opened fire with their 11- and 15-inch guns. The Confederates replied from Sullivan's Island, managing to hit the monitors seventy-one times in the dark. The Federals for their part threw 245 more shells against the already crumbling fort before retiring.

While the bombardment of Sumter continued, Gillmore did not ignore Battery Wagner. His engineers pushed their saps to within thirteen hundred yards of the earthwork as Union ship and shore batteries kept up an incessant pounding. On 6 September, Confederate Col. L. M. Keitt, then in command at Wagner, sent a message to Beauregard stating that he would sortie against the eleven thousand Union besiegers the following morning if his troops were not removed from Morris Island. He would rather see his men die in a fruitless charge than be annihilated by the deluge of shot and shell. Beauregard agreed to the evacuation that took place that same night. Gillmore had planned an attack for the following morning, but a deserter informed him of the Confederate escape.

After fifty-eight days of "possibly the heaviest artillery fire ever experienced in such a small area," one Georgia soldier who made it safely to Charleston said he wasn't "afeared of hell no more, it can't touch Wagner."[83]

Admiral Dahlgren immediately made plans to take advantage of the evacuation of Morris Island. He ordered the *Weehawken* to mark the channel between Sumter and newly captured Cummings Point. Unfortunately for the Federals, the monitor ran hard aground. Instead of making a determined attack on Sumter and Charleston, Dahlgren spent the day with the bulk of his ironclads in front of Fort Moultrie trying to prevent Confederate gunners on Sullivan's Island from noticing the stranded *Weehawken*. The next day the artillerists at Moultrie realized something was amiss with the monitor. Although at extreme range and once again under attack by Dahlgren, the Rebels managed to hit the *Weehawken* twenty-four times from guns emplaced on Sullivan's Island and at Fort Johnson. Their long-distance shots and poor ammunition, however, caused little damage. Ironically, the *Weehawken* had the upper hand in the exchange when one of its 15-inch shells bounced off the muzzle of an 8-inch Columbiad in Fort Moultrie into a box of ammunition. The resulting explosion killed sixteen men and wounded twelve. By 2:00 P.M. the tide rose, freeing the *Weehawken*. Dahlgren then retired.

In a rush to capture Sumter, both Dahlgren and Gillmore decided to launch small-boat operations against the fort on the night of 9 September. Only Dahlgren's request for army skiffs revealed the intentions of each commander to the other. Gillmore suggested a joint venture, but Dahlgren declined unless it was under naval control. Gillmore's ego did not take the suggestion lightly, so both sides went ahead with separate plans. The only thing they agreed upon was a password to prevent unwanted casualties.

The navy launches were taken under tow at 9:30 P.M. on 8 September. The army, on the other hand, was left high and dry when its boats were stranded by low tide. The landsmen were the lucky ones.

The navy operation started poorly when most of the twenty-five boats carrying four hundred marines joined the diversionary force instead of the main attack column. Many of the boats did not reach Sumter at all, and those that did received an unexpectedly vicious welcome from Maj. Stephen Elliott Jr.'s tough veterans, who had replaced the artillery units at Sumter when the remaining large guns were removed. Added to the blistering fire and bombs coming from the parapets, the batteries on Sullivan's Island aimed a few shots at the water surrounding Sumter. Without so much as a single injury, Elliott's infantry inflicted a score of casualties on the marines and captured five times that number.

Although many of the U.S. Navy's blue-water sailors mistrusted the cumbersome ironclads, and for good reason, the Confederates had nothing but respect for the mechanical monsters and tried several schemes to sink a few, particularly the flagship *New Ironsides*. On the night of 20 August, Capt. James Carlin took his jury-rigged torpedo boat out hunting but came up short. The semisubmersible *David* tried next, pushing a torpedo against the North's Goliath on the night of 5 October. Even though the crew of the little cigar-shaped torpedo boat managed to explode the weapon amidships on the *New Ironsides,* the damage was not fatal.

The escape of the *Weehawken* and *New Ironsides* deeply disappointed the Confederates. The sinking of the experimental *Keokuk* notwithstanding, it appeared that nothing the Rebels could throw at the Union fleet had the desired effect. Still, the low-freeboard monitors were extremely vulnerable and a slight gale on 6 December proved this once again. Lying at anchor off the southern end of Morris Island, the previously lucky *Weehawken* began to take water through an open hawse pipe. Within five minutes of hoisting a distress signal, the monitor was on the bottom of the channel, only her smokestack visible. Although Dahlgren hoped to raise her, she sank too deeply into the mud.

Altogether Fort Sumter weathered eleven separate bombardments. The worst began on 26 October 1863 and lasted forty-one days and nights. The firing commenced when Federal observers noticed that a protected casemate facing the channel, known from then on as the Three-Gun Battery, had been armed with two 10-inch Columbiad smoothbores and a 42-pounder rifle.[84] From Wagner and Gregg (renamed Forts Strong and Putnam respectively) and the other batteries on Morris Island, Union artillerists continued an unrelenting cascade of shot and shell on the southern gorge of the fort while the monitors *Patapsco* and *Lehigh* punished the sea face. The Confederates returned fire from Sullivan's and James islands except for a short time in early November when Jefferson Davis made an inspection tour. (The president did not mention Beauregard's gallant defense of the city and harbor during his speech at city hall earlier in his visit, straining relations between the two.)

As the bombardment continued, the ironclad *Lehigh* ran aground on 16 November. For four hours under constant fire, crew members from several ships struggled to free the stricken ship under the direct supervision of Admiral Dahlgren. At high tide the ironclad pulled away from the shoal.

The last night of November, Gillmore sent 250 troops aboard barges from Morris Island on what he called a reconnaissance of Sumter.[85] Despite the incessant shelling, Elliott was ready and waiting, and Sumter's garrison opened up with small arms before any landing was attempted. Batteries from Sullivan's and James islands, along with a Rebel gunboat anchored off Fort Johnson, once again provided heavier discouragement. The attackers did not make it closer than three hundred yards.

The fury of the bombardment reached a crescendo in the first week of December, then on the sixth of the month, it abruptly stopped. Altogether 18,677 rounds of ammunition were unleashed in the waning days of 1863.

Confederate casualties reached the century mark for the previous six weeks. On the other side, eight of Gillmore's heavy guns had burst.

Five days later, what Union firepower had failed to accomplish, an act of God or human weakness almost did. As the Confederates at Sumter lined up at the entrance of the temporary commissary to draw rations, 150 pounds of black powder stored in a magazine behind the commissary exploded. The room serving as a storehouse had not been designed for such a purpose, but with so much of the fort destroyed, the Confederates had no choice. Eleven men died in the winding passages meant to keep enemy projectiles away from the powder. Another forty-one were wounded. The actual cause of the explosion was not determined, but unofficially, everything from a flame held too close to a barrel of whiskey to ash from a pipe was blamed.[86]

The inferno could not be checked, and as soon as the Federals on Morris Island saw a hint of smoke, they opened up with every available gun, sending two hundred shells into Sumter within the next two hours. A wounded Colonel Elliott ordered the band out to the parapet to play "Dixie." When the familiar strain reached the Yankees, they ceased firing and cheered their stubborn opponents. Had they realized it, Federal troops could have waltzed into the fort since most of the arms of the unwounded defenders had been lost in the fire.

Instead, the Union gunners satisfied themselves with a Christmas bombardment of Charleston. Using the steeple of Saint Michael's Church as their target, the Federals lobbed 134 shells into the city starting soon after midnight on 25 December. Gus Smythe of the Confederate Signal Corps was stationed in the church's tower during most of the siege. Whether by divine intervention or dumb luck, none of the Northern ordnance touched Saint Michael's as Smythe watched the destructive effects of the bombardment from his perch above the city.

The Confederates had a Christmas surprise of their own planned that year. On Christmas Eve they erected three field works protecting twelve guns along the Stono River. Their commanders hoped to catch another Federal gunboat as they had ten months earlier. When the mist finally rose Christmas morning, the USS *Marblehead* appeared just a quarter mile away. The masked Rebel batteries opened fire as a regiment of Confederate infantry waited for the signal to attack the 150-man Union garrison at Legareville on Saint Johns Island on the south side of the Stono.

The noise attracted the attention of the USS *Pawnee,* anchored at the mouth of the Stono. Instead of joining the *Marblehead,* the captain of the *Pawnee* swung his ship into the mouth of the Kiawah River, a few hundred yards below the Confederate positions, and raked the flank of the Rebel batteries with his starboard 9-inch smoothbores. Caught between the concentrated fire of the two gunboats, the disappointed Confederates had to pull back, abandoning some of their weapons. The jubilant Federals landed and brought away the weapons. Although the *Marblehead* had been hit thirty times, defective Confederate ammunition allowed the ship to continuing fighting long after it should have been a hulk.[87]

The new year came in quietly, but during one nine-day period in mid-January 1864, Federal batteries sent another fifteen hundred shells toward the city, causing most of the lower part of Charleston to be abandoned. As cannon barrels wore out, the number of shells fired into the city diminished and overall activity declined as Union forces pulled out of South Carolina to bolster Northerners attempting to capture Jacksonville, Florida. On 9 February, to discourage the Confederates from withdrawing their own troops, several thousand Union soldiers probed Confederate positions on Johns Island. Both sides continued to rush reinforcements south, and by the end of February even Beauregard had left Charleston for Florida.

By spring 1864, Charleston faced a severe manpower shortage. According to a local historian, some four hundred of the city's three thousand free black males volunteered to replace members of the Charleston fire department so the firemen could be organized into a military battalion.[88] Sailors from the inactive Confederate ironclad fleet were also armed and pressed into service. Even though thousands of Federal troops had been sent to Virginia to take part in Grant's campaign against Lee, Union troops still had at least a seven-to-one advantage in the Charleston area.

Maj. Gen. John Foster, the engineering officer under Anderson at Sumter who had taken over command of the Department of the South from General Gillmore, determined to overwhelm his opponents and capture Fort Sumter. Foster planned a five-prong attack: (1) a naval bombardment of Battery Pringle, which covered the Stono River from James Island; (2) another attack on Johns Island by five thousand men whose objective was the Charleston and Savannah Railroad; (3) an amphibious assault by more than two thousand men on James Island below Battery Pringle; (4) another attempt to cut the Charleston and Savannah Railroad where it ran near the North Edisto River to prevent the sending of reinforcements from Savannah to Charleston; and (5) a one-thousand-man amphibious assault against Battery Simkins, an outerwork of Fort Johnson.

The 2 July landing below Battery Pringle, initiated under the cover of two monitors and several gunboats, made fairly short work of Confederate Maj. Edward Manigault's small force at River's Causeway. (The Rebels were supported by two field pieces that had been jettisoned the previous year from the Union tug *General Milton* at Willtown Bluff on the South Edisto River.[89]) Eventually the men in gray halted the attack on James Island, but it had been necessary to pull nearly one hundred defenders from Fort Johnson to do so. When Federals under Union Col. H. M. Hoyt navigated their boats through a narrow channel leading to a spot between Battery Simkins and Fort Johnson, only

130 Rebels remained to repel the assault. A Confederate picket sighted the craft as soon as the sun rose on 3 July. A smattering of artillery and small-arms fire commenced without causing significant damage to the attackers. Inexplicably, a mere five boats with six officers and 135 men of the Fifty-second Pennsylvania Volunteers pushed ashore. The rest of the boats withdrew.

Even so, Hoyt's Pennsylvanians overran the Brooke gun battery immediately to their front, then turned north toward Fort Johnson. Two attempts were made to breach the high earthen parapet surrounding the fort before a crossfire between Battery Simkins and Fort Johnson compelled the surrender of what remained of Hoyt's command, including Colonel Hoyt himself. At a cost of one killed and three wounded, the Confederates had halted an attack originally begun by a thousand men. Ironically, the prisoners almost outnumbered the fort's garrison and had to be kept in one of the fort's bombproofs until a guard detail arrived from Charleston.

Blame for the debacle was attributed to Col. William Gurney, in overall command of the operation. Instead of advancing with the boats, he chose to remain behind at the departure point, thus ensuring that when the majority began to withdraw, no one could stem the exodus.[90]

On the same day, another naval expedition carried Brig. Gen. William Birney's twelve hundred troops, accompanied by General Foster, up the North Edisto River to place torpedoes under the rail bridge at Jacksonboro. The Federals landed on 3 July at White Point on Slann's Island and marched unopposed until they reached a Confederate battery on King's Creek. Foster took the expedition's three gunboats up the Dawhoo River to shell the Rebels, but a few rounds fell short among friendly troops. Whether or not this proved to be a decisive factor, Birney requested permission to retreat, and Foster reluctantly assented. Foster ordered Birney's troops to support attacks on James Island and sent Birney back to Florida.[91]

As the last hope of Foster's five attacks, Brig. Gen. John P. Hatch's steamroller of five thousand men methodically advanced on the south side of the Stono River opposite Battery Pringle. Because of the intense heat, the men marched slowly, giving time for the Confederates to concentrate enough men by rail to blunt this attack as well.

Although the Federals had been stymied on land, they still had control of the waterways, and on 8 July the monitors *Lehigh* and *Montauk* and four wooden gunboats mercilessly shelled Battery Pringle from a distance of two miles as other ships downriver punished the rest of the Confederate line on James Island. Later that night Confederates wrestled into place a 7-inch Brooke rifle that forced the wooden ships to slip downriver out of range and even gave the ironclads some trouble.

Another attack on Fort Johnson was launched a week after the first, this time following a heavy preliminary bombardment. The results proved even worse than the previous attempt: Only three boats reached shore.

The next day, 11 July, after eight days and nights of continual shelling, the Federal squadron on the Stono River finally gave up and sailed back to Hilton Head. No more major land assaults would be made against the Charleston defenses for the remainder of the year, but that did not mean a decrease in activity. Beginning on 7 July and lasting until 4 September, the third major bombardment of Sumter took place.

For this cannonade, Foster lined up still more 200- and 300-pounder rifled guns and 13-inch mortars to finish off the island fort. Following three weeks of almost four hundred shots a day fired by these Union iron monsters, General Foster and Admiral Dahlgren reconnoitered Sumter aboard the *Lehigh*. The admiral wearily observed, "The northeast front still stands erect, and the work is nearly impregnable."[92] Nevertheless, he lent Foster six 11-inch guns along with crews and ammunition to replace the big guns on Morris Island that had burst because of incessant use. At the end of August, Dahlgren's navy even towed rafts filled with black powder toward Sumter on two separate occasions, but the explosives did little damage. The Union army commander still did not give up hope, and Foster promoted another amphibious operation with specially designed assault craft carrying fifty-foot ladders, but the scheme never materialized.[93] When the shelling finally let up after sixty days, Federal gunners had poured another 14,600 rounds into Sumter. Nevertheless, the defenders had actually managed to make the fort even stronger by bringing more than ten thousand sandbags a night from Charleston.[94]

By the end of 1864, Sherman was marching north from Savannah. It was only a matter of time before he would flank Charleston and force its evacuation. Before Sherman could cut Charleston's communications, however, one final tragedy struck the Federal navy. While covering picket boats at the entrance to Charleston Harbor on the evening of 15 January 1865, the USS *Patapsco* became the second monitor to fall victim to a torpedo. Like the first (the *Tecumseh*, which sank 5 August 1864, in Mobile Bay, Alabama), the *Patapsco* went down so fast that two-thirds of her crew were lost.[95]

To divert attention from Sherman and perhaps a bit reluctant to let Sherman gain all the glory they had fought for so long around Charleston, Federal troops supported by the monitors *Lehigh* and *Wissahicken* and a mortar schooner landed once more on James Island on 10 February. After a bitter fight, they overran the forward Confederate rifle pits. Instead of advancing, however, they retreated to Cole's Island. The next night another amphibious detachment approached Fort Johnson but withdrew before attempting to land.

Two days later, thirteen vessels arrived off Bull's Bay north of Charleston and stood by as sailors coaxed smaller boats through the shallow waters of the bay. Accompanying gunboats were forced to remain several miles out to sea, thus depriving the assaulting troops of supporting naval gunfire. The Confederates took advantage of the situation by meeting the attackers at the shoreline. When Union troops finally reached land on 17 February, it was anticlimactic. Plans had already been put into motion to evacuate Charleston that night. As the Rebels once again successfully retreated in the face of the enemy, they left behind them a city of ashes.[96]

The next morning the monitor *Canonicus* gingerly approached Fort Moultrie and fired two shots into the deserted works, "the last shots fired in Charleston after nearly three years of almost continuous bombardment."[97] Ignoring the threat of mines, Maj. John A. Hennessy of the Fifty-second Pennsylvania rowed out to Sumter, scaled the walls, and planted his regimental flag.

On Good Friday, 14 April 1865, Brevet Major General Anderson was ordered to commemorate the repossession of the fort by raising the flag that he had carried away four years earlier. Later that night during a dinner at the Charleston Hotel, scene of many a provocative secessionist speech in 1860, Anderson proposed a toast: "I beg you, now, that you will join me in drinking the health of . . . the great, the honest man, Abraham Lincoln." Less than an hour later, Lincoln lay dying in Washington, victim of John Wilkes Booth.[98]

If you go there . . .

The first stop any visitor to Charleston should make is the city's new **Visitor Reception Center** at 375 Meeting Street. Trained staff are available to answer questions seven days a week except Christmas and New Year's Day. Free brochures offer information about tours and points of interest.

Just a little farther down the road at 360 Meeting Street, a full-scale replica of the CSS *Hunley,* the first submarine to sink a warship, sits outside the front doors of the **Charleston Museum.** Founded in 1773, it is the oldest museum in the United States. Although only a small section in the building is devoted to the city's role in the Civil War, the museum also operates several historic homes in the city, including the **Aiken-Rhett Mansion,** 48 Elizabeth Street, two blocks north of the visitors center. Jefferson Davis visited the home in 1863, and it served as General Beauregard's headquarters the following year after his original headquarters fell within Union cannon range. Tickets for the Aiken-Rhett Mansion can be purchased in combination with several other properties at the museum, which is open 9:00 A.M.–5:00 P.M., Monday through Saturday, and 1:00-5:00 P.M. on Sunday. The cost for the museum alone is $4.00 for adults. For information, call (803) 722-2996. The mansion is open daily at 10:00 A.M. and the last tour begins at 4:00 P.M. For information, call (803) 723-1159.

Three other museums in the city exhibit Civil War–related memorabilia. **American Military Museum,** 40 Pinckney Street, in downtown Charleston, is open Monday through Saturday from 10:00 A.M. to 6:00 P.M. and Sunday from 1:00–6:00 P.M. Admission for adults is $2.00. For information, call (803) 723-9620. On The Citadel campus, **The Citadel Museum** contains items representing the uniforms, weaponry, and documents relating to the college's role in the nation's wars since its start in 1842. It is free and open to the public, Sunday through Friday, from 2:00–5:00 P.M. and on Saturday from 9:00 A.M. to 5:00 P.M. For information, call (803) 792-6846. **The Confederate Museum,** situated in 153-year-old Market Hall at the intersection of Market and Meeting streets, suffered some damage from Hurricane Hugo in September 1989. The United Daughters of the Confederacy managed in late 1993 to reopen the museum on a limited basis in the mornings. The group is presently seeking donations to ensure that the museum, which includes one of the nation's best Confederate flag collections, is fully operational. For information, call (803) 723-1541.

The best anyone interested in the Civil War could do in historic Charleston is contact Jack Thomson, a licensed tour guide with the city. His two-hour **Civil War Walking Tour of Charleston** provides a wealth of information about the historic city that, despite its destruction during the war, the 1861 fire, and subsequent hurricanes, still retains much of its antebellum charm. Although reservations are preferred, you can meet Jack at the courtyard of the restored **Mills House Hotel,** 115 Meeting Street, at 9:00 A.M., Wednesday through Sunday all year except January and February. The cost is $12.00 for adults; children under twelve can tag along free of charge. For information, contact: Jack Thomson, 17 Archdale Street, Charleston, SC 29401 (803) 722-7033.

The Mills House is not a standard Holiday Inn. Local Charlestonians worked to restore the hotel as nearly to its original configuration as possible, as delegates to the secession convention lodged here and Robert E. Lee spent the night. For reservations, call (800) 874-9600.

If you miss strolling around the city with Jack Thomson, you can still get a small taste of the military history of the city by visiting **The Battery,** or what is also called White Point Garden, which occupies the southeast corner of the peninsula. In the garden, several artillery pieces from the Civil War still point toward the harbor, including one of the 11-inch Dahlgren guns taken from the USS *Keokuk*. Anecdotes about this gun and other historical artifacts in White Point Garden have been collected in a booklet entitled "The Battery." Published by the *News and Courier* and *Charleston Evening Post,* it can be purchased at the Fort Moultrie gift shop and other locations in the city.

Another *Post-Courier* publication directs visitors to "Sixty-two Famous Houses of Charleston, South Carolina." Just a few blocks up Meeting Street from The Battery, for instance, the house at 37 Meeting served for a while as General Beauregard's office. Its nickname "Bosoms" may have as much to do with the general's reputation as a ladies' man as from the twin curved bays on the front of the structure. Federal long-range bombardment of the city forced Beauregard to move his headquarters farther up the peninsula in 1863. In the 1950s, Frank B. Gilbreth, the author of *Cheaper by the Dozen*, owned the house.

The three houses closest to White Point Garden at 1 East Battery, 5 East Battery, and 9 East Battery share an interesting relationship. During the Civil War, a giant Blakely cannon was emplaced nearby in the garden. When the Confederates abandoned the city in February 1865, a Major Bertody from a Georgia regiment was ordered to destroy the piece since it was impractical to move the thirty-ton monster with the retreating troops. One section of the destroyed gun carriage fell on the roof of 1 East Battery, the only damage the home suffered during the entire war. The carriage was removed when repairs were made to the house. A huge segment of the cannon's barrel flew over 1 East Battery and 5 East Battery and finally plunged through the roof of 9 East Battery, where it remains to this day. The leap-frogged house at 5 East Battery was owned by Dr. St. Julien Ravenel, the man who suggested the building of the torpedo boat *David*. The craft was constructed at Stony Landing, Ravenel's Cooper River plantation.

Four blocks up from The Battery at 94 Church Street, John C. Calhoun held discussions in the second-floor drawing room. These meetings led to the 1832 nullification crisis. The house had been built in 1730 by Thomas Bee, the grandfather of Bernard Bee, the officer credited with giving Thomas Jonathan Jackson the nickname "Stonewall."[99] In 1812, Theodosia Burr Alston, the wife of Gov. Joseph Alston and the daughter of Aaron Burr, left the house to visit her father. She sailed aboard the schooner *Patriot* late in the year. Neither she nor the ship were ever seen again.

Before leaving Charleston, make sure you enjoy some victuals at **Moultrie Tavern.** Owner Robert Bohrn Jr. serves wonderful game dishes amidst his collection of Civil War artifacts. For information, contact: Moultrie Tavern, 18 Vendue Range (803) 723-1862.

Charleston's most recognizable link to its role in the Civil War is, of course, **Fort Sumter.** Boat tours to Fort Sumter leave the Charleston City Marina at 17 Lockwood Boulevard along the Ashley River or Patriots Point Naval and Maritime Museum at Mount Pleasant across the Cooper River from Charleston. The tours last two and a quarter hours. For the best view of **Castle Pinckney,** which served as a prison after First Manassas, take the tour from the marina. There are still four guns at Pinckney: three 10-inch Columbiads and one 7-inch Brooke. Pinckney can be reached only by private boat.

Considering what it's been through, Fort Sumter looks pretty good. Reconstruction began in the 1870s under the supervision of Quincy

Fort Sumter *(Charleston Visitors and Convention Bureau)*

Gillmore, the man responsible for knocking much of it down. Funds ran out within a short time, and the fort stood empty except for a lighthouse keeper. Even so, thousands visited the shrine each year. At the turn of the century, two 12-inch rifles were installed in a massive concrete emplacement covering over half the original fort. Named for South Carolinian Isaac Huger (a general in the Revolutionary War), this battery still dominates the fort's parade ground. The guns were scrapped in 1943, and the fort became a national monument in 1948.

The tour at Fort Sumter is conducted by the National Park Service. The fort contains restrooms, a museum, and a gift shop, which has quite a collection of Civil War–related books. Since tour times vary according to the season, contact Fort Sumter Tours, Inc., P.O. Box 59, Charleston, SC 29402 (803) 722-1691, for a complete schedule.

The Fort Sumter tour boat also passes by the site of **Fort Johnson** on James Island. The Marine Resources Center now occupies the location of the original 1776 fort. Only one small nineteenth-century masonry powder magazine has survived. Some kind caretaker, however, has cut a window through a row of trees so that visitors can get a view of Fort Sumter in the distance behind the marker that commemorates the first shot of the Civil War. To reach the site, follow U.S. 17 south of Charleston. Take the Folly Island turnoff onto Folly Road (S.C. 171) 4.7 miles to Fort Johnson Road. The road dead-ends at the Marine Center, which is open from 8:00 A.M. to 5:00 P.M.

On the north side of the harbor, **Fort Moultrie** provides visitors with a much more visible connection with the history of Charleston's harbor defenses. Situated on Middle Street a mile and a half south of its intersection with S.C. 703 on Sullivan's Island, the fort exhibits several periods of the area's history. One section of the fort has been restored to its original 1809 appearance. From then until 1860, the fort changed very little, but at that time several advancements in armament and configuration were incorporated. Another portion of the fort emphasizes those alterations. The modernization efforts in the 1870s through its usage during the Spanish-American War to World War II are reflected in other parts of the fort.

A visitors center across the street from the fort offers an excellent orientation movie, gift shop, restrooms, and parking. To the north of the fort, artillery pieces from the Civil War and later periods line the walk to Battery Jasper, a large, concrete emplacement for four 10-inch disappearing guns completed in 1898.

Fort Moultrie is open daily from 9:00 A.M. to 6:00 P.M. in the summer and until 5:00 P.M. in the winter except Christmas. For information about Forts Sumter or Moultrie, contact: Superintendent, Drawer R., Sullivan's Island, SC 29482 (803) 883-3123.

Georgetown and Vicinity

AT THE END OF 1863, Rear Adm. John Dahlgren wrote to U.S. Secretary of the Navy Gideon Welles that "the perfect blockade of Charleston is driving speculators to the smaller ports to get cotton out and a return cargo in."[100] The admiral was referring to those inlets and harbors that penetrate the South Carolina coast north of Bull's Bay. The mouths of North and South Santee rivers usually held nine feet of water at high tide; a few miles north, eleven and a half feet passed over one of the channels into Georgetown Harbor at the head of Winyah Bay.

In June 1862, Comdr. G. A. Prentiss in the USS *Albatross*, a 378-ton screw steamer armed with one 8-inch and two 32-pounder smoothbores, passed into Winyah Bay accompanied by the *Norwich*, a similar vessel armed with four 8-inch guns and one 30-pounder rifle. A redoubt near the lighthouse was found deserted and batteries on South Island and Cat Island mounted only simulated weapons, "Quaker" guns made of logs. After dispersing some Confederate cavalry, the ships steamed to Georgetown, situated at the head of the bay, and tarried "to see if the town authorities were disposed to communicate."[101] Unprepared to hold the port, Prentiss ended his reconnaissance after capturing the steam tug *Treaty* and the schooner *Louisa*.

In mid-August, the reflagged *Treaty*, along with the USS *Pocahontas*, chased the blockade runner *Nina* into Winyah Bay. At Mayrants Bluff, the two Federal vessels came upon a Rebel battery under construction. Shortly after its cannons began to find the range of the uncompleted earthen fort, the *Pocahontas* grounded. With much difficulty, the *Treaty* was able to dislodge the gunboat. When Rebel reinforcements arrived from Georgetown, the Federals proceeded back down the bay. Confederates on shore harassed the retreating ships every chance they got.[102] The hot reception signaled the beginning of a more determined effort by the Confederates to defend the area.

By the end of the summer, the district commander, Gen. James Trapier, had completed a series of earthworks designed to confine the Federals to the lower part of Winyah Bay. Manpower continued to be a problem, however. At the newly named Battery White on Mayrants Bluff, Capt. F. F. Warley could count only fifty-three troops to work his nine guns, even though the position protected the approaches to the navy yard at Mars Bluff on the Pee Dee, where a wooden gunboat recently had been laid down.[103] Overall, Trapier had fewer than six hundred men to patrol seventy miles of coast. Fortunately for him, the bulk of the Union navy was still busy at Charleston.

The situation changed on 2 March 1864 when Federal troops landed below Battery White and easily pushed back the Rebel pickets. Trapier wrote to Gov. Milledge L. Bonham on 8 March asking for three 10-inch Columbiads and a regiment of infantry. The battery's three rifled 32-pounders and eight other smaller caliber guns could not stop an ironclad, Trapier pointed out. Neither the governor nor authorities in Richmond had anything to spare. Trapier was told that "General Lee's army was more important than Georgetown."[104] The district commander would just have to protect the coastline as effectively as possible with what he had. By the end of 1864, the district was being stripped of even these few military resources to bolster the defenses around Charleston and Petersburg, Virginia. Only one company remained behind.

On 2 January 1865, Rear Admiral Dahlgren met with General Sherman in Savannah to make plans for Sherman's march through the Carolinas. The two leaders decided that if Sherman bypassed Charleston, the navy would establish communications with his army at Georgetown. During the last week in February, Capt. Henry S. Stellwagen in the USS *Pawnee* led a squadron into Winyah Bay. As they approached Battery White, the garrison retreated. U.S. Marines occupied the earthworks on 23 February. The following day the USS *Catalpa* and USS *Mingoe* reached Georgetown, and Ens. Allen K. Noyes accepted the surrender of the city. When a group of seamen tried to raise the Stars and Stripes over the city hall, however, Confederate cavalry attacked. Reinforcements from the fleet drove them off.

Upon hearing that his naval forces had occupied Georgetown, Rear Admiral Dahlgren sailed from Charleston to see things for himself. He examined the "formidable . . . Fort White" before arriving at Georgetown on 1 March.[105] Prior to his departure, he instructed Captain Stellwagen to

Battery White, showing one of the two 10-inch Columbiads manufactured by the Tredegar Ironworks of Richmond

position the vessels under his command so they could make contact with Sherman along either the Santee or Black rivers. As Dahlgren's flagship, the *Harvest Moon,* made its way back down Winyah Bay, a torpedo shattered the partition between the admiral's cabin and the wardroom. The flagship sank in five minutes. One man was killed. The admiral escaped with only the uniform he wore.

If you go there . . .

Georgetown is the third oldest city in South Carolina. It might have been the oldest had the Spaniards who attempted to establish a colony on Winyah Bay in 1526 not been frightened away by a slave revolt. The scarcity of historical accounts of the region during the Civil War belies its importance to Dixie's war efforts. On 2 January 1861, the Georgetown Rifle Guards were the first military unit to offer service to the Confederate cause.[106] Even more significant, the lowlands around the city produced enough rice annually to feed fifty thousand troops. The history of this rice culture is presented at the **Rice Museum** in Georgetown. Situated in the old slave market at the intersection of Front and Screven streets, the museum is just one of nearly fifty antebellum structures in the immediate area. It is open 9:30 A.M. to 4:30 P.M., Monday through Saturday. It is closed holidays. The cost is $2.00 for adults. For information, contact: The Rice Museum, P.O. Box 902, Georgetown, SC 29442-0902 (803) 546-7423.

Local rice plantation owners helped fortify the inlets leading to Winyah Bay, but there were never enough troops to garrison these fortifications. They were abandoned in early 1862. The eventual establishment of a second line of earthworks closer to Georgetown, including **Battery White,** indicates how important the region's foodstuffs had become to the South, even if those defenses were never fully manned.

The guard at the gate of Belle Isle Yacht Club said that he did not think there was much left to see of Battery White, a national historic landmark on the private club's grounds, but he did write us a pass to drive down and see for ourselves. He was wrong. The massive earthworks stretch a good distance along Winyah Bay. Best of all, the view from the front is uninterrupted by trees or tall grasses. Furthermore, two 10-inch Columbiads peek out from behind gun chambers. (Whether or not these are the guns Trapier ordered, I do not know.)

A minimuseum with a few artifacts from the fort occupies a small section of one of the club's buildings next to the fort.

GEORGIA

BY THE SPRING OF 1864, three years of warfare had all but bypassed Georgia, the fifth state to join the Confederacy. This lack of attention was not in proportion to the state's importance to the Southern cause — far from it. The relatively young rail hub of Atlanta exported food, clothing, munitions, and equipment of all kinds to the Confederate field armies via the four major railroads that converged there from throughout the South.[1] One line, the Georgia Railroad, provided a direct link to Lee's Army of Northern Virginia. Furthermore, by 1862 Georgia had dressed seventy-five thousand of her sons and fathers in butternut and sent them off to war. More would follow. Although opposed to secession, one prominent Georgian, Alexander Stephens, served as vice president of the Confederacy.

Why then was Georgia clay spared for the most part from turning a darker shade of red until Sherman's 1864 campaign while the soil of the majority of Southern states was soaked with the blood of numerous battles? The answer lies in the state's geography. Its short coastline was under tight Union control from early in the war. Since Federal strategy rarely took advantage of coastal enclaves for advances toward the interior, the situation along Georgia's stretch of the Atlantic quickly stalemated. An even more important geographic factor ensuring Georgia's relative insularity was the state's lack of navigable rivers. There is no equivalent to a Mississippi, Tennessee, Cumberland, Arkansas, Red, or James River to provide the all-powerful Federal brown-water navy a highway to the heart of the state.

Saint Simons Island

CONFLICTING CLAIMS by Spain, France, England, and eventually America kept Saint Simons Island, Georgia, a battleground for much of the seventeenth and eighteenth centuries. Several times following its initial

European colonization, warriors of various nationalities, including Native Americans, raided the island along the south Georgia coast, often burning what they could not carry. Destroyed in one raid was the San Simon mission, which gave the locality its name. By the 1820s peace had prevailed and wide fields of Sea Island cotton blanketed the land. Sales of this prized commodity brought luxury to the owners of the large plantations and their children. Their idyll would be relatively brief, already threatened by sectional differences that finally split the country physically in 1861. The fine young men of a generation of islanders who had not experienced war rode off in splendid gray uniforms with the excited blessings of their kinsmen. Little did the soldiers or their families suspect their enchanted island would shortly suffer once again under the torch of passing armies.

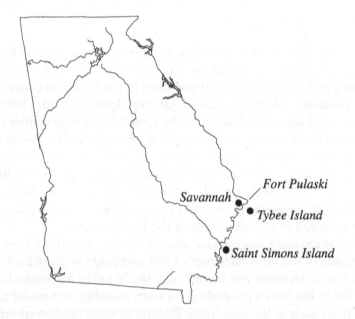

Georgia's coastal defenses were initially placed under Col. Carey Styles, a former mayor of Brunswick, a town just a few miles from Saint Simons on the mainland. Immediately following Georgia's secession in January 1861, the Jackson Artillery of Macon, Georgia, was ordered to Saint Simons, effectively blocking one of the doors to Brunswick. Slaves from Retreat, Thomas Butler King's plantation on the south side of the island, helped build fortifications consisting of earthworks covered with railroad iron and twelve feet of sand close to the lighthouse on the south end of the island.[2] The battery was named Fort Brown after Georgia's wartime governor, Joseph E. Brown. The names of local belles who vied with one another to entertain the troops found their names attached fondly to individual cannon. Batteries across the channel on Jekyll Island were of even greater strength. They were equipped with one 42-pounder and four 32-pounder navy guns.

After the fall of Port Royal, South Carolina, in December 1861, Robert E. Lee, who had been given authority over coastal defenses in Georgia, ordered the evacuation of Saint Simons and Jekyll islands. Governor Brown wrote to Lee to see if any means could be found to defend the place. Lee responded from Savannah, Georgia, on 10 February 1862, "I find it impossible to obtain guns to secure [Saint Simons and Jekyll islands] as I desire, and now everything is requisite to fortify this city."[3] Retreating troops dynamited the lighthouse and withdrew their artillery. For years afterward, ship captains had to use King's Cotton House, a four-story cotton barn, to guide their ships to the island.

On 9 March 1862 the USS *Pocahontas* and USS *Potomska* — released earlier from operations around Fernandina, Florida — anchored offshore of Saint Simons to institute Federal government control. After examining the abandoned earthworks, the Federals moved by water to Brunswick, where they found the depot and wharf afire and the town deserted.

If you go there . . .

Saint Simons and Jekyll islands are artists' colony-type places where people come to play golf and eat in trendy little restaurants. Most of the area's historical sites revolve around James Oglethorpe and Fort Frederica, the main fortress guarding the southern frontier of Britain's North American possessions in the mid-1700s. On the south tip of Saint Simons, the stone marker at the site of Fort Brown, for instance, mentions that Fort Saint Simons stood in the area from 1738–42, when the Spanish burned it. An adjacent roped area encompasses the old lighthouse built in 1810 and destroyed by retreating Confederates in 1861. The lighthouse and keeper's cottage next door were erected in 1872. The keeper's cottage now houses the **Museum of Coastal History,** which has no displays on the Civil War but does have a model of the old lighthouse. The museum costs $2.00 and is open Tuesday through Saturday from 10:00 A.M.–5:00 P.M. and on Sunday from 1:30–5:00 P.M.

The tabby ruins of **Retreat Plantation** are situated next to the Sea Island Golf Club.

For information, contact: Saint Simons Island Chamber of Commerce, 530-B Beachview Drive, Saint Simons Island, GA 31522 (912) 638-9014.

On Jekyll Island on Horton Road south of Horton House, a historical marker offers information about the Confederate battery positions situated on the island in 1861.

Savannah

MUCH OF THE urban planning for early Savannah, Georgia, was military in nature. James Oglethorpe established his buffer for Charleston, South Carolina, in 1733 on forty-foot-high Yamacraw Bluff along the Savannah River, a natural defensive site. He immediately ordered a wall to be built around the community, which had grassy squares incorporated into its design so that cattle could be grazed within the fortress should there be an attack. Catholics were not welcome because Ogle-

Fort Brown was situated near the Saint Simons Lighthouse

thorpe feared they would side with England's foe, Spain, in case of hostilities.

Twenty miles downstream, Cockspur Island (known then as "the Peeper") barely rose high enough to divide the river into two channels. But so important did Savannah's inhabitants consider these few hundred acres of mud that a portion of the eastern half was permanently set aside by the British Crown and later by the state of Georgia as a site for coastal fortifications. Begun in 1761, the pioneer fort on Cockspur Point, Fort George, was dismantled by patriots in 1776 to keep it out of the hands of the British and their powerful fleets. A great hurricane swept a second defensive structure, Fort Greene (named after Revolutionary War hero Nathanael Greene[4]), from the island in 1804, a mere nine years after it was completed.

A quarter-century later, Robert E. Lee, newly graduated from West Point, arrived on Cockspur and reported for his first duty assignment. He served as assistant to Maj. Samuel Babcock, the engineer in charge of carrying out the recommendation made by the Bernard Board for Georgia's coastal defense, a huge masonry fortress on Cockspur Island. Because of his superior's ill health, Lee designed the series of dikes that drained excess water from the island. The future Confederate general also surveyed the island and selected the final site for the fort. Credit for actual construction, however, goes to Lt. Gen. Joseph K. F. Mansfield, who served on Cockspur from 1831 until 1845. This third fort was eventually named Pulaski in honor of Polish Count Casimir Pulaski, a Revolutionary War hero who was mortally wounded at the battle of Savannah on 9 October 1779. (Also in the ranks of the American forces that day was Samuel Davis, father of Jefferson Davis.)

By the time of Lincoln's election, Fort Pulaski had consumed nearly a million dollars, and it was still not quite defensible. Of the 146 guns for which the ramparts and casemates were designed, only 20 had been mounted. In addition, its peacetime garrison consisted of only two men, a caretaker and an ordnance sergeant.

When news reached Savannah during the 1860 Christmas holiday season that Maj. Robert Anderson had occupied Fort Sumter, groups of angry citizens gathered in the city's squares to denounce the action. Col. Alexander R. Lawton, in command of the First Volunteer Regiment of Georgia, telegraphed Gov. Joseph Brown requesting his immediate presence in Savannah. The governor arrived at 9:00 P.M. on New Year's Day. Amidst speculation that Lincoln might try to garrison Fort Pulaski in force, Brown ordered the state militia to occupy the post.[5]

Early on 3 January 1861, more than two weeks before Georgia seceded, detachments from several of Savannah's volunteer companies boarded the steamboat *Ida* for the trip downriver. By noon that day they marched into the fort and found themselves in control of a coiled serpent with no fangs. The score of 32-pounder naval guns emplaced twenty years earlier were unserviceable, and the moat was filled with mud and weeds. "Had the Federal Government taken immediate and effective action, the incident on Cockspur Island might have ended quickly in complete fiasco."[6] Instead, Rebel forces had an entire year to prepare for an expected counteroffensive.

Although initially opposed to seizing the fort, Confederate Capt. Francis S. Bartow of the Oglethorpe Light Infantry took official command of Pulaski from Lawton and worked diligently to provide it with some sting. Cannon on hand were remounted, and more were ordered. A telegraph line was strung to Savannah and regular packet service established along the river. Slaves dug out the moat while state militia drilled on the parade ground and built sandbag traverses to protect the fort's magazines and the Columbiads emplaced on the ramparts. By the time shooting started at Fort Sumter in April, Bartow could take some pride in what he and his men had accomplished.[7]

On 7 November 1861, the fall of the forts guarding Port Royal, just over the border into South Carolina, marked the end of Savannah's days as a viable port. With a supply facility so near, the U.S. Navy was able to clamp a tight blockade on the sea approaches to the city. The last ship to get through to Savannah was the screw steamer *Fingal,* which arrived on 13 November. Unable to sneak back through the Union naval cordon, the *Fingal* was taken over in 1862 by the Confederate government, which contracted with Nelson and Asa Tift of Savannah to convert her into the ironclad ram *Atlanta.* The Tifts had questionable experience with ironclads, having previously built the unwieldy *Mississippi* in New Orleans.

In response to the military disaster at Port Royal, Lee, acting as Jefferson Davis's special adviser, ordered the abandonment of Georgia's Sea Islands.[8] All the batteries on Tybee Island, which is immediately south of Cockspur Island, were leveled and their guns removed to Fort Pulaski. Lee did not know it, but he had just provided the North with the key to Pulaski. Standing on the ramparts during one of two inspections he made of the fort that November, Lee pointed to Tybee Island and remarked to Charles H. Olmstead, Pulaski's new commander, "Colonel, they will make it pretty warm for you here with shells, but they cannot breach your walls at that distance."[9]

Brig. Gen. Thomas W. Sherman, in charge of the land forces at Port Royal, was not even sure he wanted to turn up the heat on Pulaski. Why not bypass the fort altogether? By utilizing one of the other waterways in the vicinity, Sherman insisted he could attack Savannah directly. The Union general approached Flag Off. Samuel F. du Pont with his plan. Du Pont listened, but when he discovered how shallow the streams were through which Sherman intended for him to operate his supply ships, du Pont balked. Stymied in his efforts to move on Savannah, Sherman oversaw the construction of a tight noose of batteries around Fort Pulaski.

Sherman understood that he could starve the garrison into surrender, but he was not planning to wait. On 19 February he sent his chief engineer, Capt. Quincy A. Gillmore, to take command of the troops on Tybee Island and secretly construct batteries facing Pulaski. Past practice indicated that beyond seven hundred yards even experimental rifled cannon would have little effect on masonry walls. Since the nearest battery to Cockspur Island sat over a mile from Fort Pulaski, Gillmore's work appeared to be in vain. Nevertheless, during the better part of the next three months, Gillmore drove his men to complete eleven batteries comprising thirty-six guns, ten of which were rifled designs of James and Parrott.

On the clear, cold morning of 10 April, officers on Pulaski's parapet watched a skiff pull out from Tybee under a flag of truce. Lt. J. H. Wilson, U.S. Topographical Engineers, landed at the south wharf with a formal demand to surrender. Olmstead refused, and, like Anderson at Sumter, he saw a single mortar round roar from a battery on Tybee, arc over the fort, and explode in the air beyond. The battle that would make obsolete practically every defensive structure in the world had begun.

When the firing slackened that first night, it was difficult for Union artillerists to tell if much damage had been done. But Gillmore, using a "powerful telescope . . . observed that the rifled projectiles were doing excellent service."[10] Federal harassment fire continued sporadically through the night to prevent the defenders from making any repairs. When both sides opened up again next morning, the immediate enlargement of two embrasures on the left of the southeast face of the fort heartened the attackers. Most of the Confederate shells, on the other hand, buried themselves in the sand of the masked batteries or flew over the Federal trenches. The effectiveness of sand and earth over stone and brick could have had no better demonstration.

Not to be left out, the Union gunboat *Norwich* closed on the northeast angle of the fort, but her shot only struck glancing blows on the brick walls, exactly the effect the fort's designers would have expected. Unlike the Port Royal expedition, this time the army would gain credit for breaching the walls of a Confederate coastal fort. As shells from the rifled cannon passed completely through the ramparts and struck Pulaski's north magazine, the possibility that the forty thousand pounds of black powder stored there might explode convinced Gillmore to surrender. Maj. Gen. David Hunter, who had taken over theater command from Sherman, understood the significance of the event. "The result of this bombardment," he reported, "must cause a change in the construction of fortifications as radical as that foreshadowed in naval architecture by the conflict between the *Monitor* and *Merrimac* [sic]. No works of stone or brick can resist the impact of rifled artillery of heavy calibre."[11] Despite Hunter's foresight, within six weeks Federal garrisons at the fort had repaired the shattered brickwork.

Had Sherman remained in command of Union land forces, he certainly would have pushed for an immediate attack upon Savannah. As it was, by June 1863 the garrison at Pulaski was reduced to a holding force and the focus of the fight for Savannah shifted to a Confederate sand battery on the Ogeechee River at Genesis Point, a few miles south of the city. Begun in 1861, the original four-gun battery underwent extensive modifications after the surrender of the forts at Port Royal. Large sand-and-sod traverses were raised between the guns so a shell exploding in one emplacement would not endanger those on either side. When Pulaski fell, the Genesis Point battery, now named Fort McAllister in honor of the family who owned the property, went from being part of a weak secondary line of defense to one of Savannah's most important protective works.

Nevertheless, the fortress did not attract the attention of the Union navy until a blockade runner raced for its protection in July 1862, bringing about a brief exchange between a pursuing U.S. warship and the fort. Soon afterward, the *Nashville* also sought safety behind McAllister's guns. When information reached the U.S. Navy that the swift side-wheeler had been

The Forty-eighth Regiment, New York Volunteers, on the Fort Pulaski parade ground, 1864 *(Georgia Department of Archives and History)*

converted to a merchant raider, an operation to destroy the vessel was mounted. On 29 July, four gunboats engaged Fort McAllister for several hours, accomplishing little more than throwing up a few geysers of sand. On 19 November three warships tried to reduce the fort again with similar results. The sand-and-sod parapets at McAllister were proving to be as difficult to knock out as the Federal sand batteries at Tybee.

Anxious to test his new ironclads gathering at Hilton Head for an attack on Charleston, du Pont decided that tough little Fort McAllister would provide the perfect warmup. So on 27 January 1863, the ironclad USS *Montauk,* accompanied by several wooden gunboats, lined up opposite the fort and traded blows for several hours. Although some of the ironclad's 15-inch shells actually tore through McAllister's twenty-foot-thick parapet, when the *Montauk* finally retired down the Ogeechee, the defenders were left shaken but unstirred. Five days later the U.S. Navy appeared at the fort again. Unbelievably, the Confederates had strengthened the works with the addition of two more gun positions, including a 32-pound rifled gun. Although the fort suffered its first and only casualty from Union naval bombardment that day,[12] the attack on 1 February did little more than prove that the *Montauk* could take it as well as dish it out. She was "struck thirty-nine times without apparent injury."[13]

Later that month, Comdr. John Worden of the *Montauk* made a reconnaissance up the Ogeechee and noticed that the *Nashville* had grounded in a
portion of the river known as Seven Mile Reach, upstream from Fort McAllister but within range of the monitor's guns. The next morning, the last day
of February 1863, the *Montauk* led the wooden screw steamers *Seneca* and
Dawn up the Ogeechee to within twelve hundred yards of the hapless
Confederate raider. Gunners from the fort managed to hit the Union ironclad
five more times as it sent shells screaming toward the *Nashville*. The *Montauk*
also set off a torpedo on its withdrawal downstream but again suffered no
damage. More important to Federal morale, Worden was finally able to report some good news to du Pont: The *Nashville* had been destroyed.

Perhaps inspired by this success, three days later the ironclads *Patapsco,*
Nahant, and *Passaic* — supported by the *Montauk,* three mortar schooners,
and two wooden gunboats — blasted Fort McAllister for seven hours. The
only Confederate loss was the garrison mascot, a tomcat. As the Federal fleet
retired, defiant Rebels even managed to fire a few parting shots.

The successful defense of Fort McAllister heartened the population of
Savannah. It seemed to be a good time to take the offensive. Flag Off. Josiah
Tatnall wanted to use the Confederate ironclads stationed on the Savannah
River to break the Federal blockade at Wassaw and Ossabaw sounds, the two
inlets south of the mouth of the Savannah River. On 19 March, upon hearing that Federal ironclads had been withdrawn from those waters, he took
the *Atlanta* through the obstructions at Elba Island, just downstream from
Confederate headquarters at old Fort Jackson. Before the *Atlanta* had gone
very far, however, Tatnall learned that his plans had been leaked to the Federals and that monitors were waiting for him at the sounds. The conservative
Tatnall ordered the Rebel ram to return upstream. For his timidity, Tatnall
was replaced by Comdr. William Page. Inactivity was forced upon him as he
waited for the *Atlanta*'s steering gear to be repaired. By the time the warship
was seaworthy, Page had been superseded by Comdr. William A. Webb.

As repair work progressed on the *Atlanta,* a third ironclad was being
made ready to join the Savannah Squadron. One of six Richmond-class ironclads built by the Confederate navy, the *Savannah* carried four heavy guns and
was powered by machinery forged at the Columbus (Georgia) Iron Works
Company. The first ironclad to join the squadron, the CSS *Georgia,* was little
better than a floating battery but still a powerful deterrent mounting ten heavy
guns. The relatively swift *Savannah,* however, could have cooperated with the
Atlanta in any of Webb's plans. Furthermore, the Miller Foundry in Savannah,
the local facility for the ironworks in Columbus, was striving to provide machinery for two more ironclads on the stocks in Savannah.

Webb, however, was not one to wait. On 30 May he moved the *Atlanta*
down the narrow south channel of the Savannah River. When one of the

ironclad's engines failed, it ran aground. An entire day was consumed pulling the warship free. At this point, Confederate Secretary of the Navy Stephen Mallory suggested that Webb delay operations until he could be supported by the *Savannah*. Webb declined and made plans to attack the two Federal monitors guarding the mouth of the Wilmington River, just below the Savannah River estuary.

As Webb approached the Federal armored vessels at dawn on 17 June, the USS *Weehawken*'s captain, John Rodgers, raised anchor and floated downstream to give his ship time to raise steam. Ten minutes later Rodgers swung about and, followed by John Downes in the *Nahant*, closed on the *Atlanta* and its two 6-inch and two 7-inch rifles. The Confederate warship fired first, but its experimental bolts had no effect on the monitor's armor. Then Webb's daring gamble backfired as the 1,006-ton *Atlanta* grounded again.

At three hundred yards the *Weehawken* opened fire. Her 15-inch Rodman, being used for the first time against an enemy warship, erupted a 440-pound ball, which caved in the *Atlanta*'s four-inch iron plate and three inches of oak backed by a foot of pine. Splinters wounded sixteen of the ironclad's gunners, and another forty or so were stunned by the shock. After firing its 11-inch gun, the *Weehawken* reversed its turret to reload. A second shot from the Rodman crushed the Rebel ironclad's pilothouse, wounding the two pilots and a helmsman. Two more 11-inch rounds from the *Weehawken* convinced the 150-man crew aboard the *Atlanta* to run up the white flag. It took just fifteen minutes and five shots from the monitor's 11- and 15-inch guns to decide the issue. Although none of the *Weehawken*'s shells penetrated the Rebel ironclad's fighting compartment, the *Atlanta*'s casemate had begun to tear loose from the hull.[14] The 15-inch Rodman had proved it was as deadly as it looked.

The loss of the *Atlanta* came as a great shock to the populace of Savannah. Webb was severely criticized, but as he indicated in his official report, none of his guns could be brought to bear on his adversaries once his ship had run aground.[15] Although the *Atlanta* had matched the *Weehawken* shot for shot, not one Rebel projectile had found a mark. The victorious Federals quickly repaired the slightly damaged *Atlanta* and commissioned her into the Union navy. As the USS *Atlanta*, the ironclad took up blockade duty on the James River in Virginia.

With Webb in a northern prison, a fourth commander, William W. Hunter, took over the Savannah Squadron. Under Hunter, the squadron would never again undertake offensive operations even though the *Savannah* became operational in July, followed by a second wooden gunboat, the *Macon*, in the spring of 1864. For the remainder of the war a dull routine of maintenance and short patrols comprised duty within the squadron as many of its naval officers and sailors received orders to report to other stations.

Only the June 1864 boarding and capture of the USS *Water Witch* within Ossabaw Sound by Hunter's men broke the monotony. Their victory was short-lived when all attempts to move the ship inland to Savannah failed. She was torched on 19 June to avoid recapture.

That fall, Savannah itself was threatened for the first time, but not from the sea. Maj. Gen. William Tecumseh Sherman was approaching from the west after howling through the heart of Georgia.

Up to that point, the city's defenses had been predicated on an attack from the east. A new defensive perimeter would have to be created to meet the new threat. Confederate Maj. Gen. William J. Hardee ordered Hunter's squadron to support his scattered units as they feverishly worked to extend the city's fortification zone. The gunboats *Macon* and *Sampson* with the tender *Resolute* proceeded upriver to protect the all-important railroad bridge across the Savannah River outside the city's main defense line. The gunboat *Isondiga* was left below the city to guard the bridge over the Savannah River near Causton's Bluff. The two ironclads, on the other hand, were of little service. The draft of the *Savannah* prevented it from moving above the city, and Hunter lacked vessels with which to tow the *Georgia* from its position near Fort Jackson.

By the second week of December, the flotilla at the railroad bridge was in danger of being cut off. The crews destroyed the bridge, then headed back toward Savannah.[16] As the three small wooden steamers retreated, they were fired upon by Federal batteries situated on bluffs overlooking the river. The two Confederate gunboats managed to turn around and escape upriver toward Augusta, Georgia, taking Hunter, who was on board one of the gunboats, along with them.

Hunter's plight was the least of Hardee's worries. The full weight of Sherman's army was pressing around his thirteen-mile-long belt of fortifications. But the Union general was having his own problems, mostly logistical. His route to the sea was still blocked, and stores were getting low. The most convenient supply line ran along the Ogeechee River right past Fort McAllister. It was the only major position of Savannah's defenses remaining outside the primary network of entrenchments running from Hutchinson Island in the Savannah River to the Little Ogeechee River a little north of Fort McAllister.

Assuming he might be isolated at some point in the upcoming battle, Maj. George W. Anderson, in command at the fort, had been preparing for just such an eventuality. Some of the earthwork's cannons were repositioned to cover the strengthened rear defenses. His men also brought a month's provisions and ammunition inside the walls. Finally, torpedoes (land mines) were positioned to protect the land approaches. On 12 December Anderson led a scouting party toward King's Bridge, near where Union forces earlier had captured the last train heading south out of Savannah. A skirmish developed when Anderson's men ran into the advance elements of Union Brig. Gen. Judson Kilpatrick's cavalry. The horsemen pursued Anderson's small group all the way back to Genesis Point, but they halted short of an actual attack on the fort.

The next day Sherman stood at the signal station built atop a rice mill looking for the U.S. Navy while keeping an eye on developments at Fort McAllister, two and a half miles away. Some three thousand men of Brig. Gen. William B. Hazen's division of the Fifteenth Corps were forming battle lines in preparation for an assault. At 4:30 P.M., while Sherman's signal team made contact with the Federal warship, Hazen's men rushed toward Fort McAllister and ripped through the chevaux-de-frise and abatis. As they hit the belt of torpedoes, men were blown to bits, but the blue wave surged forward.

Many of the 265 Confederates resisted desperately, but — as Hazen later reported — Sherman's old division "moved on without checking . . . fighting the garrison through the fort to their bombproofs, from which they still fought, and only succumbed as each man was individually overpowered."[17]

Confederate troops at Coffee Bluff on Rose Dhu Island had witnessed McAllister's fall and wired the bad news to Hardee in Savannah. Having failed to prevent Sherman's link with the U.S. Navy, the Confederate commander realized the only way to save his men was to evacuate them across the Savannah River to South Carolina.

On 18 December — as Sherman's army tightened its grip on the city and Hardee's engineers worked to float pontoon bridges over the Savannah River — Gen. P. G. T. Beauregard, in command of Confederate defenses in South Carolina and Georgia, arrived to confer with T. W. Brent, captain of the *Savannah* and temporary commander of the Savannah Squadron. The two decided to send the *Isondiga* and *Firefly* upriver to join Hunter, scuttle the immobile *Georgia* and the unfinished ironclad *Milledgeville*, burn the armored vessels still on the stocks, and use the *Savannah* to provide covering fire for Hardee's escape. Two days later, unable to steam upriver, the two wooden gunboats were set afire. Of the once-powerful squadron, only the *Savannah* remained.

Brent hoped to fight his way through the blockade and make for Charleston, but he could not get the ironclad past his own torpedoes in the Wilmington River. By early morning on 21 December, the *Savannah* was milling about Screven's Ferry across from Fort Jackson on the Savannah River. Federal troops soon appeared on the opposite bank and raised the Stars and Stripes over the former headquarters of the Savannah Squadron.[18] The ironclad opened up on the U.S. flag, the only time in Fort Jackson's fifty-six-year history it received hostile fire. A battery of U.S. field guns arrived at Bay Street along Savannah's waterfront, unlimbered, and returned the *Savannah*'s fire. Throughout the day the adversaries exchanged shots, resulting in little damage to either side. The city that had prepared itself for an attack by warships for more than three years finally was bombarded from the river. Ironically, it was a Confederate ship versus Federal shore batteries. Before being completely surrounded, the ironclad's crew set the *Savannah* afire at 7:30 P.M., then joined the rear guard of Hardee's army. Four hours later the *Savannah* exploded.

The unusually cautious Sherman with his sixty thousand hardened veterans allowed the Rebel army of ten thousand to escape. By concentrating his main effort south toward Fort McAllister rather than across the Savannah River into South Carolina, he made it evident that his primary objective was to establish contact with the U.S. Navy as quickly as possible. Still, the capture of Savannah provided a suitable ending for the march to the sea. As a Christmas gift to Lincoln, Sherman presented the president with "the city of Savannah, with one-hundred and fifty heavy guns and plenty of ammunition, also about twenty-five thousand bales of cotton."[19] Perhaps as a Christmas gift to the city, Sherman's bummers did not destroy a thing.

If you go there . . .

If you're serious about doing the region properly, find a copy of the February 1991 issue of *Blue & Gray Magazine*. The cover story is on Savannah, and it is accompanied by three excellent tour suggestions of the city and surrounding countryside. There are only two sites I would add to the author's list, which includes at least two dozen I was not aware of before seeing the article.

A second thing you might want to do is contact RSVP Georgia, a free, statewide bed-and-breakfast reservation service that also serves northern Florida and South Carolina. Often for the price of a sterile motel room, you can soak in history at a bed and breakfast. It's as easy as calling (800) 729-7787.

Next, when you enter the city on Interstate 16, drive two blocks to Liberty and turn west one block to the **Savannah History Museum and Visitors Center.** Situated in the Central of Georgia passenger depot (in use during the 1860s), the museum includes exhibits on the Civil War and a terrific show about the siege of Savannah during the American Revolution. At the visitors center you can also make reservations from coded phones for any of the several tours of the city. The center is open daily from 8:30 A.M. to

5:00 P.M. For information, contact: Savannah History Museum, 303 Martin Luther King Jr. Blvd., Savannah, GA 31499 (912) 238-1779.

One of the squares James Oglethorpe designed in the city that you won't want to miss is Madison Square. On the corner of Bull and Harris streets on the north side of the square is the Francis Sorrel residence. A historical marker indicates that G. Moxley Sorrel, an aide to General Longstreet, lived there and that Robert E. Lee was a frequent visitor during his tenure at Fort Pulaski. On the west side of the square, the fine example of Gothic Revival architecture is the **Green-Meldrim House,** presently serving as the parish house for Saint John's Episcopal Church. Charles Green, an Englishman, offered his home to Sherman as headquarters to spare any other resident the shame. Sherman eventually accepted. For a $2.50 donation, visitors are welcome to tour the residence Tuesdays, Thursdays, Fridays, and Saturdays from 10:00 A.M.–4:00 P.M. The site is closed December 15 for a month.

Farther west on Harris Street, at the northwest corner of its intersection with Barnard, sits the former home of Francis Bartow, the first Confederate commander at Fort Pulaski.

Savannah's riverfront has changed little since the Civil War. The building still standing at Seven Bay Street was utilized as Federal army headquarters during the occupation and Reconstruction. To the left is the Custom House, designed by John S. Norris, the same architect who drew the plans for Charles Green's home. From the top of the Custom House on 22 December, Sherman surveyed the conquered city.

Be sure to visit River Street, the boulevard that runs beside the Savannah River. Just watching the huge oceangoing ships leave and enter the port of Savannah, the fifteenth largest in the United States, is a treat. Don't get so caught up in the rushing tide, however, that you miss the **Ships of the Sea Museum** at 503 East River Street. The museum displays four floors of nautical items, mostly ship models, including replicas of the ironclad CSS *Atlanta* and the USS *Savannah,* a forty-four-gun frigate employed for a while as a blockader at Tybee Roads at the mouth of the Savannah River.

The museum is open daily from 10:00 A.M. to 5:00 P.M., except Thanksgiving, Christmas, New Year's, and Saint Patrick's Day. The cost is $2.00.

Traveling east on River or Bay streets, you will run into President Street. A little over a mile farther, the Savannah Country Club spreads along the south side of the street. If you drive into the entrance road, just to the east you can see the remains of **Fort Boggs,** a large earthen fort that was part of the city's Civil War defenses. You can turn around in the parking lot and head back east on President Street. Just short of a mile is Woodcock Road, which leads to **Old Fort Jackson,** the oldest standing fort in Georgia.

Begun in 1808, Fort James Jackson was built near where a Revolutionary War battery fired a few rounds at the British during the battle of Riceboats during early March 1776. A small portion of this wood-and-earth battery has been rebuilt. The brick fortress standing just to the east originally had no moat, and the rear walls and barracks were constructed of wood. A model of the fort during this period is part of the exhibits in the old bombproofs. The large brick parapet fronting the Savannah River was raised on top of the old fort between 1846–61. During the Civil War, up to eight guns guarded the river here, and forty-seven others provided backup from nearby earthworks. In addition, the CSS *Georgia* floated for thirty months on station just below the fort. Today, red buoys bobbing in the river directly in front of the fort mark the remains of this ironclad, a model of which is in the exhibit rooms. Artifacts from the ship, including cannon, are also on display in the fort. Georgia's Coastal Heritage Society is working to raise and restore this priceless hulk, which is threatened by dredging of the river channel.

Fort Jackson is open daily from 9:00 A.M. to 5:00 P.M., from 1 July to 15 August until 7:00 P.M. You pay your $2.00 admission at a small gift shop near the entrance to the nine-acre park. Special military history programs include the firing of an original 32-pounder, the largest black-powder cannon still in use in the United States. For information on these programs, contact: Old Fort Jackson, 1 Fort Jackson Road, Savannah, GA 31401 (912) 232-3945.

A little over a mile farther east on President Street, the Wilmington River passes under the road to join the Savannah. Just before the bridge, on the north side of the road, rises Causton's Bluff, the site of **Fort Bartow**, the largest earthen fort in Savannah's defense system. The area is now covered by a housing development, but you can still see a portion of the massive earth walls from President Street (U.S. 80).

About ten miles farther along the highway is the entrance to **Fort Pulaski National Monument.** After its brief moment in the spotlight, Fort Pulaski played one final cameo role during the Civil War. In an attempt to lift the bombardment of Charleston in the summer of 1864, Confederate Gen. Samuel Jones notified Union Gen. J. G. Foster that he planned to use captured officers as human shields for the city. Foster retaliated by requesting that a like number of Confederate prisoners be held on Morris Island, still under fire from Rebel guns at Fort Sumter. The standoff escalated until six hundred Federal officers were quartered in the residential section of Charleston. In October, a yellow fever epidemic gave Jones the excuse he needed to save face and move the Federals from Charleston. Foster sent the remainder of the six hundred Confederates held on Morris Island to Fort Pulaski. Today, a section of the casemates has been restored to resemble the

This aerial view of Fort Pulaski shows the damage inflicted on the southern wall
(Georgia Department of Archives and History)

prison rooms in which these prisoners lived — and died. After the war, prisoners of a different nature began to arrive at Cockspur Island, including for a brief moment, Jefferson Davis. Three of his cabinet members were held at Fort Pulaski: Secretary of State Robert M. T. Hunter, Secretary of the Treasury George A. Trenholm, and Secretary of War James A. Seddon. Three Confederate state governors and former Sen. David Yulee of Florida added to the list of distinguished guests.

Ironically, the man who brought down the third-system house of cards, Gillmore, returned to Pulaski in 1869 to upgrade the fort. He oversaw major changes in the demilune.[20] Massive concrete foundations for an Endicott-period fort in the northern end of the parade ground, however, were never used and eventually covered over.

By the beginning of the twentieth century, the moat had again filled with mud and the fort was crumbling. In 1924 the first step was taken to restore Pulaski when it was declared a national monument. Almost a decade would pass before the National Park Service began to develop the area. Today, park rangers dressed in Civil War uniforms give talks at the fort, which is one of the least-changed from its Civil War configuration of the third-system forts.

Also situated on the island are a visitors center and a statue commemorating the February 1736 arrival of John Wesley on Cockspur. Beyond them rise the concrete remains of Battery Horace Hambright, begun in 1899 to hold two 3-inch rapid-fire guns.

Fort Pulaski is open daily except Christmas from 8:30 A.M. until 5:30 P.M. Admission is $1.00 For information, contact: Superintendent, Fort Pulaski National Monument, P.O. Box 30757, Savannah, GA 31410-0757 (912) 786-5787.

Proceeding east on U.S. 80, just past the bridge over Lazeretto Creek you will see the historical marker indicating the site of Gillmore's batteries. From there, continue until you see the signs for the **Tybee Island Lighthouse.** Because of damage suffered by the lighthouse during the Civil War, workers tore away the upper portion and rebuilt it. Since Congress has refused to fund a new structure, Tybee lighthouse is the oldest active light station on the Southeast coast. Confederates constructed batteries around the lighthouse. When Union troops occupied the island, they established batteries around the nearby Martello tower, completed in 1815. The army demolished the round fifty-foot-tall tower in 1914 because it blocked the line of fire of one of the guns in Fort Screven, erected adjacent to the lighthouse just prior to the Spanish-American War as a replacement for Fort Pulaski. Battery Garland of Fort Screven (named after Gen. James Screven, a Revolutionary War leader killed in Georgia) now houses the **Tybee Museum.** For $1.50, visitors can walk through the museum, which includes a model and pictures of the Martello tower, then climb the 178 steps to the top of the Tybee lighthouse to gain a spectacular view of Savannah's defenses, particularly Fort Pulaski. The Tybee Museum is open daily from 10:00 A.M. to 6:00 P.M. in the summer, and until 5:00 P.M. in the winter. For information, contact Tybee Museum Association, P.O. Box 366, Tybee Island, GA 31328 (912) 786-4077.

If you go back to Savannah via U.S. 80, just before you reach the city, turn south on Skidaway Road. Eight miles down the road is the entrance to **Wormsloe State Historic Site.** One of the original colonists, Noble Jones, raised a fortified tabby house there to control the inland water approach to Savannah along the Skidaway River. In September 1861, Col. A. R. Lawton was charged with defending the Georgia coast and the next month (as a brigadier general) took over the Department of Georgia. He immediately posted six pieces of field artillery on the Isle of Hope near the old fort. Originally called Battery Lawton and then Fort Wimberly, the earthworks guarding the water routes around the Isle of Hope eventually boasted 176 men serving four 8-inch siege howitzers, two 4-inch Blakely rifles, and one 20-pounder Parrott.[21] A history of the plantation suggests that prior to the fall of Fort Pulaski, Federal scouts had managed to feel their way along the tidal rivers to the Isle of Hope, only to be discouraged from further progress by the batteries situated there.

Presently, the Confederate earthworks are undergoing an archaeological survey and — although still visible — are not open to the public. Besides

The Martello Tower on Tybee Island following conversion to lighthouse use *(Georgia Department of Archives and History)*

the museum, Wormsloe Historic Site offers a picnic area, interpretive trail, living history demonstrations, and access to the tabby ruins of Jones's fort. The site welcomes visitors Tuesday through Saturday, 9:00 A.M.–5:00 P.M., Sunday 2:00–5:30 P.M. It is closed Christmas and Thanksgiving. Admission is $1.50 for adults. For information, contact: Wormsloe Historic Site, 7601 Skidaway Road, Savannah, GA 31406 (912) 353-3023.

Heading south from Savannah on either U.S. 17 or I-95, you will eventually cross GA 144. About five and a half miles east, take the GA 144 (Spur). **Fort McAllister State Historic Park** is another four miles. We have Henry Ford to thank for the excellent condition of these historically important earthworks. When he built a home nearby in the 1930s, he had the fort restored. Georgia acquired the site in 1958 to establish a park, and the state has worked to create one of the best-preserved earthen forts in the United States. Most impressive are the bombproofs, one of which has been reconstructed into a field hospital, complete with wooden rafters and bunks. As far as my travels are concerned, it is the only earthen bombproof in such good condition into which visitors are allowed.

A museum and theater stand just outside the fort's walls. An excellent self-guided tour map is available at the former and explains such items as the hot-shot furnace and the types of guns within each emplacement. The

Fort McAllister, an 8-inch Columbiad overlooking the Ogeechee River

The detached mortar position at Fort McAllister

1,690-acre park also includes a campground, hiking trails, picnic areas, a boat ramp, and dock.

The cost to tour the fort is $1.50 for adults and $.75 for children over six. The park is open 7:00 A.M. to 10:00 P.M. The historic site is open from 9:00 A.M. to 5:00 P.M., Tuesday through Saturday and from 2:00–5:30 P.M. Sunday. It is closed Thanksgiving and Christmas. Special events, such as summer and winter musters, are scheduled throughout the year. For information, contact: Fort McAllister State Historic Park, Route 2, P.O. Box 394-A, Richmond Hill, GA 31324 (912) 727-2339.

FLORIDA

ANYONE FLYING over south central Florida today should be able to imagine what the state looked like in the 1800s when almost all the area between the panhandle and Key West was sparsely inhabited swamp with a few small coastal settlements. Even then the race had begun to grab a piece of paradise however. Florida's growth in the mid-1800s was at a faster pace than any other state or territory in the nation except Texas. The antebellum immigrants were not hoping to find their place in the sun, however. The prize was north central Florida soil upon which planters could harvest six hundred to eight hundred pounds of valuable Sea Island cotton[1] per acre, compared with three hundred pounds per acre in South Carolina. The seven counties in the white-gold triangle between Tallahassee and Jacksonville to just south of Gainesville contained property valued at $48 million of the state's total worth of $73 million.

Vast cotton profits fueled the demand for cheap labor until slaves made up 40 percent of the state's total population, almost two-thirds the inhabitants in some counties. With the Seminole Wars still fresh in their memories, some planters were jittery about slave uprisings and worked to promote what they felt were safeguards against any revolts. By the 1850s, blacks in Florida had to belong to someone or have a white benefactor to vouch for their integrity. Even in Key West, where many of the state's free blacks lived, laws were passed to prohibit them from walking the streets at night.[2] With an economy based on slave labor, it is logical that Florida seceded in January 1861, right behind South Carolina and Mississippi.

Before the outbreak of hostilities, much of the cotton raised in northern Florida found its way through the state's spidery water system to Gulf of Mexico or Atlantic Ocean ports at Saint Marks, Apalachicola, Pensacola, Fernandina, Jacksonville, and Saint Joseph, the last town being abandoned before the Civil War after a devastating hurricane destroyed most of it. Following the confrontations at Fort Sumter and one at Florida's Pensacola Navy Yard, the mission of the thirteen thousand Floridians who volunteered to fight in the Confederate army became to protect the remaining ports under state control and to break the Union stranglehold at Pensacola and Key West. Proving themselves "a generally undisciplined lot, as fond of drinking and brawling as fighting Yankees,"[3] Floridians failed on most counts, and by 1862 nearly all had been ordered to Tennessee, leaving the coasts open to Union incursions.

With few exceptions, the remainder of the war in Florida centered on Yankee raids, Confederate reprisals against unionist collaborators, and blockade running from the hundreds of obscure inlets that dotted the coastline.[4]

Besides smuggling and fighting, two other occupations kept Floridians busy during the war years: salt making and cattle raising. Five thousand men and boys gained exemption from the Confederate draft by boiling seawater in little shacks along the Gulf Coast. This $3-million-a-year cottage industry was the target of sporadic Union naval raids, but since all that was needed was a pot, the saltworks entrepreneurs were soon bubbling again. Selling cattle involved a larger investment and, therefore, greater risk, especially since

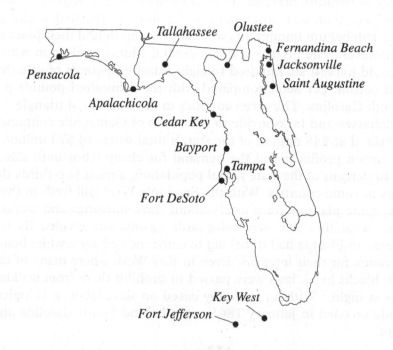

the cattlemen sold to both sides. To protect their stock, ranchers organized a "cow cavalry" to fight off Union raiders and Confederate deserters, who attacked almost every cattle drive, not just for the gold, but for the food. The Union blockade and the Confederate demand for provisions had left people with little to eat. When, for example, in April 1862 Union forces occupied Apalachicola, the few remaining inhabitants had been subsisting on fish and oysters from the bay.

In spite of a spotty military reputation, Confederates in Florida managed to hold Tallahassee throughout the war, the only Confederate state capital east of the Mississippi not to fall to Federal troops. This "honor" occurred despite attempts by Yankees to capture the city.

Although leaders in the North had the ability to send sufficient naval forces to seize any location on Florida's coast, they did not see any wisdom in holding more than a few areas permanently. Likewise, Southern leaders preferred to utilize Florida recruits in more strategic locales rather than risk them in attacks on Union enclaves. These complementary strategies left most of the state under Rebel control until the end of the war.

Despite its secondary role, the state provided some of the initial setbacks and first positive news for the U.S. government rocked by early embarrassments at its southern military posts.

Pensacola

IN 1559 the Spanish made Pensacola one of the first European settlements inside the current borders of the United States. They abandoned the harbor on Florida's panhandle two years later and did not return for almost 150 years. When they did, they showed they were serious by building some fortifications. For the next century and a half, practically every war that swept through Europe or North America created a ripple that touched Pensacola, sometimes sweeping away one occupation army only to bring it back on the next wave. In the midst of these struggles, Spain ceded Florida to the United States in 1821. Eight years later, Maj. William H. Chase began construction of a navy yard for the Gulf of Mexico Squadron. He was also to be the engineer in charge of four planned forts.

Pentagonal Fort Pickens, named for Revolutionary War Gen. Andrew Pickens, guarded Point Siguenza on Santa Rosa Island, site of one of the original Spanish stockades. The fort's five bastions were designed to hold 200–250 cannon, one tier in casemates, the other on barbettes (raised platforms). On the Pensacola mainland, Fort McRee[5] guarded Foster's Bank, west and across the channel from Pickens. Completed in 1840, McRee was designed to mount 128 cannon. Directly across the channel north of Pickens sat Fort Barrancas and its water battery, mounting a total of 33 cannon. An advanced redoubt was positioned fifteen hundred yards north to guard the land approaches to the navy yard. The three main works covered a mutually supporting triangular area of the bay.

President Franklin Buchanan's secretary of the navy, Issac Toucey, has justifiably been accused of not doing enough to prevent the seizure of federal property prior to the outbreak of actual hostilities. In fact, the commanding officer at Pensacola and his second-in-command were allowed to go on leave during the tense lame-duck period after the 1860 election. Toucey's lack of judgment might have actually worked to the North's advantage, however. Left in charge at Pensacola was 1st Lt. Adam Slemmer, a former professor at West Point. Without orders from Washington, he decided to move part of his artillery company into Fort Barrancas.

Toward midnight on 8 January 1861, sentries fired on unknown individuals approaching the fort. These are considered by some to be the first shots of the Civil War.[6] The next day instructions arrived for Slemmer and Com. James Armstrong, commandant of the navy yard, warning them to be "vigilant to protect the public property."[7] Deciding he could hold at best one fort, Slemmer chose the most remote. During the next two days, he moved his entire company and thirty-one seamen to Fort Pickens. Thirty-eight marines and a similar force of sailors remained behind with Armstrong to guard the navy yard. On 12 January, Armstrong surrendered the yard without firing a shot, an act for which he was later court-martialed.

That afternoon Slemmer declined an invitation to surrender his post to three militia officers. His audacious refusal was one of the biggest bluffs of the war as he commanded only eighty men at a facility designed for twelve hundred. Nevertheless, Slemmer drove his men to prepare for an expected assault. There was much to do. The fort had languished for a decade at the west end of forty-five-mile-long Santa Rosa Island, not out of neglect, but because of policy. Any enemy was expected to come from across the ocean, giving defenders plenty of time to make the necessary repairs. Slemmer's antagonists — up to eight hundred Southerners — waited less than three thousand yards across the bay. The U.S. troops managed to mount a few cannon, enough to prevent the secessionist Floridians and later the Confederates from using the best harbor on the Gulf of Mexico.

Within two weeks of Armstrong's surrender, Toucey sent the steam sloop *Brooklyn* under Capt. Henry Adams with reinforcements for Slemmer. Former U.S. senator from Florida and future secretary of the Confederate navy Stephen Mallory, who had a home in Pensacola, arranged a truce with President Buchanan: As long as Union troops were not landed at Pickens, Mallory pledged no attack would be made against the fort.

When administrations changed in Washington, Gideon Welles took over as secretary of the navy. He immediately ordered Adams to land the troops without informing the Florida militia at the navy yard. Adams refused. The captain of the *Brooklyn* held the draft of Mallory's agreement and could not believe his government would "engage in an act of bad faith."[8] Thinking there must be some mistake, Adams sent a messenger to Washington to clarify the situation. Upon learning the order was indeed correct, the messenger refused to carry a confirmation back. Welles ordered Lt. John L. Worden, future captain of the *Monitor,* to travel overland to Pensacola with instructions to put the soldiers ashore. Arriving at the Pensacola Navy Yard, Worden was able to convince Gen. Braxton Bragg, then in charge at the port, that his intentions were peaceful. Once on board the *Brooklyn,* Worden broke his word to the general and made sure the reinforcements were moved to Fort Pickens. Bragg was understandably upset. Although Worden was captured on his way back to Washington, he had succeeded in his mission.

Meanwhile, William Seward, Lincoln's newly appointed secretary of state, hatched a plot with the new president to start a war with Spain over Santo Domingo to "divert attention from the crisis at home."[9] As part of the plan, the warship *Powhatan* was to steam with more troops for Pensacola and Key West in case the subterfuge had the desired effect. Seward's co-conspirators in the plan to relieve Pensacola were Capt. Montgomery C. Meigs of the U.S. Army, who went on to become quartermaster-general, and Lt. David Dixon Porter, earmarked to command the *Powhatan.* They convinced Lincoln to bypass his secretary of the navy to prevent any leaks. The *Powhatan,* however, had already been selected to be a part of the Fort Sumter relief force, and a furious Welles, with a backpeddling Lincoln on his side, tried to have the ship recalled from its Pensacola assignment. It was too late. Porter refused to accept orders from anyone but Lincoln.[10]

Troops from the *Brooklyn* came ashore 11 April and Meigs's expeditionary forces landed five days later. Still no angry shots were fired. When Porter, having been delayed by bad weather, appeared on the scene the next day with the *Powhatan,* Meigs was forced to swing the sloop *Wyandotte* across the bow of the brash navy lieutenant's ship to keep him from sailing to the navy yard. For his part, Bragg continued to abide by the original agreement, although he declared martial law in Pensacola on 19 April.

The situation in Pensacola remained tense, but nothing of consequence occurred until 2 September, when a small detachment from Fort Pickens destroyed a floating dry dock that Confederate forces had earlier scuttled and were just then trying to raise. Even then Bragg's ire did not lead to action until another Federal raiding party attacked the navy yard, burned the *Judah* (reportedly being outfitted by Confederate naval authorities as a privateer), and spiked a nearby 10-inch Columbiad. In retaliation, Bragg finally ordered Gen. Dick Anderson to take Fort Pickens.

Anderson landed on 8 October with a thousand men about four miles east of the fort and easily took cantonments guarding the landward approaches manned by the Sixth New York Volunteers, who fell back until they

Confederate battery overlooking Pensacola Harbor, south of Fort McRee
(*National Archives*)

reached the protective fire of Pickens. Anderson's men stopped to loot the former Federal positions. When the Yankees rallied, well-trained Union infantry easily forced the disorganized Rebels to retreat to their boats.[11] Although insignificant compared to bloodbaths in other states (Confederates reported eighteen killed; Federals, fourteen), Anderson's abortive attack on Fort Pickens was destined to be the second largest land battle in Florida during the Civil War.

In response to Bragg's action, Flag Off. W. W. McKean, commander of the Gulf Blockading Squadron, ordered the *Richmond* and *Niagara* to bombard Fort McRee, with supporting fire from Fort Pickens. The attack began on 22 November. When the ships found their range, the Confederate fort's barbette guns were silenced immediately. The second day there was no return fire from Fort McRee, but a masked battery opened on the *Richmond* and hit her twice, killing one man. Pickens itself suffered fifteen casualties during the actual fight, two of them mortal.

During the next forty-eight-hour barrage that began on New Year's Day 1862, Union artillerists found their range and brutalized the navy yard and surrounding quarters. Fort McRee suffered the worst damage, however. A powder magazine exploded, totally destroying the fort's military worth. In mid-March, following the debacle at Forts Donelson and Henry, the already poor morale of the Rebels in Pensacola fell even lower when most of the garrison was withdrawn. President Davis had recognized the "necessity of abandoning the seaboard in order to defend the Tennessee line."[12]

Later in March, two companies from Fort Pickens destroyed a Confederate base on the mainland that had been harassing Union ships, then managed to shell a Confederate schooner on their return to the fort.[13]

By that time, the Confederates had had enough. Maj. Gen. Robert E. Lee advised Col. Thomas M. Jones, left in command at Pensacola, to send his troops to Mobile, Alabama. Jones started the evacuation on 7 May. Fires at the navy yard on 9 May alerted Fort Pickens that something was up, so the Union troops responded in the only way they knew: They began a heavy bombardment that lasted until the next morning. On 10 May Lt. Richard Jackson received the surrender of Pensacola. Moments later, Porter showed up in command of the *Harriet Lane* only to find that the army had beaten the navy to the honors.

Although Pensacola served as a staging area for nuisance raids into Alabama and the Florida panhandle, by 1863 fewer than a thousand troops remained in the city itself. Eventually Union forces moved out altogether, choosing to garrison only the two forts at the mouth of the bay. Conditions were so harsh, however, that occupation troops were regularly shuttled in and out.

Not until 1864 did a major buildup for a military operation take place in the area. Supplies for Farragut's attack on Mobile started piling up that

Reinforcements for the landing at Fort Pickens *(Harper's)*

spring. Hoping to hinder the expedition, in April 1864 Lt. James Baker, C.S.N., proposed an amphibious raid on Fort Pickens. The first part of his plan went well when he and eight men captured the sloop *Creole* near the mouth of the bay. For reasons that are unclear, Baker kept postponing the attack on the fort until it became moot following Federal operations against Fort Morgan, Alabama, on 5 August.[14]

If you go there . . .

Fort Pickens, Fort Barrancas, and the **Advanced Redoubt** are all part of the **Gulf Islands National Seashore.** The later two are situated within the Pensacola Naval Air Station. One-day passes to visit the forts and the nearby Naval Aviation Museum can be obtained at the entrances to the naval air station.

Spain raised a fort on the bluff (*barranca*) overlooking Pensacola Bay as early as 1698. Fort Barrancas, designed by Joseph Totten, was constructed between 1839–44 over the ruins of the Spanish Fort San Carlos to protect the enlarged water battery. Originally erected by the Spanish in 1797 and called Bateria de San Antonio, the water battery is one of only three Spanish fortifications left standing east of the Mississippi. Barrancas and the water battery were reconditioned by the National Park Service from 1978–80. Without a doubt, they are the best restored Civil War–era forts in the United States today. Freshly plastered, well lit, and relatively dry, Fort Barrancas belies the image of the typical third-system fortress: crumbling, dark, and damp.

Information, a slide show, exhibits, and a bookstore are available at the Fort Barrancas Visitors Contact Station. Nearby are restrooms, picnic tables, and a half-mile Woodland Nature Trail. Fort Barrancas is open daily from 9:30 A.M.–5:00 P.M. Guided tours of the fort are given daily at 11:00 A.M. and 2:00 P.M. For further information, call (904) 455-5167.

With the completion of Fort Barrancas in 1844, all that remained to carry through Simon Bernard's recommendations for Pensacola's fortifications was to construct a northern anchor for the navy yard's land defenses, which were flanked on the south at Fort Barrancas. Starting in 1845 and taking nearly fifteen years, contracted slave labor assembled the Advanced Redoubt, a deceptive name for the masonry stronghold since it is nearly as large as Fort Barrancas. A series of trenches covered the eight hundred yards between the two positions. Anyone trying to approach the navy yard by land would have to breach this solid line, as the yard sits on a peninsula formed by Pensacola Bay and Bayou Grande. This perimeter defense was tested only once: Alabama cavalry approached in 1863 but withdrew after a brief skirmish.

Fort Pickens

The Advanced Redoubt was the first of the Pensacola forts to be restored by the National Park Service. After two years of work, it was opened in 1976. It is a short drive north of Fort Barrancas and has its own parking lot but is open at irregular times. Check with the Fort Barrancas Visitors Center for information.

The complete disappearance of Fort McRee into the Pensacola Bay channel during a 1906 hurricane is a shame because the fort's design was unique for the period. It resembled a "large, stubby airplane wing, 450 feet long, 150 feet wide, with rounded ends."[15] The closest comparison would be Fort Wool in Hampton Roads. Two tiers of guns in casemates and barbette guns on the terreplein (the platform behind the parapet on which heavy guns were mounted) faced the channel. There were enough emplacements for 128 cannon, but Federal troops spiked many of the 24- and 32-pounders before they fled to Fort Pickens.

Starting in 1837, workers took just three years to finish McRee, a record for third-system forts. Part of the reason for this seems to be the considerable incorporation of wood into its construction, much more than in other forts of the period. For example, the second tier of guns in the casemate sat on timber platforms, and old photographs seem to indicate that some of the open casemates were enclosed with wooden walls. No doubt the great amount of lumber contributed to the spread of fires throughout the fort during the intermittent bombardments during 1861–62. When Confederates departed in May 1862, they burned what was left. The part of one wall left standing after the hurricane of September 1906 was used as fill to protect the foundations of Battery Center on Foster's Bank.

An aerial view of Fort Barrancas and Battery San Carlos *(Gulf Islands National Seashore)*

The **Pensacola Navy Yard** has a few reminders of the Civil War. The old entrance gate dates back to the Civil War, and a portion of the wall surrounding the original yard still stands.

Within the city, the **Pensacola Historic Museum** occupies the oldest Protestant church building still standing in the state. Used by Federal troops as a barracks and hospital, the former church now contains exhibits, a historical library, and an extensive collection of old photographs. The museum is open daily except Sunday and holidays. For information, contact: Pensacola Historic Museum, 405 South Adams St., Pensacola, FL 32501 (904) 433-1559.

Also in downtown Pensacola, the **Civil War Soldiers Museum** offers visitors a chance to learn about the city's involvement in the war through letters, diaries, and life-size dioramas. In addition, the bookstore at the museum stocks more than five hundred different titles related to the Civil War period. Admission to the museum, which is open Monday through Saturday from 10:00 A.M.–4:30 P.M., is $3.00 for adults and $1.50 for children. For more information, contact: Civil War Soldiers Museum, 108 South Palafox Place, Pensacola, FL 32501 (904) 468-1900.

Although Fort Pickens lies just over a mile across the bay from Fort Barrancas, the overland drive covers almost thirty miles. Gulf Islands National Seashore, which encompasses the fort, provides camping, fishing (no license is required in saltwater), nature programs, lectures, and movies. The Fort Pickens Area Museum and Auditorium, open 9:00 A.M.–5:00 P.M. daily, stands a small distance northwest of the fort. Many of the lectures take place there. The Fort Pickens Visitors Center, situated just inside the entrance to the fort, is open 9:30 A.M.–5:00 P.M. daily. A small gift shop offers some great books on the forts and has program schedules. For information, call (904) 934-2635. Just to the left as you enter the fort are former officers' quarters that were used to house the Apache prisoner Geronimo and his followers from 1886–88. One of the more interesting features of Fort Pickens is a missing wall. Fire ignited a magazine containing black powder under the northwest bastion on 20 June 1899. That day it rained bricks on towns surrounding the navy yard a mile and a half away.

Inside, on the fort's parade ground, rises Battery Pensacola, an Endicott-period work built during the Spanish-American War. It is only one of several interesting concrete batteries at or near Fort Pickens. If you decide to hike for a look at the other "modern" forts, be aware there are poisonous snakes in the area. If you don't bother them, they won't bother you. I would especially recommend driving to Battery Number 234 and Battery Cooper, situated near one another on a one-way drive. Battery Number 234 contains two 6-inch shielded guns. These guns were added in 1976 by the National Park Service and the Smithsonian Institution. Likewise at Battery Cooper, one 6-inch disappearing gun mount was installed by the park service.

All sites are open free of charge. For further information about any of the forts in the Pensacola area, contact: Gulf Islands National Seashore, 1801 Gulf Breeze Parkway, Gulf Breeze, FL 32561 (904) 934-2600.

Gulf Coast

THERE WERE probably several reasons why the War Department chose to station ships near certain harbors and risk missing a few blockade runners when it would have been relatively easy to capture the ports and shut them down completely. Since the Confederacy had no navy to speak of, warships lying offshore were practically immune from attack. Garrisons in port towns, on the other hand, always faced the risk of defeat by a larger raiding force. Strategically speaking, Union generals probably felt the same way about many other ports as William Tecumseh Sherman felt about Mobile, Alabama: he "preferred to have a Confederate garrison tied up there than a Union garrison."[16] More than likely, life aboard ships was healthier than duty in some of the pestilential ports of call, if only because there were fewer malarial insects hovering about. As long as steady supplies of fruit and fresh water could be obtained, saltwater tars could thank providence they weren't marching in long blue lines toward orange sheets of flame erupting from Rebel guns.

Monetary rewards could have also influenced Northern strategies on occasion. Prize courts awarded a portion of captured cargoes to the men who seized them. Since cotton, the South's only hard currency, brought a high price in Northern mills, a few open Southern ports provided captains and crews a chance to gain extra money if they could confiscate cotton bales waiting to be loaded on outward-bound steamers. The potential earnings from contraband cotton and other goods taken by blockaders were staggering. Union Adm. Samuel P. Lee, a relative of Robert E. Lee and at one time commander of the North Atlantic Squadron, reaped $109,689 in prize money, making him the U.S. Navy's biggest wartime winner.[17] In all, by war's end, naval personnel had earned more than $10 million from confiscated cargo.[18]

Rowena Reed, in her prize-winning book *Combined Operations in the Civil War*, indicated that Lincoln ordered a blockade in lieu of declaring Confederate ports closed for political, not strictly military, reasons: "removing the incentive for patrol duty — the prize money from captured ships — would weaken the Navy."[19] Additionally, Reed argued, closing the ports would hurt financially powerful Northerners engaged in covert trade with the Confederacy.

Confederate authorities certainly had little or no way to stop the sporadic Federal naval sorties in search of cotton. Brig. Gen. John H. Forney, C.S.A., commander of the Department of Alabama and West Florida, tried to take away the temptation in his department in mid-1862 by ordering "all cotton at or near navigable waters within the Military Command shall be forthwith removed by the owner to some point in the interior of the country near to which no approach can be made by water, or shall be burned."[20]

In the long run, the benefits to the Southern cause gained by open seaports far outweighed the nuisance factor caused by the infrequent capture of a blockade runner. Historian Stephen R. Wise observed, "Without blockade running, the Confederacy could not have properly armed, clothed, or fed its soldiers. As long as there were open ports that the steamers could utilize, the Confederacy survived; but once the seaports were captured, the nation was destined to die."[21]

A case in point is Apalachicola, Florida. Pensacola had the naval base, but the Gulf Coast city of Apalachicola was "the largest exporting and importing port in Florida."[22] Nestled next to its namesake river that flowed past Georgia and Alabama plantations, Apalachicola was the port of choice for the transportation of cotton from a large number of inland farms via the Gulf of Mexico. In early 1862, however, the Confederate Secretary of War Judah P. Benjamin ordered most troops on duty along Florida's coast to join A. S. Johnston's army in Tennessee. Northern strategists knew this, but they did not put a definite end to Apalachicola's use as a haven for blockade runners by garrisoning the port. Federals did not occupy the town until more than two weeks after Lee surrendered at Appomattox Court House.

Up until then, Union activity in the area mainly involved impounding harvested cotton. As early as August 1861 sailors from the USS *R. R. Cuyler* burned a ship preparing to receive a cargo of cotton at Apalachicola. In April 1862, armed boats from the USS *Mercedita* and the USS *Sagamore* showed just how easy the pickings were by going into town and seizing two pilot boats, three schooners, and a sloop.[23] In the fall of 1862, boats from the USS *Fort Henry* proceeded up the Apalachicola River and captured more cotton. In 1863, the crew of the USS *Port Royal* struck it rich when they landed three times that year at or near Apalachicola and hauled off baled cotton.

Only once, it seems, did any Federal excursion encounter resistance. On 12 May 1864, rumors reached the USS *Somerset* of a possible Confederate attack on the USS *Adela,* a blockader stationed outside Apalachicola. Boats were launched, and once on shore, Yankee sailors easily dispersed the crew of the CSS *Chattahoochee,* landlocked after a boiler explosion. Besides this attempt to capture a Union naval vessel, about the most warlike act undertaken by Confederate authorities was the incapacitation of the Cape Saint George and Cape San Blas lighthouses.

While the Confederates appreciated the futility of trying to stop the Federals at the shoreline, they certainly were not willing to concede the interior. With that in mind, in 1862 Confederate authorities stationed some infantry, cavalry, and four cannon at Fort Gadsden (about fifteen miles upriver from Apalachicola), a site first fortified by Great Britain during the War of 1812. In 1818 Andrew Jackson ordered Lt. James Gadsden, best known for the 1853 Gadsden Purchase that added territory in what is now Arizona and New Mexico, to erect a smaller fort on the same site. When Florida was ceded to the United States in 1821, Gadsden's fort was abandoned and not occupied again until Confederate troops manned the earthworks in 1862. They remained for just over a year. Malaria forced them away from the river in July 1863, apparently without anyone ever firing an angry shot.

Apalachee Bay, just south of Tallahassee and east of Apalachicola, however, brought out the fighting spirit on both sides much sooner. By the summer of 1861, Confederates had built a battery at the mouth of the Saint Marks River near the lighthouse. On the same spot in 1539, Hernando de Soto had tied banners to the trees to help guide ships to the river's mouth. Spaniards arriving later built a series of forts upriver at the junction of the Saint Marks and Wakulla rivers. In 1739, a permanent stone fort was begun but never finished despite, or perhaps because of, several battles in the area involving Spain, England, and the United States. In 1839 much of the stone from the fort was utilized by the U.S. government to build a marine hospital for victims of yellow fever. Confederates later used what remained of the old stone fort at the town of Saint Marks as a starting point on which to build earthworks.

Long before the fortifications were completed, the USS *Tahoma* and *Somerset* crossed the bar of the Saint Marks River. On 15 June 1862, the two warships shelled Fort William, the Confederate battery at the lighthouse, for forty minutes. The artillery company defending the position withdrew. The victorious sailors landed, destroyed the battery, and burned the barracks buildings.

Further patrols brought little action until February 1863 when the USS *Stars and Stripes* fired upon a Confederate camp on Long Bar, near Saint Marks. The Rebel steamer *Spray,* a former towboat armed with two guns, came downriver to investigate but quickly retreated to the protection of the batteries at Saint Marks when challenged by the *Stars and Stripes.*

Five months later, Lt. Comdr. Alexander Crossman, U.S.N., commenced an operation to capture the *Spray.* Under cover of darkness, Crossman led a force of 130 men in boats from the *Somerset* and *Stars and Stripes* into the Saint Marks River. His plan was to land above the earthworks, spike the guns, then make a dash for Newport farther up the river. Reports from Newport indicated that besides the *Spray,* he would find a large shipment of cotton being loaded aboard a schooner there. When Crossman's raiding party reached Port Leon below the town of Saint Marks, a Confederate picket called out. Crossman tried to convince the Rebel soldier that the accompanying boats belonged to fishermen, but as the Yankees moved closer, the guard fired, wounding a man in Crossman's boat. Fires on the shore immediately blazed higher and the batteries of the old fort at Saint Marks thundered. Without the element of surprise, Crossman decided that to continue upriver would be useless, so the Federals retreated to their ships.[24]

Crossman proposed another expedition up the Saint Marks to Acting Rear Adm. Theodorus Bailey, commander of the East Gulf Blockading Squadron, but was turned down. Then, early in 1864, Maj. Gen. Quincy A. Gillmore, commander of the Department of the South, proposed a campaign into Florida to strengthen the presidential bid of Secretary of the Treasury Salmon P. Chase. Gillmore planned to garrison the east Florida towns of Jacksonville, Baldwin, and Palatka "to see the lumber and turpentine trade on the Saint John's [sic] River revived by loyal men,"[25] men loyal to Chase, Gillmore hoped.

Unfortunately, the general in charge of the invasion, Truman A. Seymour, prematurely embarked on a march from Baldwin west along the Florida, Atlantic, and Gulf Railroad toward Florida's capital at Tallahassee. When the news of Seymour's advance reached Gillmore at his Beaufort, South Carolina, headquarters, he tried to stop the projected movement, but his orders arrived too late. Although Adm. David Farragut, commander of the West Gulf Blockading Squadron, was willing to send fifteen hundred men with the necessary transport and escorts to Saint Marks to create a diversion for Seymour's attack, the information reached Admiral Bailey "so late that it would have been to no avail."[26] As Gillmore predicted, without "coastal demonstrations"[27] to contend with, Confederate Brig. Gen. Joseph Finegan, commander of the District of East Florida, was able to defeat Seymour at Olustee, Florida, the largest land battle in Florida during the Civil War.

The year following Seymour's failed invasion of the Florida panhandle, crew members from the *Tahoma* rowed ashore on two occasions near Saint Marks to destroy saltworks. Other than that, little happened until March 1865 when a combined U.S. Army-Navy operation commenced. Its goal was to capture the fort at Saint Marks and eventually occupy Tallahassee. Early that month, sixteen ships anchored off the Saint Marks River lighthouse. Retreating Confederates mined the structure before approximately a thousand Federals came ashore. On 3 March, some three hundred Union seamen surprised Confederate pickets and seized the East River bridge four miles north of the lighthouse. Shallow water kept the Union warships from approaching the Confederate batteries at the old Spanish fort, so after crossing the East River, Union Brig. Gen. John Newton pressed forward his soldiers and sailors in an attempt to find a place to cross the Saint Marks River farther upstream. The Fifth Florida Cavalry blocked the Newport bridge, so Newton left a small diversionary force there and continued up the east bank of the Saint Marks toward Natural Bridge. Confederate Gen. William Miller, anticipating the move, sent forces under Lt. Col. George Scott to defend the area.

From the foggy hours before dawn on 6 March until mid-afternoon, some five hundred to seven hundred Confederates, including boys and old men from nearby Woodville, held off a similar number of Union troops along the narrow natural bridge from behind previously constructed breastworks. The third-largest land confrontation during the Civil War in Florida, the battle of Natural Bridge left twenty-one dead Yankees and three dead Rebels on the field.[28] By sundown the next day, the Union forces had returned to the protection of the fleet.

Newton's complaints that he had not been supported in his movements were true, but it was not just the grounded Federal warships that had hurt his chances. Almost four hundred Federal soldiers at Cedar Key had also been ordered to reinforce Newton's attack on Tallahassee, but they did not accomplish their mission either.

Cedar Key, although remote, served as the gulf terminus of Florida's first coast-to-coast railroad, which originated in Fernandina. The railroad was built by David Yulee, the state's first U.S. senator. The inaugural train did not pull into Cedar Key until March 1861. Within a short time, Federal blockade ships were on station, and Yulee "became heavily involved in the enterprise of blockade running."[29] In the fall of 1862, crews from the busy *Somerset* and *Tahoma* destroyed Confederate saltworks in the vicinity, and by the end of the year Federal troops occupied the town.

Not much happened until 8 February 1865 when Union Maj. Edmund C. Weeks led his command from the mainland near Cedar Key up the east bank of the Suwannee River. Five days later, Confederate irregulars commanded by Capt. John Dickison and augmented by local militia attacked Weeks's four hundred men. In a running fight, the Confederates pushed Weeks all the way back to the gulf. By the time Weeks reached his base, Newton's push on Tallahassee had failed.

Between Cedar Key and Tampa Bay, a favorite stop for blockade runners in the later part of the war, was Bayport. In early April 1863 an armed-boat expedition of U.S. sailors and marines engaged and forced the evacuation of a Confederate battery defending the port. The crews of several blockade runners in the area drove their ships aground to avoid being sunk and set fire to a schooner loaded with cotton to prevent its capture. The Federals also destroyed a sloop carrying a cargo of corn. When Rebels brought up a rifled cannon, the attackers retired out of range.

During the following months, several blockade runners — including three flying British colors — were captured off Bayport. The area's continued use as a haven for Rebel ships prompted another Federal raid in July 1864. This time the Yankees managed to capture some cotton as well as burn the town's custom house. Nevertheless, once the Federals retired, it was business as usual at Bayport. As late as February 1865, the USS *Mahaska* seized the schooner *Delia* off Bayport with a cargo of pig lead and sabers.

Although open ports were good as gold for the Confederacy, another treasure also existed along Florida's Gulf Coast: salt. Essential in the all-important preservation of food, salt also retarded the spoilage of hides bound for tanneries where they would become leather harnesses and shoes. For these purposes, Southern states needed six million bushels of salt a year.[30] To meet this demand, early in the war the Confederate government turned to Florida. Particularly suited to this soon-to-be-booming wartime industry was Florida's "wild and almost uninhabited Gulf Coast, from Choctawhatchee Bay south to Tampa,"[31] where anyone who owned a kettle and was able to stoke a fire could produce salt. Perhaps fortuitously for salt makers, a three-year drought in the region had also increased the brine content of the already abnormally high saline concentration in the area's marshes.

Eventually the salt industry in and around Tampa became too important for Northerners to ignore. In a series of naval raids the last two months of 1863, Federal troops destroyed five hundred saltworks, "wreaking such havoc that the Union officer in command exultantly proclaimed that it was a greater blow to the Southern cause than the fall of Charleston."[32]

Late the next spring, three Union ships returned to Tampa, offloaded army troops supported by a naval landing party, and captured the town in three days, taking forty prisoners. Salt production continued in the area, however, and during the month of July 1864, separate naval raids destroyed two large salt-making operations near Tampa Bay. On 12 November, a combined-forces operation in the same vicinity as the earlier sorties was turned back by Rebel cavalry. Three weeks later, a larger Federal force succeeded in capturing the saltworks.

Because of the ease with which destroyed salt operations could be brought back into business, the South's leaders had confidently assumed that it would be impossible for the North to crush salt production completely. Only a few feeble efforts were made in Florida to protect the manufacture of salt. Consequently, a mere handful of Federal raiders were able to cause the loss of millions of dollars of salt and manufacturing equipment. Even though the salt industry continued to operate along Florida's coast throughout the war, the rise in the price of salt from seventy-five cents a bushel in 1861 to forty-five dollars a bushel for black-market salt during the last weeks of April 1865 provides some proof that the North belatedly won this round of ship-versus-shore confrontations.

If you go there . . .

Fort Gadsden State Historic Site lies on the southwest corner of the Apalachicola National Forest off State Highway 65. Possibly it's the highest spot along the Apalachicola River for miles in either direction, but the middle of the old British fort was one big puddle the day I visited. The fairly well-preserved earthen ramparts of the smaller Fort Gadsden still edge right up to the riverbank. Since the battery was already built, I can understand why Confederates chose to emplace cannon there. But after a short visit, I could also appreciate why they left.

The seventy-eight-acre park contains a picnic area and playground. An interpretive trail winds through the vestiges of the two forts to an old cemetery, and a boat landing makes traveling to the park by water very convenient. Also of interest is an interpretive kiosk containing a nice model of the original British fort and some information on the site's role during the Civil War.

The park is open free of charge from 8:00 A.M. until sundown daily. For more information, contact: Fort Gadsden State Historic Site, P.O. Box 157, Sumatra, FL 32334 (904) 670-8988.

San Marcos de Apalache State Historic Site includes some rock walls left over from the old Spanish fort, a huge mound of earth that once protected the Confederate magazine of what Federal reports mistakenly called Fort Ward,[33] a military cemetery, and lots of trees. The visitors center, built on the foundation of the old marine hospital, has a picture of the lighthouse battery called Fort William and a drawing of the Confederate batteries at the old Spanish fort. No actual photographs seem to have been taken nor any contemporary drawings made of the Confederate fort at Saint Marks.

The Federal advance on Tallahassee was turned back at Natural Bridge

The historic site is open, Thursday through Monday, from 9:00 A.M.–5:00 P.M. except Thanksgiving, Christmas, and New Year's Day. For more information, contact: San Marcos de Apalache State Historic Site, P.O. Box 27, Saint Marks, FL 32355 (904) 925-6216.

Visitors may also walk around the grounds of the **Saint Marks Lighthouse,** part of the Saint Marks National Wildlife Refuge, the site of Confederate Fort Williams. Take Route 59 off U.S. 98 at Newport.

The spot marked "Natural Bridge" at the **Natural Bridge Battlefield State Historic Site** is now a manufactured bridge because the county dug a channel through the 150-foot cavern to keep the road from being flooded during high water. The battle site consists of a monument, two markers, a parking lot, and a picnic area. Reproduction log-breastworks in the park are used by reenactors on the Sunday nearest March 6 each year. The site is open at 8:00 A.M. and closes at sunset year-round. For information, contact: Florida Department of Natural Resources, Marjory Stoneman Douglas Building, 3900 Commonwealth Blvd., Tallahassee, FL 32399.

Cedar Key, a small, isolated community linked by a single bridge to the mainland, has two historical museums. Two cannon on the front lawn of **Cedar Key State Museum** may have come from a Confederate battery on Sea Horse Key. The strongpoint was built to protect the harbor and railroad. The museum also has a small diorama of the engagement between the troops of Dickison and Weeks, and an interesting exhibit on the Civil War. Closed on Tuesdays and Wednesdays, the museum is open the rest of the week from 9:00 A.M.–5:00 P.M. The cost is $1.00. To get there, follow the signs from State Road 24. You will think you are lost, but you won't be. For information, contact: Cedar Key State Museum, P.O. Box 538, Cedar Key, FL 32625 (904) 543-5350.

On the edge of downtown Cedar Key stands the **Cedar Key Historical Society Museum.** Although closed when I was there, the museum reportedly has some displays pertaining to the Civil War. It is open, Monday through Saturday, from 11:00 A.M.–4:00 P.M. and Sunday from 1:00–4:00 P.M. at a cost of $1.00. For information, contact: Cedar Key Historical Society, Second Street at State Road 24, P.O. Box 222, Cedar Key, FL 32625.

According to a park officer at **Fort DeSoto Park** on Mullet Key near the mouth of Tampa Bay, a parking lot covers the site of Fort Brooke, the focus of several ship-versus-shore engagements at Tampa. Although a lieutenant colonel by the name of Robert E. Lee visited Mullet Key in February 1849 and recommended a fort be erected there, no coastal defenses had been started by the time the Civil War erupted. However, Federal forces occupied Mullet and Egmont keys, the latter being the site of the lighthouse rebuilt in 1858 and still active today.

The present concrete-and-earth battery on Mullet Key was constructed during the Spanish-American War to protect eight 12-inch mortars, half of which are still in place. Two 6-inch rapid-fire rifles from Egmont Key are also displayed at Fort DeSoto.

The present battery at Fort DeSoto was constructed during the Spanish-American War

Gamble Plantation, refuge of Judah P. Benjamin in May 1865

The park also offers swimming beaches with showers, fishing piers, picnic areas, campgrounds, and a boat-launching ramp. There is no charge to enter the park, but you have to travel there by way of two toll bridges.

Near Tampa, **Gamble Plantation** is the only surviving antebellum plantation house left in south Florida. It was purchased by the United Daughters of the Confederacy as a memorial to Confederate Secretary of State Judah P. Benjamin. During his May 1865 escape from Richmond, Benjamin hid at the mansion, which at that time was owned by Archibald McNeil, the Confederacy's deputy commissary for the Manatee District.

The site, which includes an interpretive center, is open from 8:00 A.M. until sunset every day, but tours of the house are only given Thursday through Monday at various times from 9:30 A.M. until 4:00 P.M. During the third weekend in March, demonstrations of sugar-cane processing are conducted on the property.

For further information, contact: Gamble Plantation State Historic Site, 3708 Patten Avenue, Ellenton, FL 34222 (813) 723-4536.

Key West

KEY WEST started life as a swampy, almost uninhabitable high spot at the end of the Florida keys. Only brigands lived there until 1822 when Com. Matthew Perry drove them out. What had attracted the pirates was one of the largest deep-water anchorages in the country. Soon after Perry planted the U.S. flag, many vessels sought refuge in the waters west of the island. "Wreckers," men who legally salvaged cargo from unattended ships stranded on the many reefs surrounding the Florida keys, continued to practice another form of plunder off the small island. According to local lore, some wreckers disabled the Key West lighthouse to improve their already lucrative business. So much money was made wrecking that Key West became the largest city in Florida for a time and certainly the richest in the state.

With its impressive natural harbor situated on the border of the Atlantic Ocean and the Gulf of Mexico, Key West soon came to the attention of Joseph G. Totten, a graduate of the first class at West Point in 1806. Along with French engineer Simon Bernard, Totten helped lay out plans for a series of fifty or so forts from Maine to California. When Bernard returned to France in 1831, Totten completed the design work on the two major works guarding the Key West anchorage. In 1836, he persuaded Congress to appropriate $3 million "to insure the protection of the [Florida] Straits and . . . deny their harbors to enemy vessels."[34] In 1844, Capt. J. G. Barnard, assistant to Totten and later designer of the ring of Civil War fortifications around Washington, D.C., made arrangements to acquire the land for the first fortress protecting Key West Harbor. Construction began the following year.

Hurricanes, yellow fever, labor shortages, racial problems, and the isolation of the position guaranteed that work on the fort at Key West proceeded at a turtle's pace. Two years later, sixty-eight miles into the gulf on Garden Key in the Dry Tortugas chain, Lt. Horatio G. Wright, U.S. Army, laid out the lines of the most ambitious of all Bernard and Totten's designs, a hexagonal monstrosity designed to hold 450 guns. Using windmills and steam-powered pumps, Wright drained areas enclosed by cofferdams to construct the fourteen-foot-wide, two-foot-thick foundations for the walls. It was one of the first big sub-marine construction jobs ever attempted by the U.S. Engineer Corps.

In 1850, the first two forts received names. The one on Key West island was called Fort Taylor after Zachary Taylor, who had just died of typhus while serving as president of the United States. His son-in-law Jefferson Davis held the chairmanship of the Senate Military Affairs Committee. Fort Jefferson was named after the nation's third president.

One of the first warlike acts committed by the U.S. Navy during the early days of the secession crisis occurred in the waters surrounding Key West. On 15 November 1860, Lt. Thomas A. Craven, commander of the U.S. naval forces at Key West, notified Secretary of the Navy Isaac Toucey that he was defending Fort Jefferson from the decks of the USS *Mohawk* and had ordered the USS *Wyandotte* to protect Fort Taylor, which sat a distance offshore, from "any bands of lawless men" among Key West's inhabitants.[35]

The night before Florida seceded from the Union, U.S. Army Capt. John Brannan attended church services, then led his forty-five men through the center of town into Fort Taylor, effectively keeping it out of

Fort Taylor, Key West *(Leslie's)*

Southern hands.[36] For the most part, islanders chose to ignore Brannan's action, preferring instead to fight the war in their drawing rooms by arguing with high-ranking Yankees over shipwrecked brandy. Besides, as early as April 1855, 8-inch smoothbores had been emplaced in Taylor's casemates, more than a match for anything the locals could bring to bear. Eventually 800 troops and 198 cannons convinced everyone, particularly the weak Confederate navy, that trying to capture Key West or its harbor would be foolish.

By June 1861 the USS *Mississippi* took up blockade duty at Key West and within a week captured a schooner, the first of many ships seized by naval forces stationed at Key West. In early 1862, the still unfinished Fort Taylor, along with Key West Harbor, became headquarters for a brief time of the East Gulf Blockading Squadron under the command of Flag Off. David Farragut. The hero of New Orleans would return to Key West in 1864, this time on his way to greater glory at Mobile Bay.

The deadliest enemy at Key West, as at many other locations during the Civil War, proved to be disease. In July 1864 a yellow fever outbreak almost crippled the Federal squadron stationed there, according to Adm. Theodorus Bailey.[37]

Despite the lack of military threat, eventually Dutton's request for a ring of protective bastions around Key West gained approval, but only two were begun. These were known as Martello towers, the circular-shaped defensive structures erected in Europe from which guards would warn residents of attack by ringing bells with a hammer or *martello*. Both East and West Martello were intended to be simple towers protecting the landward approaches to Fort Taylor, but plans were expanded to include two-tiered casemated batteries facing the sea. Laborers did not begin work on East Martello until the spring of 1862. Progress continued sporadically through yellow fever outbreaks and fiscal restraint until 1873, when construction halted on the last Martello tower to be built in the world.[38] West Martello was begun in 1863 and abandoned three years later.

Work on Fort Jefferson's eight-foot-thick, three-quarter-mile ring of brick was only partially completed when the Civil War began. Engineers, who thought the foundations rested upon solid coral reef, had actually placed the fort on sand and coral boulders washed up by the gulf. The huge pile of 16 million imported bricks started sinking and cracking almost immediately. Only a fraction of the guns for which the fort was intended could possibly be mounted. To Capt. Montgomery Meigs and his thirty men guarding the fort, questions of load and stress were entirely academic. By the election of 1860, there were still no cannon in the fort.

On 18 January the news arrived at Fort Jefferson that Florida had seceded. Meigs ordered a fishing smack to race to Key West for cannon. The next day, a large steamer flying no colors anchored off the reef and a small boat entered the harbor. Much to Meigs's relief, the rowboat carried Union Maj. L. G. Arnold. He had brought sixty-six artillerymen and some cannon from Boston.[39] Three days later a fully armed Rebel schooner arrived at Garden Key. A messenger from the ship approached the drawbridge and demanded that Arnold surrender.

"Tell your captain I will blow his ship out of the water if he is not gone in ten minutes," Arnold shouted from an empty embrasure. As a parting shot, he added: "I think I will open fire anyway as soon as you get back on board."[40]

A good scare was about the best the Union major could accomplish. He and his men were still mounting the fort's first cannon. Arnold proved to have a good poker face. The Confederates sailed away, never to threaten the isolated position again. Without a navy to support the barren outpost, it is doubtful the Confederates could have held Fort Jefferson for very long. But had Rebel forces managed to capture the forts on Key West and Fort Jefferson, communication with Fort Pickens in Pensacola would have been critically affected and the history of the Civil War in the Gulf of Mexico drastically changed. As it was, by the time Fort Sumter was fired upon, sixty-eight guns had arrived at Fort Jefferson. Although many of the cannon were not ready for service, their presence ensured a safe Federal supply line to any coastal area on the gulf.

Fort Jefferson *(Harper's)*

The most interesting events related to Key West's forts and their role in the Civil War happened *after* the war. In June 1865, Dr. Samuel Mudd arrived at Fort Jefferson. He was the man who had set John Wilkes Booth's broken ankle and given his name to the saying, "Your name is Mudd." Now he was a prisoner serving a life term after being found guilty of conspiracy in the assassination of Lincoln. In 1959 a joint resolution of Congress signed by President Dwight Eisenhower authorized a bronze tablet to be hung at Fort Jefferson honoring the doctor-prisoner for his work in a yellow fever epidemic that swept the prison in 1867.

If you go there . . .

Getting to the Dry Tortugas, so-called because there is no fresh water available, is easy — if you have the money. Chartered planes and boats *start* at around $100 per person. For that reason, **Dry Tortugas National Park** is one of the country's least used national park sites, attracting only twenty-five thousand visitors in 1988, the year renovation began to strengthen some of the fort's 16 million bricks, many of which are crumbling into dust. Of the ten park rangers assigned to Fort Jefferson, some are brick masons. Still, for history buffs, Fort Jefferson is well worth the extra effort required for a visit.

In May 1991 the royal yacht *Brittania* anchored off Garden Key while Queen Elizabeth II and Prince Philip enjoyed a picnic and toured Fort Jefferson. One of their countrymen, George St. Leger Grenfel, was sentenced to life on Garden Key in the summer of 1866 for conspiring to free Confederates in Northern prisons during the Civil War. During the yellow fever epidemic of 1867, Grenfel offered to assist Dr. Mudd. For three deadly months he nursed the critically ill. When his lawyer's plea for a commutation of his sentence based on these humanitarian deeds was denied, Grenfel and three other prisoners, one with a thirty-pound ball bolted to his leg, made plans to escape. Unfortunately, they chose to flee in a stolen fishing boat on the night of one of the worst storms ever to hit the area. No one heard from them again.

The park is in an area of great natural beauty and offers a shaded picnic area, a secluded beach, and a drinking fountain, but no food or other beverages are available for sale. If you don't have your own vessel like the queen, you can travel to the fort on a chartered boat. But flying offers the most impressive angles for picture taking. A plane ride also allows a good view of marine life in the shallows between Key West and the fort. Key West Seaplane Service, 5603 W. Jr. College Road, Key West, FL 33040 (305) 294-6978, offers half-day trips with free snorkel gear for $139 per person.

An aerial view of Fort Jefferson

Shark fishing, one of the only breaks in monotony for garrison troops, is still good around the Tortugas, but the biggest natural attraction is the excellent bird watching from March to September. Camping is permitted on Garden Key, and there are limited docking facilities, but if you plan to arrive in your own boat, you should contact the Superintendent of Everglades National Park, Box 279, Homestead, FL 33030.

Fort Zachary Taylor State Historic Site barely rises out of the surrounding sand at the end of Southard Street in Key West. Just a stub of its former self, the fort bears little resemblance to its original design. During modernization in 1898, its height was reduced by the removal of its top tier of casemates. Obsolete cannon and sand were thrown between the walls on the seaward side of the fort, then concrete batteries were added.

Those additions dominate the fort today: emplacements for a two-gun battery of heavy 12-inch rifles facing south and four 3-inch rapid-fire rifles facing west to defend Key West Harbor against enemy torpedo boats. Soldiers manned both batteries through World War I, after which the 3-inch guns were removed. The 12-inch guns were dismounted in 1942 and sent to England, but just in case, antiaircraft guns were situated on the west wall. Fill from the nearby submarine basin was dumped around the fort, so that even though it was completely surrounded by water when first built, the fort is now entirely landlocked. As late as the Cuban missile crisis of 1962, Fort Taylor was ready to defend America's shores, this time with four missile batteries and radar.

An aerial view of Fort Taylor, c. 1930s *(Fort Taylor Historic Site)*

Efforts to renovate Fort Taylor, at least partially to its Civil War configuration, were begun in 1968 when workers discovered the richest store of Civil War guns and ammunition on any post in the United States. The fort was named a national historic landmark in 1973. Recent work on a water-filled moat to surround the fort revealed more artifacts, and much of what has been recovered is on display around the grounds or in the fort's museum, which houses a large cross-section model of the original fort. Tours of the fort are given daily at 2:00 P.M.

Although the park, which opens at 8:00 A.M., closes at sundown, Fort Taylor is an ideal spot to watch the sun slip below the edge of the gulf if you want to get away from the crowds at Mallory Square. The site also includes a beach with barbecue grills, picnic tables, fresh-water showers, and changing rooms. The cost to enter the park is $3.25 for a car with a surcharge of $.50 per person. You do not need a car on Key West, so save $2.25 by riding a bike. For information, contact: Fort Zachary Taylor State Historic Site, P.O. Box 289, Key West, FL 33040 (305) 292-6713.

As at Fort Taylor, batteries were emplaced at West Martello, situated just west of White Street on Atlantic Boulevard, after the start of the Spanish-American War. As the years passed, bored gunners from Fort Taylor used West Martello for target practice, which explains the dilapidated condition of the walls facing Fort Taylor. Only the construction of railroad magnate Henry Flagler's Casa Marina Hotel in 1920, which stood in the pathway of the shells, and the efforts of County Commissioner Joe Allen saved the fort from complete destruction. In the early 1950s Allen convinced the county to let him create a garden center at West Martello.

The Key West Garden Club took up where Allen left off, and today **West Martello Tower Joe Allen Garden Center** is listed on the National Register of Historic Places. For a voluntary donation, visitors can stroll through the lush gardens in the parts of the old fort left standing. The club also provides classes in horticulture and holds special exhibits. The garden gates are opened at 10:00 A.M., Wednesday through Sunday. The last entry is at 3:30 P.M. For information, write: West Martello Tower Garden Center, Atlantic Boulevard, Key West, FL 33040.

Like its western counterpart, East Martello was employed for defensive purposes during the Spanish-American War and both world wars. It also served a stint as a cattle pen. But unlike its neighbor to the west, East Martello remains fairly intact today.

The Key West Art and Historical Society acquired the property in 1950 and created a museum and art gallery. The **East Martello Museum** now offers exhibits from Key West's past and displays concerning the town's more prominent writers and artists, including Ernest Hemingway and Tennessee Williams. For a $3.00 entrance fee, visitors can contemplate the art and historical displays in the casemates, climb the central tower to get a view of the nearby airport, and browse through the gift shop daily except Christmas. The museum opens at 9:30 A.M. The last entry is at 4:15 P.M. For information, contact: East Martello Museum, 3501 South Roosevelt Boulevard, Key West, FL 33040 (305) 296-3913.

One last site with some Civil War connections in Key West is the **Key West Lighthouse Museum.** Situated across the street from the island's most popular attraction, the Ernest Hemingway home, the lighthouse was built in 1847. The light keeper's quarters house the museum's collection of artifacts, including the sword lost by Maj. Gen. George Gordon Meade during the battle at Fredericksburg. Meade, who went on to command Union forces at Gettysburg, was a topographical engineer before the Civil War and designed screw-pile lighthouses for the Florida Keys.

The museum is open daily from 9:30 A.M.–5:00 P.M. The cost is $4.00 for adults and $1.00 for children six to twelve. For information, contact: Key West Lighthouse Museum, 938 Whitehead Street, Key West, FL 33040 (305) 294-0012.

Fernandina, Saint Augustine, and Jacksonville

WHEN THE UNION navy sought a coaling station on the South Atlantic in late 1861, one of the points under consideration was Fernandina, a town of two thousand on Amelia Island, Florida. The city served as the eastern terminus of the Cedar Keys Railroad, a line running westward across the peninsula to the Gulf of Mexico. For this reason, Union Secretary of the Navy Welles called Fernandina "probably the most important port to close up on the eastern coast of Florida."[41]

On the last day of February 1862, Flag Off. Samuel Francis du Pont cleared Port Royal, South Carolina, with his flotilla and turned south toward Florida. The previous week, Robert E. Lee had ordered Fernandina's fifteen-hundred-man garrison to pull back with as many of its heavy guns as possible. When a telegram arrived at Fernandina on 2 March from Brunswick, Georgia, reporting a fleet of twenty-four Federal ships at Saint Andrew's Inlet, just north of the Florida border, the Confederates hastily completed arrangements for their withdrawal from the port at Fernandina. They fled inland with eighteen of thirty-three guns from batteries protecting the various approaches to the city.[42] When du Pont heard that the enemy had abandoned the forts protecting the sea entrance to Fernandina, he decided to send the lighter-draft vessels under Comdr. Percival Drayton down Cumberland Sound toward Fernandina's back door while he took the heavier vessels to the main ship entrance. By the next morning, Drayton and his armed launches had navigated the shallow waters of the sound all the way to Fort Clinch, the strongest defensive position on the main shipping channel. As reported, the great brick fortress sat empty.

An officer was dispatched to raise the American flag to signal du Pont, who was waiting on the other side of the bar. The moment was historic. Fort Clinch was the first of the national properties seized by the Confederacy to be retaken by the Federals.

Continuing toward the town of Fernandina in their armed boats, Drayton's men engaged in one of the most unusual ship-versus-shore confrontations of the war. A train loaded with the last of the retreating Confederates was just leaving the station. The tracks ran for a distance along the Amelia River, so Yankees from their launches and Rebels on the train exchanged shots during a two-mile running fight. Finally the two locomotives and their cars successfully escaped.

The weather finally moderated on 4 March, allowing du Pont to cross the bar on board the *Mohican*. He and the other officers expressed surprise that the formidable defenses of Fernandina had been abandoned without a fight. Our "forces had captured Port Royal," he reported, "but the enemy had given us Fernandina."[43] Du Pont's statements were partly theatrical. Soldiers at Fort Clinch "possessed only four guns, all lacking ammunition."[44] Furthermore, most of the Confederate batteries, including Fort Clinch, protected the sea entrance. Once the Federals established themselves inside the bar of Cumberland Sound, the Fernandina defenses were outflanked. Even if the defenders had not already been retreating, any ap-

Fort Marion (*Castillo de San Marcos*), the parade ground in front of the chapel door (*National Archives*)

proach to the city from the sound would have put the Rebels in an untenable position.

Brig. Gen. H. G. Wright and his brigade entered the harbor on 5 March. Flag Officer du Pont immediately turned over responsibility for the forts and public property to him so he could continue his expedition down the Florida coast. By the evening of 8 March, the *Wabash*, a heavily armed screw frigate now serving as flagship, anchored off Saint Augustine. As soon as he realized no armed resistance was forthcoming, du Pont dispatched several gunboats to the Saint Johns River, forty miles north, to cross the bar when the tides permitted. Du Pont and the *Wabash* remained behind at Saint Augustine until a boat could be sent ashore. When the seas finally cooperated, Commander Rodgers approached the city under a flag of truce. At his appearance, a white flag rose over Fort Marion, the old Spanish castillo (fort) that contained three 32-pounders and two 8-inch howitzers. The mayor of the city met Rodgers at the wharf and led him to the town hall. City officials informed him that the two companies of Florida troops who had garrisoned the area had moved out the previous night.

Fort Marion, named after the Revolutionary War Swamp Fox, had originally been seized by secessionists on 7 January 1861. Immediately,

Florida troops removed some of the cannon and sent them to Fernandina and other points around the state. Most of the town's young men in gray eventually followed suit. By November 1861, Robert E. Lee declared, "The small force posted at Saint Augustine serves only as an invitation to attack."[45]

The few men remaining in Saint Augustine after the Confederates abandoned the port indicated their willingness to submit to Federal authority, according to Rodgers, but he added there "is much violent and pestilent feeling among the women. They seem to mistake treason for courage, and have a desire to figure as heroines."[46] Local ladies chopped down the town's flagpole so that the Stars and Stripes could not be raised, and a woman "marched up to [Rodgers] and declared that 'the men had behaved like cowards, but there were stout hearts in other bosoms (striking her own).'"[47]

Ten days after the first Union troops arrived, Lt. J. W. A. Nicholson, commanding officer of the *Isaac Smith*, brought his ship into Saint Augustine's harbor and saw to it that an 8-inch gun was mounted on the ramparts of Fort Marion to command the main road into the city. After overseeing arrangements for these somewhat meager defenses, du Pont steamed north in his flagship to the Saint Johns River. The sailors he had dispatched previously had sounded the bar and placed marker buoys, but a rough sea prevented all but a small side-wheel steamer, the *Ellen*, and two of the flagship's armed launches from entering the river. The earthworks guarding the entrance at Talbot Island north of the river and Fort Steele south of the river at Mayport Mills had been deserted, so the crews raised the Stars and Stripes over the lighthouse at the latter point. On 10 March three more gunboats crossed the bar, each warship carrying a company of the Fourth New Hampshire.

Du Pont, aboard the *Wabash*, next proceeded to Mosquito Inlet, fifty-one miles south of Saint Augustine, to join two gunboats sent to protect a shipment of live oak. Confederate defenders managed to kill or capture seven crewmen sent ashore near an abandoned earthwork. The remainder of the raiders escaped from the inlet under cover of darkness to the Federal vessels waiting offshore.

The occupation of Jacksonville on the Saint Johns River went much more smoothly. On the night of 11 March, retreating Confederates "burned a nearly completed warship, seven sawmills, four million board feet of lumber, two iron foundries and the railroad depot."[48] The next day at noon, Union troops landed at Jacksonville without incident, captured two pieces of heavy ordnance on the wharf, and picketed the town. Having accomplished his mission in Florida, du Pont returned to Port Royal. In Washington, Secretary of State William H. Seward declared, "One half of the coast of South Carolina, the whole coast of Georgia, and the harbors, cities and coasts of

East Florida, are occupied. . . . There is scarce a harbor on the whole coast . . . which is not hermetically sealed."[49]

On 24 March, Wright assumed command in Jacksonville. Local unionists organized themselves to create a loyal state government, but the day before the 10 April convention, Federal troops evacuated the city and returned to Fernandina. Union gunboats continued to patrol the Saint Johns, however, so Brig. Gen. Joseph Finegan, the Confederate commander in East Florida, ordered batteries to be constructed at both Yellow Bluff, where sharpshooters had been harassing Union boats since April, and Saint Johns Bluff. By the second week in September the Saint Johns Bluff battery was regularly exchanging iron greetings with patrols from the Union fleet.

On the last day of September four transports disembarked Union troops at Mayport Mills under orders to capture the troublesome battery six miles upriver. Lt. Col. C. F. Hopkins, the Confederate commander at Saint Johns Bluff, requested reinforcements from Capt. Joseph L. Dunham at Yellow Bluff, five miles farther upriver. Dunham ferried over three companies of dismounted cavalry on 1 October as six Union gunboats began to pound the earthworks. Despite the reinforcements, the next night Hopkins pulled his five hundred men out of the fortifications, and by 3 October Union forces reoccupied Jacksonville. After four days, the boys in blue returned to Hilton Head, South Carolina, and the boys in gray marched back in.

Even though it served as the primary Confederate defensive position between Jacksonville and the Atlantic, Yellow Bluff never managed to become as powerful a bastion as the Rebels hoped. After mid-October 1862, when guns from the steamer USS *Uncas* "devastated" the fort, very little appears in official records concerning activity there.[50] In fact, on 10 March 1863 when transports carried fourteen hundred black troopers to Jacksonville, they met no opposition. With the presence of such a large group of freed slaves, General Finegan feared a general slave uprising in Florida, so he attacked the town on 25 March with an 8-inch rifled cannon mounted on a flat car. "Seven rounds were fired before a Federal gunboat returned the fire and the Confederates withdrew."[51] The Federals mounted their own 4-inch gun on a handcar and chased the retreating Rebels west on the rails. When the pursuers pumped out of range of their supporting gunboats, the Confederates reappeared and forced them to retreat. Following another four-day stay, these Union raiders also departed Jacksonville, leaving behind a smoldering ruin of a city.

In February 1864, Union soldiers returned to Jacksonville. Although defeated at Olustee later that month, the Federals could not be coerced out of Jacksonville, which they heavily fortified and occupied the remainder of the war. A chain of breastworks supported by seven batteries protected twelve thousand hurried reinforcements. In addition, Union gunboats continued to patrol the Saint Johns. The former Confederate earthworks along the river at Yellow Bluff and Saint Johns Bluff served as signal stations.

If you go there . . .

Fort Clinch, named after Gen. Duncan Clinch of Seminole War fame, is operated as a living-history program. Park rangers dressed as Union soldiers cook meals, maintain the fort, and perform sentry duty as though the year is 1864.

Whether or not you're fond of living history, the Fernandina area and especially Fort Clinch State Park deserve more attention among Civil War enthusiasts than they have previously enjoyed. Although the fort was garrisoned during the Spanish-American War, it was not bastardized with intrusive, architecturally sterile concrete batteries like so many of the other third-system forts. Furthermore, because fighting bypassed the fort, one of its barracks actually has survived and has been restored to reflect the Civil War era. Best of all, more cannon have been emplaced *en barbette* on carriages here than at any other Civil War fort I have seen.

The 1,086-acre park also offers a swimming beach with bathhouse, picnic area, nature trail, and fishing areas. All this fun comes at a price. Up to eight people in a car can enter the park for $3.25. It costs another $1.00 per person to see the fort. The park is open year-round from 8:00 A.M. until sunset. The fort and its interpretive center/gift shop are open daily from 9:00 A.M.–5:00 P.M. For information, contact: Fort Clinch State Park, 2601 Atlantic Ave., Fernandina Beach, FL 32034 (904) 261-4212.

An aerial view of Fort Clinch *(Fort Clinch State Park)*

Fort Clinch, the western bastion

On the drive back toward Fernandina Beach along Atlantic Avenue you will pass the **Amelia Island Lighthouse.** Built in 1839, the lighthouse has changed very little in the intervening years. Now fully automated, it is not open to the public.

The town of Fernandina Beach can claim a tastefully restored Centre Street, which runs down to the old railroad line along the docks. Still standing in town are many pre–Civil War buildings, including the **First Presbyterian Church** on North Sixth Street a half-block north of Centre. Completed in 1859, the church was used to garrison Federal troops. Some Yankees considered using the church's tower bell to make armaments, but Maj. William B. C. Duryee interceded. After the war, he also made sure the building was returned to its congregation.

Yellow Bluff Fort, situated on a ninety-foot bluff along the Saint Johns River downstream from Jacksonville, is a little hard to find and barely worth the effort. Perhaps the most interesting thing about the fort is that a sign there claims it was designed by Robert E. Lee, but even that is questionable.[52] Because the earthwork resembles little more than a pile of dirt, it's difficult to get an idea of more than just its general T-shape. The park, a half-mile east of the new Highway 9A bridge on New Berlin Road, has a few picnic tables and is open from 8:00 A.M. to sunset.

At various times several monuments and markers relating to the Civil War were spread throughout Jacksonville, but try as I might, I could not find any of them. However, a propitious stop at the Jacksonville Landing, a shopping and entertainment complex right along the Saint Johns River in downtown Jacksonville, led me to a wonderful discovery. The landing is the temporary home of the **Jacksonville Maritime Museum.** Besides

The Olustee Battlefield. Lacking naval support, Federal forces were thwarted here from advancing on Tallahassee.

many nice ship models, the museum is the repository for artifacts from two Union ships sunk in the river.

The *Columbine,* a steam side-wheel tug armed with two 20-pounder Parrott rifles, was captured by Dickison's men 23 May 1864 at Horse Landing, three miles north of Walaka, Florida. Part of the haul from the Union gunboat included a 12-pound case shot fired by Dickison's troops into the tug. Other artifacts on display come from the four-hundred-ton cargo ship *Maple Leaf,* one of three ships sunk by mines in the Saint Johns in the spring of 1864.

The museum is open from 11:00 A.M.–7:00 P.M. free of charge. For information about the museum or how to join the nonprofit Maritime Museum Society, contact: Jacksonville Maritime Museum Society, 1504 Jessie Street, Jacksonville, FL 32206-6042 (904) 633-9469.

About a fifty-minute drive west from downtown Jacksonville along U.S. 90 lies **Olustee Battlefield State Historic Site,** site of the largest land battle during the Civil War in Florida. Union Gen. Truman Seymour led his expeditionary force out of Jacksonville toward Tallahassee, and although his black regiments, including the Fifty-fourth Massachusetts (which was the last Northern regiment to leave the field), fought well, within two days he was leading his men back into Jacksonville.

The historic site is open, Thursday through Monday, from 9:00 A.M. to 5:00 P.M., except for holidays from November through April. There is an interpretive center with several displays relating to the battle and a marked trail that runs along the battle lines through swampy terrain. The battle is reenacted each February. For information, contact: Olustee Battlefield State Historic Site, P.O. Box 40, Olustee, FL 32072 (904) 752-3866.

An aerial view of Fort Marion/Castillo de San Marcos
(Saint Augustine Chamber of Commerce)

East of Jacksonville the **Saint Johns River Lighthouse,** completed in 1859, still stands at the Mayport Naval Station. The last pre–Civil War keeper shot out the lens to prevent its use by Federal gunboats. It is open to the public on weekends.

Saint Augustine, Florida, was one of the few cities in the United States during the Civil War whose main complaint was the war's adverse effect on its tourist trade. In 1884, perhaps partly in recognition of the importance of tourism to the area, the U.S. Congress appropriated $5,000 for restoration work on Fort Marion, the first instance of the use of public funds for historic preservation. In 1942, Congress changed the fort's name back to its Spanish original, **Castillo de San Marcos,** as a tribute to Spain's influence in the area. Today the castillo is one of the more popular attractions in the oldest, continuously occupied European-founded city in the United States. For $1.00, visitors can walk along ramparts that had already stood eighty years by the start of the American Revolution.

Today park rangers at the castillo provide tours and special programs. The fort also has a small museum and nice gift shop with at least one book on the area's Civil War history. The castillo is open April through October from 9:00 A.M.–7:45 P.M. and the rest of the year from 9:00 A.M.–5:15 P.M. For information, contact: Castillo de San Marcos, 1 Castillo Drive, Saint Augustine, FL 32085 (904) 829-6506.

Some Union soldiers stationed in Saint Augustine — especially, no doubt, those quartered right across the street at **Saint Francis Barracks** (still serving the military as headquarters for the Florida National Guard)— could not resist taking chunks of tabby from the **Oldest House** site.

Fort Marion, the parade ground

Continuously occupied since the early 1600s, it was designated a national historic landmark in 1970. In the early 1700s Oldest House belonged to an artilleryman at the castillo. Your $5.00 ticket to Oldest House, at 14 Saint Francis Street, admits you to several other sites as well, including the **Museum of Florida's Army,** situated next door in a home occupied at one point by Union Civil War Gen. Martin D. Hardin. Oldest House opens at 9:00 A.M. daily except Christmas. The last tour is at 4:30 P.M. For information, contact: Saint Augustine Historical Society, 271 Charlotte Street, Saint Augustine, FL 32084 (904) 824-2872.

The **Museum of Weapons and Early American History** boasts a "large Confederate display." For $2.50 you can judge for yourself. Open daily at 10:00 A.M., the museum is on King Street just west of Zorayda, a reproduction of Spain's Alhambra palace. For information, contact: Museum of Weapons and Early American History, 81C King Street, Saint Augustine, FL 32084 (904) 829-3727.

Back east on King Street, you can walk by **Government House,** which served as the U.S. Provost Guard House during the occupation by Federal forces. Throughout the centuries, troops from many nations trained across Saint George Street from Government House in the **Plaza de la Constitucion.** Today a **Confederate War Memorial** stands in the plaza just west of the Old Market.

CHAPTER 6

ALABAMA

THE STATE OF Alabama nursed the infant Confederacy for a little over three months after leaders from six Deep South states met on 4 February 1861 in Montgomery to form a new nation. Operating out of the capital of Alabama, the Confederate States of America rushed to form a government and hold elections. A bronze star at the capitol in Montgomery marks the spot on which Jefferson Davis was inaugurated on 18 February. Less than two months later a Montgomery telegraph operator tapped out the order to fire on Fort Sumter.

The focus of this action in Montgomery belies the significant unionist sentiment in the northern part of the state, separated by geography and loyalties from the Black Belt of slaveholding areas closer to the Gulf of Mexico.[1] Citizens from several northern counties talked openly of seceding from Alabama and forming a separate state with disenfranchised unionists from East Tennessee and Georgia. The plan never developed beyond threats, but thousands of men from Alabama joined the Union army and many others deserted from the Confederate army once the opportunity arose. Sectional differences in the state eventually erupted into violent feuds similar to those taking place in Missouri, feuds that would simmer long after the war was over. Animosities in some areas did not fade until well into the twentieth century. Confederate Gen. Joseph "Fighting Joe" Wheeler, for example, serving in the U.S. Army at San Juan Hill in 1898 was reported to have screeched at his men: "Charge the damn yankees!"[2]

Despite internal rebellion, many Alabamans were second to none when it came to supporting the South. Their attitude helped cement the state's integral role in the Southern confederation during the Civil War and its continued lost cause loyalty today. In both these endeavors, the state's spirited women took up the slack if not the lead. "Women played a considerable part in arousing enthusiasm for the Confederacy. Young women of slaveholding families who ordinarily would not associate with farm boys spoke openly of the honors of war, tempting many 'foolish boys' to enlist in the Confederacy."[3] Postwar sympathies were kept alive by groups such as the Daughters of the Confederacy, which created shrines of Alabama locales important to the history of the Southern states' war for independence.

Whatever state claims bragging rights for the grayest blood, Alabama certainly held a significant position in the Confederacy during the Civil War. Even before the loss of the Middle Tennessee iron country, some of the iron for the CSS *Virginia* came from the Cane Creek furnace in Alabama. After Tennessee's Iron Belt came under Federal control in early 1862, Alabama's ore gained even greater importance. The respected Brooke cannons of Selma, Alabama, were cast from local ore. Even so, the state's most famous export was Confederate Adm. Raphael Semmes, a Marylander by birth but a Mobile lawyer by choice, who gained immortality as the captain of the South's greatest raider, the CSS *Alabama*.

The North's most admired admiral, David Glasgow Farragut, a native Tennessean, considered Semmes and the *Alabama* one of the few worthy enemies he could face. For fifty-three of his sixty-two years before leading the attack on Alabama's most important port of Mobile, Farragut had served in the navy, earning his first independent command at the age of twelve when he took charge of a prize ship during the War of 1812. Before his attack on Mobile, he had captured New Orleans and Baton Rouge, navigated the tricky waters of the Mississippi River through enemy territory, run the batteries of Port Hudson, and taken part in the reduction of Vicksburg, but he longed for a chance to unfurl sails in the open ocean and face an enemy of wooden walls and iron men, instead of the other way around. Hearing of the *Kearsarge*'s victory over the *Alabama* during a deadly pas de deux in the Atlantic Ocean outside Cherbourg, France, in June 1864, the rear admiral sent a card to Mrs. Winslow, wife of the commander on the victorious Union ship, with these words written on the back: "I would rather have fought that fight with the *Alabama* than all I have done in the war."[4]

Alabama the state would give Farragut his last chance at naval glory. Two months after Semmes's setback an ocean away, the battle of Mobile Bay would, in the eyes of seamen, always be Farragut's "surest claim to glory."[5] Although the forts and torpedoes protecting the channel caused some concern within the ranks of the accompanying tars, it was the great ironclad

Tennessee, covered with three layers of iron plate from the Shelby Company of Selma, that Farragut wanted a chance to conquer or destroy.[6]

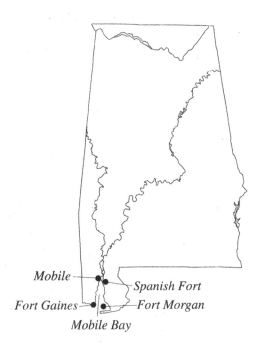

Mobile
Spanish Fort
Fort Gaines
Fort Morgan
Mobile Bay

Mobile Bay

THE PORT AT Pensacola, Florida, is deeper, but the shallow, wide bay running thirty miles from Mobile — a bustling antebellum city of thirty thousand — to the Gulf of Mexico possessed an even greater asset: excellent interior communications. Emptying into this bay were two large rivers with a spider web of tributary systems, "more navigable river miles than any [other] state in the nation."[7] Furthermore, the Mobile and Ohio Railroad, one of the South's longest lines, snaked northwest out of Mobile all the way to Columbus, Kentucky. For protection, two large masonry forts guarded the bay's entrance channel. Second only to New Orleans in exports and imports, Mobile clearly was an important asset to the Southern effort from the beginning of the secession crisis.

Flag Off. David Farragut, U.S.N., desired to immobilize Mobile immediately after he knocked New Orleans out of the war, but other objectives always had more priority for the decision makers in Washington. President Lincoln wanted to clear the Mississippi first, so Farragut committed his sloops to the river campaign. Comdr. David D. Porter's gunboats, however, headed to Mobile where he hoped to place channel markers to guide

David W. Farragut

Farragut's ships when they arrived. Bad weather ended the operation before it ever really began.

After the failure of the 1862 Vicksburg campaign, Farragut wanted to tackle Mobile again, but Union Gen. Benjamin Butler in New Orleans said he could spare no troops for a combined operation. When Maj. Gen. Nathaniel Banks relieved Butler in December, he had specific orders for Farragut to aid in the reduction of Port Hudson, Louisiana. After suffering disaster at Port Hudson followed by aiding Grant's victory at Vicksburg in July 1863, the sexagenarian Farragut took a much-needed leave. Generals Grant, Banks, and Sherman desired a move against Mobile, but for political reasons Lincoln sent Banks's troops to Texas, allowing Confederate Gen. Joe Johnston to transport almost half his army via Mobile to assist Braxton Bragg at Chickamauga.

When Farragut returned to duty at the beginning of 1864, he surmised the mouth of Mobile Bay could not be forced without the aid of ironclads. While running between New Orleans and Pensacola and supervising block-ade duty off Mobile Bay, Farragut organized an invasion armada for Mobile but had to wait for armored warships.

Even before strategists in Washington decided to allow Farragut to neu-tralize Mobile Bay in 1864, it had become the most important gulf port in the Confederacy. Several havens for Southern blockade runners remained open on the Texas Gulf Coast, but the trip through the trans-Mississippi to the Confederate armies east of the Mississippi River was all but impossible. That meant an extensive cat-and-mouse game developed around the entrance to Mobile Bay. In October 1862, for instance, one of Farragut's felines stopped some prey after a six-hour chase. When the vessel's captain was brought before the commander of the West Gulf Blockading Squadron, the desperate mariner protested that he was not headed for Mobile but for the neutral port of Matamoros, Mexico, as his clearance papers indicated. Exhibiting a bit of humor, Farragut responded: "I do not take you for running the blockade but for your damned poor navigation. Any man bound for Matamoras [sic] from Havana and coming within twelve miles of Mobile Light has no business to have a steamer."[8]

All this fun and frustration began on 4 January 1861 when Alabama state militia took over the two brick bastions at the mouth of Mobile Bay: Forts Morgan and Gaines. The property included five thousand shot and shell.

As their compatriots had discovered at most of the other seized forts throughout the South, the Alabama volunteers at Morgan and Gaines found themselves in possession of two defensive works far from ready to withstand any attack. While workers cleaned cisterns for rainwater and began to sod the outer walls, the new Confederate government looked for ordnance. On 7 March 1861, two 10-inch Columbiads arrived from Richmond. With their mile-and-a-half range, these guns became the most powerful in Mobile's defenses.

Not until the end of May 1861 did David D. Porter arrive in command of the *Powhatan* to bring permanent enforcement of Lincoln's blockade proclamation.[9] For most of the remainder of the year, only a loose watch was kept on the bay because the U.S. Navy could spare only a few ships. Even as late as April 1863, cotton valued at almost $2 million had left Mobile the preceding twelve months. Total violations of the blockade would run just over two hundred, with slightly more than 80 percent successful.[10]

In February 1862, Confederate Secretary of the Navy Stephen Mallory appointed Victor Randolph, a native of Alabama, to command the naval forces at Mobile. As the leader of a group that had captured the Pensacola Navy Yard in January 1861, Randolph was a hero in the South. In early April 1862, he tried to uphold his image by taking his wooden gunboats out to challenge the Federal blockaders. He broke off the action before either side suffered any damage. Because the blockaders consisted almost entirely of sailing vessels, Randolph might have challenged the Federal squadron successfully with his steamers if he had chosen to press the attack.[11] Losing patience, Mallory replaced Randolph with another bona fide hero, Franklin Buchanan. The Maryland native had gone to sea at the age of fifteen and counted among his posts the first superintendency of the U.S. Naval Academy (1845–47) and subsequent command of the Washington Navy Yard. But it was as captain of the *Virginia* at Hampton Roads that he had earned celebrity status. Still suffering from wounds received during his battle with the *Monitor,* Buchanan arrived at Mobile in August 1862 to assume his duties.

If Mallory had great expectations, they were soon dashed. Buchanan was even less willing to risk his precious fleet than was his predecessor. Instead, the man who had taken the *Virginia* into battle on her shakedown cruise waited for blockade-breaking ironclads, several of which were in various stages of construction up the Tombigbee and Alabama rivers. In February 1863, three of these wonder weapons slid into the waters at Selma, Alabama: the *Huntsville, Tuscaloosa,* and *Tennessee.* All were brought down to Mobile for fitting out.

During trials that spring, the first two proved to be seagoing sloths, barely making three knots in calm weather. Both were relegated to duty as floating batteries. Buchanan had greater hopes for the *Tennessee* and a fourth vessel, the *Nashville.* Laid down in Montgomery, the *Nashville* was the larger, and for that reason Buchanan elected to finish the *Tennessee* first. He did not have enough resources to outfit both warships, and the smaller of the two could be commissioned more quickly. With five to six inches of iron backed by twenty-five inches of wood and two 7-inch and four 6.4-inch Brooke rifles, the *Tennessee* was a formidable weapon of war.

Nonetheless, it had some glaring weaknesses. Lacking speed, the ironclad could use her ram only with an incredible stroke of luck and her gun ports jammed easily, but the most conspicuous defect was that her steering chains ran over her armored deck, exposing them to enemy fire.[12] What these deficiencies meant was that the ram had the distinct chance of becoming a floating iron box with no speed to run, no way to shoot, and no method to steer. None of this conjecture would matter, however, if Buchanan could not get the *Tennessee* over Dog River Bar, mud flats about nine feet in depth twenty miles down the bay from Mobile. Using "camels," large floats made to fit below the water line, the Confederates managed to coax the ironclad over the bar on the night of 17 May. Buchanan, finally showing a bit of the spunk for which he was famous, planned to run the blockade that night and capture Fort Pickens at Pensacola.[13] The ship ran aground before it could start and was discovered the next day by the blockaders. At that point, Buchanan, perhaps awed by the number of ships arrayed against him, dropped any pretense of offensive action. To be fair to Buchanan, by 1862 Jefferson Davis's overall strategy revolved primarily around defense, particularly along the coasts. The expected contributions of the Confederate navy were essentially passive and reactive.

Confederate land forces were not idle during this time. On the night of 17 April 1863, Maj. James T. Gee left Fort Morgan with men from his First Alabama Artillery Battalion and two field pieces. They marched nine miles along the beach until they saw a blockader close against Swash Channel to the east of Fort Morgan. At daylight, the Confederates opened fire, striking the Federal vessel several times. Two more gunboats came up, and all three fired at the Rebels. After two and a half hours, the blockaders retired and Gee's men returned to Fort Morgan having accomplished their mission: forcing the Union fleet to stay farther away from Swash Channel.

Even so, blockade runners still took risks approaching Mobile along the eastern shore of Mobile Point. On 31 January 1864 the British blockade runner *Denbigh* ran aground in Swash Channel east of Fort Morgan. The blockading fleet moved in to destroy the steamer, but artillery fire from Fort Morgan drove it away. Several days later the Confederates managed to tow the *Denbigh* into port. Six months later the *Ivanhoe* was not as lucky. Although gunners in Fort Morgan managed to keep the blockaders away from the blockade runner grounded east of the fort, on the night of 5 July, Federal launches managed to sneak men aboard the *Ivanhoe*. The raiders then set her afire. Four days later the *Virgin* grounded in the same spot. Once again, the Confederates had the good fortune to get her into the bay.

Although Farragut disliked ironclads, he had grown to respect them, especially since the one inside Mobile Bay was commanded by Buchanan. Despite a few earlier setbacks, Farragut continued to exhibit only contempt for fixed defenses and practically dismissed from his plans those in Mobile Bay, although the entrance channels contained some of the strongest in the South. Between Dauphin Island and the mainland, the channel from Mississippi Sound to the bay was guarded by Fort Powell, named after the former commander of Mobile Bay's lower defenses. The small but unfinished earthwork covered Grant's Pass, the deepest of the passages through the shoal water, with one 10-inch and two 8-inch guns, one 32-pounder, and two 7-inch Brooke rifles.

In August 1863, the gunboats *J. P. Jackson* and *Genesse* opened fire at long range on Fort Powell. The earthwork's only casualty resulted from the explosion of its own gun, the only one that could strike back at the attackers. The next month the two gunboats returned with a third, the *Calhoun*. Although the ships sent 175 shells toward the fort, just 15 hit the island, and none caused any damage. The most serious threat came in February 1864. Reportedly as a diversionary attack to support Sherman's move toward Meridian, Mississippi (but just as much a diversion for his own bored men), Farragut undertook another bombardment of Fort Powell. Only shallow-draft vessels were involved, but they could not get closer than four thousand yards without running the risk of grounding. For several days six mortar schooners and four gunboats pounded the earthen walls with virtually no effect. Percival Drayton, commenting on the exchange, wrote a fellow officer: "We are hammering away at the fort here, which minds us about as much as if we did not fire."[14] The Confederates also had little to show for the exchange, except for their continued hold on the island. None of the torpedoes placed in the waters west of Grant's Pass exploded, even though

Federal vessels struck many of them, and in each bombardment the Confederate guns had been silenced.

On Dauphin Island, five-sided Fort Gaines mounted twenty-seven guns of various calibers on barbettes. Since it sat too far away from the main ship channel to influence the action, Farragut paid no attention to it when he drew up final plans for his run at Mobile Bay. Across the channel, pentagonal Fort Morgan on Mobile Point posed a more serious problem. It boasted approximately forty-five guns of varying sizes on barbettes and in casemates, as well as in a water battery. Obstructions and approximately one hundred torpedoes covered all but a narrow passage stretching a mere 160 yards away from Morgan's guns. To avoid the torpedoes, blockade runners had to keep to the east of a red buoy.

Farragut held this new wonder weapon in more contempt than he held shore defenses. Writing Rear Adm. Theodorus Bailey at Key West on 26 May 1864, Farragut again displayed his wit: "I can see [Buchanan's] boats very industriously laying down torpedoes, so I judge that he is quite as much afraid of our going in as we are of his coming out; but I have come to the conclusion to fight the devil with fire, and therefore shall attach a torpedo to the bow of each ship, and see how it will work on the rebels — if they can stand blowing up any better than we can."[15]

By the beginning of July 1864, ironclads began to join the Union fleet outside Mobile. Although the army insisted it could not spare enough troops to attack both forts at the same time, Farragut concluded that the troops on hand could overwhelm Fort Gaines first, then turn their attention to the tougher Fort Morgan once the fleet passed into the bay. By August, only the arrival of the *Tecumseh* delayed the impending ship-versus-shore battle. On the fourth of the month, Farragut committed himself by landing several thousand troops on Dauphin Island to invest Fort Gaines while six gunboats renewed the attack on Fort Powell. Toward sunset the *Tecumseh* finally made its way to the fleet anchorage. The next morning's tide would sweep the Federal fleet toward its destiny.

At dawn on 5 August the wind blew from the southwest, a good omen for the Federals since it would blow the smoke of battle toward Fort Morgan. By 6:30 A.M. the *Tecumseh*, the lead ironclad, opened fire. Within an hour, the warship steamed abreast of the fort. Three more ironclads followed, providing covering fire for Farragut's wooden ships that were formed obliquely off their port sides. The *Tecumseh* and *Manhattan* each carried two 15-inch guns, the heaviest afloat. This pair led the *Winnebago* and *Chickasaw*, each with four 11-inch guns in two turrets.

Perhaps in the confusion of the struggle, the *Tecumseh*'s captain, Tunis Craven, misunderstood his orders, having had only one night to study the plan of attack. As his warship neared the buoy that marked the minefield, the CSS *Tennessee* edged out from behind Mobile Point to block the passage.

Craven, worried that he would miss the opportunity to engage the Rebel ram, turned to his pilot and said, "It is impossible that the admiral means us to go inside that buoy; I cannot turn my ship."[16] This is exactly what Buchanan had hoped for.

Irritated, Farragut watched from his flagship, the *Hartford,* as Craven began to cross the line of the wooden fleet to cut off the advance of the *Tennessee.* As at New Orleans, Farragut's subordinates had talked him into not taking the lead in the *Hartford.* They argued that the *Brooklyn* was better suited to hold the position of honor since she had a rig to catch torpedoes. Farragut acquiesced but regretted it when Capt. James Alden of the *Brooklyn* stopped his vessel to avoid overtaking the monitors. The army signal officer who received and translated for Farragut the message from the *Brooklyn* sent back the admiral's signal, "Order the monitors ahead, and go on."[17] Only later in his report to Farragut after the battle did Alden mention stopping and backing up to avoid crossing into a line of buoys.

Moments later, the admiral's anger turned to horror as the *Tecumseh* struck a torpedo.[18] She lurched and within minutes slid bow first under the water. In one of the most-dramatic scenes during a battle with many memorable moments, Craven stepped back to allow his pilot to escape first. The pilot was saved; Craven was not. A mere twenty-one survivors struggled in the water. Lt. Comdr. J. E. Jouett of the *Metacomet* ordered a small boat to go to their rescue. For his part, Brig. Gen. Richard L. Page, the commander at Fort Morgan, ordered his men not to fire on the rescuers.

With the Union fleet in danger of becoming entangled under the guns of Fort Morgan, Farragut learned from his pilot, Martin Freemantle, that the channel was wide enough to pass the *Brooklyn* on its port side. The admiral said, "I will take the lead," and ordered the *Hartford* ahead at full speed. The most famous quote of the battle, "Damn the torpedoes! Full steam ahead!" was not attributed to Farragut until fourteen years after the battle.[19] It was a fateful moment. If the *Hartford* struck a mine or if the other ship captains faltered, the fleet's momentum could easily be lost, and with it, the battle. With little or no hesitation, the remainder of the fleet, including the *Brooklyn,* followed Farragut's flag.

Only after most of the Federal fleet had passed the fort could Morgan's gunners safely work their cannon. Consequently, the *Oneida,* bringing up the rear of Farragut's line, was incapacitated by the fort's batteries. Farragut had planned for the eventuality and had smaller steamers lashed to the port sides of all the wooden ships. A similar plan had failed at Port Hudson, but this time the current was favorable, and the *Oneida*'s consort was able to bring the two of them into the bay.

The only loss to the Union fleet was the *Philippi,* a supply ship. After delivering some stores to vessels outside the bar, its commander, Acting Master James T. Seaver, decided on his own to shadow the fighting fleet as it approached the forts in case any ship needed help. The small steamer ran aground within range of Fort Morgan and was easily set afire by gunners who were no longer under the hot breath of Farragut's warships. After the war, in his starch-stiff style, Adm. David Dixon Porter, who had not been present, passed judgment on Seaver: "There is always some one person who will, for want of common sense, do his best to defeat the object of his commander."[20] Apparently Farragut agreed. He recommended to Secretary of the Navy Gideon Welles that Seaver be dishonorably dismissed from the service and ordered him sent North under arrest.

When the Federal warships entered the bay, the small Confederate fleet tried to engage the Federal vessels. As the *Hartford* passed over the minefield, the three Confederate gunboats in the vicinity took up positions to rake the Union flagship. Unable to reply with any but her bow guns, the *Hartford* suffered more from the Rebel naval force than she had while passing Fort Morgan: "The quarters of her forward division became a slaughter pen; a single shot killing ten and wounding five men, while splinters and shreds of bodies were hurled aft and on to the decks of her consort."[21] The *Tennessee* came on next, but the slower warship could not overtake Farragut and turned to pass down the line of the rest of the Federal saltwater fleet. After blasting several well-aimed shots into every ship, the Confederate ironclad pounced on the hapless *Oneida*. Having delayed before the fort to occupy its guns, the Federal ironclads finally came to the *Oneida*'s rescue, placing themselves between the wooden gunboat and the Confederate ironclad.

The *Tennessee*'s captain broke off his attack, then took such a long time to maneuver back up the bay that Farragut assumed he had sought shelter under the guns of the fort like two of the other gunboats in the Rebel fleet, the *Morgan* and *Gaines*. As it became apparent that "Old Buck" Buchanan had no such intention, Farragut ordered his seventeen ships to prepare for another round.

The *Tennessee* had no chance. Besides having to face 199 guns, the Rebel ironclad could not count on her own half-dozen weapons. Faulty primers caused the superior Brooke rifles to misfire more than they fired, giving the Federals an even greater advantage.[22] Within a short time, most of her gun ports were jammed and her steering mechanism shattered by relentless Federal shelling. After the *Tennessee* served twenty minutes as a target for Union gunners, Capt. J. D. Johnston mounted the forecastle and waved a white flag. Just over three hours had passed since Fort Morgan opened fire on the advancing Union ironclads. Not counting the hundred men who went down with the *Tecumseh*, the Federals had suffered fifty-two killed, half of those being aboard the *Hartford*. The three main forts were still under Rebel control, but for Farragut the only battle that counted was over. He had conquered the South's most powerful remaining warship.

Later that night, the ironclad *Chickasaw*,[23] which had doggedly stuck to the *Tennessee*, fired on the unprotected rear of Fort Powell. Not prepared to

The *Hartford* engaging the Confederate ram *Tennessee (Leslie's)*

repel attacks from two sides, the defenders evacuated the works and then destroyed them. The next day the busy *Chickasaw* shelled Fort Gaines. The fort's gunners replied with the two 10-inch Columbiads facing the bay, but they did not manage to hit the monitor.

The actual attack on Fort Gaines had begun three days earlier when Maj. Gen. Gordon Granger landed with three thousand men and several pieces of artillery on Dauphin Island. The following night, six 3-inch Rodmans were in position to begin bombarding the Confederates. Col. Charles D. Anderson, in charge at Fort Gaines, was not in a totally hopeless position. Under his command were 46 officers and 818 men who could bring to bear four 10-inch Columbiads, two 7-inch Brooke rifles, twelve to fifteen smoothbores consisting of 24- and 32-pounders, and five flank casement howitzers. Two of the Columbiads and six of the 24-pounders protected the land approaches. Remarkably, both ammunition and food were plentiful.[24] Forty-eight hours of constant shelling from the land batteries supplemented by the huge guns of the navy, however, convinced Anderson to seek terms on 7 August despite the fact that General Page, commander of Fort Morgan, personally visited Fort Gaines in an attempt to stop the proceedings. The surrender was formalized the next day, and Page condemned the act as a "deed of dishonor and disgrace."[25]

The army under Gen. Gordon Granger was then transferred to Mobile Point. On 13 August, Union Brig. Gen. Alexander Asboth departed

Pensacola with fourteen hundred troops and some artillery on a march toward the Perdido River. Dabney Maury, in overall charge of the defenses of Mobile, had considered sending troops to assault Granger's rear, but he abandoned his plans in order to protect the east side of Mobile Bay against Asboth, who subsequently returned to Pensacola without a fight.

A Federal siege train from New Orleans landed near Fort Morgan on 17 August. Three days later thirty-four guns were in position to complete the encirclement of the fort. Ironically, the damage to the *Tennessee* had been quickly repaired, and it was towed into position to join in the bombardment.

While arrangements were progressing for the final onslaught against Morgan, Farragut made a personal reconnaissance up Mobile Bay with his shallow-draft vessels and ironclads. He was disappointed to find his way to the city blocked by the unfinished ironclad *Phoenix*, sunk across the main channel approaching Mobile. His warships could not get within two miles of the surrounding forts and so would be unable to force their capitulation without a large supporting army.

At daylight on 22 August a coordinated cannonade commenced upon Fort Morgan and continued throughout the day. With all but two of his guns destroyed, breaches in his walls, and a fire threatening his magazine, General Page soaked his remaining powder. He raised a white flag the next morning as soon as there was light enough to see. Once more, Farragut reported to his superiors that he had accomplished a difficult and dangerous mission.

Immediately, Secretary of the Navy Welles wanted him to take over the North Atlantic Blockading Squadron. Farragut was too tired and told Welles so. The secretary persisted, but the hero of the North insisted he needed a rest. Welles relented, and Farragut came home to parades and a promotion to vice admiral.[26]

Although the Confederates continued to operate in the upper bay, by 1865 few military reasons existed for the North to capture Mobile itself. Nevertheless, in January 1865, Grant ordered E. S. R. Canby, Nathaniel Banks's replacement as commander of the Army of West Mississippi, to move against Mobile to prevent reinforcements from being shifted to Virginia. Canby planned to move up the east side of the bay supported by Rear Adm. H. K. Thatcher, the new naval commander at Mobile. Operations against Rebel positions began 21 March when Canby's troops landed under the protection of gunboats to invest Spanish Fort, the strongest of the defenses on that side of the bay. Another army under Gen. Frederick Steele moved overland to Fort Blakeley, which guarded the mouth of the Blakeley River farther north. At least one company of free blacks formed to defend the city.[27]

Up to this point the Federal fleet had remained outside Dog River Bar, partly because of shallow water but also because of torpedoes. When the Union army landed, several of Thatcher's gunboats moved over the bar to cut both garrisons' communications with Mobile. Although the area had been swept for torpedoes, the ironclad *Milwaukee* sank 28 March after closing to attack a transport off Spanish Fort and striking a mine. The next day the ironclad *Osage* hit a torpedo and settled to the bottom, her turret rising above the shallows.[28] On 1 April the steamer *Randolph* struck a mine and sank while trying to raise the *Milwaukee*.

On land, things were not going much better. The ironclad CSS *Nashville* and the gunboat *Morgan* provided relief to Confederate commander Randall Gibson's hard-pressed left until Federal Parrott guns drove them back. The bitter fight at Spanish Fort did not end until 8 April, the day before Lee laid down his arms at Appomattox Court House. On 10 April the *Metacomet* swept for torpedoes above Spanish Fort, allowing several ironclads to blast positions at Blakeley under attack from Steele's troops. The next day these positions were abandoned also, allowing Thatcher's ships to use the river system to approach to within a mile of Mobile. The city, literally under the gun, surrendered.

Several more boats were lost sweeping for mines, but for the most part, the navy's job was finished at Mobile. On 4 May Confederate Gen. Richard Taylor surrendered what was left of his command in Alabama and Mississippi to Canby, and Com. Ebenezer Farrand, C.S.N., delivered the ships that had managed to escape up the Tombigbee River to Admiral Thatcher.

The war was over.

If you go there . . .

As part of its American bicentennial observance, the city of Mobile reconstructed part of an old French fortress that had protected the city for around a century beginning in the 1720s. Today's Fort Condé serves as the **City of Mobile Visitor and Welcome Center** and is open free to the public daily except Christmas and Mardi Gras from 8:00 A.M.–5:00 P.M. Although the fort no longer existed by the time the Civil War began, anyone interested in military history will enjoy walking its ramparts (made with brick supplied by the same company that provided building materials for the original fort) and looking through its museum. Questions about any of the other attractions in the area can be answered at the information building, situated in one of the replica barracks.

Within a short drive of the visitors center, the USS *Alabama*, BB60, acts as a floating museum permanently moored at Battleship Park. Also at the park, Alabama Cruises offers a ninety-minute tour of Mobile Bay and Mobile River. The captain narrates the trip with stories about the Civil War, including tidbits about **Battery McIntosh,** one of two strongpoints built by the Confederates on one of the small islands that the cruise ship passes. Along with Battery Gladden, Battery McIntosh protected the ship channel leading to the Mobile River. According to the manager of Alabama Cruises, each of the batteries mounted a dozen cannon.[29] With three lines of earthworks guarding the land approaches and with various forts, obstructions, and torpedoes barring the route from the sea, Mobile was considered by Gen. Joseph E. Johnston to be the best fortified city in the Confederacy.

The narrated boat tours, which cost $6.00 for adults and $3.00 for children, leave Battleship Park daily except for the month of January. There is also a $1.00 entrance fee to get into the park. For more information, contact: Alabama Cruises, Inc., Box 101, Mobile AL 36601 (205) 433-6101.

Driving south from Mobile on Highway 163 toward **Fort Gaines Historic Site,** you will cross a bridge to Dauphin Island that passes the former location of Fort Powell. Nothing remains of the battery. Fort Gaines covers the eastern tip of Dauphin Island. The area's strategic worth was recognized by the earliest French explorers, who named the island after the son of Louis XIV. Wooden forts occupied the spot as early as 1717, when Dauphin Island was capital of all French Louisiana. The Americans, however, were the first to erect permanent battlements there. Preliminary work began in 1821, but it was not until a quarter-century later that construction began in earnest on the fort to be named after Edmond Pendleton Gaines, the captor of Aaron Burr.

The design of Fort Gaines is very similar to that of Fort Clinch at Fernandina, Florida. Were it not for the Endicott emplacements at the former, aerial views of the two would be almost identical. Past the entrance to Fort Gaines Historic Site, open seven days a week, is a small bookshop where visitors can pay $2.00 for a terrific walking-tour guide. In the courtyard rests an anchor from the *Hartford.*

An aerial view of Fort Gaines. Note the Endicott modifications along the sea face. *(Alabama Historical Commission)*

An aerial view of Fort Morgan. Endicott construction practically divides the fort in half. *(Alabama Historical Commission)*

The adjacent Fort Gaines Campground has washers and dryers, a playground, and a private beach surrounded by the 160-acre Audubon bird sanctuary. A fishing pier and public boat launch are nearby.

The staff at Fort Gaines organize a wide variety of Civil War programs throughout the year, ranging from a Civil War ball and Civil War meal to salt making and reenactments of the land battle around Fort Gaines. For information on activities, contact: Fort Gaines Historic Site, P.O. Box 97, Dauphin Island, AL 36528 (205) 861-6992.

The ferry across the channel from Dauphin Island to Mobile Point, the location of **Fort Morgan National Historic Landmark,** is $9.00 per car and driver, plus $1.00 for each other adult passenger. If you drive from the east, the cost to enter the fort grounds is $2.00. A self-guided tour map of the fort is available, but park employees also lead walking tours starting at the new museum, which has a fine display of materials from the Civil War.

Fort Morgan is very similar in appearance to Fort Jackson, situated at the mouth of the Mississippi River. Each possessed interior defensive barracks or citadels that were destroyed during Farragut's attacks

Mobile Bay's two guardians and the other massive, vertical-walled third-system forts embodied the best technology of the eighteenth century. Against nineteenth-century advances in weaponry, however, most served as little better than targets. Torpedoes (or mines) inflicted the greatest damage during the battles at Mobile Bay. One testimony to that fact lies under a red buoy about three hundred yards west of the fort's wharf. The remains of the ironclad *Tecumseh* have been placed on the National Register, but any attempts to raise the well-preserved monitor must await perfected anticorrosive techniques.

Fort Morgan National Historic Landmark is open daily, 8:00 A.M. until sunset. Besides the fort, the immediate surroundings offer beaches, a fishing pier, and a picnic area. The **James B. Allen Museum** is open daily from 8:00 A.M.–5:00 P.M. For more information, contact: Fort Morgan, Route 1, Box 3540, Gulf Shores, AL 36542 (205) 540-7125.

The town of Spanish Fort, on I-10 across the bay from Mobile, was named after a Spanish-built fort in the area that repelled a British attack in January 1781. On the city's Confederate Drive, a street that meanders next to the bay, a historical marker indicates the site of Confederate **Fort McDermott**. For eighteen days, positions anchored at the fort held off elements of two Union army corps and five ironclads.

Four miles north on Highway 225, remnants of earthen forts, rifle pits, redoubts, and battery positions dot **Historic Blakeley State Park.** At thirty-eight hundred acres, Blakeley is the largest site listed on the National Register of Historic Places east of the Mississippi River. The sheer length of the opposing earthworks make Blakeley one of the best places in the country to view siege works uncluttered by any postwar developments or well-intentioned monuments. Moving toward the Confederate line from the Union trenches, visitors can gain some appreciation for what faced attacking troops trying to reach the Tensaw River. Two hundred yards in front of the main Confederate works, a series of well-preserved rifle pits gave advanced pickets a bit of shelter. Behind these, the main line appears as just a small hump in the distance, but the mounds of earth gain stature as the yards tick off. Some modern abatis provide only a small indication of what Federal soldiers must have had to contend with before conquering the Confederate trenches and reaching the town of Blakeley.

The city prospered through some boom years after Josiah Blakeley chartered it in 1814, but by the BOOM! years of the Civil War, the former port had been a ghost town for almost two decades, destroyed by a yellow fever epidemic and silt in its harbor. Today archaeological research continues at the town site, and markers relate its history to visitors.

Besides the historical attractions, the park offers a campground and picnic area. The cost to enter the park is $2.00. It is open from 9:30 A.M.–6:30 P.M. in the spring and summer and from 9:00 A.M. to 6:00 P.M. in the winter. The park is closed Christmas Eve and Christmas Day. On a weekend early in April, a reenactment of the battle at Blakeley takes place. The first Saturday in October marks the Blakeley Cajun-Bluegrass Festival. For information, contact: Historic Blakeley Authority, 33707 State Highway 225, Spanish Fort, AL 36527 (205) 626-0798.

MISSISSIPPI

DELEGATES TO Mississippi's secession convention did not mince words when it came to presenting their feelings regarding the issues of the day. In "A Declaration of the Immediate Causes Which Induce and Justify the Secession of the State of Mississippi from the Federal Union," the opening paragraph reads: "Our position is thoroughly identified with the institution of slavery — the greatest material interest of the world."[1] There was not one word in the document about states' rights. Reflecting the South in general, however, the largest slaveholders in Mississippi did not usually favor the breakup of the Union. James Lusk Alcorn, a prominent Mississippi plantation owner and future U.S. senator, signed the ordinance of secession despite the fact that he did not believe "disunion would best protect slavery."[2] He was rewarded for his grudging support with the rank of brigadier general in the state army. Still, the prevailing attitude among most of the white male population was that they would rather die than free the slaves, which for the most part did not even "belong" to them.[3]

Mississippi backed up this sentiment with action. Approximately seventy-eight thousand men from the state served in the Confederate armies. Perhaps one of the best indications of just how much the state's soldiers gave to the cause occurred the year after the war ended. In 1866 Mississippi lawmakers appropriated $30,000 for the purchase of artificial limbs for veterans. By comparison, only $20,000 went to the state university.[4]

With the exception of Charleston and Richmond, no other southern city received as much unwanted attention from Federal troops as Vicksburg, Mississippi. Although President Davis appeared unable to formulate a successful defense of the city, it was not due to any lack of interest on his part. He had spent the thirty years preceding the war at Brierfield, his mansion twenty miles below Vicksburg. When Union troops moved up from New Orleans in the summer of 1862, they burned the adjoining plantation that was owned by Davis's brother, but they spared Brierfield. Uncertainty about his safety kept Davis from visiting his property in December of that year when he made a tour of Mississippi's defenses.

The next spring Grant's troops did everything to Brierfield but burn the big house down. They stole all items of value and destroyed what they could not carry. One soldier even took Davis's inscribed copy of the U.S. Constitution. Although he was fighting for the principles implied in the document, the soldier did not regard the parchment very highly. William Tecumseh Sherman found the manuscript beside the road while on his way to the battle at Champion's Hill.[5]

Imprisoned for two years, Davis was not able to return to Brierfield immediately after the war. When he came home in 1875, someone else owned the property, so he retired to Beauvoir on Mississippi's Gulf Coast. If Davis could see far enough into the "beautiful view" directly south of his property, he would see a rise in the gulf called Ship Island, where the story of Mississippi's introduction to combat in the Civil War begins.

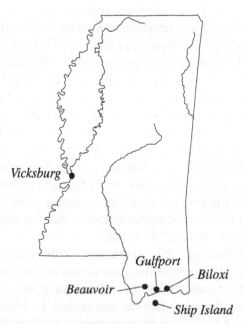

Vicksburg

Gulfport

Biloxi

Beauvoir

Ship Island

Ship Island

AS EARLY AS 9 February 1699 the Comte de Surgères, one of Sieur d'Iberville's men, sighted Ship Island, just off the coast of present-day Mississippi and west of what would become the state of Louisiana.[6] Because of its excellent deep-water harbor, it was eventually called Isle aux Vaisseaux or Ship Island. Although a fort stood there as early as 1717, the importance of the position was overshadowed by that of New Orleans. When France ceded the area to England after the French and Indian Wars, lists of French properties did not even mention Ship Island.

The Gulf of Mexico sand pile might have faded into obscurity during the next century except that Maj. Gen. Edward Pakenham used it as a base for nearly sixty ships during his preparations for the attack on New Orleans in 1815. To prevent any foreign countries from capitalizing on Ship Island's harbor in the future, U.S. engineers began a semicircular bastion guarding the anchorage as part of the post–War of 1812 shore defenses construction boom.

The next conflict to engulf Ship Island began in a rather benign, almost comical way. On 13 January 1861 a party of armed men arrived on the island and informed 1st Lt. Frederick E. Prime, the engineer in charge of raising the fort on Ship Island, that they had come to take possession. Work on the brick casemates continued, and the visitors left later in the day. The same afternoon, another group landed with a similar message. These men also did not interfere with the fort's construction and eventually departed as well. A week later, a third force reached the island. These would-be occupiers would ultimately vacate Ship Island, too, perhaps after learning how boring life on a cay in the Gulf of Mexico can be, but not before Prime tired of his rude visitors and abandoned his building project.

The upshot of this coming and going was that when war finally broke out, the island was deserted. In May 1861, Confederate Secretary of War Leroy P. Walker ordered Brig. Gen. James Trudeau of New Orleans to take possession of the island, but there was one problem: Trudeau commanded no troops. Not until 6 July did Capt. Edward Higgins land a party of fifty-five marines and some cannon on the island. If being assigned to a deserted island were not bad enough, they found that Brig. Gen. William J. Hardee, the commander at Mobile, Alabama, had ordered the burning of all the buildings on the island after hearing rumors of an impending Union attempt to reoccupy the position. Depending upon one's sectional interests, Higgins's unhappy Confederates were just in time. On 9 July Comdr. Melancton Smith of the screw steamer USS *Massachusetts* approached Ship Island and found four gun emplacements in the process of being constructed by Higgins's party. Seventy-five militiamen had also arrived just the day before.

Smith and Lt. A. F. Warley, C.S.N., ordered their respective commands to fire. The Union gunboat retired toward Mobile after a twenty-minute "intense, wild-firing fight."[7] Eventually Col. Henry W. Allen of the Fourth Louisiana Infantry took charge of the defenses at the island. He continued work on the fort, now named Fort Twiggs in honor of seventy-one-year-old Maj. Gen. David Twiggs, commander of Department Number 1, which consisted of southern Alabama and Mississippi and all of Louisiana. Because of Allen's continuing efforts, Twiggs reported to his superiors on 19 July that the island fortress "was strong enough to resist any force the Federals could send against it."[8]

On 3 September, Col. Johnson K. Duncan of the First Louisiana Artillery was given temporary command of the fortification. Because the fort's brickwork had not been finished by U.S. engineers, a temporary wood-and-sandbag roof covered the embrasures. Duncan felt that the timbers would collapse onto the gun crews and suggested the nine 32-pounders, two 24-pounders, one 8-inch shell gun, and one 9-inch Dahlgren be mounted outside the fort behind sandbag parapets. Even so, the most powerful of these could not cover the channel between Ship Island and Cat Island to the west. For this reason, Duncan recommended that the position be abandoned.

His report was forwarded by Twiggs, who had never visited the fort himself, to Samuel Cooper, adjutant general of the Confederacy. Reversing President Davis's stance of just four months earlier, Cooper ordered the island evacuated. Flames from the burning lighthouse brought the *Massachusetts* and two Federal sloops to investigate. Smith gave the retiring Confederates a parting shot.

The Federals began work once again on the fortress, renamed Fort Massachusetts in honor of the ship that had loitered in the area for so long. On 3 December the steamer *Constitution* arrived with two thousand reinforcements for the meager Federal garrison. The next day, as an indication of the importance that the North attributed to the position, the U.S. Navy Department designated Ship Island as headquarters of the West Gulf Blockading Squadron. Even at that late date, Confederate commanders in the area thought little of the Federal buildup.[9] Although many historians have pointed out that the withdrawal of Rebel forces from Ship Island was among the most crucial mistakes of the war,[10] in retrospect it is difficult to believe the isolated post could have been held in the face of any determined thrust by the Federal navy considering what happened to more strongly fortified positions throughout the South.

Whatever feelings Southern commanders may have held in early 1862, undoubtedly those among them who encouraged a continued presence on the island[11] felt vindicated in their views when Flag Off. David Farragut employed the island as his base of operations for his successful attack on New Orleans. Throughout the remainder of the war, the Federal navy used Ship Island as the major command post and rendezvous point for the ships of its Gulf Squadron. Furthermore, the eighteen-gun sloop-of-war *Vincennes* was stationed there from October 1862 until after the war to discourage any Rebel reconsiderations.

If you go there . . .

In August 1969 Hurricane Camille cut through Ship Island. Fort Massachusetts, on the western surviving half, was not severely damaged, although the breakwater around it was swept away. The fort and what is now called West Ship Island are part of the Mississippi District of the **Gulf Islands National Seashore.** The Ship Island Excursion Ferry departs from either Gulfport or Biloxi on a seventy-minute cruise to West Ship Island once or twice a day from March to October.

Obviously the fort is not the only, or even primary, attraction for those taking the day-long junkets. Sand, sun, and surf are the magnets. Still, park service suggestions for those traveling to the island carry a reminder of what the area must have been like for those who were held on the island as prisoners toward the end of the Civil War. Although today there is a boardwalk, snack bar, lifeguards, and picnic shelters, park employees suggest you bring shoes, a hat, some good sunscreen, and protective clothing. The sun can turn a great adventure into a slow burn. Two other cautions: Glass bottles and camping are prohibited on Ship Island, and the ferry will not carry pets or bulky items.

Park rangers offer guided tours of the fort twice a day during the summer, although special tours are held in the spring and fall. Exhibits and publication sales are available for tourists visiting the fort.

Ticket offices and docks for the ferries are at Gulfport Yacht Harbor, Highway 90 at Highway 49, Gulfport, MS (601) 864-1014 and next to the Buena Vista Beach Club Inn, Highway 90 near the I-110 overpass, Biloxi, MS (601) 432-2197. The cost is $12.00 for an adult round trip and $5.00 for children three to ten years old.

Even if you're not sure about a day in the sun, a side trip to Biloxi will not be wasted. **Beauvoir** estate, the last home of Jefferson Davis, faces the gulf just west of Biloxi on Highway 90. Visitors to the historic home can look through a glass partition into the statesman's sleeping quarters and see,

An aerial view of Fort Massachusetts, headquarters of the West Gulf Blockading Squadron *(Gulf Islands National Seashore)*

Beauvoir sits on eighty-eight acres dedicated to the memory of Jefferson Davis

besides the typical furnishings of a bedroom, Davis's French-manufactured telescope. The brass instrument indeed looks out over a "beautiful view," the rough translation of the estate's French name. It would also have allowed Davis to scan some of the barrier islands, including Ship Island.

The small outlying cottage that he employed as an office and study still has the desk upon which he wrote *The Rise and Fall of the Confederate Government* and the bookshelves that he fashioned to hold his library. The eighty-eight-acre grounds also include a museum dedicated to the former president, a gift shop, and a Confederate cemetery. The home is open from 9:00 A.M.–5:00 P.M. daily. Admission is $4.00. For more information, contact: Beauvoir, 2244 Beach Boulevard, Biloxi, MS 39531 (601) 388-1313.

At one time twelve lighthouses existed on the Mississippi Gulf Coast. Today only two remain. One is the **Biloxi Lighthouse.** Situated on

The outlying cottage-study *(left)* in which Davis wrote *The Rise and Fall of the Confederate Government*. Davis's telescope *(right)* looks out from his bedroom toward Ship Island, the staging area from which Farragut launched his armada against New Orleans.

Highway 90 between Biloxi and Beauvoir, it was the first cast-iron lighthouse in the South and has shone continuously from 1848 except for a brief time during the Civil War when its lens was hidden by the home guard.

The other lighthouse still standing is the **Round Island Lighthouse** in neighboring Pascagoula. David Farragut's father owned a plantation in the area, and the young future admiral made occasional visits. Even before Union troops burned the town 13 December 1864, the war was not popular with the locals, according to the curator at **Old Spanish Fort.** Built in 1718, this cottagelike structure on the Pascagoula River loosely claims to be the oldest building in the United States between the Appalachian and Rocky mountains. The "fort" began as part of the estate of Joseph Simon de La Pointe and was surrounded by a stockade at one time, thus giving rise to its present name. Even though the Spanish did not build it or ever control it, a battle between settlers and Spanish troops did take place there in 1810 when disputes arose between the boundaries of old French Louisiana and Spanish Florida.

Old Spanish Fort is now run by the Jackson County Historical Society and includes, besides the original 1718 carpenter shop, a small but interesting museum. Some exhibits relate to the Civil War, such as artifacts from the *Barataria,* a Union transport. Originally a Confederate gunboat captured at New Orleans, it was used by Union forces for troop support on Lakes Pontchartrain and Maurepas, Louisiana. On 7 April 1863, the boat hit upon a snag at the mouth of the Amite River, which flows into Lake Maurepas. The crew set it afire to prevent its recapture by Confederate troops.

The museum and grounds are open Monday through Saturday 10:00 A.M.–5:00 P.M. and Sunday 12:30–5:00 P.M., except major holidays. The cost is $2.00. Old Spanish Fort is two blocks north of Highway 90 off Lake Avenue. For information, contact: Old Spanish Fort Museum, 4602 Fort Drive, Pascagoula, MS 39567 (601) 769-1505.

Vicksburg

ON 12 JANUARY 1861, months before the first angry shots of the Civil War split the nation, Gov. James Pettus of Mississippi ordered a battery of guns to be emplaced at Vicksburg, the cultured, county-seat town set atop imposing three-hundred-foot bluffs along the Mississippi River about halfway between Memphis and New Orleans.[12] State governors in the Old Northwest reacted angrily, and an embarrassed Pettus had the artillery withdrawn. As postelection tempers simmered just below the boiling level, the governor had inadvertently drawn attention to the "Queen City of the Bluff" and its royal position on the Midwest's commercial lifeline. For the next two and a half years, Vicksburg would not be far from the thoughts of anxious leaders on both sides of the secession issue.[13]

"Valuable as New Orleans will be to us," President Lincoln told Comdr. David Dixon Porter in early 1862, "Vicksburg will be even more so. We may take all the northern parts of the Confederacy, and they can still defy us from Vicksburg. . . . [S]ee what a lot of land those fellows hold, of which Vicksburg is the key. . . . The war can never be brought to a close until that key is in our pocket."[14] When David Glasgow Farragut left Washington that spring to strike New Orleans, he carried orders to open the *entire* Mississippi River. Since Andrew Hull Foote's successful naval attack on Fort Henry had outflanked Confederate defenses all the way to Memphis, Tennessee, from the north, Farragut's instructions meant he had only to capture Vicksburg to fulfill his orders once New Orleans fell on 26 April. If he had sailed immediately to Vicksburg instead of taking two weeks to prepare his ships, Farragut would have arrived at an undefended city. As it was, the Rebels had just enough time to bring in troops and a few heavy guns.

Farragut's initial ascent of the river began well enough. After occupying Louisiana's capital at Baton Rouge without firing a shot, the fleet moved on to Natchez, Mississippi. The citizens came out in their Sunday best to see the Yankees, and — unlike his counterparts in New Orleans and Baton Rouge — the mayor of Natchez surrendered when requested to do so. One young girl standing by the shoreline even took out a U.S. flag. Her daring boosted the spirits of the fourteen-hundred-man Vicksburg occupation force crammed aboard transports, but their good humor was short-lived.

When Comdr. Samuel Phillips Lee demanded the capitulation of Vicksburg on 18 May 1862, the military governor of the city, perhaps unaware of what had transpired in Natchez, brazenly replied: "Mississippians don't know, and refuse to learn, how to surrender."[15] Like many of his men, Farragut felt physically unwell and did not accept Col. James L. Autrey's invitation to "come and try" if the Federals thought otherwise. Charles H. Davis's ironclads had been mauled at Plum Point just north of Fort Pillow, Tennessee, a week before, or else they might have appeared on the scene soon enough to change the odds. As it was, Farragut decided to return to Baton Rouge, where he arrived on 28 May.

Navy Secretary Gideon Welles informed Farragut he must try to subdue Vicksburg again, so by 24 June the commander of the West Gulf Blockading Squadron led an even larger force northward, expecting to meet Davis and his flotilla. Having just witnessed the capitulation of Memphis, a correspondent for the *Illustrated London News* wrote prematurely on 10 June, "By the time this letter appears in print the 'Father of Waters' will pursue his course uninterrupted by cannon from his source to the Gulf of Mexico, and Vicksburg, the final stand-point of the Confederates, will have been wrenched from them by Davis and Farragut."[16]

Davis suffered a setback 13 June on the White River in Arkansas while attempting to resupply a Federal army led by Maj. Gen. Samuel Ryan

Charles H. Davis

Curtis. The commander of the Mississippi Squadron was still licking his wounds when Farragut dropped anchor below Vicksburg. Alfred Ellet, having replaced his mortally wounded brother as commander of the Federal river rams, managed to cut through the swamps to reach Farragut with the message that Davis would not be coming.

Still on an emotional roller coaster, Farragut chose to tackle the wild river ride upstream to Davis. On 26 June Porter signaled his mortarboats to unleash their iron rain on Vicksburg. As at the forts below New Orleans, the resulting fireworks were grand but had little actual effect on the fighting capacity of the defenders. Two days later Farragut ordered his squadron to make its way through the horseshoe bend in front of the city. By breakfast, the fleet dropped anchor above Vicksburg three miles below the mouth of the Yazoo River. The worst damage occurred aboard the mortarboat *Clifton*. A shot had burst her boiler, scalding seven crewmen to death. Trying to escape the infernal steam, another sailor drowned. Seven other Federals in the fleet were killed, and thirty were wounded.

Running the batteries with minimal losses provided good copy to a North starved for positive news after George McClellan's setbacks around Richmond that summer. But for the feat to have any military value, there should have been something on the other side. All Farragut found was Davis and his ironclads, which finally appeared 1 July — hardly a meaningful accomplishment. While Davis and Farragut commiserated about the inability of those in

Washington to appreciate their situation, army commander Gen. Thomas Williams set his men to digging a canal to bypass the bothersome batteries, a task accomplished at Island Number 10 earlier that year with mixed results.

Farragut's morale began a downward slide as his fleet baked in the sun north of its target. There were good reasons for concern. During the summer, the countryside around Vicksburg was a malarial trap.[17] Even worse, the river began its customary dip in water level at that time of year. Besides negating all Williams's digging, the falling depth of the river meant that if Farragut kept the fleet upriver much longer, it could be stranded there for months.

Confederate commander Isaac Brown's worries also rose as the river fell. The captain of the unfinished ironclad ram *Arkansas* had successfully escaped Memphis as Davis approached and managed to continue work near Liverpool, Mississippi, on the Yazoo River. Without the proper materials, Brown did what he could. By July the *Arkansas* was as ready as she would ever be, and Brown ordered her closer to the Mississippi and the combined Federal fleets.

Federal scouts suspected something lurked up the Yazoo, and the enterprising Alfred Ellet conveyed those fears to Farragut. The deep-water vessels could not navigate the narrow river, so Farragut asked Davis for help. On 15 July the *Queen of the West*, *Carondelet*, and *Tyler* nosed into the sinewy Yazoo.

Davis's earlier setbacks were not caused by a lack of courage among his crews. But on this warm, calm morning, his boat commanders appeared to lose their nerve after spotting a worrisome beast stalking them from the shadows along the bank. *Carondelet*'s forward guns boomed immediately before its pilot attempted to turn the ironclad in the narrow channel. The unarmed ram *Queen of the West* started forward, then backed hard after shrapnel played a staccato tune on her deck. The crew of the *Arkansas* concentrated its fire on the *Carondelet*. Hit at least twenty times, the Union ironclad drifted out of control toward shoal water. The Confederates, unable to ram their nemesis in shallow water, had to settle for raking their larger adversary one more time at a range of forty feet.

The Rebel ram had not escaped punishment either, and it did little better than limp after the two timberclads scurrying downriver. The *Arkansas*'s pilot was mortally wounded, then Brown suffered two head wounds. His men were laying him next to the dead and dying when he miraculously popped up to his feet. He took over the con when the pilot's assistant was also incapacitated. Since the pipe connecting the armorclad's furnace to its smokestack had been shot away, boiler fires were unable to get a good draw and almost died out. Steam pressure dropped from 120 to 20 pounds, barely enough to allow Brown to steer. Undaunted, Brown knew the current would carry the still-deadly warship to Vicksburg only ten miles away. Not having many options, he decided to aim his wounded metal monster toward the enemy fleet.

The exchange between the *Carondelet* and the *Arkansas* at the mouth of the Yazoo River (*Leslie's*)

Luckily for Brown, boiler fires on the Federal vessels had been kept low, both to conserve fuel and to leave the area below decks as cool as possible. When the Union timberclads broke into the Mississippi in the early morning, followed closely by the *Arkansas*, Farragut was literally caught sleeping; he rushed on deck in his nightshirt.

Brown's gunners could not miss nor could his ten cannon fail to find a target within the forest of masts and smokestacks among Farragut's oceangoing ships or the turtlebacks of Davis's Mississippi Squadron. Unable to maneuver without steam, the Federal warships could fight back only with the guns they could immediately bring to bear. Worse, they risked striking friends anchored on both sides of the river. Although badly damaged during its passage through the explosive canyon between the Federal fleets, the *Arkansas* reached a jubilant Vicksburg. Cheers gave way to chills when townspeople saw the brains, hair, and blood strewn about the gun deck "as though [they] had been thrown by hand from a sausage mill."[18] Still, it was a singular victory.

The scene among the Federal soldiers and sailors was, if possible, even more dismal. Had Farragut's blood been in his ships' boilers, his fleet could have steamed after Brown immediately. As it was, he impulsively decided to return downstream both to escape the falling river and to gain revenge against the *Arkansas*.[19] The flotilla reached Vicksburg just as the sun began to set, making it difficult to pick out the rust-colored ram hunkered under the red clay of the bluffs. Nevertheless, an 11-inch shell from the *Oneida*'s pivot gun smashed through the engine room, killing or wounding five men and preventing the ram from joining battle the third time that day. The Union ships passed Vicksburg safely, leaving in their wake a battered but unbroken *Arkansas.* Ironically, Farragut was promoted to rear admiral the next day, the first officer to hold that rank in the history of the U.S. Navy.[20]

During the following week, the Union squadrons probed Vicksburg's waterfront with their huge 13-inch mortars. A single hit would have destroyed the *Arkansas,* but none found the mark. Farragut then convinced Davis to make one more attempt at the stubborn ironclad. The *Queen of the West* did not back away this time, and both she and the *Essex* managed to ram the Rebel warship. Neither blow produced a mortal wound, however. Two days later on 24 July, Farragut departed for New Orleans as Davis headed upstream to his new base at Helena, Arkansas, thus ending the first phase of the campaign to capture the new Gibraltar of the Confederacy.

Captain Brown took a well-deserved rest in Grenada, Mississippi, only to fall ill. In his absence, his second-in-command, Lt. Henry Stevens, was ordered by Gen. Earl Van Dorn to take the *Arkansas* south to assist in the battle developing at Baton Rouge in early August. The ram's machinery could not manage the distance. The starboard engine broke down twice, but engineers managed to fix it both times. At dawn on 6 August, with the USS *Essex* approaching upstream, Stevens nosed the ram into the current, intending to swing her around and bear down on the Union ship at full speed. Before he could, the port engine locked. Out of control, the *Arkansas* stuck deep into the river's west bank, her lightly armored stern offering the perfect target for the 9-inch bow guns of the *Essex.* With tears in his eyes, Stevens ordered the ship set afire.[21]

Confederate Secretary of the Navy Stephen Mallory had lost his four most powerful ironclads — *Virginia, Arkansas, Mississippi,* and *Louisiana* — in the last five months. Pressure increased for him to do something about the situation around Vicksburg, but there was little he could accomplish. The South did not have the kind of resources needed to mount an effective naval counteroffensive.

As the campaign for Vicksburg shifted in focus from the rivers to the land, Union gunboats continued to keep a high profile. In mid-August Lt. Comdr. Samuel Ledyard Phelps cast off from the wharf at Helena at the head of a fleet of three gunboats and four of Alfred Ellet's rams. The seven raiders steamed to the Yazoo, then headed thirty-five miles up that river, destroying Rebel communication lines and supplies before retiring to Helena. The navy may have temporarily ceded the primary role of capturing Vicksburg to the army, but it refused to concede control of the area's waterways to the Confederates.

By October the principal personalities of the battle for Vicksburg were established. Grant had been given command of the Army of the Tennessee, in whose theater of operations Vicksburg fell. Porter took over command of the Mississippi Squadron, reorganized under the Navy Department after serving as part of the army since the beginning of the war.

The USS *Cairo*, the first warship to ever be lost to a mine *(Library of Congress)*

Newly promoted Confederate Lt. Gen. John C. Pemberton was appointed to replace Van Dorn.

Grant planned to hold Pemberton at bay while William Tecumseh Sherman took thirty thousand men down the Mississippi from Helena to attack Vicksburg via Chickasaw Bluffs. Scouting the Yazoo for Sherman's drive, the USS *Cairo* struck an "infernal machine" and sank on 12 December, the first ship in history to fall prey to a mine. This was just the beginning of what would be a disastrous month for the Federals around Vicksburg. A week later Grant halted his squeeze on Pemberton when he learned that Confederate cavalry genius Nathan Bedford Forrest had wreaked havoc on his railroad supply lines. The next day more cavalry under Van Dorn destroyed Grant's new supply base at Holly Springs, Mississippi. That was enough. On 23 December Grant sent a note to Sherman informing him that he was withdrawing to Memphis.

Unfortunately for Sherman, the note had to travel by a circuitous route. Before it reached him, Sherman had already made his plans for attacking entrenched Rebels on the bluffs north of Vicksburg behind Chickasaw Bayou. On the day Grant began his withdrawal, Porter sent the gunboats *DeKalb* and *Signal,* the ram *Queen of the West,* and a tug back up the Yazoo. A day later they neared the *Cairo* wreck where the *Queen* ran over a torpedo wire. No repeat of the earlier disaster occurred, but when boats were lowered, Confederate sharpshooters forced them back to their mother ships. Both sides blasted away the duration of Christmas Eve.

Sherman's troops followed the naval scouts on 27 December. They tested the Confederate defenses south of the Yazoo River on 28 December, then Sherman ordered a bloody frontal assault the next day. Almost two

David Dixon Porter

thousand Federals fell, compared to fewer than two hundred Confederates, in a replay of what had transpired two weeks earlier at Fredericksburg, Virginia.[22] As Sherman's men returned to their transports, the Union commander received Grant's message warning him that Pemberton could now reinforce his positions around Vicksburg. Sherman had already found out the hard way; indeed, only a thick fog had kept him from ordering further attacks.

By 1863 Federal forces had been turned back three times at Vicksburg, the navy twice and the army once. Grant now determined to grapple with his foe until Vicksburg was subdued. A record rise in the Mississippi's water level gave the army commander several ideas. Two more canals on the west side of the river were attempted, accomplishing nothing more than keeping idle soldiers busy. On 3 February it was Porter's turn to try a new tack. He ordered a portion of the levee just east of Helena, Arkansas, destroyed. By the next day, floodwaters connected the Mississippi to the upper tributaries of the Yazoo. Unfortunately, Lt. Comdr. Watson Smith did not manage to move his flotilla through the levee for more than two weeks. By that time, any pretense of surprise had disappeared, but the operation proceeded as planned. Smith commanded seven gunboats and transports carrying forty-five hundred men under Gen. Leonard Ross. It took ten days to overcome overhanging trees, enemy snipers, heat, and insects to reach the Tallahatchie River. Ten more days brought the force within striking distance of the point where the Tallahatchie and Yalobusha join to form the Yazoo and where

Confederate Gen. William Loring waited behind makeshift Fort Pemberton, a cotton-bale-and-sandbag strongpoint situated in a narrow bend of the Yazoo near Greenwood, Mississippi.

When Smith arrived, the fortifications were so advanced and well placed that Ross could not land his troops in the marshy surroundings. The brown-water navy would have to silence the fortress. As before, at Forts Henry, Donelson, and Hindman, Federal gunboats held the advantage in firepower, but Smith was neither a Porter nor a Foote.

Around 10:00 A.M. on 11 March, the ironclad USS *Chillicothe* nosed around a bend in the Tallahatchie and approached Fort Pemberton. Two well-placed shots struck the gunboat almost immediately.[23] The ironclad backed up until only the bow, which held two 11-inch Dahlgren smooth-bores, could be seen from the Confederate works. After an hour of exchanging iron insults with the fort's defenders, the gunboat withdrew. The *DeKalb* took up the fight later in the afternoon for another two hours. The battle ended with Smith withdrawing his gunboats for repairs.

The next day the Federals erected a shore battery eleven hundred yards in front of the fort in a thickly wooded area. On Friday the thirteenth, the Yankees had only slightly better luck. They opened fire on the Rebel works from two gunboats abreast, their land batteries, and a 13-inch mortar. The Confederates once again "severely handled" the Union warships,[24] but not before the gunboats exacted some retribution. An 11-inch shell punched through the fort's parapet, displacing a cotton bale and igniting a gun magazine; the resulting explosion wounded a lieutenant and fifteen men. A shell also killed a crew member at another battery. Sporadic fighting occurred throughout the next afternoon, but both sides kept the Sabbath. Monday's grand assault was canceled almost before it began when a shot from a Confederate heavy artillery piece penetrated the *Chillicothe*.

Claiming he was too ill to continue, Smith turned his armada over to Lt. Comdr. James P. Foster, who prepared to retreat. The arrival of reinforcements changed his plans. The gunboats threw a few rounds into the Confederate embankments on 19 March expecting the bolstered army to advance, but after one look at the Confederate defenses, the troops turned around and headed back north. The gunboats followed.

In the meantime, fearing that Smith and Ross might be cut off, Grant and Porter had headed up Steele's Bayou north of Vicksburg on 14 March to come to their aid. This time Porter led the expedition himself. The admiral discovered what Smith already knew: The swamps could swallow heavily armed gunboats. When a coal barge sank and blocked his retreat, Porter began to fear he might have to abandon his flotilla to the Confederate infantry and artillery that had driven his sailors from their outpost on top of an old Indian burial mound. Sherman arrived, however, on 21 March, just in time to save Porter's fleet. Because the river was too narrow to turn the gunboats around, it took almost another week for them to back all the way to their base.[25] The Federals contented themselves by loading all their gunboats with cotton as they retreated—$25,000 worth on the USS *Cincinnati* alone.

During the aborted attacks on Fort Pemberton and up Steele's Bayou, the remaining Federal naval forces around Vicksburg had not been idle. Eight mortars on rafts continued to shell the town and its defenses around the clock.[26] Except for the water batteries (mounting eleven and thirteen guns respectively), the artillery pieces defending Vicksburg had been scattered about and concealed within the city. Unable to locate them, Federal gunners could only lob shells haphazardly into the Confederate positions. In what was one of the first instances of military photo analysis, a navy photographer enlarged a picture of the bluffs and used a magnifying glass to pinpoint Confederate guns.[27] Even so, hitting the targets proved difficult. When Ross returned from Fort Pemberton, a dejected Sherman suggested another total withdrawal. Grant refused.

The army commander knew a retreat would be politically disastrous for the Lincoln administration already stinging from poor mid-term election results. Also, as spring progressed and the river dropped, Grant could finally get his army south of Vicksburg by moving down the east bank of the Mississippi. Farragut tried to bring his fleet upriver past the guns at Port Hudson, Louisiana, on 14 March to support Grant's movement, but only two ships made it. Farragut asked for help from Porter. The request came to the attention of General Ellet, who pledged to send the rams *Switzerland* and *Lancaster* to join Farragut in a bombardment of Warrenton. Capt. Henry Walke, commanding the upper squadron in Porter's absence, refused to dispatch an ironclad to protect the rams. The rash Ellet decided to run the batteries anyway.

Worried more about running aground than being sunk by gunfire, Ellet decided to pass fortress Vicksburg in daylight on 25 March. A shell through the *Lancaster*'s steam drum, followed by a large-caliber plunging shot, cracked the old boat's hull, sinking her almost immediately. The *Switzerland* was disabled but drifted down to Farragut. Accusations flew between Porter and Ellet until Farragut became disgusted and withdrew downriver without making the assault on Warrenton. Grant made a personal reconnaissance up the Yazoo on 1 April. The scouts looked foolish when the gun deck on the new ironclad *Tuscumbia* collapsed after a few shots had been fired to provoke a response from the defenders. In any case, Grant had seen enough and decided to forego another attack on Haynes's Bluff. Now all he had to do was convince Porter to run the batteries of Vicksburg to support his army downstream.

At nine in the evening of 16 April, Porter's fleet headed for a surprise appointment with Confederate gunners at Vicksburg. The flagship *Benton* led six other gunboats and several auxiliaries in single file at fifty-yard intervals. Running silently, the fleet managed to avoid detection until it reached the first battery. Heavy and rapid fire from the massed guns of Porter's ironclads kept the Confederates off balance. Despite the fearsome pyrotechnics, after two hours Porter's fleet was below the city with the loss of only one transport. The next morning the squadron lay at New Carthage, Louisiana. Six days later a half-dozen transports also ran the batteries stretching from Vicksburg to Warrenton to bring supplies downstream to Grant's army.

As part of his two-hundred-mile-long front from Vicksburg to Port Hudson, Pemberton had enough foresight to garrison Grand Gulf, Mississippi, where a large contingent under Maj. Gen. J. S. Bowen had dug in several cannon. This was the same spot Grant chose to land his army. The gunboats were to reduce the defenses before the army crossed, but Porter did not want to attack such a strong position. Grant, on the other hand, favored a direct approach. On the morning of 29 April, the Union gunboats pushed their way across a six-knot current to exchange fire with Confederate heavy ordnance. Caught in swirling eddies, the gunboats became spinning targets for Rebel gunners. During the five-and-a-half-hour slugfest, Porter's gunboats managed to silence the batteries farthest downstream without losing a single boat, but it was clear a river crossing was out of the question. Much of the casemate armor on the unlucky *Tuscumbia* had been knocked off and the USS *Benton* had been disabled.

Having control of the river, Grant did what Porter had wanted to do in the first place: outflank Grand Gulf. On 30 April Grant made an unopposed landing a few miles south at Bruinsburg. Bowen marched his outnumbered force from its prepared position to meet Grant, only to be routed. His men stopped long enough on their retreat toward Vicksburg to blow up the munitions and guns at Grand Gulf.

Gen. Joseph Johnston then wired Pemberton to unite his forces to whip Grant: "Success will give you back what was abandoned to win it."[28] Pemberton hesitated. On the same day Grant's troops disembarked, Sherman — with the aid of several gunboats and three mortarboats under Lt. Comdr. K. R. Breese — attacked Haynes's Bluff[29] and Drumgould's Bluff on the Yazoo north of Vicksburg. For two days soldiers and sailors stood toe to toe with Confederates and exchanged blows. Concentrating their fire on the Union warships, Rebel gunners managed to hit the USS *Choctaw* fifty-three times. The damage may have been a small price to pay to confuse the enemy. When Federals observed ox teams hauling heavy guns to reinforce Confederate positions along the bluffs, they knew their feint had worked. Still trying to determine which attack — Sherman's or Grant's — was the main thrust, Pemberton did what he thought best: not much of anything. The Confederate commander's inaction guaranteed that Grant and his army, not Porter and his navy, would capture the city.

During the next eighteen days, Grant won five battles with a series of movements matched only by Stonewall Jackson's Shenandoah campaign of

March–June 1862. By mid-May, Pemberton had withdrawn his army behind the fortifications at Vicksburg. Johnston advised him to escape, but he refused. Worried about the news from his home state, Davis called Lee to Richmond on 15 May. The general assured the cabinet that if the summer weather in Mississippi did not drive Grant away from Vicksburg, an invasion of Pennsylvania would draw the invaders north.[30] Postmaster General John Reagan, the only member of the cabinet from west of the Mississippi (Texas), insisted that Vicksburg was the most crucial point in the Confederacy and that its relief should have the highest priority. Gen. James Longstreet proposed moving west with two of his divisions. Davis liked the idea, but such was Lee's standing that he got his way.

Once Porter was below Vicksburg, he had to suffer the indignity of relieving Farragut, who was blockading the mouth of the Red River. Porter wanted to rejoin Grant and continue the Vicksburg assault.[31] Quickly accomplishing the task of seizing Alexandria, Louisiana, for Gen. Nathaniel Banks, Porter returned to the Mississippi. On the way back to the supply base at Young's Point just above Vicksburg, one of Porter's commanders noticed that the Confederate works at Warrenton seemed deserted. A party from the *Mound City* was sent to reconnoiter. A few defenders were hiding behind parapets, but a lucky shot from the gunboat set their cottonclad earthworks aflame. What the Confederates failed to destroy as they withdrew, the men of the *Mound City* gladly finished off. By 15 May, Porter was once again ready to assist Grant. The next day, threatened from the rear by Grant's advance, Confederate forces quickly evacuated Haynes's Bluff, and Sherman's men — supported in their attack by the gunboat *DeKalb* — planted the Stars and Stripes on the pesky entrenchments.

Porter's boats now prowled the Mississippi above and below the city and almost a hundred miles up the Yazoo. There would be no reinforcements from the trans-Mississippi for the hard-pressed population of Vicksburg. In addition, mortarboats fired thousands of naval shells onto the defenders. They caused little material damage, but the constant shelling psychologically devastated the soldiers and townspeople. Even Grant's drinking, driven by the boredom of siege warfare, could not alter the inevitable.[32]

One of the first things Porter did after his return was to send a fleet once more up the Yazoo, after the obstructions around Haynes's Bluff were cleared. He intended to destroy any Rebel vessels under construction at Yazoo City. At the approach of the Yankees on 21 May, the former commander of the *Arkansas*, Isaac Brown, destroyed three rams in various phases of completion. The Federals only needed to watch the flames.[33] On the way back down the river, the fleet came under attack by sharpshooters and artillery at Liverpool Landing, but it suffered only nine casualties.

During the second general attack by Grant's troops on Vicksburg's defenses the next day, the Confederate cannon known as Widow Blakely lost the tip of its barrel when one of its own shells burst prematurely during a fight with Union gunboats supporting the Federal assault. The barrel of the 7.44-inch rifled gun was trimmed, and the piece was used as a mortar for the rest of the siege. The Confederates got some revenge on 27 May. Grant had ordered one of Porter's ironclads to engage the rifle pits near Fort Hill, the northwestern anchor of the Confederate lines. When the *Cincinnati* turned upstream to hold its position, an 18-pound smoothbore (which had been rifled) known as Whistling Dick put a shot through the boat's unarmored stern. According to crewman Daniel F. Kemp, "Every battery at Vicksburg was pouring shot and shell into our poor doomed Gunboat and they had the range so perfect that almost every shot struck us and came thro' and did a lot of damage."[34]

Lt. George M. Bache, miraculously unscathed when a round smashed the pilothouse, killing the pilot and wounding a quartermaster, managed to bring the *Cincinnati* to shore. It slid into deeper water, however, and "careen[ed] to one side — her hull fill[ed] with water & slowly she settle[d] down in the water & [sank] to the bottom."[35] she was the only ironclad vessel sunk solely by gunfire. Under cover of darkness, Sherman's troops removed the 9-inch guns from the boat and mounted them in front of their position. Lt. Comdr. T. O. Selfridge, formerly captain of the *Cairo*, handled the battery, which eventually bore his name.

Another expedition on the Yazoo came within fifteen miles of Fort Pemberton but had to turn back when sunken steamers blocked the way. On their way back, Federals once again landed at Yazoo City. This time they carried away all the remaining iron that could be used for armoring ships. Confederates on shore tried to inflict some damage, but they were easily driven off.

Before dawn on 7 June, Brig. Gen. Henry E. McCulloch's Texans attacked the Federal outpost at Milliken's Bend, Louisiana, across the river from Vicksburg. Here again, black soldiers proved they would fight and die as 1,500 Confederates pushed back the Federals, killing or capturing more than 660 of the 1,000 defenders. Two gunboats sent downriver by Porter from their base at Young's Point arrived in time to drive off the Texans. Confederate Maj. Gen. John G. Walker wrote: "It must be remembered that the enemy behind a Mississippi levee, protected on the flanks by gunboats, is as securely posted as it is possible to be outside a regular fortification."[36]

Growing impatient, Grant ordered a deadly six-hour cannonade for Vicksburg on 20 June. The extent of devastation already within the city was demonstrated when Porter's fleet met no opposition.[37] Five days later Yankee miners set off a charge under a Rebel redan northeast of Vicksburg. For the next three days both sides fought over the resulting hole before the Federals pulled back after losing two hundred men. At the beginning of the next month, another charge exploded under the same redan, but the wary blue troopers did not attack this time. It was clear to the exhausted soldiers of both sides that the end was near.

On 3 July Pemberton sought terms from Grant while men in blue and gray bled in the fields and hills surrounding a little Pennsylvania town called Gettysburg. As Lee prepared to retreat across the Potomac on the anniversary of the nation's Declaration of Independence, the official surrender of Vicksburg took place. The Fourth of July would not be celebrated in Vicksburg again for the next eighty-one years.

One of the first orders Grant gave after riding into Vicksburg was to Porter, suggesting he send still another fleet up the Yazoo River. Four armored gunboats and five thousand troops under Maj. Gen. Francis J. Herron entered the hotly contested waterway the second week in July. As they crawled cautiously along on 13 July, the *Cairo*-class ironclad *DeKalb* was forced to withdraw after encountering an enemy battery across from the navy yard below Yazoo City, the operation's objective. Herron's troops landed and captured the city, with support from the ships. While moving back upstream, the *DeKalb* was shaken by two torpedo explosions and sank within fifteen minutes. The capture of three thousand bales of cotton lessened the sting of a second major loss to torpedoes on the Yazoo. The value of the cotton was equal to the cost of the lost gunboat.[38]

If you go there . . .

Natchez, Mississippi, is being invaded by Yankees via the river once again, and today's residents are reacting to the appearance of the ship-borne northerners as their ancestors did 130 years earlier. They are more curious than cantankerous, even though this time there will definitely be some bandits along — the one-armed kind — as an Iowa company brings riverboat gambling to the town's historic Under-the-Hill area, the traditional docking site below the Natchez bluff.

Preservation-minded community leaders express confidence that the influx of gamblers will not alter the flavor of the state's oldest city, whose main tourist dollars formerly came from the well-known spring and fall Natchez Pilgrimage tours of the city's landmark mansions. Prior to the Civil War, more millionaires settled in the countryside surrounding Natchez than anywhere else in the country.

Two factors have allowed more than five hundred antebellum buildings in and about Natchez to survive to the present day. To begin with, very little fighting took place in Natchez during the Civil War. Even so, **The Burn**, a Greek Revival bed and breakfast at 712 North Union Street, was used as a hospital for Union troops. Second, a decline in local cotton production brought about the collapse of a postwar economic boom by the turn of the century, guaranteeing that there would be no money for new construction. Finally, an interest in historic preservation by some citizens as early as the 1930s ensured that architecturally and historically important structures would be retained and restored, if possible. Consequently, many of the stately plantation homes capping the hillsides surrounding the town appear much the same as they did when the Civil War began.

One house, **Longwood,** at 140 Lower Woodville Road, stands as a testament to the disruption of the antebellum plantation lifestyle. Begun at the end of the 1850s, the octagonal, thirty-two-room oriental villa was designed to serve as the symbol of success for Dr. Haller Nutt, a southern-born planter and slaveowner. Like many of the wealthy landowners in the South, Dr. Nutt was a unionist, even proclaiming his "unswerving loyalty to the Union at all times."[39] Despite the sectional strife, he tried to run his plantation during the war to earn enough money to complete his house. But by 1863, his freed slaves chose to leave. In addition, Union troops began to occupy his land and buildings, confiscate his crops, and burn what they couldn't carry on their way to Vicksburg. Depressed at finding himself a poor man, Dr. Nutt took ill and died at his unfinished home in June 1864. Recognizing the justness of Nutt's claims of wrongdoing by the Union army, the federal government paid his widow approximately $200,000 over a period of some thirty years. When the property was turned over to the Pilgrimage Garden Club of Natchez in 1970, thought was given to finishing Dr. Nutt's dream, but it was decided to leave the home as a reminder of war's disruption. The home is open for tours daily. For more information, contact: The Pilgrimage Garden Club, P.O. Box 347, Natchez, MS 39120 (800) 647-6742.

The best place to start any study of Grant's anabasis at Vicksburg is the visitors center at **Vicksburg National Military Park,** just off I-20. The bookstore there sells separate battlefield guides to several of the related campaigns, including Sherman's Chickasaw Bayou debacle. Business 61, just north of the National Military Park, runs roughly parallel to the Confederate lines that halted Sherman's advance in December 1862.

Other sites to see in Vicksburg include the **Old Court House.** Used as a museum since 1948, the building stood on the highest hill in town and was employed during the war as a signal station and prison. Despite being the target of several Union bombardments, the building suffered only one serious hit before the city's surrender. As can be expected, many of the displays in the museum deal with the Civil War. Included are models of the *Virginia, Monitor,* and *Cairo.* The museum is open, Monday through Saturday, 8:30 A.M.–4:30 P.M. and on Sunday from 1:30–4:30 P.M. It is closed Thanksgiving, Christmas Eve and Day, and New Year's Day. Admission is $1.75 for adults and $1.00 for students in grades one through twelve. For information,

The Old Vicksburg Court House

contact: Old Court House Museum, 1008 Cherry Street, Vicksburg, MS 39180 (601) 636-0741.

Just south of the courthouse, the **Toys and Soldiers Museum** occupies the corner of Cherry and Grove. During the Civil War the building served as a grocery store and was the first business Grant allowed to reopen. Today visitors can walk through an incredible collection of twenty-six thousand soldiers and other toys, including a dozen or so $1/72$-scale models of Civil War ships involved in battles around Vicksburg. Admission is $2.00 for adults and $1.50 for students grades one through twelve. The museum is open Monday through Saturday 9:00 A.M.–4:30 P.M. and Sunday from 1:30–4:30 P.M. For information, contact: Toys and Soldiers Museum, 1100 Cherry Street, Vicksburg, MS 39180 (601) 638-1986.

The newest museum in Vicksburg is **The Gray and Blue Naval Museum.** Advertising "The World's Largest Collection of Civil War Gunboat Models," the museum offers naval enthusiasts thirty-five $1/8$-scale models by Bill Atteridge of Arcadia Crafts and fifteen paintings on naval subjects from the collection of Lamar Roberts. A gift shop sells model kits and books. Admission to the museum, open from 9:00 A.M.–5:00 P.M. Monday through Saturday and 1:00–5:00 P.M. on Sunday, is $1.50 for adults, $1.00 for twelve and under, and $5.00 for the whole family. For information, contact: The Gray and Blue Naval Museum, 1823 Clay Street, Vicksburg, MS 39180 (601) 638-6500.

The **Vicksburg Convention and Visitors Bureau,** situated just across Clay Street from the National Military Park, offers an excellent city guide that pinpoints many of the buildings related to the town's role in the Civil War. Although there are too many places to name, keep in mind two bed and breakfasts if you want to sleep surrounded by history. **Balfour House,** a small bed and breakfast, served as the site of a Christmas gala attended by Maj. Gen. Martin Luther Smith who announced, "This ball is at an end" when told of the approach of Sherman's troops. Two doors east is the Willis-Cowan House, General Pemberton's headquarters the following summer. Union troops utilized Balfour House as headquarters after the city fell. A cannonball and other artifacts found in the walls are on display. The price is approximately $85 for double occupancy. For information, contact: Balfour House, 1002 Crawford Street (601) 638-3690 or (800) 844-2500.

A bit larger, the **Duff Green Mansion** provided soldiers on both sides with a place to sleep and something to eat during its role as a hospital. The cost for bed and breakfast today is $75–$150 for two people and includes modern amenities such as a pool and cable television. For information, contact: The Duff Green Mansion, 1114 First East Street (601) 636-6968 or (800) 992-0037.

The Vicksburg tour home with one of the most interesting connections to the Civil War is **McRaven.** Near the site of the battle of the Railroad Redoubt, the grounds did not escape the crossfire of opposing armies. But the most notorious event surrounding the property occurred after the fall of the city when the home's owner, John H. Bobb, was murdered in 1864. No one was ever brought to trial. A bit of shooting still resounds around the gardens since the former Confederate campsite is now used for battle reenactments. Tours of the estate are given daily during the fall and spring, Monday through Saturday from 9:00 A.M. to 5:00 P.M. and Sunday from 10:00 A.M. to 5:00 P.M. From June through August, tours run from 9:00 A.M. to 6:00 P.M. seven days a week. The cost is $4.50 for adults. For information, contact: McRaven Tour Home, 1445 Harrison Street, Vicksburg, MS 39180 (601) 636-1663.

Certainly any stop at Vicksburg would include a trip through **Vicksburg National Military Park,** arguably the most beautiful military park in the nation. Approximately eight miles into the drive just below the Navy Monument and Battery Selfridge lie the restored remains of the ironclad USS *Cairo.* Because there was little time to abandon ship, almost all the supplies and many of the sailors' personal possessions sank with her. Mud and sand preserved this treasure, which was raised with the ship and put on display in the **Cairo Museum,** making the *Cairo* alone worth a special trip to Vicksburg.

The circumstances that brought the ironclad from its building site south of Saint Louis to its final berth next to Vicksburg National Cemetery provide a glimpse into the overall strategy in the Civil War's western theater. Unable to stop the Union navy with ships or shore fortifications, Confederates began searching for novel methods to deal with the North's naval advantage.

In the autumn of 1862 a Confederate officer who would affect the fate of the *Cairo* and alter the course of naval warfare appeared in Vicksburg.

Earlier on Lake Pontchartrain near New Orleans, C.S.N. Lt. Beverly Kennon had been conducting experiments based on work done earlier in Virginia by Matthew Fontaine Maury. The result was an electrically activated torpedo (mine) that Kennon planned to use for the defense of New Orleans until the capture of the city forced him to abandon that idea.

Neither Kennon nor Maury, a former U.S. Navy officer who had resigned his commission at the beginning of the war, were the first to come up with a practical mine. David Bushnell had devised a keg torpedo during the American Revolution. Mines were also used at Canton, China, in 1857–58, and the Russians employed them during the Crimean War. None of these managed to sink an enemy ship, however.

Kennon had not been any more successful than the others, but he imparted his knowledge to Zedikiah McDaniel and Francis M. Ewing, both of the Submarine Battery Service, a branch of the Confederate military authorized to oversee mining operations throughout the South. McDaniel and Ewing had been sent to help the defenders of Vicksburg, and they used Kennon's information to develop torpedoes that were placed in the Yazoo River.

On the other side, Union naval forces had become proud, almost to the point of insolence, of the way they had been able to deal with Confederate shore defenses. Although there had been some setbacks, for the most part the Federals did what they pleased on the oceans and inland waterways. Many tars wanted a share of this glory, and the crew members of the *Cairo* were no exception. They considered it unfortunate that their ironclad had not been completed in time for the engagements at Forts Henry and Donelson in Tennessee. Furthermore, she just missed the battle at Shiloh where the fire of gunboats on the Tennessee River is given a large share of credit for saving Grant's army. The *Cairo* was able to get in some shots during one of the few fleet actions of the entire war above Fort Pillow, Tennessee, at Plum Point on the Mississippi River, but it had been a disappointing affair. Both the ship's crew and its captain were eager for more. Vicksburg might be their chance.

During an operation in conjunction with Sherman's army late in 1862, the navy sought a route up the Yazoo to cut off Pemberton's army from Vicksburg. Tinclads were sent to reconnoiter. They reported Confederate batteries dug in at Drumgould's and Snyder's bluffs. The waterway leading to them was protected by torpedoes, or "infernal machines." Having successfully swept for mines at Fort Henry and Columbus, Kentucky, Comdr. Henry Walke, who was in charge of the entire Yazoo River operation, decided to send tinclads escorted by gunboats to destroy the torpedoes. The mines had been no real threat so far, but they were a menace with which the navy would have to deal.

Lieutenant Commander Selfridge was put in charge of the minesweeping expedition that got under way 12 December 1862, a cool and

The resurrected USS *Cairo*, undergoing restoration work at the Vicksburg National Military Park

cloudy day. Three tinclads led the way, followed by the ironclads *Cairo* and *Pittsburg*. Just before reaching the objective, Selfridge heard firing from the direction of the lead tinclad, the *Marmora,* then saw that it had reversed its wheel. Thinking it under attack by sharpshooters, Selfridge ordered the *Cairo* forward only to discover that the captain of the tinclad had stopped to blow up some torpedoes. Selfridge, impatient to attack the Confederates who had opened fire from Drumgould's Bluff, again ordered the *Cairo* to proceed upriver.

Within a minute, two explosions shook the craft. Twelve minutes later it sank, miraculously without any loss of life. The unlucky *Cairo* became the first warship ever to be lost to enemy torpedoes, thus opening a new chapter in naval history. By the end of the Civil War, nearly fifty more ships on both sides would be sunk or damaged by those "infernal machines."

The sinking of the *Cairo* did not end the Yazoo mission. Eventually, the crew of the *Pittsburg* destroyed twelve torpedoes while a tinclad pulled down the *Cairo*'s chimneys and jackstaffs to hide her location from the Confederates. Bluejackets from the flotilla also discovered the point ashore from which McDaniel, Ewing, and Lt. Isaac M. Brown, former commander of the ram *Arkansas,* had watched the sinking. At that spot, sailors found and destroyed supplies to produce more torpedoes.[40]

At first, Admiral Porter blamed the mishap on the fact that "due caution was not observed and that the vessels went ahead too fast."[41] In his later massive tome, *The Naval History of the Civil War,* Porter was less critical, stating: "It was an accident liable to occur to any gallant officer whose zeal carries him to the post of danger, and who is loath to let others do what he thinks he ought to do himself."[42]

For the next century the *Cairo* lived on only in stories told by locals. Then in 1956 Edwin C. Bearss, the new historian for Vicksburg National Military Park; Warren Grabau, a Civil War buff; and Don Jacks, a park maintenance person, used compasses to pinpoint the location of the wreck. Three years passed before divers were able to bring back positive proof and set serious recovery work in motion.

In September 1960 the pilothouse and a naval cannon were raised. This success helped bring money into the project. One of the most unusual donations came from Bearss himself who appeared on the television game show "100 Grand" in 1963 and won $10,000 for the project. Navy personnel helped to disarm projectiles, volunteers and others working for cost brought out the remaining cannons, and finally, late in October 1964, the ironclad saw daylight again. It was almost salvaged when lifting wires cut the hulk in three sections. The parts were eventually raised separately, the last coming to rest on its barge 12 December 1964, exactly 102 years to the day after it sank.

In 1965 the three sections were towed to Ingalls shipyard in Pascagoula, Mississippi. Hurricane Camille bypassed the hard-luck ironclad in 1969, providing one of its few brushes with good fortune. It took eight more years to raise enough money to return the *Cairo* to Vicksburg for restoration. The project was completed in 1984.

One final irony occurred in the ironclad's long history. In 1876, the Mississippi River took the shortcut south of Vicksburg that Grant so desperately sought, and the city no longer occupied a commanding spot on the river.[43] In 1902 the Army Corps of Engineers diverted the Yazoo from its old channel to run past the city. So the *Cairo* rests under its own shed next to the river that had been its grave for over a century.

Both the park and the Cairo Museum are open daily except Christmas. The ironclad can be reached from the park tour road or through the city of Vicksburg via Fort Hill Drive and Connecting Avenue. For information, call: Cairo Museum (601) 636-2199.

To follow Grant's final amphibious campaign for Vicksburg, the best guide to acquire is "Claiborne County Historical Tours," a brochure available from Tour Headquarters, Port Gibson, MS 39150.

One of the tours outlined in the brochure will lead you ten miles northwest of Port Gibson to **Grand Gulf Military Monument Park.** In the early 1840s the Mississippi River port of Grand Gulf had high expectations, but a yellow fever epidemic and tornado devastated the small town. Then the Mississippi ate away fifty-five city blocks, the entire business district. What remained, Union forces burned during the second of their occasional occupations. When Southerners returned, they came back to stay. Pemberton, in anticipation of Grant's flanking movement, ordered General Bowen to arm both Fort Wade and Fort Cobun at Grand Gulf with heavy mortars.

Today students at the Army War College take frequent pilgrimages to the park, which features a museum, campground, picnic area, hiking trails, several restored buildings, and portions of both the earthen forts. Confederates tried to destroy their own magazine at Fort Wade when they abandoned the position, but the powder room's walls, which utilized iron from an old jail, partially survived. Admission to the museum (open Monday through Saturday, 8:00 A.M.–noon and 1:00–5:00 P.M., and Sunday from 9:00 A.M.–noon and 1:00–6:00 P.M.) is $2.00. Included among its myriad Civil War artifacts are models of many of the warships that fought in the waters around Grand Gulf. For more information, contact: Grand Gulf Military Monument Park, Route 2, Box 389, Port Gibson, MS 39150 (601) 437-5911.

One of the restored buildings at Grand Gulf is the Catholic church from **Rodney,** a small port town just south of where Grant eventually landed at Bruinsburg. A stop on the Claiborne County tour, Rodney lies just south of the county line and is not easy to find. Its claim to fame is the Old Rodney Presbyterian Church. While on blockade duty, sailors from the USS *Rattler* decided to attend services there one Sunday. The unarmed Yankees were attacked by "little old ladies armed with their prayer books," according to the curator at Vicksburg's Old Court House Museum, in what has been called the battle of hymnals. Although one Southern belle gallantly hid a frightened Federal worshiper under her petticoats, the rest of the Northerners feared for their safety and somehow managed to call down a cannonade from the *Rattler.* A round shot is still embedded in the church. The *Rattler's* remains are buried near the Grand Gulf Military Park, and historians are trying to dig them up. Behind the church some Confederate trenches line the hills.

The Rodney Presbyterian Church. A cannonball is embedded just above the middle top window.

Most visitors to Vicksburg don't bother to scout Smith's 1863 naval excursion down the tributaries of the Yazoo toward **Fort Pemberton.** But if Henry McCabe gets his way, more will likely make the effort. Although the county has built a small park on the north side of the highway with markers telling of the Federal naval attack on the fort, McCabe wants more to be done. He has been trying for several years to start renovation work on the earth-covered cotton-bale fort, whose unprepossessing breastworks are bisected by Highway 82W just west of Greenwood.

The site of Fort Pemberton, one of the few cotton-bale forts built in the South. This area constitutes the fort's northeast bastion.

Just north of the fort, the *Star of the West*, the first ship to be fired on in the Civil War as it came to the aid of Fort Sumter, lies scuttled in the Talla-hatchie River. Following its unsuccessful attempt to reprovision Fort Sumter, the *Star* was ordered to Texas where it was captured near Indianola by troops under Col. Earl Van Dorn. As the men of Union Gen. Benjamin Butler closed in on New Orleans in 1862, the reflagged *Star* was sent to Vicksburg with gold, silver, and currency from the banks of New Orleans. In 1863 it was towed to Fort Pemberton and scuttled as a block ship.

The **Cottonlandia Museum** on Highway 82 in Greenwood has some of the recovered portions of the *Star*. For information or donations, contact: Cottonlandia Museum, Highway 82 Bypass West, Greenwood, MS 38930, or call Henry McCabe at (601) 453-5922.

CHAPTER 8

TENNESSEE

●N 8 JUNE 1861 Tennessee became the last state to join the Confederate States of America. Its tardiness was indicative of the divided loyalties of the state's population. Gov. Isham G. Harris, unable to gain secession through an earlier vote, used President Lincoln's call for troops after the fall of Fort Sumter as an excuse to sever relations with the North. Whether or not South Carolina and her followers were justified in leaving the Union, Harris — like many other Southerners — felt that Lincoln had no right to use force to compel individual states to remain in the republic. That summer, Tennessee prepared for war.

In retrospect, the key to the South's survival as a viable independent nation rested predominantly with the Volunteer State. Had the Confederate capital remained in Alabama, more emphasis on the protection of that state's northern border might have kept Tennessee in the Confederacy long enough to change the outcome of the war. With the wisdom of hindsight, the reasons for Tennessee's paramount importance are obvious.

To begin with, Tennessee was one of the South's major producers of foodstuffs: "in the total production of corn, hogs, cattle, mules and horses, the lower Middle Tennessee zone was one of the richest areas in the *entire Confederacy.*"[1] Furthermore, the capital of Tennessee — Nashville — was the most cosmopolitan city south of the Ohio River, with the exception of New Orleans. Art and affectation obviously do not win wars, but Nashville also served as the leading war production center in the West. Local companies manufactured artillery, small arms, copper percussion caps (90 percent of the South's copper came from around Ducktown, Tennessee), cartridges, saddles, blankets, and other accouterments of war. Even more important, the Confederacy's largest gunpowder mills lay along the Cumberland River northwest of the city,[2] utilizing saltpeter from the cave regions of East Tennessee. Nashville also blocked the invasion path to the industrial centers of Chattanooga and Atlanta.

If that were not enough, the South's greatest iron production region lay between the Cumberland and Tennessee rivers. Thousands of black, white, and Chinese laborers toiled to produce millions of pounds of raw iron in this Great Western Iron Belt, iron used for muskets, swords, and artillery.

Despite Tennessee's essential resources, few on either side of the Mason-Dixon Line regarded the state as deserving immediate attention. Politics dictated that energies would be focused in the region between the two national capitals. Robert E. Lee, who continued to serve as Jefferson Davis's military adviser even after assuming command of the Army of Northern Virginia, "did not grasp fully the importance of the munitions-producing area of Georgia, Tennessee, and Alabama."[3] In addition, Northern Commander in Chief Winfield Scott's Anaconda Plan emphasized control of the Mississippi River. Thus Tennessee Governor Harris and his second-in-command, Gideon Pillow, not only expected the North to follow Scott's plan but also trusted Kentucky's neutrality to protect all the overland invasion routes into Tennessee. As a result, most of the state's troops, engineers, and artillery went to bolster the defenses of a chain of forts along the Mississippi from Memphis to Island Number 10 to protect against an attack from Missouri. Only four thousand troops guarded the vital iron ore region of Middle Tennessee. Another token force guarded the Cumberland Pass.[4]

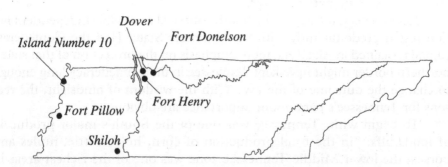

When Gen. Leonidas Polk, the Fighting Bishop, arrived in July 1861 to oversee the state's military forces, the situation did not improve. Polk, like Harris and Pillow, remained intent on controlling the vital Mississippi. The results were both predictable and disastrous for the South.

Forts Henry and Donelson

EVEN BEFORE the state had officially seceded from the Union, a group of prominent Middle Tennessee businessmen sent a telegram to Adna

Anderson, an engineer for the Edgefield and Kentucky Railroad, imploring him to do something about the weak nature of the defenses in the strategically important twin rivers region, the narrow neck of land between the Cumberland and Tennessee rivers that produced most of the South's iron. Anderson passed on their concerns to Governor Harris's assistant, Gen. Gideon J. Pillow, who replied there was "no present danger . . . nothing of military importance to be gained by ascending [the] Tennessee River."[5] Because the Federals were having their own difficulties preparing an advance, the first part of Pillow's statement was indeed true. The latter sentiment, that the enemy could gain no military advantage by an attack up the Tennessee River, would cripple Confederate strategic planning for the coming campaign, contribute to the eventual loss of Kentucky and Tennessee, and lead to the defeat of the South as perhaps no other single military misconception during the Civil War.

Henry Halleck, posted in November 1861 as senior Union commander in the West, reported to his Washington superiors prior to the battles at Forts Henry and Donelson that the struggle between the twin rivers would be "the turning point of the war."[6] Although he may have been promoting his own department's importance to the war effort, the fact that a Union officer with no small amount of authority made the observation is a telling one.

Governor Harris eventually sent several engineers to survey the best sites for forts to protect the twin rivers. Electing not to violate Kentucky's neutrality, Harris opted for positions in Tennessee less desirable than areas farther downstream in Kentucky (the rivers flow north in that section). Sluggish work began on two main forts: one on the Tennessee named Henry (for Gustavus A. Henry, senior Confederate senator from the state) and the other twelve miles away on the Cumberland eventually named Donelson (for the state's attorney general, Daniel S. Donelson).

On 4 September Leonidas Polk ordered Pillow to fortify Columbus, Kentucky, violating that state's neutrality and providing the North with the justification to do righteously what it had planned to do in any case. Two days later, acting on his own, Ulysses S. Grant seized the Ohio River town of Paducah, Kentucky, situated at the mouth of the Tennessee River.[7] Grant followed up by positioning troops in Smithfield at the mouth of the Cumberland. Union troops also swept across the Ohio River from Grant's base at Cairo, Illinois, to build a fort on Kentucky soil. So much for neutrality protecting Tennessee's long northern border.

That same month Albert Sidney Johnston, C.S.A., arrived in Tennessee to take over command in the West. Little remains to suggest Johnston had more than a "cursory appreciation"[8] for the importance of the Confederate heartland. Although Johnston desired to protect the capital city of Nashville, he practically ignored any threat to the twin rivers and concentrated his defenses at Columbus on the Mississippi River and Bowling Green, Kentucky, northeast of Nashville. Perhaps his dispositions had been swayed by Kentuckian Simon Bolivar Buckner who "wanted no Yankee invader's heel treading upon [Kentucky] soil,"[9] and Polk, who was mainly concerned with the threat of a Union advance down the Mississippi. Whatever Johnston's reasons, anyone with military training could see a thrust along the Tennessee River would flank both positions.

Splitting his command was a calculated risk for another reason: Johnston had no reliable method to bring reinforcements quickly to threatened areas. Some 281 regular and transient packet boats had worked the prewar Cumberland River. By the fall of 1861 most were tied along the shore, their owners and hands departed for army service, either voluntarily or otherwise. Scarcely a dozen remained available for Johnston's use. Although blessed with more railroads than many Southern states, locomotives and rolling stock wore out from the increased demands placed upon them by the military; they could not be replaced and were repaired with great difficulty.

Fortunately for the Confederates, money problems, logistics, and departmental squabbling prohibited a Union river offensive in 1861. Most of the delay resulted from the brown-water navy's difficulties. Comdr. John Rodgers had managed to get three converted timberclad gunboats to Cairo by 12 August 1861. Rodgers, however, blew the whistle once too often on irregularities in the letting of civilian contracts, and Maj. Gen. John Frémont — Halleck's predecessor in Saint Louis — replaced him at the end of August with Andrew Hull Foote.[10] At age fifty-three, Foote had spent well over half of that time in the navy, fighting Malayan pirates in the East Indies, slavers off Africa, and forts in China. He made sure he could hold his own with the army by insisting upon flag rank. Of greatest importance to the coming campaign, civilian contractor James B. Eads performed minor miracles in putting together a fleet of ironclads, but they were not fully operational until early in 1862.

Grant, anxious to implement a plan for a strike down the Tennessee, petitioned Saint Louis for permission.[11] General Halleck did not feel as kindly toward Grant as Frémont had and he stalled any operations, even though reports from several sources suggested a thrust into central Tennessee would meet little opposition and could break the backbone of the Confederacy's western defense. All that Union subordinates had to do was convince the high command that an attack was feasible.

South of the Ohio the situation was somewhat similar. Both Polk in Columbus and Johnston in Bowling Green received letters about the sad state of affairs as Union gunboats began incursions up the Tennessee in October 1861. Col. Adolphus Heiman and his Tenth Tennessee (720 men

Andrew Hull Foote

armed with flintlocks) had begun work on Fort Henry and Fort Heiman[12] that fall. The Confederates also made noises about constructing a river defense fleet. Still, the overall state of preparedness was comical. During part of the summer, the unfinished Fort Donelson was garrisoned by forty unarmed men and was later totally abandoned until October. Fall floods inundated Fort Henry and covered torpedo defenses with thirty feet of water, more than enough to allow the unimpeded progress of gunboats. Johnston did not seem overly concerned; not once did he inspect the forts in person.[13]

When Halleck heard that Confederate reinforcements might be coming from Virginia, he quit stalling. On 29 January 1862 he authorized Grant to capture Fort Henry. Once he had permission, Grant acted quickly. By the time Confederates realized that his 4 February landing was more than a diversion, Foote had already put Grant's troops ashore below Fort Henry. Grant, however, had almost been too anxious. Hoping to land John McClernand's division past Panther Creek a little over a mile north of the fort, Grant and Comdr. W. D. Porter were almost killed while scouting the area. The general wisely chose to disembark the troops farther downstream.

On 4 February three Union gunboats also pushed to within two miles of Fort Henry and began a lackadaisical half-hour bombardment before retiring. None of the gunboats' shells fell into the fort. Fearful lest the large charges of powder required to reach the Federal warships should dismount one of the two guns capable of hitting the Federals, Heiman ordered his crews to cease firing almost as soon as they began.

Hearing the firing, Lloyd Tilghman, temporarily in command of the twin rivers defenses, rushed to Fort Henry. No fool, Tilghman realized the fight was over even before it began. "Only 2,600 men protected [Fort Henry], and most were armed with antiquated muskets used by Andy Jackson's militia in the War of 1812."[14] Worse yet, cold rainwater was so deep in the fort that the few reinforcements who arrived from Columbus could not enter the earthworks. Agreeing with Heiman that it would be suicidal to garrison Fort Heiman, Tilghman immediately ordered its evacuation even though much time and effort had been expended on the position. Selecting fifty men to service the water batteries, Tilghman sent the rest of his command toward Fort Donelson and resolved to fight a holding action against the dreaded Union ironclads. He did not have long to wait.

Two days after his first probing attack, Foote ordered his entire flotilla forward, not knowing that Grant's foot sloggers had gotten off to a late start. High water meant the gunboats could fire point-blank at the forts, but victory was not a foregone conclusion. Twelve of Fort Henry's heaviest guns would bear upon the fleet from behind the eight-foot-high, fourteen-foot-wide parapets. Jesse Taylor, commanding the artillery within the fort, ordered each gun captain to concentrate upon one particular vessel.

Army or no army, Foote determined to capture the forts on his own. As he signaled his fleet to close, Confederate gunners unleashed a punishing barrage. A round from a Columbiad struck the *Essex,* tore through its armor, and struck its middle boiler. Escaping steam killed ten men and wounded another score, including the gunboat's commander, William D. Porter, brother of Adm. David Dixon Porter. Fortunately for the remaining crew, the current swept the *Essex* back toward secure Union positions. Accurate fire from the fort took a toll on the other ironclads as well, a close shot even knocking the breath out of Foote. Just when the Confederates sensed a remarkable victory could be stolen, the tables turned. A 24-pounder burst, killing or disabling its entire crew. The Columbiad was then inadvertently spiked when a priming wire jammed and the blacksmith could not open the vent. Tilghman joined the men at the remaining guns, but by 1:30 P.M., just an hour after the battle began, only four guns remained serviceable. When Foote tried to maneuver the *Cincinnati* to enfilade the last artillery pieces, two shots from Tilghman's 32-pounder caused the flagship to alter its course.[15]

In another twenty minutes, fellow officers convinced Tilghman that continued resistance would only entail a useless loss of life. Wavering in his resolve, the Confederate commander finally ordered Taylor to strike the

The naval bombardment of Fort Henry *(Leslie's)*

fort's colors. The crew of the gunboats mightily celebrated the first major Union victory in Halleck's department and raced each other to be the first to the fort.[16] No one from Grant's army gained the forts until later in the afternoon.

When announced simultaneously with another Union naval victory at Roanoke Island, North Carolina, the fall of Fort Henry gave Northerners some positive results after all the false starts and empty promises of the previous year. In the South, the defeat came as a shock. As often happens in all-or-nothing situations, Tilghman, who came so close to being a hero, bore the enmity of his fellow secessionists for the surrender. Those who knew the truth about his predicament tried to defend his actions, but the fact remained that those in charge at Fort Donelson feared Foote's metal monsters could not be stopped. Whatever was going on in their minds, the men and commanders at Donelson would have time to think and prepare while Grant waited for the roads to Fort Donelson to dry out and for Foote's ironclads to be repaired and transferred to the Cumberland.

In the meantime, Foote detached S. L. Phelps with three timberclads to steam up the Tennessee River and capture the railroad bridge near Danville. Confederate guards fled before the fearsome gunboats, and Phelps's men tried to render the bridge inoperable without destroying it — Federal armies would want to use it later.

Phelps continued to a Hardin County landing known as Cerro Gordo in time for his busy crew to save the *Eastport* from being scuttled. Claiming the fast steamer as well as hundreds of feet of ship lumber as prizes of war, Phelps pushed on to Florence, Alabama, where in an attempt to win over the locals, he spared the railroad bridge linking that town to Tuscumbia. The Union gunboats could have pressed all the way to Chattanooga were it not for Muscle Shoals, forty miles of rapids that prohibited any advance beyond Florence except for small boats. The raid was a clear demonstration of the power of gunboats.

In the meantime, with his river protection gone and floodwaters at his back, Grant had reason for concern. For one thing, the remaining Confederates between the rivers outnumbered his forces. A determined counteroffensive by Johnston would probably have destroyed Grant, his career, and possibly any chance for the Union. But Johnston could not make up his mind. Although Halleck was not much better at formulating a plan than his Confederate counterpart and was scheming behind the scenes to have Grant replaced, he worked hard in the rear areas to make sure Grant received adequate supplies via the Tennessee and that Grant's flank was protected against any demonstrations from Columbus. By the time the timberclads returned on 10 February after destroying a Confederate encampment near Savannah, Tennessee, close to an unknown country church by the name of Shiloh, the immediate crisis had passed. Two days later, Grant started his legions from Fort Foote (the Union name for Fort Henry) and across the neck of land toward Fort Donelson.

Confederate decision-making seemed as frozen as the winter ground, the general officers in particular suffering from ironclad fever. Brig. Gen. John Bell Floyd, who would take over command at the fort within several days, reported that the "[ironclads] are nearly invulnerable, and therefore they can probably go wherever sufficient fuel and depth of water can be found."[17] Johnston shared his subordinate's views and admitted his fears to Richmond: "I think the gunboats of the enemy will probably take Fort Donelson without the necessity of employing their land force."[18]

Under different circumstances, Foote would have found these misgivings humorous. Not only had the flag officer lost valuable men during the struggle against Fort Henry, but several of his tars deserted on the trip back to Cairo. Replacements balked. They feared being scalded to death in Foote's iron coffins. Having tasted sweet victory, however, Foote was hooked by that powerful drug. Although insisting his ironclads were not prepared for another battle, he hated to miss the action. With a strong push from Halleck and others, Foote ordered the three city-series ironclads he deemed sufficiently repaired into the Cumberland the night of 11 February. The *Essex* and *Cincinnati* remained tied to the levee at Cairo.

The first test of the water defenses at Donelson came at 9:05 A.M. the next day. As C. F. Smith's division probed the Rebel outworks, the ironclad *Carondelet,* on station below Fort Donelson since shortly after the victory at Fort Henry, exchanged a few shots with the water batteries. The outcome was a draw.

Remarkably, despite an early superiority in numbers, the confused Confederate leadership did not strongly contest Grant's almost total investment of their landward position. Even so, the troops in Fort Donelson expressed confidence in their ability to turn back any Yankee approach.

On 14 February the remnants of Foote's Western Flotilla arrived on the scene. Foote continued to have doubts about his patched ironclads, but with an advantage of fifty-seven heavy guns to twelve, the fleet hove into the floodwaters of the Cumberland beneath Fort Donelson at 1:45 P.M. At worst, any boats put out of action would drift into friendly hands. On the other hand, Foote had the opportunity to score another decisive victory. Within fifty minutes the first long-range shots were exchanged between the gunboats and the two largest Confederate cannon. When a priming wire stuck in the 6.5-inch rifle at the upper battery, a repeat of Fort Henry seemed likely, but cool heads and skilled hands unjammed the vent. By 3:30 P.M. Foote had brought his fleet to within four hundred yards, hoping to mirror his close-quarters success on the Tennessee River.

As bleak as the early situation appeared for the men behind the earthworks, the situation was even worse inside the boats. A 32-pound steel Valentine struck the pilothouse on the *Saint Louis,* wounding Foote in his ankle. The quick-thinking commander managed to grab the wheel from the mortally wounded pilot, but further damage rendered the vessel useless. The command ship drifted out of the fight. Later Foote told a reporter he had participated in six other ship-versus-shore engagements, "but never was under so severe a fire before."[19] The *Louisville* was next. After taking at least four shots into the fighting compartment, the boat retired when its tiller was severed. The *Pittsburg* also retreated because it began to flood; the crew could not serve the guns and the pumps at the same time. Only one ironclad, the *Carondelet,* remained to face the jubilant Rebels, but not for long. In a matter of minutes, the defenders turned it into a shambles. Embarrassingly, the retreating *Pittsburg* accidentally rammed *Carondelet's* stern. By 4:30 P.M. the contest was over. Cheer after cheer rolled over the Confederate positions.

Foote tried to make the most of the defeat. Writing in disjointed English, he officially reported, "Would in fifteen minutes more, could the action have continued, have resulted in the capture of the fort bearing upon us."[20] As the defenders lost no guns in the point-blank duel, Foote's boastful words ring hollow. Playing armchair admiral, Rodgers suggested Foote's mistake was closing too quickly. The long-range cannon of the Union fleet could have overwhelmed the defenses if kept at a safe distance. Foote, however, showed an understanding of what maneuver could accomplish. The aging flag officer indicated that he intended to pass the batteries, as he had also vainly attempted at Fort Henry, and take the defenders from their exposed flank, a tactic used successfully at Port Royal, South Carolina, the previous year.

The naval bombardment of Fort Donelson *(Harper's)*

Once again the army was conspicuous by its absence. Grant had done nothing but watch the battle. Joint army-navy cooperation still had a long way to go.

The victory put a little spine back into the local Confederate command. Floyd, Pillow, and Brig. Gen. Simon Bolivar Buckner planned an early morning attack for 15 February to break the blue encirclement. Grant was visiting the wounded Foote when the Rebel yell burst upon the Federal right wing. Pillow and Buckner, with the help of a relatively unknown cavalry commander named Nathan Bedford Forrest, punched a hole in the Union lines literally large enough to march an army through. The situation was saved from becoming a total disaster for the Federal forces by Brig. Gen. Lew Wallace, later author of *Ben-Hur,* who, without orders, sent his brigades to reinforce McClernand.

For some reason, possibly because they had not counted on such a huge success, the Confederate generals had not reached an understanding concerning what to do once their men rolled back the Yankee lines. Buckner proposed marching the army to Nashville via the now-open Wynn's Ferry Road. Pillow, the senior officer on the field, astonishingly ordered Buckner back to the trenches. Buckner had not liked Pillow before and refused to obey at first. Finally, with the steam gone out of the advance, Buckner pulled his troops back and went in search of Floyd. The Confederate commander could not believe Pillow's order either. Pillow defended himself by stating reports that the Union army was reportedly receiving twenty thousand reinforcements. If Grant chose to attack the Rebel army in the open as they marched toward Nashville, Pillow argued, the tired, cold, and hungry men who were running low on ammunition would surely be slaughtered.

Whether or not Pillow was correct no longer mattered. The damage had been done.

Grant did not reach the scene of the battle until it was almost over. Shaken, he immediately penned a note to Foote asking him to make a demonstration with his gunboats to save the army. After regaining his composure, Grant showed his true talent for command. Quickly surmising that whoever attacked first would win the battle, he did just that, ordering Smith's division forward on the left. Without firing a shot, the Northerners took the outerworks, just as Grant had foreseen. As darkness fell over the battlefield, Confederates and Federals hugged roughly the same earth they had in the morning.

That night, rather then relish their victory, a gloom settled over the Confederate high command. Buckner, the one most insistent about breaking out earlier, reached some sort of personal breaking point. He suggested there was no other recourse but surrender, adding that Foote's gunboats would cut them to pieces if they tried either to cross the river or to forge icy Lick Creek. Floyd also caved in, but both he and Pillow did not want to be captured. The Rebel commander had served as secretary of war during the Buchanan administration and had been accused of sending arms and munitions south during his tenure. Pillow had his own reasons. Buckner volunteered to stay behind.

Forrest exploded with anger. Insisting there was more fight in the army than the generals gave it credit for, Forrest vowed not to surrender. Asking for volunteers, the wily Forrest made his way twenty miles toward Nashville the next day. Although the march was arduous, no one died from exposure, as Confederate doctors and Pillow had predicted. Even more important, no Federal troops were encountered. After arriving in Nashville, Forrest helped organize the evacuation of the city while the local government fled to Memphis.

Floyd and Pillow commandeered two steamboats arriving at Fort Donelson with supplies and made good their escape, leaving Buckner and his disappointed rank-and-file to accept unconditional surrender from Grant. Benjamin F. Dove of the U.S. Navy arrived before Grant at the Dover Hotel and would have accepted Buckner's sword if Wallace had not been there first. Dove left after a somewhat heated discussion, only to be suspended by the Navy Department for failure to take the surrender.[21] Grant eventually appeared and came around to discussing terms with Buckner. The Union commander allowed the captured officers to retain their sidearms and servants.[22]

On 19 February, after returning to Cairo to announce the victory at Donelson, Foote took the gunboats *Conestoga* and *Cairo* up the Cumberland toward Nashville to reconnoiter. At a small fort near Clarksville, the reputation of Foote's ironclads preceded them. Upon hearing that the gunboats were approaching, the commander of the fort wired General Floyd asking for instructions within ten minutes, "as I will have to go in a hurry when I go."[23] When Foote arrived, Federal troops found only a white flag. Lieutenant Phelps and Grant's chief of staff took possession of the fort. Foote wanted to send the Union fleet upriver immediately to capture Nashville, but Halleck hung back.

Several reasons have been offered for Halleck's decision. The department commander may have been concerned about a possible attack toward Cairo, Paducah, or Fort Henry by Polk's troops in Columbus, certainly a possibility if Polk had not been so wedded to his position. Foote attributed Halleck's refusal to jealousy within the army ranks.[24] Not all questions regarding ship-versus-shore contests were to be resolved between enemies: much to Foote's chagrin, glory, it seemed, had to be divided. An even more Machiavellian machination could have been behind Halleck's orders. He may have planned to allow Johnston to evacuate Nashville safely to demonstrate the result of a divided command in the western theater. The city lay in Gen. Don Buell's jurisdiction, not Halleck's.[25] If this was a ploy by Old Brains, it worked. At the beginning of March, Lincoln gave Halleck what he desired: command of all the armies in the West. The victory at the twin rivers, coupled with Maj. Gen. Samuel Curtis's victory at Pea Ridge, Arkansas, the following week, placed two feathers in Halleck's cap that seemed to presage the end of the Confederacy. But the obituary that Grant and others penned for the South after the collapse of Johnston's Tennessee line proved to be premature.

In the fall of 1864, Forrest, the only person to advance from the rank of private to lieutenant general in a single war,[26] departed Corinth, Mississippi, on what would be his last independent command in the war. With his mixed force, he would attempt "to cut Sherman's line of communication"[27] during the Union general's famed March to the Sea. By 28 October, Forrest's men arrived at Fort Heiman. They emplaced two 20-pound Parrotts in the old Confederate works and a section of Capt. John W. Morton's battery six hundred yards downstream. Other batteries would shut the trap at Paris Landing, five miles upstream. By late afternoon, the Federal Tennessee River supply line was broken, and Fort Heiman was prepared to accomplish what it had been intended to do when started two years earlier: obstruct Union advances on the Tennessee.

The first boats that appeared that day were riding high, empties going back to Cairo for more supplies, so Confederate Brig. Gen. Abraham Buford ordered the raiders to let them pass unmolested. The next day, the *Mazeppa* strained into view from the north towing a barge right into the Rebel trap. The quick-witted pilot, after taking a few shots, ran her ashore on the opposite bank and the crew escaped. The Southerners had no way to retrieve their booty. Capt. Frank Gracey volunteered to float across the river

Nathan Bedford Forrest

and bring back one of the boat's lines, which he did with the help of the victim's yawl. The ragged Rebel troopers pulled the abandoned transport to them and began to unload seven hundred tons of supplies. Three gunboats arrived and opened fire on the temporary longshoremen, only to be driven off by Rebel artillery crews.

The next morning when the *Anna* sped downriver past the concealed Confederates, Buford changed his mind about attacking empties. Wanting to capture an unharmed ship, the general hailed the transport and promised not to fire if she would surrender. The pilot agreed, then at the last minute ordered full steam. The Rebel gunners loosed a well-aimed volley into the disappearing steamer, but the damaged boat got away. A few miles upstream, the men of the escort *Undine* heard the cannon fire and turned around to investigate. The gunboat opened on the Confederate positions with its eight 24-pounders but got the worst end of the forty-five-minute shootout. The captain nosed her ashore midway between the enemy batteries at a point neither one could reach. Southern foot soldiers took up the fight, dodging case shot while trying to prevent the crew from effecting repairs.

During this time, the transport *Venus* hove into view. Ignoring signals from the *Undine*, the ship tried to run the blockade. Its daring captain was killed, and the steamer took shelter behind the stricken gunboat. Within twenty minutes, the *J. W. Cheeseman*, also oblivious to signals from the *Undine*, made a dash at the gray gauntlet. This time fire from the shore batteries forced the transport ashore at a spot where it could be unloaded before being torched.

Col. E. W. Rucker, C.S.A., then arrived on the scene with two more batteries and personally found a place for them from which to blast the remaining two stubborn boats. A few rounds convinced the *Venus* to surrender, but the gunboat crossed to the opposite shore. Confederates boarded the *Venus*, followed the *Undine*, and finally seized her. Another gunboat, the *Tawah*, was driven off by the Confederates at Fort Heiman.

Forrest then decided he wanted a navy. He placed two of his Parrotts on the *Venus* and ordered it and the *Undine* to follow him upriver toward the Union supply depot at Johnsonville, Tennessee, the raid's actual target. On Halloween, the new sailors treated themselves to a little practice before getting underway.

The crew members of the *Venus* became a bit too bold and were caught by the *Tawah* and another gunboat, the *Key West*, out of range of their consorts. The little transport was quickly overwhelmed. This time Yankees celebrated as Rebels fled the abandoned steamer. A fierce thunderstorm broke up further action.

The next day, 3 November, Forrest masked his intentions by emplacing two small batteries across from Reynoldsburg Island,[28] two miles north of Johnsonville, then sending the *Undine* to tease Union gunboats into range of the shore positions. The Federal commanders thought they were pretty smart to avoid the trap, but while they waited for reinforcements from Cairo, Forrest continued toward the supply dump at Johnsonville. When finally the two Federal flotillas were in position above and below Reynoldsburg, the crew of the *Undine* destroyed the last warship in Forrest's fleet. The land batteries, however, still had their sting. After taking nineteen hits in twenty minutes, the upper force under Acting Lt. Edward M. King retired back to Johnsonville. The six gunboats from Cairo under Lt. Comdr. LeRoy Fitch dared not pass the narrow chute alongside the shore and sat impotently as the first muffled explosions sounded upriver.

Under cover of darkness, Forrest had hidden his batteries across the Tennessee from the fort protecting the town and supply depot. His artillery commander, not satisfied with the positions after viewing them in daylight, requested permission from Forrest to move some of the guns. Forrest was not happy, but reluctantly assented. By 2:00 P.M. Rebel gunners were taking aim at the pesky gunboats to put them out of action first. When Forrest gave the order to fire, his well-placed artillery spewed forth instant destruction. Within forty minutes, everything afloat — four gunboats, fourteen transports, and seventeen loaded barges — was burning furiously. The acres of supplies on shore received the attackers' attentions next, particularly a pile of barrels which exploded into a blue-orange fireball and sent burning rivers of whiskey flowing toward the Tennessee.[29]

That night, as Confederate forces withdrew, Forrest returned to watch the flames of seventy-five thousand tons of burning supplies reflected in the river. Talking to his artillery officer, Capt. John W. Morton, Forrest observed, "if they'd give you enough guns and me enough men, we could whip Old Sherman off the face of the earth."[30]

That same day, Sherman had given orders to burn Rome, Georgia. It was the first part of a plan to cut his own supply lines, feed off the country, march to the sea, and make Georgia howl. Forrest was too late.

If you go there . . .

The marker for **Fort Heiman** stands beside Kentucky Highway 121, just north of the Tennessee border at New Mount Carmel Church. On 15 February 1862, the day the Confederates opened a route to Nashville from Fort Donelson, a Confederate company advanced from Paris, Tennessee, and attacked some Federals encamped in the churchyard.[31] The actual site of the fort is being developed for housing. To see what remains of the earthworks, turn off Kentucky Highway 121 and follow the road that runs west of the church. After a quarter-mile, bear right at the fork in the road. After another mile and a half, you should see signs for the Fort Heiman housing development. Turn right off the main road a half-mile beyond the signs. After another quarter-mile, the road cuts through some earthworks that were once Fort Heiman. Remember, you are on private property.

To reach the outerworks of **Fort Henry,** go back to Highway 121 and turn south. Two miles farther you will enter Tennessee, where the road becomes Tennessee Route 119. After several miles you will run into U.S. 79. Turn east and you will cross Kentucky Lake. A mile past the lake, turn north onto Fort Henry Road. About two miles farther, turn west at a sign indicating Boswell Landing. In less than a half-mile, the paved road bears right, but you should go straight onto a dirt road. After one-tenth mile you will find the outer works of Fort Henry stretching from both sides of the road. Just ahead is Kentucky Lake, the watery grave of Fort Henry.

Fort Donelson National Battlefield, about six miles farther east of Fort Henry Road on U.S. 7, encompasses the fifteen-acre fort as well as several miles of Confederate outerworks and the Dover Hotel. More than a hundred log huts stood within the original ten-foot-high walls. Reproductions of several of these huts are used by reenactors to exemplify how the garrison lived.

The most picturesque spot in the park is the lower water battery. Lake Barkley, created by a dam on the Cumberland River, stretches to the north,

Entrance to the main earthworks at Fort Donelson *(left)*, and the lower water battery overlooking the Cumberland River *(right)*

the direction from which Foote attacked. One of the gun positions has been restored to resemble how it appeared in 1862. Several cannon tubes are also on display next to the battery. A picnic area with grills is nearby.

The visitors center, which houses a small museum and gift shop, is open from 8:00 A.M.–4:30 P.M. daily except Christmas. Maps available at the visitors center highlight the major sites within the park, most of which can be reached by car. One of those is the **Dover Hotel,** the site of Buckner's surrender. Restored in the 1970s, the hotel is open daily from 11:00 A.M.–4:00 P.M., June through August, and from 1:00–4:00 P.M., September through May.

After Dover was almost completely destroyed by Confederate Gen. Joseph Wheeler's attack in 1863, the Union garrison in the town built another fort, which is now the site of the National Cemetery, the final resting place for 655 Union soldiers. For more information, contact: Superintendent, P.O. Box 434, Dover TN 37058.

The **Nathan Bedford Forrest State Historic Site** focuses more on recreation than history, but it does occupy the ground upon which Forrest placed his artillery for his ambush of Johnsonville, Tennessee. The park has two campgrounds, more than thirty miles of trails, picnic grounds, and regularly scheduled summer programs and demonstrations. Those interested in Forrest's exploits will find information and maps at the visitors center at the entrance to the park. Items on display in the center include a safe and other relics from the *Cheeseman,* one of the boats that Forrest captured on the Tennessee River. Another place to stop within the park is the interpretive center that sits atop Pilot Knob, the highest elevation in West Tennessee. The interpretive center features information about folk customs of the region, but there is a monument to Forrest on the overlook, which provides a clear view of the entire battle area.

From the I-40 Nathan Bedford Forrest exit, turn north to Camden and follow the signs to the park. It is open from 8:00 A.M.–10:00 P.M. in the

The Dover Hotel

summer and from 8:00 A.M. until sundown in the winter. For information, contact: Superintendent's Office, Nathan Bedford Forrest State Historic Area, Eva, TN 38333 (901) 584-6356.

Island Number 10

AS U. S. GRANT took his troops for a February 1862 cruise toward Fort Henry on the Tennessee River, Union Gen. John Pope ferried twenty-five thousand men from Cairo, Illinois, across the Mississippi River to Birds Point and pushed them through the Missouri mud toward the hamlet of New Madrid, situated on the Mississippi at the southern end of the Kings Highway from Saint Louis. There the forty-year-old West Pointer faced Gen. John McCown, C.S.A., and his seven-thousand-man garrison.

After Fort Henry fell, Leonidas Polk pulled his outflanked gray-clad de-fenders out of Columbus, Kentucky, and repositioned his heavy guns at Island Number 10, so-called because it was the tenth island downstream from Cairo. The island, a two-mile piece of high ground at the bottom of a horseshoe bend, was surrounded by swamps and the river. For that reason both sides thought it impregnable to land attack, but if an enemy could straddle the one road that passed south through Tiptonville to the Tennessee mainland, the garrison would be trapped. As part of their defense of this stretch of river — which looped six miles to the west before flowing south again — the Confederates erected two earthen forts on either side of New Madrid. Fort Thompson on the west held fourteen guns. East of the city at Wilson's Bayou stood Fort Bankhead with seven guns.[32]

On 3 March Pope's advance guard brushed aside Confederate pickets and invested the town. Fire from the forts and Confederate Com. George N.

Hollins's gunboats convinced Pope that any attack would be fruitless until he could mount siege guns. While waiting for the ordnance from Cairo, Pope sent Col. J. B. Plummer around New Madrid to the south to occupy the town of Point Pleasant. Southern warships prevented him from advancing until Plummer's sharpshooters forced the gunboats to withdraw. Union troops then moved into the town and dug in a few pieces of artillery. Although Plummer's guns could not do lethal damage to the Confederate gunboats, their presence forced the Rebels to land their unarmed supply vessels bound for Island Number 10 six miles farther downriver.

When three 24-pounders and one 8-inch howitzer arrived from Cairo, Pope's engineers quickly emplaced them under cover of darkness within a half-mile of the New Madrid forts. The next morning an artillery duel developed, pitting the guns from the Confederate forts and Rebel gunboats against the Federal siege train. Although neither the forts nor the tinclads were heavily damaged, Hollins expressed the opinion that his warships lacked enough armor protection to continue the fight. Without gunboat protection, McCown decided to withdraw across the river. Under cover of the first of several thunderstorms that would follow during the next month, the Rebels abandoned the town by 13 March, leaving behind everything they could not carry on their backs. The Yankees did not discover the retreat until the next morning.

P. G. T. Beauregard, second-in-command of Confederate forces in the West, replaced the disgraced McCown with Gen. W. W. Mackall, who took over the defenses at Island Number 10. Although Grant's success at Fort Henry the previous month had flanked the Confederate position, the defenders felt relatively secure since any movement by Grant toward the Mississippi would be quickly reported, giving the garrison ample warning to evacuate if necessary. Pope also presented no immediate threat, as six to eight gunboats under Hollins still controlled the river below New Madrid and could prevent any unguarded crossing by Pope's troops. Also, Pope's transports were upriver. It was true that the Federals had an enviable ironclad armada that could savage the Rebel fleet, but Mackall was confident they could not pass his gauntlet of guns on Island Number 10.

Pope, in fact, had been expecting help from Foote's Western Flotilla any day. The warships, roughly handled at Forts Henry and Donelson, were still undergoing repairs and were not in position above Island Number 10 until 15 March. Still in pain from the wound in his ankle suffered at Donelson, Foote held back. The Eads ironclads could not be anchored by their sterns,[33] and Foote feared, rightfully so, that any disabled ships would drift helplessly in the swift current toward the fortifications, either to be destroyed or captured by the Confederates. Henry Halleck, senior commander in the West, had been encouraging Foote to cooperate with Pope, but Halleck also had no desire to gamble with his most powerful assets and deferred to Foote's judgment concerning a run past the batteries. Foote preferred to let

The naval bombardment of Island Number 10 *(Leslie's)*

his newly finished mortarboats lob shells into the Rebel redoubts from a safe anchorage around a bend in the river.

After two days of ineffectual bombardment, Foote edged his ironclad fleet closer, but not too close. With the lessons from Henry-Donelson still fresh in his mind, Foote kept his boats two thousand yards from the enemy earthworks. After trading blows for seven hours with the enemy, Foote's gunboats retired with the coming of night.

Sloshing about in two feet of water like their kinsman at Fort Henry, the defenders lost one killed and seven wounded. A gun explosion on the USS *Saint Louis* killed two and wounded fifteen.

To get a better idea of the effect of the shelling on Rebel positions, a balloon was dispatched to Foote's fleet on 21 March. The report from the observer indicated few perceptible results from the cannonade, but it appeared to the balloonist that the Confederates might be evacuating the island anyway.[34] Realizing the futility of the long-distance siege, Pope continued to urge Foote to bring his ironclads past Island Number 10, then to silence the batteries protecting landing sites downstream by Tiptonville. Once that was accomplished, the Union army commander planned to ferry his men across the Mississippi. Foote held a council of his officers. All but Henry Walke, captain of the *Carondelet,* voted against forcing a passage.

Impatient with the navy, Pope ordered a canal to be dug, bypassing Island Number 10. More than six hundred engineers toiled nineteen days in the mire and muck to dig a six-mile water detour. When the river dropped, only the transports had a shallow enough draft to make it to New Madrid. But that was an important first step. At least Foote would not have to worry about the thin-skinned transports during any runs past the island. All his brown-water navy had to do was sneak two ironclads past the Confederates. That should be enough to protect Pope's river crossing. Walke volunteered to make the first attempt. As the *Carondelet*'s captain waited for bad weather to mask his movement, his compatriots tried to improve their chances by creating some of their own luck.

On the night of 1 April a combined army-navy expedition under Master John V. Johnston, U.S.N., made fools of the Confederates by landing at Fort Number 1 on the Tennessee shore above Island Number 10. No defenders were on station to stop the Federals as they spiked the guns and retired to safety. Three days later, the Confederates' floating battery of six guns was cut loose from its moorings by a concentrated bombardment. That night, three weeks before David G. Farragut's more-famous run into New Orleans, Walke ordered the lines cast off the *Carondelet* as a tempest brewed in the west. Once again, the defenders were taken by surprise, firing randomly into the blackness of the storm. The gunboat reached New Madrid by 1:00 A.M. unscathed. Two days later Walke made a reconnaissance as far as Tiptonville, exchanging shots with shore batteries and at one point putting ashore some men to spike some cannon. As another storm swept the river that night, the *Pittsburg* proved the first run was no accident. The two gunboats combined to destroy the remaining batteries guarding Tiptonville, then stood watch as the transports ferried Pope's army across the river. The Confederates were cut off.

On 7 April 1862, as twenty-four thousand men in blue and gray lay bleeding or dead at Shiloh, Mackall surrendered seven thousand soldiers, an equal number of small arms, more than a hundred heavy guns, two dozen field pieces, and hundreds of crates of ammunition. Comdr. A. H. Kitty of *Mound City* even managed to capture a Confederate signal book — all this for the loss of less than a hundred men on *both* sides. If anyone needed proof of the incredible ability of steam-powered, iron-sheathed weapons of war to win battles by maneuver, the ship-versus-shore confrontation at Island Number 10 provided plenty of evidence.

If you go there . . .

The Mississippi River is a fickle geographical entity. The Father of Waters constantly seeks the shortest way to the Gulf of Mexico. Without the efforts of engineers, for example, New Orleans might already have lost its position on the main channel. Sometime in the future, the Mississippi may force itself into the Atchafalaya River basin, leaving the Crescent City surrounded by dry land. Both Vicksburg and Port Hudson, scenes of the bloodiest fighting on the Mississippi in the Civil War, are no longer on the river that made them so strategically important. Fort Pillow, another in the chain of Tennessee forts along the Mississippi, silently guards backwaters today. The fate of Island Number 10 was even more dramatic. Constantly wearing at the sandbar's upper end, the river eventually swept away the entire land mass. Where Confederate guns once blasted at Foote's ironclads, a deep current now runs. Within twenty years of the Civil War, a new Island Number 10 arose on the opposite shore, "not standing as the old one, in the stream with a channel on either side, but near a point and surrounded by shoal water," wrote A. T. Mahan in the 1880s. "It has perhaps gathered around a steamer, which was sunk by the Confederates to block the passage through a chute then existing across the opposite point."[35]

Seismologists predict that Pope's initial target, New Madrid, Missouri, may again be the epicenter of a major earthquake, as happened in 1811–12 when the Mississippi ran backward for a while. The publicity is good for local businesses. The town's museum, standing on the Mississippi River–end of Main Street, sells T-shirts and sweatshirts that read "Visit New Madrid While It's Still There."

For those with a more historical bent, the museum also has on display several artifacts from the siege of New Madrid and the battle at Island Number 10, including cannonballs, a remnant of the Stars and Bars captured on the island, map cases, knapsacks, medical bags, swords, and other items belonging to the forces of Generals Pope and McCown. A driving-tour map available at the museum pinpoints the location of Fort Thompson.

Perhaps the most interesting exhibit involves the scuttled Confederate steamer *Winchester*, the boat to which Mahan referred. The same day that Mackall surrendered, Union forces burned the abandoned steamer to its waterline. Almost a century later, members of the New Madrid County Historical Society found what they thought to be the *Winchester* in a chute near the former location of Island Number 10. For more information, contact: New Madrid Historical Museum, 1 Main Street, New Madrid, MO 63869 (314) 748-5944.

Finished just before the beginning of the Civil War, the **Hunter-Dawson home** on the northern edge of town on Dawson Road reportedly served as Pope's headquarters during the campaign. Although the house was situated close to the fighting, it survived the battle with no serious damage. Open daily for tours, it is being restored to its appearance during and after the war. There is an admission charge. For information, call (314) 748-5340.

Unlike many of the other battlefield parks along the Mississippi River, **Columbus-Belmont Battlefield State Park** in Kentucky continues to overlook a commanding promontory along the river. Although the terrain has changed some, the strategic significance of the high bluff is apparent from its clear view both up and down the great river.

The restored Confederate redoubt is impressive, but the most noteworthy earthworks are those along a hiking trail to a spot called Arrowhead Point. They are the highest Civil War embankments I have seen outside Fort Fisher, North Carolina. Other items of note in the 156-acre park are a section of the massive chain that was deployed via rafts across the Mississippi to prevent the Federal fleet from moving downriver. A building that served as an infirmary then now houses a museum offering an audiovisual program on the battle of Belmont for a twenty-five-cent admission. Two gift shops sell Civil War relics and books.

The park, which is open April through October, also includes picnic shelters, a playground, a campground, and a snack shop. For information, contact: Columbus-Belmont Battlefield State Park, Columbus, KY 42032 (502) 677-2327.

Fort Pillow

AFTER TENNESSEE voted to secede in June 1861, leaders in both that state and Kentucky expected Federal and Confederate authorities to respect Kentucky's neutrality. Consequently, any Union invasion of Tennessee would have to come down or across the Mississippi River. Based on this faulty premise, military commanders in the Volunteer State believed that a series of forts constructed along the Chickasaw Bluffs would provide the best defense against such an eventuality. The largest of these works, Fort Pillow, was situated just north of Fulton, Tennessee. The steamboat channel at that point on the Mississippi River ran within musket-range of the bank, which provided ample shelter and positions from which to aim plunging fire.

As Confederate Gen. Leonidas Polk moved to fortify, first, Island Number 10, then Columbus in Kentucky, Fort Pillow became a third-line backup position. Roughly in the shape of a semicircle, its outerworks could accommodate a garrison of six thousand men. Capt. Montgomery Lynch, the post's commander, made sure the fortress, forty miles north of Memphis, could withstand a major siege.

After the fall of Forts Henry and Donelson in February 1862, Polk was outflanked and withdrew from Columbus. He reinforced the defenses of Island Number 10 and sent a small detachment to Fort Pillow under Brig. Gen. John B. Villepigue. With the simultaneous setbacks at Island Number 10 and Shiloh in the first week of April, P. G. T. Beauregard, who had

The main battery at Fort Pillow *(London Illustrated News)*

replaced Albert Sidney Johnston — killed at Shiloh — as overall commander in the West, employed a thousand slaves to improve the entrenchments at Fort Pillow. Dismissing Island Number 10 as an outpost for Fort Pillow, Beauregard insisted that Fort Pillow was far more important and easily defended. Since it was the last major stronghold between Island Number 10 and Memphis, the Confederate commander had few choices. He also had very few men. Still, Fort Pillow, with batteries on the bluffs and near the water's edge and surrounded by extensive earthworks, could pose formidable obstacles to any Union advance.

Union forces under Flag Off. Andrew Hull Foote and Gen. John Pope hoped to be as successful at Fort Pillow as they had been at Island Number 10. Pope would land his army north of the Confederates this time and work his way to the rear as Foote's gunboats and mortars blasted the fortress from the river. Pope's twenty thousand men were in position by 14 April, but the next day Henry Halleck, in overall command in the West, ordered Pope and his troops to Shiloh to help destroy Beauregard at Corinth, Mississippi. Pope left behind fifteen hundred men should the bombardment by the gunboats show any exploitable results.

Whatever the reasoning, Foote felt abandoned.[36] Furthermore, the foot injury he suffered at Donelson continued to plague him. A board of surgeons examined the inflamed wound and declared that the flotilla commander would soon be unfit for duty. Foote asked his old friend, Secretary of the

Naval engagement off Fort Pillow between Federal and Confederate gunboats
(*London Illustrated News*)

Navy Welles, to send Charles Davis as his replacement. On 9 May, Davis arrived and, to the cheers of his men, Foote took his leave.[37]

Captain Davis was not given much time to get acclimated. The day after he took command, right on schedule, mortarboat number 16 was towed to a spot within range of Fort Pillow for the daily exchange of unpleasantries. Standing nearby was the Eads ironclad *Cincinnati*. The first round left the mammoth mortar at 6:00 A.M. Several more followed until smoke was noticed coming around Plum Point, exhaust from the eight gunboats of the Confederate River Defense Fleet dashing toward their Union antagonists. Lightly armed and unarmored, the Confederate steamers were no match for the iron-plated warships under Davis. But with speed and surprise, they could generate some havoc.

The CSS *Bragg* and *Sterling Price* raced for the *Cincinnati*. Both ships managed to ram the ironclad, which swung into the river only to take a blow from the CSS *Sumter*. When the *Cincinnati*'s commander came on deck to get a better view, a Confederate sharpshooter immediately cut him down. Two tugs managed to push the sinking gunboat toward shore before it sank in twelve feet of water. The USS *Mound City* and *Carondelet* eventually joined the fray only to have a shot from the CSS *Van Dorn* open a four-foot gash in the *Mound City*, which also limped off into shoal water to settle into the Mississippi mud. When the USS *Pittsburg* and *Benton* approached the battle area, Confederate Comdr. J. E. Montgomery signaled his ships to withdraw. The Federal fleet followed the faster Confederates until they came within range of the batteries at Fort Pillow. At that point, the Union boats broke off their pursuit.

Montgomery had won a considerable victory, but its impact was limited. Davis still had an overwhelming advantage in strength and firepower.

The two flotillas continued to play a game of cat and mouse the remainder of the month of May, with the gunners at Fort Pillow joining the action whenever the Federals got close enough. Events in Mississippi put an end to this standoff: Beauregard opted for a strategic withdrawal from Corinth rather than risk losing his entire army. On the night of 29–30 May he pulled his forces behind a new defense line along the Tuscumbia River in Alabama.

Now it was Fort Pillow's turn to be outflanked. On the night of 4 June Confederate steamers helped evacuate the defenders. Villepigue's men saved much of their powder and artillery but were unable to remove the larger guns. These they spiked. Within hours, Federal troops moved into the former Confederate stronghold.

Because of Fort Pillow's position above Memphis rather than below, the Union high command never intended that it serve as a major post. Only a small garrison was kept there, mostly to prevent Confederate raiders from bottling up river traffic from their former trenches on the bluffs. Except for the naval battle at Plum Point, Fort Pillow would have been nothing more than a footnote in history were it not for a land battle almost two years after the Confederates withdrew. Nathan Bedford Forrest attacked the fort on the night of 11 April 1864. At the time Fort Pillow held six artillery pieces and approximately 560 men, half of whom were black. Forrest's force overwhelmed the fort, and more than half the garrison was lost.[38]

The next day the Union gunboat *Silver Cloud* arrived and began to bombard the fort. A flag of truce went up, and soon both parties agreed to allow wounded prisoners to be evacuated to hospitals in Cairo, Illinois. Forrest's troops left soon afterward to threaten Columbus and Paducah, Kentucky. Neither Union nor Confederate forces occupied Fort Pillow again.

If you go there . . .

Fort Pillow State Historic Area may be reached by turning west off U.S. Highway 51 onto State Highway 87 for seventeen miles before turning north on State Highway 207. The park entrance is another mile up the bluff. A visitors center is situated near the park entrance. You may want to stop because Edward Williams's booklet ($1.50) about the battle and other historical books are available for purchase there and not at the interpretive center. Several miles farther into the park, the interpretive center houses displays and provides an audiovisual program about the history of the fort. You can also pick up a free pamphlet about the park and a map of the fifteen miles of hiking trails.

The restored earthworks at Fort Pillow

Today the original breastworks remain in good condition. A five-mile trail begins at the interpretive center and follows the entire line of outer-works. The rugged half-mile walk from the interpretive center to the main redoubt gives visitors a taste of the longer trails through the hills and woods of the park and is definitely not for the faint of heart. The path dips into a large ravine that once held a trading post and other buildings at its mouth. An impressive swinging suspension bridge leads across the chasm to the 1864 battle site. Interpretive signs along the route relate information about the battle. At the other end of the bridge, the earthworks defended by Union forces against Forrest have been restored. Some canvas tents and artillery pieces add to the authenticity. From the bluff, hikers can see Cold Creek and Cold Creek Chute, but like many other former strongpoints along the river, Fort Pillow has been abandoned by the Mississippi. The main river channel is now about a mile to the south.

Although Fort Pillow State Historic Area is worth a visit by any student of the Civil War, the park's main assets have been given to it by nature. The surrounding forests and ravines are every bit as impressive as those at Port Hudson, Louisiana. Because it is a designated Wildlife Observation Area, no hunting is allowed on park property. However, Fort Pillow Lake is stocked with bass, bream, crappie, and catfish. A park fishing permit (for a small fee) is required for angling in Fort Pillow Lake and can be obtained in the inter-pretive center. A boat ramp is available, but there are no rental boats. Gas motors are not allowed. Next to the lake is a picnic area with tables, grills, restrooms, a playground, and a pavilion that may be reserved with a three-day notice and a fee.

The park also offers several different camping areas. The family campground has forty sites. Designed primarily for tent camping, this camping area has tables, grills, two modern bathhouses, restrooms, a laundry facility, and water faucets, but there are no electrical hookups. Campsites there are given out on a first-come, first-served basis. Reservations can be made at the group tent camping area near the pavilion for parties of up to two hundred persons.

For more rugged adventurers, the Chickasaw Bluff Camping Area is nestled in the south end of the park overlooking the Mississippi River along the Chickasaw Bluff State Scenic Trail. It can only be reached by hiking. Water, fire rings, and an outhouse are provided. A camping permit (free of charge) can be picked up at the interpretive center.

The park is open all year from 8:00 A.M. to 10:00 P.M. The interpretive center is open from 8:00 A.M. to 4:30 P.M. The visitors center is closed some afternoons during the winter months. For further information, contact: Fort Pillow State Historic Area, Route 2, Box 108 B-1, Henning, TN 38041 (901) 738-5581.

Farther to the south, the city of Memphis holds some interest for those interested in the Civil War. Situated on Mud Island, the **Mississippi River Museum** provides a fascinating history of the river, including a section on the river war. One gallery displays a half-dozen or so impressive models of Union and Confederate warships, but the highlight of that section of the museum has to be the full-scale replica of the front third of a Union city-class ironclad. After walking through the ironclad, visitors climb a ramp that leads them to a replica Confederate battery overlooking the ironclad. A sound-and-light show mimics a ship-versus-shore confrontation.

Just off Riverside Drive, Mud Island's season generally runs from Memorial Day through Labor Day. The cost for adults is $6.00, children ages four to twelve are $4.00. This price includes a monorail ride to the attraction since there is no parking on the island. Parking at the monorail station is extra. For information, contact: Mud Island, 125 N. Front Street, Memphis, TN 38103 (901) 576-7241.

Shiloh

SHILOH SHOULD have marked the zenith of Ulysses S. Grant's meteoric rise. When Albert Sidney Johnston's army attacked at 6:00 A.M. on 6 April 1862, Grant was breakfasting at Savannah, Tennessee, downriver from his main camp. Critics went so far as to claim he was drinking.[39] Grant's men were just as unprepared for the fight as their commander. They, too, were taking their morning meal when the gray horde descended.

A few hours later, just as the Confederates appeared to be headed for a major victory, Grant's naval support entered the fray. Confederate Maj. Gen. Leonidas Polk reported that his forces "were within from 150 to 400 yards of the enemy's position, and nothing seemed wanting to complete the most brilliant victory of the war but to press forward and make a vigorous assault on the demoralized remnant of his forces. At this juncture [Union] gunboats dropped down the river, near the landing where [Grant's] troops were collected, and opened a tremendous cannonade of shot and shell over the bank, in the direction from where our forces were approaching."[40] It was this enfilading fire of the gunboats *Lexington* and *Tyler* that led P. G. T. Beauregard (who had replaced the mortally wounded Johnston) to order his advanced lines "to desist from further attacks and to retire out of range of the gunboats."[41]

As at Fort Donelson, Grant had not been on the battlefield during the most critical fighting. He arrived by boat around mid-day. If he had any doubts about the effectiveness of naval support, they disappeared that fateful spring day. "In this repulse," Grant later wrote about the attack on 6 April, "much is due to the presence of the gunboats."[42] He might have added river transports to his list of things for which to be thankful. Facing a steamboat delivery of William Nelson's division of Gen. Don Carlos Buell's Army of the Ohio across the Tennessee River to Pittsburg Landing, Beauregard decided to halt the attack until the next day. Although many on both sides did not know it, the issue had already been decided. Confederate Willie Micajah Barrow, for instance, wrote in his diary: "April 6th 1862. Battle this morning we marched in battle array one of the finest armies in the Confederacy hard fighting all day. We whipped the yankees."[43]

As men in butternut and blue tried to regroup or rest for the next morning's onslaught, the gunboats kept up a continual fire that broke the spirits of the Confederates even further. General Beauregard wrote: "During the night [of the sixth] the rain fell in torrents, adding to the discomforts and harassed condition of the men. The enemy, moreover, had broken their rest by a discharge at measured intervals of heavy shells thrown from the gunboats; therefore, on the following morning the troops under my command were not in condition to cope with an equal force of fresh troops . . . sheltered by such an auxillary [sic] as the enemy's gunboats."[44]

The next day diarist Barrow's fortunes took a tremendous swing in the opposite direction: "April 7th 1862. This morning I awoke early after having slept in a yankee tent. the weather was bad it rained nearly all night. the regiment was drawn up in Line (what was left of it) we marched to battle and I was taken prisoner about one o'clock."

In partial defense of Grant, Pittsburg Landing had not been his choice as a battlefield. On 15 February 1862, the day Confederate commanders threw away the advantage their troops had gained at Fort Donelson on Tennessee's Cumberland River, Lt. Comdr. William Gwin embarked from

Cairo, Illinois, in command of the gunboat USS *Tyler* and steamed up the Tennessee River past the recently captured Fort Henry. His object was to destroy the 240-foot-long Memphis and Charleston Railroad bridge over Bear Creek, a tributary of the Tennessee in extreme northeastern Mississippi. When Gwin reached Eastport, Mississippi, at the mouth of Bear Creek, he discovered that "the Rebels had sent a force of approximately one thousand men to guard the railroad bridge."[45]

A week after he left Cairo, Gwin returned to Illinois. He suggested to his superiors that a larger force be dispatched to Eastport to cut the railroad. In preparation for such a move, a scouting force composed of the gunboats *Lexington,* under the command of Lt. James Shirk, and *Tyler* proceeded back up the Tennessee. The two timberclads reached Pittsburg Landing on 1 March, where they came under fire from a Confederate battery. These were the first shots fired on the Shiloh battlefield. After a brief engagement the Rebels were driven off. Two companies of the Thirty-second Illinois infantry moved ashore and captured two 32-pounders before being driven back to the boats by the Eighteenth Louisiana.

The two gunboats pulled back into the channel and continued upriver. At Bear Creek, the Federals discovered Confederates erecting batteries at Chickasaw, Mississippi, just across the creek from Eastport. After reconnoitering as far as Florence, Alabama, the scouting force slipped back downriver to Pittsburg Landing on 4 March. A week later the *Tyler* and *Lexington* pulled out from Pittsburg Landing once again to test the strength of Confederate works covering the landing at Eastport. During the ensuing ship-versus-shore conflict, the "*Tyler* expended sixty shells and the *Lexington* twenty-five."[46] Shirk and Gwin concurred that the range of the guns at Chickasaw was great enough "to prevent the landing of troops at Eastport."[47]

Nevertheless, on 15 March, Union Gen. C. F. Smith sent William Tecumseh Sherman from Fort Henry up the Tennessee with a convoy of nineteen transports to Eastport. If resistance was encountered, Sherman was to retreat. Finding the batteries at Eastport still manned, the Federals made their way back to Pittsburg Landing. While awaiting further instructions from Grant, who had replaced Smith as department commander, Gwin continued to harass the Rebels at Bear Creek with the guns of the *Tyler.* By the end of March, he suspected the area had been evacuated.

Just to make sure, Grant ordered Sherman to return to Bear Creek with a large force to destroy the pesky land defenses once and for all. On 1 April, Sherman and his men waited on two transports while their naval support, the ironclad *Cairo* and the gunboats *Lexington* and *Tyler,* bombarded every spot from which the Confederates had previously fired on them. Seeing no response from the shore, Sherman landed his two battalions, one on either side of Bear Creek. Satisfied that he had accomplished his mission and reluctant to push his troops inland beyond the support of his gunboats,

A few hundred yards from Pittsburg Landing, a trio of Parrotts marks the site of Grant's headquarters.

Sherman ordered the entire force back to Pittsburg Landing.

Still not quite satisfied that Eastport (according to Sherman, the best landing on the Tennessee) was safe for full-scale operations, Union commanders ordered Col. J. D. Webster to cruise on the *Tyler* once more to the vicinity of Bear Creek. His 3 April report confirmed Sherman's earlier observations.

Before Grant could pull together his legions for a major assault on the Charleston and Memphis Railroad via Eastport, Confederate General Johnston was pushing his army toward Pittsburg Landing from its base at Corinth, Mississippi. Whether Grant wanted it or not, he was about to have a real fight on his hands.

Besides depriving the Confederacy of a gifted leader, the battle of Shiloh accomplished little. It did, however, convince those on both sides that the struggle would be long and bloody and that Northern naval supremacy would play a key role. In the North, General in Chief Halleck, "in spite of his contempt for the Navy, had concluded that only the Union gunboats *Tyler* and *Lexington* had kept Grant's army from being destroyed before Buell arrived."[48] In New Orleans, where citizens were preparing for Commodore Farragut's onslaught, the *Daily Delta* commented on 18 April: "[The battle at Shiloh] has taught us that we have nothing to fear from a land invasion of the enemy if he is unsupported by his naval armaments. It has taught us that the right arm of his power in this war is in his gunboats on our seacoast; and that our only assurance of saving the Mississippi from his grasp is to paralyze that arm upon its waters."[49]

If you go there . . .

Shiloh National Military Park lies literally in the middle of nowhere. For this reason, I would guess the almost four thousand acres of park and the

A marker at the Shiloh National Battlefield Park adjacent to Pittsburg Landing explains the first ship-versus-shore confrontation at Shiloh.

surrounding countryside have been altered less by humans than most other major national battlefields. Because of its pastoral setting, I would suggest bringing your bicycle. A lot of people prefer to see a battlefield from their cars, but biking seems a better way to me.

Another suspicion I have about Shiloh is that there are more artillery pieces inside the park boundaries now than during the actual fighting. Large clusters of cannon, including many naval guns, mark many of the important positions on the field.

Visitors can pick up a map of the 9.5-mile auto-tour route at the visitors center, which is open every day except Christmas. Starting at the center daily in the summer and on weekends in the spring and fall, park rangers lead brief walks and talks and conduct infantry and artillery demonstrations. A program schedule is available at the visitors center, which also offers a twenty-five-minute film on the battle shown every hour and a small museum. A fine book and gift shop is in a separate building a short distance away.

Before you start your tour, walk through the National Cemetery to the Tennessee River and Pittsburg Landing. On the river side of the cemetery stands a plaque that tells about the first ship-versus-shore engagement at Pittsburg Landing.

A picnic area with a pavilion, grills, and restrooms is available on Highway 22, a mile south of the park entrance. The park is open 8:00 A.M. to 6:00 P.M. from Memorial Day to Labor Day, and 8:00 A.M. to 5:00 P.M. the rest of the year. There is a $1.00-per-person charge at the visitors

When Grant's army was attacked at Shiloh, he was several miles down-river at Cherry Mansion, near Savannah, Tennessee.

center. For information, contact: Superintendent, Shiloh, TN 38376 (901) 689-5275.

North of Pittsburg landing at Savannah, Tennessee, you will find the reason Grant spent so much time away from his army: **Cherry Mansion.** The mansion hosted the headquarters of Maj. Gen. C. F. Smith before he died of infection from a foot injury suffered after leaping from one boat to another early in the upper–Tennessee River campaign. According to the mansion caretaker, a piano upon which Grant played is still in the private home. On the morning of Johnston's attack, the general was not at the piano, but eating his breakfast when he heard cannon fire coming from upriver. Major General Buell also used the house for a short time, and Maj. Gen. W. H. L. Wallace, mortally wounded at Shiloh, died there. The house is not open to the public.

CHAPTER 9

LOUISIANA

●N 26 JANUARY 1861 Louisiana seceded from the Union and remained an independent republic for six weeks before joining the Confederacy. A small majority of the state's eligible voters had supported states'-rights-advocate John Breckinridge in the previous November's presidential election. Many of the richest parishes, however, backed the conservative and cautious John Bell, including Orleans Parish, home to the South's most important port; Tensas, a rich cotton parish with many large slaveholders; and East Baton Rouge Parish, site of the state capital.[1] Initially, the Pelican State's position far below the war's initial battle sites gave its citizens a false sense of security. They were only too happy to send captured munitions and their sons to the defense of distant sister states. With a large population, Louisiana raised sixty-five thousand troops for the Confederacy, 20 percent of whom did not make it home after the war. This number included three thousand free blacks, many of whom professed strong patriotism and a desire to hold on to their property, including slaves.[2] Soon, unfortunately, the state's position astride the mouth of the Mississippi River made it one of the most important military targets in the war, and its bayou-dotted coastline left it particularly vulnerable to Federal naval excursions.

At the beginning of the war, Alexander Dallas Bache, as superintendent of the U.S. Coast Survey, probably knew more about the nation's shoreline, including Louisiana's, than any other person in the North. When Navy Secretary Gideon Welles had to formulate a blockading strategy to fulfill President Lincoln's orders, he turned naturally to Bache, who recommended the formation of an advisory board. This hard-working committee produced five reports for Welles. The last one, dealing with the Gulf of Mexico, was presented 9 August 1861.

Concentrating on New Orleans, the board virtually ignored the remainder of the Gulf Coast "as too remote and inaccessible to be of any importance."[3] With its population of 170,000 (by far the Confederacy's largest urban area), its position near the mouth of the Mississippi River, and its immense volume of trade (exceeded only by New York City[4]), New Orleans was arguably the most important port in Confederate hands. Even so, the board assumed that the South would protect this vital metropolis with formidable defensive measures and concluded that an attack against New Orleans would be "incompatible with the other nearer and more urgent naval and military operations in which the Government is now and will be for some time hereafter engaged."[5]

What the board did to undermine a seaborne attack on New Orleans, politicians did to discourage adoption of General in Chief Winfield Scott's Anaconda Plan, which called for a well-trained army to advance down the Mississippi River to split the Confederacy while the U.S. Navy strangled Southern coastal shipping. Although Scott's strategy did not find favor in the North, its existence greatly influenced Southern defensive strategy. Thinking that the main attack along the Mississippi would come from the north, military leaders in Richmond and New Orleans concentrated the port's defenses for that contingency, leaving the Crescent City with a soft underbelly.[6] Unfortunately for Southern interests, U.S. Assistant Secretary of the Navy Gustavus Fox had commanded merchantmen in and out of New Orleans and knew its waters well. True, five formidable brick fortresses guarded the passes to the city from the gulf,[7] but once past the pair of antiquated forts guarding the lower Mississippi, a fleet could easily steam into the port. Rather than take the time to slog down the Mississippi Valley as Scott had suggested, the sly Fox hoped to sever the South's main river artery in a single operation.

To find out if the plan was feasible, Welles summoned David Dixon Porter, who had just finished seventy-six days on gulf blockading duty. Porter brought with him his own ideas for capturing the Queen City of the South. Welles and Porter reached an understanding, then approached Lincoln, who remarked, "Of course, such a piece of work could not be done too soon."[8] Lincoln, in turn, convinced Gen. George B. McClellan to have ready by early 1862 the small number of troops the plan required.

Two issues remained. After the army and navy had subdued New Orleans, Porter pushed for proceeding up the Mississippi River to Vicksburg, Mississippi, the only spot between Port Hudson, Louisiana, and Memphis, Tennessee, where the river touched defensible bluffs. Welles was skeptical, but the fighter in him eventually agreed to what sounded like a professional wrestling move: a reverse Anaconda. After that came the choice of a commander. Porter suggested his foster brother, David Glasgow Farragut, and so did Hiram Paulding, the commandant of the New York Navy Yard.

Unlike other coastal cities occupied by the navy during the Civil War, New Orleans was used as a significant staging area for further movements, including campaigns around Baton Rouge, the Bayou Country, up the Red River, and the Texas coast. The object of several of these raids had more to do with economic concerns than with military realities as Northern factory owners pressured politicians to provide them with cotton, sugar, and salt. Perhaps for that reason, many of these operations ended up as partial or complete failures. The fact that attempts were made at all, however, marks the capture of New Orleans as one of the most important long-term strategic events in the war. Certainly, the loss of the city's manufacturing and port facilities hurt the Southern war effort, but the cooperation — weak though it sometimes was — between army and navy units based in New Orleans set the stage for forthcoming operations in the Civil War as well as wars to come.

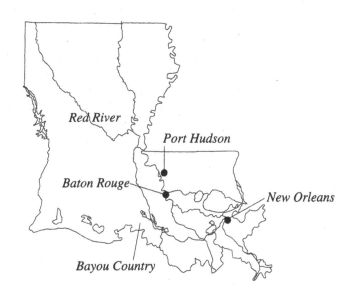

New Orleans

WHILE STILL in his sixties, Capt. David Farragut was doing handstands, but these physical acrobatics were nothing compared to the mental gymnastics he would have to perform to prove his loyalty to the Union. Although Farragut had been born in Tennessee, lived for a time in New Orleans, made his home in Norfolk, Virginia, married a southern belle, and could claim to have many friends and relatives throughout the South, he professed that secession was treason and moved north when Virginia left the Union.

As an officer during the Mexican War, Farragut had drawn up a plan for a naval attack against Veracruz. The scheme had been turned down but left a lasting impression on now Secretary of the Navy Welles. Passing over officers with much higher seniority, the navy secretary asked Farragut to adapt the plan for use against the South's most industrialized city, New Orleans. In December 1861 Gustavus Fox, assistant secretary of the navy, asked Farragut if the ships being fitted out for the coming operation could accomplish the job. Farragut replied "that he would engage to run by the forts and capture New Orleans with two thirds of the number."[9] In January 1862 Farragut was appointed commander of the West Gulf Blockading Squadron.

Although by 1862 many of its best local units had been sent north, New Orleans was not totally helpless against the forthcoming juggernaut. In January 1861 local militia forces had seized Forts Jackson and Saint Philip for the Confederacy. Situated seventy-five miles downriver from the port, these two defensive works were thought to be impregnable, not only by the citizens of New Orleans, but by many in Washington. Fort Saint Philip — an older, open work — had gained a fearsome reputation by holding off an attacking British squadron during the War of 1812. Sod covered its strong brick walls, which along with its water batteries mounted fifty-three guns. Across the river sprawled Fort Jackson. Considered an outstanding example of contemporary military architecture, its casemated walls bristled with seventy-five guns. Unfortunately for the seven hundred defenders, almost half the guns at both forts were 24-pounders, the same cannon used half a century earlier to stop the British.

Maj. P. G. T. Beauregard, former superintendent of the U.S. Military Academy at West Point and a native Louisianian, recognized the forts' weaknesses. He told the Military Board of the state: "In the present condition of Forts Jackson and Saint Philip any steamer can pass them in broad daylight."[10] Beauregard's plans to strengthen the city's defenses were at first ignored, then only partially carried out. Upset that Braxton Bragg was given command of state forces, Beauregard took his engineering skills to the port of Charleston, which held out three years longer than New Orleans.

Five months after the Mississippi forts fell into the hands of the Louisiana militia, the USS *Brooklyn* set up a blockade of New Orleans at the mouth of the Mississippi River. Initially, there was not much a weak Confederate navy could do. As of February 1861, the New Orleans naval squadron consisted of two captured revenue cutters. At the end of July, however, Capt. George N. Hollins, a popular figure around the Crescent City, took over as fleet commander. He put together a motley group of a half-dozen or so steamboats, including several tugs, most of which carried only four guns.

Hollins was content to let the U.S. Navy dart around the mouth of the Mississippi until a Federal expedition began to erect a shore battery at Head of Passes, the two-mile-wide bay in the alluvial fan below New Orleans where the five river channels leading to the gulf diverge. On 9 October the side-wheel steamer CSS *Ivy* bombarded the blockading vessels. The incident caused more concern than destruction among the Northern fleet, but it was followed three days later with an attack by the CSS *Manassas,* a metal-sheathed ram carrying only one gun and looking like a half-submerged cigar. The *Manassas,* the *Ivy,* the side-wheeler *James L. Day,* and several fire-raft tugs approached the five Union warships near Head of Passes in the predawn darkness and rammed the USS *Richmond,* a sloop armed with twenty 9-inch smoothbores and one 80-pounder. When Capt. John Pope, in charge of the operation, saw fire rafts approaching his ships, he ordered them to retreat. The Confederates were no less confused. The *Manassas* managed to ground itself along the bank and a fire-raft tug grounded farther up.

When the sun rose, the USS *Water Witch,* a side-wheeler with three guns, found itself alone at Head of Passes. Her captain decided to follow the remainder of the Federal ships toward the gulf. Curious, Hollins turned the retreating Rebel fleet downriver, only to find Head of Passes abandoned. He seized a coal schooner and a cutter and burned the lumber on shore intended for use in the Federal fort.

As the calendar flipped to 1862, Porter was putting together a mortar flotilla to assist Farragut's passage up the river. Altogether he amassed twenty-two ships mounting twenty 13-inch mortars and various other guns. His men stowed on board more than thirty thousand shells. Farragut himself was no less busy. He assembled an all-wooden fleet of nineteen ships boasting almost two hundred guns.

On 20 February 1862 Farragut landed at Ship Island off the Mississippi coast. There he was met by the eighteen-thousand-strong occupation army under Gen. Benjamin Butler, who had managed to get troops into Washington, D.C., during the early, dark days of the war and was being rewarded for his effort.[11] Although Farragut had overall command, Butler's troops would ensure the fall of the forts by landing at Isle au Breton and taking the forts from the rear if necessary. Early in the spring, Porter's fleet easily entered the Mississippi through Pass à l'Outre, but Farragut had trouble in the deeper Southwest Pass. Nevertheless, by 8 April the entire fleet was over the bars except for the *Colorado,* which drew twenty-three feet. It was left behind.

Ten days later Porter had his mortar fleet positioned down the river from Fort Jackson in approximately the same location from which a British fleet had bombarded Fort Saint Philip in January 1815. Protected by woods and a bend in the river, Porter's fleet rested out of sight of the forts. On the first day mortars threw a thousand rounds toward the Confederates. Porter bragged he would reduce the forts in two days. The wooden defensive barracks inside Fort Jackson — meant to act as a bomb shelter — were destroyed. Pennsylvania-native Brig. Gen. Johnson Duncan, in charge at both forts, feared for a while that the magazines were in danger. Only a few defenders had been wounded, however, and the effectiveness of both bastions was only slightly diminished.

Porter's sailors tried to mask their presence from Confederate artillery by camouflaging their vessels with tree cuttings. *(Leslie's)*

At 10:00 A.M. on the second day of the bombardment, the Confederates earned a small payback. A Rebel shell found one of the mortar schooners, which later sunk, the only vessel in the mortar flotilla destroyed by shore fire.[12] The greatest threat to Porter's fleet, however, was not counterfire from the forts, whose guns for the most part did not have the range, but a massive ironclad anchored just above Fort Saint Philip. Confederate sailors had managed to float the unfinished *Louisiana* downriver from New Orleans in time for the battle. Construction workers toiled to finish her armored roof, and only six of the behemoth's sixteen guns were ready for battle, but Duncan wanted her to attack the fleet anyway. Her captain, not subject to Duncan's authority, refused.

Two days after the bombardment began, the Easter sun was rising and so was Farragut's impatience. Like his Confederate counterpart, he wanted to get his ships moving. Unlike Duncan, he had final authority over the entire operation. That night he sent two gunboats to break the chain that stretched across the river from Fort Jackson. A rocket fired from shore lighted the river, and cannon added their deadly glow. Union crews attempted to use a torpedo to destroy the links, but that failed. Fortunately for the raiders, Confederate gunners were having trouble distinguishing the Union ships from hulks sunk across the channel. Although accounts differ concerning just how Capt. H. H. Bell and two other officers managed to break the chain, the deed was accomplished.

By 23 April approximately 16,800 mortar shells had been lobbed toward the forts. Still Porter asked for more time.[13] As the days dragged on, fire from the gunboats decreased in effectiveness. Not only did fatigue hamper the crews, but faulty fuses caused many of the shells to explode in mid-air. Farragut ordered his signal officer, B. S. Osbon, to climb a mizzenmast and wave a red flag for every shell that fell within Fort Jackson and a white flag for every shell that missed. The red flag flew only rarely. "There's the score," Farragut concluded. "I guess we'll go up the river tonight."[14]

Sailors lowered chains to cover the ships' sides; Jacob's ladders were hung so carpenters could quickly descend and repair any holes in the wooden hulls. Sandbags protected engines and powder magazines. Mud was smeared on the sides of the ships to hide them in the moonless night, and sand was spread on the decks to absorb blood. The decks were whitewashed to provide as much light as possible to the gun crews during the night action. At 2:00 A.M. on 24 April, two red lanterns were hoisted atop the flagship *Hartford*'s mizzen to signal the fleet to get underway. Ninety minutes later the screw steamer *Cayuga*, the flagship of Capt. Theodorus Bailey's First Division, slipped unnoticed through the break in the chain.

Earlier, Farragut had warned his friends in the South that they were "going to catch hell."[15] Now his warning seemed prophetic as he viewed the conflagration that broke out between his ships and the shore defenses. From the deck of the *Hartford*, the lead ship of the center division, Farragut recalled that it seemed "as if the artillery of heaven were playing upon the earth."[16]

Early in the donnybrook, it was Farragut who almost caught hell. Attempting to elude a fire raft, the *Hartford* grounded. According to many accounts, as flames licked up the sides of flagship, the usually confident Farragut lost his composure — and his eyebrows. Except for the "powerful voice" of Richard Wainwright, captain of the *Hartford*, the situation could have been fatal.[17] Fortunately, the emergency passed quickly. The ship's guns sank the tug pushing the raft, and crew members doused the fire gobbling up the rigging.

By this time the small Confederate fleet of about a dozen ships had stormed into the Union line of battle. Although under the overall command of John K. Mitchell, who had replaced Hollins, the Rebel armada contained vessels from three separate organizations, each acting independently. Even without overwhelming numerical superiority in ships and guns, the Union fleet's central command gave the attackers a tremendous advantage. Undaunted, Lt. Alexander F. Warley, in command of the CSS *Manassas*, struck a glancing blow on the USS *Mississippi*, a ship on which he had served before the war. Later Warley managed a solid hit on the *Brooklyn*, which had taken some damage from the guns of Fort Saint Philip. The chains slung along its sides may have prevented the *Brooklyn* from sinking.

By daybreak, however, the Rebel fleet was in shambles. Only one Federal ship, the plucky screw steamer *Varuna*, was lost. All but three of the Confederate ships were dispatched, including the bothersome *Manassas*, run

Passage of the second division under the guns of Fort Saint Philip *(Leslie's)*

aground by Warley, then sunk by a broadside from the USS *Mississippi*. One Rebel gunboat escaped upriver, and two others found protection under the guns of Fort Jackson.

The closest calls in the Federal fleet occurred among the vessels of the third division commanded by Captain Bell. Two craft got tangled among the sunken hulks scuttled between Fort Jackson and the opposite shore, and another was put out of action with a shot in the boiler. The worst disaster took place on board the USS *Iroquois* when a sailor misunderstood the command "starboard" to mean "stop her" and shut off the engines. The river's current pushed the steam sloop under the guns of the *Louisiana*. Weak though it was, the blast of the Confederate ironclad's broadside killed eight and wounded twenty-four on board the *Iroquois*, the greatest casualties of the whole fleet in proportion to her complement.[18]

The heavy bombardment by Porter's fleet over the previous days had caused only superficial damage to the forts. One participant, in fact, reported that no guns in Fort Jackson had been silenced. As a precaution against such a situation, Porter had brought his mortarboats as close to the forts as he dared to support Farragut's run past the batteries. As soon as the center of Farragut's column had cleared his path of fire, Porter began to fire grape and canister into the Rebel positions. Despite the pounding, the Rebels stuck to their posts. When the sun rose on 24 April, however, the entire Union fleet but three had steamed beyond the range of enemy guns, having lost only 37 men killed and 147 wounded.

Mansfield Lovell, in charge of the defenses at New Orleans, had steamed south from the city when Porter's bombardment began. He barely eluded capture when Farragut's warships passed the forts. At that point, Lovell knew the city was doomed. With most of his troops fighting in Virginia, the Confederate commander had only three thousand untrained militia to defend against Farragut's fleet. Capt. Theodorus Bailey in the speedy USS *Cayuga* was already accepting the surrender of three hundred men at a Confederate camp at Quarantine, just above the Mississippi forts.

The next morning Bailey arrived at the Rebel batteries at Chalmette. Built upon lines constructed by Andrew Jackson during his successful defense of the city in January 1815, they were meant to stop an attacking army, not a powerful navy. Still, as the *Cayuga* steamed within range, hidden gunners poured fourteen shots into the screw steamer. Retiring, Bailey waited for the larger men-of-war. As expected, Farragut brushed past the Rebel forces stationed there: a thousand infantry and five batteries of artillery consisting of ten 32-pounders and two 8-inch Columbiads, half on each side of the river.[19] Moving toward the city, his fleet also witnessed the burning remains of the unfinished armorclad *Mississippi*. The second of what could have been a powerful ironclad fleet had been torched when efforts to tow her upstream failed.

Farragut arrived in New Orleans at 1:00 P.M. on 25 April. He was met by more destruction as cotton and stocks of foodstuffs went up in flames. An angry crowd had also gathered. Lovell and Mayor John Monroe were at that moment meeting in the latter's office. The military guardian of New Orleans announced that he planned to evacuate the city, fearing that if he remained and put up a resistance, the Federals would destroy the town, as high water allowed the fleet's guns to be at the same level as the city. To save lives and limit property damage, Lovell felt he had no choice.

Farragut sent Bailey, Lt. George Perkins, and a small guard of sailors ashore. The two officers left their escort behind and marched through a mob toward city hall. A witness called it "one the bravest deeds I ever saw done."[20] Mayor Monroe told the two officers he had no authority to surrender the city since it was under martial law. Lovell was summoned. He reassigned governing authority to the mayor and council, then took the last Confederate train out of town. The mayor still refused to surrender but showed Bailey and Perkins a rear door from which they could exit and return safely to the fleet. Farragut did not wish to provoke bloodshed, but he also had no intention of continuing the stalemate. Pride was at stake. If Butler's troops arrived before the city surrendered, the army would get credit for capturing New Orleans.

Meanwhile, below the city, half the garrison at Fort Jackson had mutinied, spiked the guns, and fled into the bayous.[21] To General Duncan's surprise, Commander Mitchell, who had earlier refused to confront Porter's flotilla, now proposed to continue the battle in the *Louisiana* by attacking the mortarboats and Butler's men, who had landed that day and were approaching the forts by land. Duncan dismissed Mitchell, saying that his offer was several days too late. He then went to Porter and told him that he intended to surrender the forts but had no control over the fleet. The next day the *Louisiana* closed on the fleet and then exploded before reaching any of the Union vessels. The two remaining Confederate gunboats in the area, the *Defiance* and *McRae,* were also destroyed.

The following day Duncan reached New Orleans with news of the capitulation of the forts. Sailors aboard Farragut's ships raised a cheer, and the marines were then ordered to lower all Confederate and Louisiana flags in the city. In his dispatch outlining the fall of the city and the capture of the two bastions covering the Mississippi River, Farragut also mentioned that the enemy had abandoned Forts Pike and Macomb guarding the passes to Lake Pontchartrain northeast of New Orleans and Fort Livingston looming over the entrance to Barataria Bay southwest of the city. By 1 May the Federal army began occupation duties under General Butler. The battle for New Orleans was over.

As drastic as the economic consequences were to the South after the capture of its largest city, the psychological trauma was even worse. How the city fell so easily was a question no one seemed able to answer. Lovell was relieved of command in December, but on 9 July 1863 a Confederate court of inquiry exonerated him and Secretary of the Navy Stephen Mallory for any misconduct at New Orleans. Southerners, it seems, were still analyzing the first act of the Mississippi River drama after the denouement at Vicksburg and Port Hudson.

Part of the Confederacy's military problems lay with its weak command and control systems. The same right of self-determination that had fueled the South's secession oftentimes prevented a unified command, which in turn plagued the defense of specific locations, such as New Orleans.

In the North, initial reports credited Porter and Butler with the capture of the city. These misleading accounts were soon corrected, and Farragut reached hero status. According to author W. M. Fowler Jr., "It would be nearly two years before President Lincoln found a commander on land who could equal his new commander at sea."[22]

If you go there . . .

The delta of the Mississippi River received considerable attention in War Department plans for the protection of the American coastline. No fewer than nine coastal forts were built or begun in Louisiana before the Civil War. Two are open to the public and a few others can be reached by adventurous boaters.

Sixty-four miles south of Business 90 on Louisiana Highway 23 squats **Fort Jackson,** named after the hero of the battle of New Orleans, Andrew Jackson. Work on the post, which lies opposite **Fort Saint Philip,** began in 1822 on a bend in the Mississippi that had been fortified since the 1700s. A decade passed before troops first garrisoned the five-bastioned, casemated work constructed of clam shells, faced with brick, trimmed with granite, and covered with sod. Another decade of relative inactivity reduced the effectiveness of both forts, which finally saw a brief resurgence of life during the Mexican War in 1846 but then lapsed into disuse with only caretaker garrisons. Events in early 1861 quickly changed the importance of the positions, and Louisiana militia seized both bastions.

After the fall of New Orleans, Fort Jackson was used as a prison for a brief time, then as a training ground until it was abandoned altogether. During the Spanish-American War two large coastal batteries were installed in and near the fort. During World War I, the fort served as a training base once more. At the end of the war, both Forts Jackson and Saint Philip were declared surplus and eventually sold.

The New Orleans couple who purchased Fort Jackson donated the property to Plaquemines Parish in 1960, the year it and Fort Saint Philip were declared national historical landmarks. A year later, the Parish Council undertook restoration work to preserve Fort Jackson for tourists. Part of the job required the dredging of the mud-filled moats, which now hold water and an occasional guardian alligator. The historic and recreational park was opened in May 1962.

The fort is open free daily during daylight hours. A museum-gift shop in a former powder magazine displays relics found on the site. Open from 9:00 A.M. to 4:00 P.M., the museum also offers a slide show to visitors. A free walking-tour map highlights the various areas of the fort, including the former location of the fort's citadel that was destroyed by Porter's bombardment in April 1862. On display in the fort's parade ground is one of the 6-inch Rodman cannon formerly placed on the outer wall.

Spring 1991 marked the first gathering of Civil War reenactors at the fort. Regular events at the fort include a July 4 celebration, pirogue races the second Sunday in August, and the Plaquemines Parish Fair and Orange Festival the first weekend in December. For more information, contact: Plaquemines Parish, Route 1, Box 640, Port Sulphur, LA 70083 or call (504) 564-2925.

Nearby Fort Jackson Campground offers fifty campsites with water and electrical hookups at $5.00 per night. However, there are no toilet or shower facilities. For reservations or information, contact: Fort Jackson Campground, P.O. Box 7043, Buras, LA 70041 (504) 392-6692.

An aerial view of Fort Jackson *(Louisiana Division of Historic Preservation)*

Barely visible across the Mississippi, Fort Saint Philip peeks above the bayous. Begun in the eighteenth century, it was rebuilt in 1803 by the Spanish, then turned over to the French who sold it along with the entire Mississippi Valley to the United States in time to withstand a British attack during the War of 1812. The fort can now be reached only by boat.

Another of the forts built to protect New Orleans guards the main deep-water channel into Barataria Bay, the city's back door. Also accessible only by water, **Fort Livingston** slumps on the west end of Grande Terre island (west of Fort Jackson on the Gulf of Mexico).

The pirate Jean Lafitte first fortified the east end of Grande Terre, but Col. George Ross destroyed Lafitte's headquarters in September 1814. U.S. government plans for the fortification of Barataria Pass had been drawn up as early as 1813, but it was not until 1841 that work began on a permanent fortification. The brick-faced, cemented-shell walls of Fort Livingston (named after Andrew Jackson's secretary of state) suffered from the elements, perhaps more than any other of the third-system forts. Lt. P. G. T. Beauregard assisted Capt. J. G. Barnard for a time on the construction, but even these brilliant engineers could not prevent the pounding of hurricanes, the erosion of the shoreline, and the settling of the walls into the clay soil. Nonetheless, the fort took shape slowly and within a decade Chief Engineer Joseph Totten was able to report that the post could be finished "by a few weeks' work."[23] The reason for further delay, Totten admitted, was the fact that the fort was continuing to sink into the island. Five years later, only four 6-pounders had been emplaced. By the fall of 1860, the War Department had all but given up its battle against the elements.

Still, even a partially finished fort covering a strategic position has some value, and in January 1861 Louisiana militiamen occupied the crumbling structure. Confederates did little to strengthen the fort until that autumn when General Lovell ordered the installation of gun platforms. Soon fifteen pieces had been mounted and a battery of two small-caliber guns had been placed on a shell midden in Barataria Bay above the fort.[24]

When word of the capitulation of New Orleans reached the fort, the three-hundred-man garrison evacuated the island. At 7:30 on the morning of 27 April 1862, naval officers from several Union vessels in the vicinity spied a flag of truce over the fort. Upon investigation, they found it to be deserted. A few locals indicated the garrison, mostly French and Italian troops, had been poorly clothed and fed.

No longer of military importance, the fort remained unoccupied until October 1863 when units of the Sixteenth Maine Volunteer Infantry garrisoned the post. Later, when Capt. Albert Loring arrived to take command on 23 November 1864, he arrested two officers for abusing the 130 soldiers of Company C, Tenth U.S. Heavy Artillery (colored). The unit and its sixteen guns remained until September 1866. For a few months afterward, one officer and fifteen men held down the fort. By December only an ordnance sergeant watched over the artillery, which workers eventually dismounted in April 1872.

On occasion minor repairs to the fort and its grounds were undertaken as plans shuffled around various offices regarding the upgrading of the position. However, in 1888 the fort was abandoned. Hurricanes in 1893 and 1915 destroyed the south wall, so the surf now pounds into the parade

Half the garrison at Fort Jackson mutinied when Farragut's flotilla landed at New Orleans

An aerial view of Fort Livingston. Hurricanes have, over time, destroyed one wall.
(Louisiana State Archives)

ground. The remains, which were entered on the National Register of Historic Places in 1974, lie on a state wildlife and fisheries reserve.

The fort can be seen from **Grand Isle State Park,** a 140-acre site at the end of LA 1 on the state's only inhabited barrier island. During the summer season, there is an entrance fee of $2.00 per car. The park's visitors center has a small display on Fort Livingston and an observation platform from which to survey the surroundings, including the fort, but the beach at the farthest eastern tip of the park provides the best view. The camping area can accommodate up to a hundred groups. No utilities are available, but there is a bathhouse with running water and a dump station. For information, contact: Grand Isle State Park, P.O. Box 741, Grand Isle, LA 70358 (504) 787-2559.

Another series of masonry forts protected the eastern approaches to New Orleans from Lake Borgne, which connects to Lake Pontchartrain through two passes. At the northern pass, called the Rigolets (from the French *rigole*, meaning "trench" or "gutter") stands **Fort Pike.** Begun in 1818 near the original wooden Fort Petites Coquilles, the post was named after the explorer-general, Zebulon Montgomery Pike. Completed in just under ten years, the fort served in the 1830s as a staging area for soldiers heading east during the Seminole Wars and later held Seminole prisoners and their black slaves being shipped west to Oklahoma. During the Mexican War, the post became a stopping point for soldiers moving into Texas and

Fort Pike protected Rigolets Pass into Lake Pontchartrain but never fired a shot in anger.

Mexico. From that time until the Civil War, a single ordnance sergeant maintained the fort's weaponry, which originally consisted of twenty-four 32-pounders, fifteen 24-pounders, and four 13-inch and two 10-inch mortars.

Louisiana militia garrisoned the fort from early 1861 until New Orleans fell. Retreating Confederates burned the central citadel, which was repaired by Union occupation troops. After the war the area was once again left in the care of an ordnance sergeant. Except for a fire in 1887 that reduced the citadel once again to a brick skeleton and completely destroyed the two-story, columned officers' quarters, excitement bypassed this remote corner of Louisiana. The fort was officially abandoned in 1890.

Fort Pike, placed on the National Register of Historic Places in 1972, now functions as a state commemorative area situated approximately twenty-three miles east of downtown New Orleans via U.S. 90. The structure is architecturally important since its vaulted casemates can only be reached through narrow passageways, a design feature on many of Simon Bernard's fortification plans that was changed on most of the other coastal forts in the United States. The fort is open, Wednesday through Sunday, from 9:00 A.M. to 5:00 P.M. at a cost of $2.00 per person. A brochure allows visitors to take a self-guided walk through the fort, the present configuration of which varies only slightly from the original Bernard Board design. Facilities include a small museum, picnic area, shelters, restrooms, and a boat launch. For

The entrance to Fort Pike (*left*) and the citadel (*right*), once a two-story barracks, now a museum. Torched by retreating Confederates in 1862, the fort burned again in 1887.

information, contact: Fort Pike State Commemorative Area, Route 6, Box 194, New Orleans, LA 70129 (504) 662-5703.

Just a few miles south of Fort Pike on U.S. 90 hunches **Fort Macomb** (also known as Fort Wood). A chain-link fence surrounds the undeveloped site, which was built to guard Chef Menteur, the southern channel connecting Lakes Borgne and Pontchartrain. The Fort Macomb Marina utilizes part of the fort's moat, and if you ask permission you can drive into the marina for a closer look at the fort.

While you're at the marina, if you want to see the three forts guarding the bayou passes from Lake Borgne into the Mississippi, you'll have to rent a boat. Head down Chef Menteur Pass from Fort Macomb into Lake Borgne, then follow the coastline down to Bayou Bienvenu. At its confluence with Bayou Villere languish the ruins of **Battery Bienvenu.** Construction began on a simple earthwork to hold three guns as soon as the British left the area in 1815. Modifications and renovations changed the final design until Battery Bienvenu developed into an "open work . . . surrounded by a moat . . . closed by four brick buildings."[25] A Confederate garrison abandoned the earthen fort in April 1862. Various Union black infantry and artillery units manned the post throughout the remainder of the war. Six guns — a 24-pounder, a 32-pounder, and four 42-pounders — can be seen on the property today. The area is now privately owned; you'll have to get the owner's permission if you wish to visit the site.[26]

Farther east on the southern shores of Lake Borgne rises **Martello Castle** (Dupre Tower), still marking the channel into Bayou Dupre. Work on the two-story hexagonal tower began in 1827 and continued through several design modifications until 1855. Confederates from the Twenty-first Infantry manned its five 24-pounders through 1861–62, but abandoned the post when New Orleans fell. The property, surplussed in 1883 and now completely surrounded by water, is privately owned. Farther east along the shoreline around Proctor Point, the remains of **Old Fort Beauregard** (Fort

Proctor) crumble into Lake Borgne a few hundred yards west of the mouth of Bayou Yscloskey. Started five years before the outbreak of the Civil War near the former site of Proctorville, the terminus of the Mexican Gulf Railroad, the structure is remarkable in that engineers under Maj. P. G. T. Beauregard utilized rolled I-beams and poured concrete in its construction. However, all work had stopped prior to the Civil War because of lack of funds. A storm in 1860 leveled the town and damaged the fort's glacis and revetment. It, too, is accessible only by boat.

Back toward New Orleans via U.S. 90, you can take LA 47 south to LA 46 (Saint Bernard Highway). Turn west and you will pass the ruins of the **De La Ronde Mansion** where Sir Edward Pakenham died of his wounds after the battle of New Orleans in 1815. **Chalmette National Historical Park** is just a short distance down the highway. Exhibits are primarily concerned with Andrew Jackson's victory over the British, but on the same site Confederate troops made a last futile attempt to halt Farragut's ships before they reached New Orleans. **Chalmette National Cemetery** occupies land adjacent to the battlefield. Most interments are Union veterans of the Civil War. For more information, call (504) 589-4428.

For the most enjoyable visit to Chalmette take the Creole Queen River Plantation and Battlefield Cruise. Paddle wheels depart four times a day from Riverwalk in New Orleans for $12.00 a person. Although the trip down the river is relaxing, the stay at the park is somewhat rushed. If you feel the urge to return, Chalmette is a short drive from New Orleans. For information on the cruises, call (504) 529-4567.

Fort Macomb, just a few miles from Fort Pike, is identical in layout and purpose, guarding one of the passes to Lake Pontchartrain northeast of New Orleans.

Back toward New Orleans, Saint Bernard Highway merges into Saint Claude Avenue. On the north side of the street one mile from Chalmette at 6400 Saint Claude sits the **Louisiana National Guard Military History and State Weapons Museum.** It is in a restored powder magazine built in 1837 for **Jackson Barracks,** an army post established in 1826 that was eventually used by both the North and the South. Almost every major leader during the Civil War spent time here: Jefferson Davis (whose father-in-law, Zachary Taylor, also served at the post), Robert E. Lee, Ulysses S. Grant, William Tecumseh Sherman, James Longstreet, Albert Sidney Johnston, Joseph E. Johnston, and Braxton Bragg.

The museum has an excellent display of Civil War weapons, including the most complete example of an 1861 10-pounder Parrott rifle in the state. Within the Civil War weapons display is a picture of Fort Proctor. Admission and parking are free. The museum is open 8:00 A.M. to 4:00 P.M., Monday through Friday, except holidays. For information, contact: Jackson Barracks, 6400 Saint Claude Ave., New Orleans, LA 70146-0330 (504) 278-6242.

Of course, the raison d'être of the outlying fortifications was and still is New Orleans. The best place to start a Civil War tour of the city is the **Confederate Museum** at 929 Camp Street, just south of Lee Circle, which is on the Saint Charles streetcar line. The statue of Lee in the circle was sculpted by Alexander Doyle. Both Davis and Beauregard were present at its unveiling in 1884. The museum is the oldest in Louisiana, dedicated in 1891. Two years later, the remains of Jefferson Davis lay in state there before being moved to Richmond.

In front of the museum looms an 8-inch Columbiad that defended Spanish Fort at Mobile Bay from the attacking Union army. Thirteen members of Fifth Company, Slocomb's Battery Battalion, Washington Artillery of New Orleans fell before the gun was disabled on the tenth day of the attack, 5 April 1865. Inside, the museum houses such noteworthy items as P. G. T. Beauregard's uniform and the Confederate battle flag that he designed. Paintings of the *Arkansas* and *Tennessee* line the walls, and a piece of metal from the *Virginia* is also on display. A small gift shop sells a wide variety of Civil War books and other items. Admission is $3.00, and the museum is open from 10:00 A.M. to 4:00 P.M., Monday through Saturday. For information, contact: Confederate Museum, 929 Camp Street, New Orleans, LA 70130 or call (504) 523-4522.

Beauregard, a native of Louisiana, lived at 1113 Chartres Street for eighteen months after the war. The house was slated to be demolished when a group of ladies saved it because of its ties to the general. Author Francis Parkinson Keyes completed the restoration of the property, which includes bedroom furniture belonging to the general donated by Beauregard's granddaughter, Laure. Portraits of the general and his wife, Marie Laure, the granddaughter of the first native-born governor of Louisiana, hang in the ballroom. The home is open for tours on the hour from 10:00 A.M. to 3:00 P.M. The cost is $4.00. For information, contact: **Beauregard-Keyes House,** 1113 Chartres Street, New Orleans, LA 70116 (504) 523-7257. Another Beauregard granddaughter, Hilda, was present at the 1913 unveiling of the general's equestrian statue, sculpted by Alexander Doyle, at the Esplanade Avenue entrance to City Park.

Beauregard also lived for a while at 934 Royal Street, an apartment house that apparently has not changed much outwardly from the time the general lived there. He died at 1631 Esplanade Avenue and was buried in the **Metairie Cemetery** at 5100 Pontchartrain Boulevard along with twenty-five hundred men of Thomas Jackson's Louisiana Brigade and Confederate Gens. Richard Taylor and John Bell Hood, who died with two members of his family at 1206 Third Street during the yellow fever epidemic of 1879.

The **U.S. Mint** where William Mumford tore down the U.S. flag and was hanged for doing so occupies the corner of Esplanade Avenue and Decatur Street. The building, renovated in the 1850s by Beauregard, served for a short time in 1861 as the Confederacy's only mint. Now part of the **Louisiana State Museum,** the mint is open 10:00 A.M. to 5:00 P.M., Wednesday through Sunday. Each of three buildings in the museum complex costs $3.00 to enter, but multiple building discount tickets are available.

Also part of the museum complex, the **Presbytère** occupies a spot on Jackson Square next to the Saint Louis Cathedral. Outside the Presbytère languishes the Mystery Sub of Jackson Square. Thought for a while to be the prototype for the CSS *Hunley,* which sank the Federal warship *Houstonic* in 1864, the primitive vessel is of unknown origin. A submarine designed to attack Farragut's fleet was built in New Orleans, but it was sunk in Lake Pontchartrain to avoid capture. The submersible resting in front of the Presbytère was discovered in the Mississippi River in 1878 just west of Spanish Fort, a defensive work erected south of New Orleans on the Mississippi in 1770 by Baron de Carondelet. Only a few bricks mark the site of the fort today. Displays at the Presbytère change regularly, but the permanent exhibit includes Napoleon's death mask, military artifacts from the battle of New Orleans, and memorabilia collected by President Zachary Taylor, much of it having to do with his Mexican campaign. For a current schedule, write Louisiana State Museum, P.O. Box 2448, New Orleans, LA 70176, or call (504) 568-6972. Inside **Jackson Square,** General Butler had an inscription cut on the base of the equestrian statue of Andrew Jackson that reads: The Union Must and Shall Be Preserved.

The **Historic New Orleans Collection,** 533 Royal Street, includes a research center holding many manuscripts and images associated with the Civil War. A small gift shop sells discriminating Civil War memorabilia. For information, call (504) 523-4662. John Slidell, a Confederate emissary whose capture by U.S. personnel while en route to England on board an English ship created an international embarrassment for the Lincoln administration, lived nearby at 312 Royal Street.

Several other sites associated with the Civil War are scattered throughout New Orleans. The **U.S. Custom House** at Decatur and Canal streets. Unfinished at the start of the war, it was used by Butler for a headquarters and prison. Jefferson Davis died in 1889 while visiting the **Forsyth House** at 1134 First Street. A small stone monument sits in front of the home. Many tourists stopping at the **Cornstalk Hotel,** at 915 Royal Street, to have their picture taken in front of the unusual cast-iron fence are unaware that it was here that Harriet Beecher Stowe was inspired to write *Uncle Tom's Cabin* after viewing the neighborhood slave markets. For information or reservations, contact: The Cornstalk Hotel, 915 Royal Street, New Orleans, LA 70116 (504) 523-1515.

Confederate statesman Judah P. Benjamin for a time lived in a house at 327 Bourbon Street. Benjamin would not recognize his lodgings today as they are part of a striptease joint called the Bourbon Burlesque. Union troops occupied the **Hermann-Grima House,** 820 Saint Louis Street, during the war. They left the house in good shape except for a bullet hole in the brass banister at the bottom of the main staircase. The house is open for tours, Monday through Saturday, from 10:00 A.M. to 3:30 P.M. and on Sunday from 1:00 to 4:30 P.M. The cost is $3.00 per person. For information, call (504) 525-5661.

A sign on the **Old Absinthe House** at the corner of Bourbon and Bienville brags that everyone who was anyone stopped by for a drink, including Jackson, Lee, Davis, Beauregard, Pershing, and FDR. Farther east on Bourbon Street at Conti, another message tells visitors the bar there is the original location of the Old Absinthe House. Believe what you will.

If you want to pick up some Civil War artifacts, do not miss **James H. Cohen & Sons, Inc.,** at 437 Royal. The large shop features cannon balls, swords, rifles, and pistols from the Civil War as well as weapons and uniforms from other conflicts. **Gentique's,** in the Riverwalk Mall along the Mississippi, features old prints, many of them from the original *Harper's Weekly* coverage of the Civil War.

For variety, hop aboard the Saint Charles streetcar on Canal Street and head west toward the Garden District. You will pass the **City Hall** at 543 Saint Charles, a scene of great emotion for many locals when the state flag was lowered by Farragut's sailors. Farther down at 2919 Saint Charles is the **Christ Church Cathedral,** burial place of the bishop-general, Leonidas Polk.

Originally Confederate leaders in New Orleans thought they had more to fear from an attack by Andrew Foote's fleet coming down the Mississippi than from Farragut's advancing from below. The forts protecting the city from the south could not be passed, they incorrectly assumed. Consequently, a line of earthen fortifications stretching along the present route of Causeway Boulevard several miles west of the city were thrown up just in case Foote made it that far. On the east bank of the river sprawled **Camp Parapet,** and on the west bank ran a smaller work to provide cross-fire in case of a river invasion. These earthworks were also situated to guard the railroads leading north and west from New Orleans: the New Orleans, Opelousas, and Great Western Railroad on the west bank and the New Orleans, Jackson, and Great Northern Railroad on the east bank. Much of the land surrounding the entrenchments was swampy and unhealthy, making life unpleasant for the troops stationed there. As a consequence, most of the Rebels were transferred to Camp Moore in the healthier piney woods country north of Lake Pontchartrain.

When Union troops took over the earthworks after withdrawing from Baton Rouge during the summer of 1862, they strengthened them into quite formidable defenses. All that is left of these fortifications is a former powder magazine just south of U.S. 90 on Causeway Boulevard. A sign at the fenced-off mound of dirt mentions that tours can be made by appointment, but the phone number listed has been disconnected.

Baton Rouge

AFTER CAPTURING New Orleans in April 1862, Flag Off. David Farragut continued up the Mississippi to join the siege of Vicksburg. En route the Federals occupied Baton Rouge, but the fleet moved on upriver and Confederate guerrillas moved into the capital. Foiled at Vicksburg, Farragut returned to Baton Rouge on 28 May and easily retook the city. Then he tried once more for the prize of Vicksburg. In late July Farragut retreated once again from Vicksburg and on the way back to New Orleans with the fleet, he landed Brig. Gen. Thomas Williams's depleted brigade at Baton Rouge.[27] On 25 July in Vicksburg, Confederate Gen. Earl Van Dorn ordered Brig. Gen. John Breckinridge, former vice president of the United States, to attack the former capital of Louisiana.

Sickness slashed the ranks of the Southerners. Breckinridge was not totally discouraged, however. He knew the enemy had to be suffering equally from the heat. Furthermore, he had received word that the CSS *Arkansas* was at Bayou Sara, a few miles above Port Hudson, Louisiana, and would attack Union ships protecting Baton Rouge the next day. Lt. Henry Stevens, in temporary command of the Confederate ironclad, had been ordered by Van Dorn to support Breckinridge despite earlier instructions by Comdr. Isaac N. Brown not to move the warship because it was undergoing repairs after its debut at Vicksburg and was not yet ready for combat.

The land battle at Baton Rouge began poorly for the Confederates. Undaunted, Breckinridge ordered his troops into the early morning fog covering Baton Rouge. Making slow but steady progress, the weakened Confederates struggled toward the wary Federals. The brunt of the attack hit the Twenty-first Indiana, which soon lost all its field officers. General Williams rode up to rally the men, but as the men finished their cheer in answer to his call, Williams was shot and fell dead from his saddle. Seeing its commander fall, the Twenty-first Indiana shattered, opening a gap in the Federal lines. By 10:00 A.M. the city was ripe for the plucking.

Unfortunately for him, Breckinridge was not in a position to pick the fruits of his men's labor. His troops were thirsty; many had run out of ammunition. Worse, the Federal gunboats *Sumter, Cayuga, Kineo,* and *Katahdin,* which had lain quietly up to that point for fear of raking their own men, suddenly opened up with a fearful barrage now that the Union army was crowding toward the river and safety. A Federal officer on the roof of the statehouse spotted for the warships.

Breckinridge could do nothing but call a halt until the *Arkansas* arrived. What he did not know was that the ram was in pieces on the bottom of the Mississippi, her engines having failed just above Baton Rouge. When he heard the news later in the day, Breckinridge retired with his worn troops.

The Confederate attack surprisingly turned out to be a strategic victory when ten days later Union army commander Benjamin Butler, fearful that the Confederates would attack New Orleans next, pulled his men back to the port. After the withdrawal of Federal troops from Baton Rouge, Confederate control of the Mississippi increased from the three miles their batteries covered at Vicksburg to 250 miles, opening the important Red River pipeline from the trans-Mississippi states. When the Confederates moved into the city, they found a city in ruins, burned or stripped of valuables by the retreating Yankees.

Recognizing the folly of the move, Farragut recommended reoccupation of Baton Rouge to Nathaniel Banks, Butler's replacement, who at one point had been considered for the post of navy secretary in Lincoln's administration. In mid-December, Federal troops boarded transports once again, steamed for Baton Rouge, brushed aside only minor enemy resistance, and began preparations for a deadly assault on Port Hudson.

If you go there . . .

If you take a tour that leads through Louisiana State University in Baton Rouge, the guide may tell you that William Tecumseh Sherman was the university's first president and that he resigned when the Louisiana militia seized the U.S. Arsenal at Baton Rouge. That's true to a degree. Sherman was president of the Louisiana Seminary of Learning in Pineville, and the school moved to Baton Rouge after the war to become LSU.

Sherman spent time in Baton Rouge, however. Highlighting the importance of what was then the nation's southwesternmost state, the U.S. Army built the **Pentagon Barracks** on the Mississippi riverfront just north of town in 1819–22. Among the U.S. officers quartered there were Sherman, Ulysses S. Grant, George Custer, and Jefferson Davis. On 12 January 1861 Louisiana state troops captured the position from its Federal contingent. The original buildings are still in use, and one holds a small museum that includes a display concerning the town's role in the Civil War and a small gift shop. The museum, on the state capitol grounds, is open free to the public from 10:00 A.M. to 4:00 P.M.

On the other side of the capitol stands the **Old Arsenal Museum.** Constructed around 1838, its walls are fifty-four inches thick. A ten-foot-high brick wall surrounds the main building. The arsenal has been closed indefinitely for renovation.

The Arsenal, just east of Pentagon Barracks, now houses a museum.

Federal forces, having reoccupied the area in 1862, surrounded the garrison buildings on the capitol grounds with earthworks. Part of this defensive ring, an old **Indian mound,** still rises just northwest of the arsenal. From atop the mound, two cannon overlook Bayou Gross, a stream that has been dammed to form a lake. A plaque explains the history of the mound, including its small part in the Civil War.

Farther south along the Mississippi River juts the **Old State Capitol.** Looking like some Arabian Nights fantasy, the neo-Gothic building housed

The Old State Capitol was gutted by fire in December 1862 while
Federal troops were bivouacked on the grounds.

Union soldiers and Confederate prisoners during the war. An out-of-control
cooking fire gutted the building on 28 December 1862. After the war, the
building was renovated, and in May 1882 the Louisiana legislature again
met in the Old State Capitol. Samuel Clemens, better known as Mark
Twain, counted himself among those who thought the castle unworthy of reconstruction efforts: "It would have been so easy to let dynamite finish what
a charitable fire began."[28] At least three more restoration projects have been
undertaken on the Old Capitol, the latest one turning the building into a
museum. Portions of the structure are open to the public while development
of the museum continues.

Downstream from the Old Capitol adjacent to the USS *Kidd* National
Landmark is **The Louisiana Naval War Memorial Museum and Nautical Center.** The entrance fee is $2.00 to visit the museum. It costs $2.00
more to board the World War II destroyer USS *Kidd.* The Baton Rouge Ship
Modelers club has provided models of the USS *Mississippi* (destroyed while
running the batteries at Port Hudson above Baton Rouge) and the CSS *Alabama.* The models are part of a display of the Civil War navy in Baton Rouge.
Available at the center's gift shop is a book by William Spedale on the battle
of Baton Rouge. The author outlines Yankee earthworks in Baton Rouge, including a stockade south of town on Highland Road, remnants of which still
exist. For information on the museum, contact: Naval War Memorial Museum, 305 S. River Road, Baton Rouge, LA 70802 (504) 342-1942.

Bayou Country

ON 28 JULY 1862 Confederate Maj. Gen. Richard Taylor was assigned to command the District of Western Louisiana. He had learned his fighting from his father, U.S. President Zachary Taylor, and gained patronage from his former brother-in-law, Confederate President Jefferson Davis. Even more important to the coming campaign, he owned a sugar plantation in the watery expanses west of New Orleans that had been ransacked by the troops of the Union district commander, Benjamin Butler, and he was determined to protect the region from further assaults. Later that fall he got his chance when Gen. Godfrey Weitzel loaded his brigade aboard transports at Carrollton, Louisiana, and — protected by four gunboats — landed on 24 October at Miner's Point, six miles below Donaldsonville, Louisiana, on the Mississippi River. The next day his men entered the city, which had been bombarded and torched on 9 August by Rear Adm. David G. Farragut after his boats had been fired upon near the town. Weitzel then followed Bayou Lafourche south toward Thibodaux, Louisiana, headquarters of Confederate Brig. Gen. Alfred Mouton. Heavily outnumbered, Mouton ordered a retreat west along the railroad to Brashear City (now Morgan City), on the east side of Berwick Bay.

General Butler responded by sending a naval force under Thomas Buchanan to prevent the Confederates from retreating across the bay.[29] Partisans had moved local channel markers, so by the time Buchanan found his way and arrived at the bay on 30 October, Mouton was safely across.

Despite their failure to bag Mouton's fourteen hundred troops, Buchanan's gunboats still posed a big threat to the Confederacy. From Berwick Bay, the warships could proceed west on Bayou Teche and cut off the South's major supply of salt, which came from the nation's first rock salt discovery made the previous May a few miles southwest of New Iberia at Petite Anse Island.

On 3 November, Buchanan began to steam up the Teche with his four gunboats. Mouton ordered the Rebel gunboat *Cotton* to hold up Buchanan while his troops completed entrenchments farther up the river. Because the Teche is not very wide, Confederate Capt. E. W. Fuller almost won an impressive victory, tackling one Union vessel at a time during a three-hour brawl. Although Confederate light artillery on the shore was able to add some firepower during the last half-hour, the battle ended when ammunition ran out on the *Cotton* and both sides retreated. Buchanan tried to move up the Teche again on 5 November with similar results.

Hoping to flank the stubborn defenders, another Union fleet traveled via the Gulf of Mexico to Vermilion Bay, then up Bayou Petite Anse to the salt works. Confederate commanders learned of the movement and sent artillery, which beat back a small landing party on 21 November. The entire Federal task force then retreated. Even had they managed to reach the salt operations, what Union troops could have done to destroy solid rock salt just below the surface of the island apparently had not been thought out.

Butler's replacement by Maj. Gen. Nathaniel Banks and the latter's abortive attack on Galveston at the end of 1862 caused a short lull in the bayou fighting, but by January 1863 Weitzel was planning a joint naval and land attack up the Teche. At the outset, the battle that developed on 13 January between rival naval forces appeared to be a repeat of the November river battles, but Union gunboat commander Buchanan was killed. Only the timely arrival of the forward detail of the Seventy-fifth New York Regiment preserved the Union position. Advancing Union troops outflanked the *Cotton*, and it became that ship's turn to suffer. Captain Fuller, wounded in both arms, managed to retreat by steering the *Cotton*'s wheel with his feet. That night the *Cotton* was scuttled and became an additional obstruction in the Teche. The next morning Weitzel retreated to Berwick Bay satisfied that the destruction of the *Cotton* had made the foray a success.

On 28 March, as the various Union commands in the region tried to agree on an overall plan, Capt. Thomas Peterson took his gunboat, the *Diana*, toward Pattersonville against the advice of Weitzel's aide-de-camp, Lt. Pickering Dodge Allen. Peterson got into a sharp fight with dismounted Texas cavalry and some infantry, both under the command of Col. Henry Gray. After a three-hour bloodfest during which both Peterson and Allen were shot down, the *Diana* surrendered. This gave the Confederates three gunboats on the Teche.

By 8 April, Banks had established headquarters at Brashear City at the head of an army of eighteen thousand men. A three-time governor of Massachusetts, Banks had also served as Speaker of the U.S. House of Representatives. The small man with the large mustache harbored presidential ambitions, but his lack of military training threatened to sidetrack his career as a soldier. Relying on personal courage rather than insight, Banks had managed to escape serious criticism, but he knew his political life was on the line in Louisiana. Hoping for a great victory, he ordered his troops to cross Berwick Bay on 9 April as their supporting fleet dispersed some Confederate light artillery halfway to Pattersonville.

Although the Union army outnumbered the Confederates four to one, General Taylor, who had arrived to take personal charge of the defense, was determined to stop the invaders. The Rebel line was anchored on a fortified position known as Camp Bisland five miles beyond Pattersonville. As Banks and his men advanced on 12 April, they came under the concentrated fire of these defenses, which included a few Parrott shells from the former *Diana*, now under the command of Capt. O. J. Semmes, the son of the commander of the *Alabama*, Raphael Semmes. Banks was resolute in his desire to push forward, almost losing his life as he reconnoitered with Gen. William Emory ahead of his advancing army. After a day-long struggle, the Federals broke off their attack, which they resumed the following morning. Fighting raged throughout the day, the Federals finally gaining an advantage when the *Diana* was disabled and the Confederate right flank gave way. However, at 4:00 P.M., upon learning that Gen. Cuvier Grover had successfully landed with his ten thousand troops on the shores of Grand Lake behind Taylor, Banks halted the attack and allowed his tired troops to rest.

Taylor did not learn the same information until five hours later.[30] He promptly ordered his small army to retreat up the Teche toward Franklin, where he hoped the *Diana* would once again be able to join the battle. Fortunately for Taylor, troops he had deployed to protect against a threat to his rear had been able to slow Grover's advance. This gave him the time he needed to reposition some of his Fort Bisland forces to guard his line of retreat. By the next day Taylor's men were waiting to meet Grover at a place called Nerson's Woods, about a mile and a half above Franklin. With the aid of the *Diana*, Taylor held back the Yankees long enough at the battle of Irish Bend to get the remainder of his army to safety. The Confederates burned everything they were forced to leave behind, including the *Diana* and several other ships. Since any other choice seeming suicidal, Taylor continued to retreat.

Banks's slow advance north outflanked Fort Burton at Butte la Rose on the Atchafalaya. On 19 April Federal troop transports accompanied by gunboats approached the post and captured it after the two Rebel gunboats lying nearby withdrew, but not before shells from the retreating ships and the two old 32-pounder siege guns in the fort struck the attacking Union flotilla several times. The Confederate gunboats made their way to Fort de Russy on the Red River, where they helped hinder Adm. David Porter's Mississippi Squadron. After assaulting Grand Gulf, Mississippi, on 3 May and guarding Grant's river crossing below Vicksburg, Porter's flotilla was advancing to meet Banks's troops at Alexandria. The town surrendered to the Union gunboats without a fight on 7 May. Later that same day Banks's troops marched into the city. Taylor continued his long retreat, this time up the Red River toward Shreveport.

Unable to proceed upriver because of the low water level, Porter's gunboats returned to Fort de Russy and partially destroyed it. The admiral then sent five warships up the Black River on reconnaissance. Before reaching Harrisonburg, on 10 May these ships ran into Fort Beauregard, one of four heavily defended casemated earthen batteries stretching below the city. Unable to overwhelm the defenders and their two 32-pounders despite a two-day bombardment, the Federal fleet made its way back to the Red River and Porter returned to Grand Gulf.[31]

Without naval protection, Banks decided to march east and reduce Port Hudson above Baton Rouge on the Mississippi.

By 28 May, Col. Thomas Chickering, whom Banks had left behind at Opelousas to strip the bayou country of its possessions, was back in Brashear City. The next month, hoping to draw Banks away from beleaguered Port Hudson, Taylor ordered his men to build an armada with which to attack Chickering from the rear. At dawn on 22 June the surprise waterborne attack by 325 Confederates successfully captured the 700-man Union garrison at Brashear City.[32] Two days later Taylor's covering forces took Bayou Boeuf, but not before Lt. Col. A. J. Duganne of the 176th New York destroyed personal property Union officers had stored just before beginning their crossing of Berwick Bay in April.

Confederate Gen. Tom Green left Brashear City and continued with his Texans toward the Mississippi River. On 27 June, as Banks and Grant tightened their respective strangleholds on Port Hudson and Vicksburg, Green attacked Donaldsonville, where Banks's bayou campaign had begun eight months earlier. During a rare night engagement, Union gunboats finally drove off Green's men assaulting the Union fortifications protecting the town.[33] In the meantime, Confederate General Mouton recaptured Thibodaux and pushed patrols within twenty miles of New Orleans. The nervous Federal commander at New Orleans, Brig. Gen. William Emory, wrote Banks at Port Hudson that "something must be done for this city."[34] Instead of pushing forward toward New Orleans, Taylor instead concentrated his efforts on the Mississippi below Donaldsonville. By the time twelve guns had been manhandled from Brashear, however, it was too late to help the doomed garrison at Port Hudson. Realizing his folly, Taylor ordered the guns to Bayou Lafourche. When Federals started once again down the bayou, Taylor ordered Mouton back to Brashear.

Weitzel and Grover took six thousand men as far as Cox's Plantation, but after a sharp fight with Green's Texans, they retreated to the Mississippi. Even though Taylor had recaptured all the territory lost to Banks during the previous months, his accomplishments were completely overshadowed by the fall of Vicksburg and Port Hudson.

If you go there . . .

At New Iberia, Banks used **Shadows-on-the-Teche** for his headquarters. Situated on the main road along the Teche, the mansion is now part of the National Trust for Historic Preservation and can be toured daily except Thanksgiving, Christmas, and New Year's from 9:00 A.M. to 4:30 P.M. The cost is $5.00 per person. Members of the National Trust may tour free of charge.

David Weeks, the home's builder, made his fortune as a sugar planter but died before the mansion was complete. His wife, Mary Clara Conrad,

Shadows-on-the-Teche served as headquarters for Banks's 1863 campaign.

married Judge John Moore, who made the Shadows his home until his death in 1867. The former Mrs. Weeks confined herself to the second floor during the Union army occupation of her property, and she died there in 1863.

The home fell into disrepair during the economic hard times following the war, but revenues from salt mining allowed a descendent of the Weeks family to restore the family home. Thus Shadows became known as "the house sugar built and salt saved."

A Civil War reenactment is held annually on the property the first week of March. For more information, contact: Shadows-on-the-Teche, 317 East Main Street, New Iberia, LA 70560 (318) 369-6446.

Also in New Iberia, the **Church of the Epiphany,** 301 West Main Street, was used as a military hospital during the Civil War.

Avery Island, the object of Federal raids against the salt works there, is now home to a two-hundred-acre tropical garden and bird-wildlife sanctuary open to the public from 9:00 A.M. to 5:00 P.M. including holidays. For information, call: (318) 369-6243.

Highway 182 heading southeast out of New Iberia parallels the Teche and passes many of the beautiful antebellum homes Banks left untouched. One of the more famous is **Oaklawn Manor,** on Highway 28 (Irish Bend Road) just off LA 182. From Oaklawn Manor, residents watched General Grover's attempt to cut off Taylor's line of retreat at the battle of Irish Bend. The home is open for tours year-round except for major holidays from 10:00

A marker is all that remains of Fort Star.

A.M. to 4:00 P.M. For information, contact: Oaklawn Manor, Route 1, Box 153, Franklin, LA 70538 (318) 828-0434.

Closer to the town of Franklin nearer the actual site of the battle just off LA 182 on LA 233, **Grevemberg House,** an 1851 Greek Revival structure, now houses a museum. Civil War relics from the battle are on display. The museum is open, Thursday through Sunday, from 10:00 A.M. to 4:00 P.M. For information, call (318) 828-2092.

The sign marking the location of **Camp Bisland** had been knocked down by some erratic driver when I passed through the area on my way to **Morgan City** (formerly Brashear City). But I was lucky enough to find the Morgan City archives in the city's library, across from Lawrence Park. Personnel in the archives directed me to **Fort Star,** the largest of five earthen forts erected by Federal troops to protect the city and its railroad. One of the fort's bastions covers the front lawn of Atkinson Memorial Presbyterian Church on Fourth Street. For more information, contact: Morgan City Archives, 220 Everett Street, P.O. Box 430, Morgan City, LA 70381 (504) 380-4621.

Port Hudson

AFTER CONFEDERATE Maj. Gen. John C. Breckinridge abandoned his 5 August 1862 attack on Baton Rouge, he ordered Brig. Gen. Daniel Ruggles to occupy and fortify the eighty-foot bluffs at Port Hudson, situated twenty-five river miles north of Baton Rouge on a 150-degree bend in the

Mississippi River. Any ships cruising with the current had to slow considerably at the turn, and working against the current had always been a tedious venture on any stretch of the river. Both sides knew that batteries sited at Port Hudson could rake slowly passing ships with blistering fire.

The Confederates easily pushed aside the few Union troops in the immediate vicinity of the port and began to strengthen the defensive works around what would become the southern anchor of their Mississippi line. Deep ravines on the landward side and bluffs on the riverfront made the town easily defensible.

Despite its relative obscurity today, the importance of Port Hudson to the Confederacy cannot be overemphasized. The Mississippi does not touch bluffs again until Grand Gulf, sixty river miles below Vicksburg. Not only did these three fortified positions prevent Federal traffic from flowing freely to the sea, they also allowed important commerce from the trans-Mississippi states of the Confederacy to reach the eastern theater. Louisiana salt and sugar moved through this gaping hole in the Union blockade of the third coast. Even long-horned cattle driven from Texas swam the Mississippi at Port Hudson.

Soon after occupying Port Hudson, Confederates gave the Federal navy a taste of what it would be up against. On 7 September 1862, David D. Porter, commander of the mortar flotilla at New Orleans, descended the river on the USS *Essex*. The former crew of the *Arkansas,* now stationed at Port Hudson, managed to exact some revenge on this gunboat that had forced them to destroy their vessel above Baton Rouge the previous month. Firing two 32-pounders, a 20-pound Parrott, and some field pieces, gunners put one shot through a porthole on the *Essex,* causing extensive damage. Fourteen other Confederate projectiles found their mark, three penetrating the ironclad. As a testament to the efficiency of the Southern gunners, Porter indicated, "As nearly as I can judge, the enemy had in position from thirty-five to forty guns" of large caliber.[35]

Porter's observation was obviously self-serving. Even by 24 October, a mere thirteen heavy guns guarded the bluffs, including one rifled 32-pounder. The paucity of weapons was more a result of the difficulties encountered bringing cannon to the area than a reflection of what the Confederate high command felt was the worth of the position. In fact, as an indication of just how important Port Hudson was to the Southern cause, Brig. Gen. John Bordenave Villepigue was given command of its defenses. Gen. P. G. T. Beauregard called him "the most energetic officer available."[36] Unfortunately for the Confederates, Villepigue became ill and died within a month of his arrival. He was replaced with the equally gifted Maj. Gen. Franklin Gardner, a civil engineer before the war who graduated in the same West Point class as Grant. If the Federals did not do something quickly, Port Hudson would become another Vicksburg.

Maj. Gen. Benjamin Butler, commander of the Department of the Gulf, insisted he could do no more than protect New Orleans, and he made no moves up the river. In fact, he had abandoned Baton Rouge the previous August because he thought it was impossible to defend. Butler's inactivity, as well as his brutal treatment of the citizens of New Orleans, which earned him the nickname "the Beast," caused Lincoln to replace him in November 1862 with Maj. Gen. Nathaniel P. Banks, Stonewall Jackson's opponent in the Shenandoah Valley. General in Chief Henry W. Halleck, commander of the Department of Missouri, suggested to Banks that his first objective should be to open the Mississippi. To ensure Banks's cooperation, Halleck offered him this carrot: "You will exercise superior authority as far north as you may ascend the river."[37] Halleck wanted Grant superseded.

Banks arrived in New Orleans on 14 December 1862. Three days later, Brig. Gen. Cuvier Grover landed with forty-five hundred troops at Baton Rouge and dispersed the few Confederates defending the city. Banks, unwilling to instigate a direct attack against Port Hudson, decided to starve out the town's defenders by cutting off their supplies. He began a long swing through the Louisiana bayou country the following February. Chasing the Confederates out of southwestern Louisiana, Banks returned to Baton Rouge on 8 March.

To cut supplies further, Flag Off. David G. Farragut planned to run the Port Hudson batteries at night in conjunction with an attack by Banks. Once above the town, his fleet would be able to stop supplies moving down from Shreveport on the Red River. To give the squadron a better chance, smaller gunboats were lashed alongside the larger ships for mutual support and to increase the mobility of both vessels by supplementing the power of their steam-driven screws. Another novel idea tried by the sailors was the installation of howitzers in the fore- and maintops to confuse the Confederates' aim. Farragut also ordered a voice trumpet to be run from the *Hartford*'s wheel to its mizzentop so that his pilot, Thomas R. Carrell, could give commands from above the fog and smoke of battle.

A foulup in communications caused the army to make no diversionary attacks, and Farragut proceeded on his own. Mortar fire the morning of 14 March led Port Hudson's defenders to suspect something was afoot. About 11:20 that night, Farragut's flagship, the *Hartford*, appeared below their batteries. To avoid obstacles on the west side of the river, the ship passed so close to the Confederate-held bank that its rigging brushed against the trees. Ten minutes later the Rebel lookouts finally set off a signal rocket and huge bonfires flared on the opposite shore, their flames magnified in reflectors placed behind the fires for better illumination.[38] In some cases, gunners on shore could not lower their pieces enough to take aim, but a few shots

One of Port Hudson's batteries (*National Archives*)

managed to come close. Loyall Farragut, the admiral's son, was serving aboard the flagship when a shell whizzed by. He flinched. "Don't duck, my son," his father cautioned. "There is no use in trying to dodge God Almighty."[39] God was with Farragut that night, and the *Hartford* passed the last batteries at 12:15 A.M., relatively unscathed.[40]

The remainder of the fleet was not so fortunate. The *Richmond,* second in line, began almost immediately to suffer at the hands of the Confederates, who were angered by the safe passage of the *Hartford.* Nevertheless, she might also have succeeded in turning the corner above the city had not an enemy shell broken her boiler's safety valve. Upon hearing the steam escape, Lt. Comdr. A. B. Cummings, who lost his foot to a cannonball and his leg to surgeons during the run, said, "I would rather lose the other leg than go back."[41] Four firemen received Congressional Medals of Honor for their work putting out fires in the damaged starboard boiler.[42] Unknown to the crew trying to pick out landmarks in the dense smoke, the five-knot current had swung the *Richmond* and its companion around so that the ship was headed back down the river. Mistaking flashes off the port for the enemy, the ship's gunners accidentally fired on the *Mississippi.*

The third ship in line, the *Monongahela,* was caught in an eddy and surrendered, but she drifted downstream before the Confederates could take her and her eleven valuable guns as a prize. The last ship, the *Mississippi,* with Lt. George Dewey (the future victor at Manilla Bay) aboard, also. grounded. Because the ship was a side-wheeler, she did not have a companion lashed to her side and was not able to pull free. Hot shot from shore

The engagement at Port Hudson (*Harper's*)

batteries set her on fire, and she and her seventeen guns were abandoned by her crew at 3:00 A.M.[43] After making sure no living person remained aboard, Dewey and Capt. Melancton Smith boarded the last lifeboat, which floated down to the *Richmond*. Lightened, the *Mississippi* slid off the shoal, swung around in the current, and floated back downstream. Heat reached friction primers in the loaded port guns, and a ghost crew fired a final broadside before the *Mississippi*, which had served as Com. Matthew Perry's flagship during the Mexican War and expedition to Japan, disintegrated in a spectacular explosion. Federals on guard duty as far away as New Orleans were startled by the resulting fireworks.

Farragut did not know it, but he had lost thirty-five dead and seventy-seven wounded, compared to a total of eight Confederate casualties, to bring two ships past the Port Hudson defenses. He waited until morning, then slipped back downstream, hoping to contact his compatriots below Port Hudson. Unable to do so, he steamed upriver to confer with Grant at Vicksburg after running the batteries at Grand Gulf.

Gardner was not overly concerned with the passage of the *Hartford*. He assumed she would go the way of the *Queen of the West* and *Indianola*, both captured between Vicksburg and Port Hudson in February, but that was not to be the case. After receiving supplies that were floated downriver past Vicksburg, Farragut took the *Hartford* back to the Red River where he waited for Rear Adm. David D. Porter, who was working with Grant to get his army below Vicksburg. With the arrival of Porter in mid-May at the mouth of the

Red River, Farragut returned to Baton Rouge via the Atchafalaya River, a circuitous line of communication between New Orleans and the Mississippi above Port Hudson.

By this time, Banks — possibly fearing that Grant would reduce Vicksburg before he could arrive to take overall command — was determined to capture Port Hudson. He recalled three divisions from Alexandria, which landed at Bayou Sara north of Port Hudson near Saint Francisville. Confederate Gen. Joseph E. Johnston, appointed supreme commander of all forces in the western theater the previous November, ordered Gardner to withdraw his forces before they were surrounded. Determined to follow Jefferson Davis's instructions to resist as long as possible, Gardner refused.[44] By May 22, it no longer mattered. Port Hudson was cut off.

The navy began softening up the defenses on 24 May by bombarding installations at the southern end of Gardner's lines for two and a half hours. The next day Union land batteries added their firepower. During one of these ship-versus-shore contests, the screw sloop *Monongahela,* which was almost captured earlier by the Confederates, dropped out of the line to confront a battery it had been ordered to silence. In the midst of the shootout, the quartermaster reported to Lt. Winfield Scott Schley that the *Hartford* was signaling but he could not decipher the message. Since he was under orders to destroy the battery, Schley ignored the signal. After knocking out the enemy guns and falling back downriver, Schley reported to Farragut, who confronted him for disobeying orders. The lieutenant protested that he could not read the signal. Farragut told him not to use that tired excuse, then called the young officer into his quarters. In private, Farragut said he had to chastise the commander in public, but that he desired to commend him and his officers and men for doing what he believed was right under the circumstances. He added, "Do it again whenever in your judgment it is necessary to carry out your conception of duty."[45]

The Confederates were not diffident about the threat posed by the Union fleet. Without gunboats, their options were limited but imaginative. They sent torpedoes floating down the river, but lookouts on the ships spotted the clumsy contraptions and foiled the plan. Capt. Robert L. Pruyn of the Fourth Louisiana and some other officers even built a torpedo boat and launched it against the fleet. It, too, failed. The shelling continued.

Banks ordered a general assault for 27 May. Had he attacked two days earlier, while Gardner's northern perimeter was still unprotected, or two days later, when his commanders would have had a better grasp of the terrain, his attack might have succeeded.

As it was, mortar vessels shelled the garrison throughout the night of 26 May. The fleets above and below the town approached early the next morning, but they ceased firing after an hour for fear of hitting their own

men. The attack on the northern end of Gardner's fortress, the area farthest from the river, commenced at 6:00 A.M. but quickly stalled in the hills
and ravines. The Southerners had nailed white crosses on trees to mark
ranges and zeroed in on opposing batteries. Additional Federal artillery finally arrived and knocked out almost every Confederate gun on that portion of the line, but the damage had already been done. The formidable
terrain prohibited almost anything but piecemeal attacks. Losing cohesion,
many Federals simply dropped into thickets to wait until nightfall covered
their retreat.

On the far right, the river side, of the Federal's northern pincer that
morning were stationed the First and Third Louisiana Native Guards. The
First, including a majority of its line officers, was composed of free blacks
from New Orleans. Brig. Gen. William Dwight, in overall command of
that sector, did not intend to order the First and Third forward. Like many
officers, he thought little of the fighting ability of former slaves and freed-
men. But when his main assault faltered, he changed his mind. Into the
most demanding landscape of the whole battlefield, Capt. Andre Cailloux
— a free black — led the charge with a dangling left arm, broken above the
elbow by a cannonball. A second shell, however, killed him. After suffering 50 percent casualties (more than any white regiment on the northern
sector), the First and Third withdrew to the woods only to endure continued artillery fire for hours as they sniped with enemy gunners.

At that point, the focus of the Federals' northern flank shifted to the
left, where Confederate Col. Benjamin Johnson and his men at "Fort Desperate" literally thrust bayonets over the tops of earthworks at the few Yankees determined enough to advance that far. Despite facing more than
three regiments, Johnson's 292 men held on until 11:00 A.M. in some of
the most furious combat of the entire siege. By that time, fighting on the
Union right ended.

Although Federals on the northern end of the line made a poor showing, some of the blame must be shared by other Union commanders. Brig.
Gen. Thomas W. Sherman, who had opposed the frontal assault when it
was first proposed, contented himself with an artillery exchange throughout the morning on the southwest portion of Gardner's lines. When Banks
threatened to have him replaced, Sherman proved it was not lack of
courage that kept him from attacking. He was struck down twice by enemy
fire while finally leading his men forward at 2:00 P.M. Confederate Col.
William Miles told his men facing Sherman, "Shoot low, boys, it takes two
men to take away a man who is wounded, and they never come back."[46]
Canister finally broke the Union attack across Slaughter's field, named
after the owner of the property, but appropriate all the same.

Finally hearing action on his left, Banks ordered Maj. Gen. Christopher Augur to advance on the Confederate center. Southern gunners used

"railroad rails and broken chains for grape and rusty nails and other bits of scrap for canister."[47] Augur did not meet with success either.

Banks ordered up nine additional regiments, more than enough to replace his losses. On 14 June he launched another assault. This time the major brunt of the fighting occurred in the Confederate center at a point called the Priest Cap. More than two thousand Union troops went forward, running into a string of torpedoes made from unexploded shells. This was the "first time in military history a mine field was ever used in a battle."[48] Only once did Federal troops slip past the six hundred Confederate defenders. Under cover of fog, Northern soldiers found a spot in the defenses momentarily undefended. Lt. Col. A. S. Hamilton's First Mississippi temporarily pulled out of the Priest Cap to meet the threat, capturing or killing all the Yankees who entered the Confederate lines. After several more unsuccessful Union assaults that day, both sides settled into a war of attrition.

For Banks the inevitable did not take place soon enough. Still hoping to preempt Grant, he planned another attack for 5 July. Heavy rains caused a postponement until 7 July, when news of the fall of Vicksburg reached Port Hudson. Since continuing the struggle would now be pointless, Gardner decided to surrender what was the last Confederate fortress on the Mississippi. He had done his duty. He had held nearly forty thousand Federals at bay for two months, inflicted five thousand casualties (sunstroke and disease accounted for another four thousand Federals), sustained only five hundred casualties, and allowed Maj. Gen. Richard Taylor to reoccupy western Louisiana.[49]

Even in victory, Banks had to face defeat. It was Grant, and not he, who would become supreme commander. Banks's initial caution may have contributed to his failure to overwhelm quickly Port Hudson, but once he made up his mind, Banks cannot be criticized for lack of ingenuity. He attempted to utilize "two machine guns, and a well developed communications system, based on the military field telegraph."[50] The Confederates fought back with land and naval mines, a torpedo boat, telescopic rifle sights, a Columbiad mounted on a rail car, two English-made breech-loading 2.65-inch field guns, and a calcium-powered searchlight — all a preview of trench warfare a half-century later.

A week after Port Hudson surrendered, an unarmed merchant ship arrived in New Orleans following an unmolested trip down the Mississippi. "The Father of Waters again goes unvexed to the Sea," announced Lincoln.[51]

The battle at Port Hudson lasted forty-eight days, making it the longest siege involving Americans until Vietnam. Lawrence Hewitt in his book *Port Hudson: Confederate Bastion on the Mississippi,* suggested the determined resistance of Port Hudson's sixty-eight hundred Confederates against more than thirty thousand Union troops supported by gunboats actually *shortened* the war. The assistant professor of history at Southeastern Louisiana University argued that if Banks had captured the town before Grant reduced Vicksburg, the former would certainly have been given overall command of the Mississippi operations. He, not Grant, would have gained credit for the seizure of Vicksburg. That pivotal victory, along with his political connections, may have eventually catapulted Banks up the ladder of command with possible dire consequences for the North.

The participation of black troops in the battle also shortened the war, according to Hewitt. The attack on Port Hudson was the first time black troops in the regular U.S. Army took part in a major assault. Although the Corps D'Afrique was repelled by cannon fire from the bluffs and Mississippi sharpshooters in rifle pits, its bravery played a vital role in convincing Northerners to accept more black enlistees. By sponsoring a recruitment poster heralding the "valor and heroism" displayed by the black soldiers at Port Hudson, abolitionists in Philadelphia alone induced more than 8,000 blacks to enlist. By the war's end, the number of black troops in the Union army (nearly 180,000) almost equaled Confederate infantrymen present for duty. The 18 July 1863 attack by the more famous Fifty-fourth Massachusetts regiment on Battery Wagner outside Charleston only served to confirm what had been proven at Port Hudson.

If you go there . . .

The military significance of Port Hudson is much greater than its limited coverage in most Civil War histories might suggest, and a trip to the **Port Hudson State Commemorative Area** should be included in any itinerary that brings persons interested in the Civil War to the Baton Rouge area. In fact, Frances Kennedy of the Conservation Fund calls Port Hudson the "best preserved Civil War battlefield in any state park system today."[52]

The story of the park began soon after the battle ended. Since most of the three hundred buildings in the city had been destroyed by the conflict, little reason existed for anyone to move back. In addition, the Mississippi River got "lazy," as locals call the river's tendency to straighten its curves, and moved a mile away from Port Hudson. The battlefield was not included when the federal government purchased the battle sites at Vicksburg, Gettysburg, and Antietam. Consequently, except for a few trenches on flatlands that were reduced under the plow, the fortifications remained virtually untouched. Thus some of the earliest tourists were European military leaders who came during World War I to study the trenches designed by Gardner a half-century earlier.

"When I was a little boy, you could walk from one end of the 4½ miles [of Confederate entrenchments] to the other," said Kennedy. "You could see the earthworks, the rifle pits, the gun emplacements. . . . They were just like the day, July 9, 1863, that the Confederates surrendered and walked off. It was there for people to see. The landowners were glad to show it to you."

But in the 1960s, the science of greed visited the battlefield. Modern grave robbers began to use metal detectors to locate and steal artifacts from the area. According to a Louisiana State University archaeologist just finishing a 1990 survey of part of the battlefield, "Each time the technology of metal detecting improves, a new swarm of fortune seekers ravages the area."[53]

To preserve at least part of the battlefield, the state of Louisiana purchased 643 acres comprising the northeast sector of the defenses.[54] The area was slated for development in a 1975 master plan, but the seven miles of trails winding through the redoubts and trenches were not completed until 1982. Even then, the park remained fairly anonymous since signs directing visitors did not explain that it was a Civil War battlefield. Although improvements are continuing and a visitors center finally opened in the fall of 1989, it was not until 27 May 1990 — the 127th anniversary of the first major Union ground attack on Port Hudson — that the battlefield received some much-deserved publicity. A Union and a Confederate officer found buried side by side during a 1987 joint excavation by the Smithsonian Institution and LSU archaeologists were reinterred with full military honors near a peace monument erected by Georgia-Pacific Corporation, the present owners of the southern end of the Confederate lines. Local historians think the Union officer died while being treated at the Confederate hospital. (There are several recorded instances of Confederates going outside their own trenches to help wounded Federal troops during the battle.) Even so, according to Civil War experts, it was unusual for antagonists to be placed in the same grave. The fact that they were shows once again the humanitarian side to one of America's most brutal conflicts.

Port Hudson State Commemorative Area is a fifteen-minute drive north of Baton Rouge on Highway 61. Besides the visitors center, the park offers a shaded picnic area and walking paths. Two free brochures have maps that pinpoint significant portions of the battlefield along the trails. Outdoor displays include a section of trench and some artillery pieces. One of the guns, an 1841 model, 8-inch navy smoothbore, is the only surviving example of that type. It was manufactured in West Point. The Confederates had it emplaced at Battery Number 8 until 6 July 1863 when, just two days before the garrison surrendered, its trunnion was knocked off by a remarkable

Confederate trenches at Port Hudson

thirteen-hundred-yard shot. The gun was taken to West Point where it was displayed until 1983 when it was returned to Port Hudson.

The rustic nature of most of the park is perhaps its greatest asset. The tangled vines, fallen trees, and deep defiles offer a rare glimpse of a battle-field that has changed little in the last 130 years. To all but the most focused observers, the giant trees, lush vegetation, and natural wildness of the park's steep ravines overwhelm the remains of the Confederate trenches. In fact, since it requires a strenuous climb, the walk from the visitors center to the Alabama-Arkansas redoubt should not be attempted by anyone who is out of shape. For those who do manage it, the hike will provide — as no amount of reading can — a true picture of what Federal troops were up against that summer of 1863.

A shorter, less-strenuous route over a blacktopped path will take more casual hikers to the scene of some of the battle's most brutal fighting, Fort Desperate. Here, 292 officers and men under Col. Benjamin Johnson held a three-quarter-mile-long front against fantastic odds at the extreme north-eastern salient of the Confederate earthworks. A wooden boardwalk and tower provide a complete overview of the immediate area. Longer walks lead to the Mississippi Redoubt, near where black troops attempted to break the Confederate line.

To rectify the apparent lack of historical context for the relatively small mounds of earth snaking through the hills, exhibits featuring photographs, maps, and information on the fighting that occurred at each point are being prepared by the Louisiana Office of State Parks. Before those are emplaced on the battle sites, however, the displays and slide show at the visitors center relate enough information about the battle to provide anyone who visits an adequate understanding of the struggle that took place in the surrounding hills and fields. There is also a small gift shop. Future plans include an annual Civil War reenactment the third weekend of March. For further information, contact: Port Hudson State Commemorative Area, P.O. Box 453, Zachary, LA 70791 (504) 654-3775.

As you head south from the park toward Baton Rouge on Highway 61, if you turn west after one mile on the Plains-Port Hudson Road, you can drive along some of the earthworks still in private hands. Signs along Highway 61 will also direct you to **Port Hudson National Cemetery,** three miles south of the battlefield park. Locals say that during the Depression a bounty was paid to anyone finding the body of one of the fifteen hundred men who fell on the battlefield. Today, most artifacts illegally obtained on the battlefield wind up in antique shops in New Orleans.

Saint Francisville is worthy of a short side trip. Just below the hill on which the town sits lies Bayou Sara, the port used by Banks to land his troops for the Port Hudson campaign. The town of Bayou Sara had been shelled by the *Essex* on 23–24 August 1862, and from 1863 on, a gunboat was kept just off the port to prevent the Confederates from making use of the area as a landing site for supplies coming from the trans-Mississippi.

On 11 June 1863 the citizens of Saint Francisville were approached by officers from the USS *Albatross* and asked if there were any Masons in the town. The captain of the gunboat, Lt. Comdr. J. E. Hart, had shot himself while delirious with fever, and he had requested a Masonic burial before he died.

Confederate Capt. Walter W. Leake, in the area on furlough to visit his wife, conducted the services at **Grace Episcopal Church** in Saint Francisville. Hart's tombstone can still be seen behind the church. A free brochure can be picked up in the vestibule and offers a self-guided tour of the church's interior and the haunting cemetery that surrounds the restored building. Ironically, on 16 January 1864 the USS *Lafayette* shelled Saint Francisville, called a "perfect hotbed of secession,"[55] for several hours. The heaviest damage was sustained by Grace Church, which lost its bell tower and a stained-glass window. After the war, Captain Leake placed flowers on Hart's tombstone, and for years his children placed flowers on the grave that soldiers stopped a war to dig.

Grace Episcopal Church

Across the street to the south, a plaque describes the damage done to the former courthouse that stood on the site during the war. The former Leake home, now the **Barrow House Bed and Breakfast,** stands one block south at 524 Royal Street. For further information, contact: Barrow House, P.O. Box 1461, Saint Francisville, LA 70775 (504) 635-4791.

The Red River

SECRETARY OF STATE William Seward originally urged a campaign up the Red River in the summer of 1863 for political and economic reasons. Concerns about French designs for their puppet Maximilian in Mexico and a declining cotton supply for Northern mills necessitated some remedial action. A drive to Shreveport, Louisiana, Seward argued, would give the Federals a base from which to advance upon Texas and prevent the French from getting any ideas about reestablishing Mexico's old borders. The expedition could also open Louisiana and Texas cotton markets for exploitation.

After the failure of a combined operations attack on Sabine Pass, Texas, in September 1863, a push up the Red River was given high priority. During the winter of 1863–64, Adm. David Porter made plans with Maj. Gen. Nathaniel P. Banks for the expedition. By the beginning of March 1864, Porter had assembled a naval force of fifteen ironclads and four wooden gunboats at the mouth of the Red River. Transports bearing a corps from Gen. William Tecumseh Sherman's army under the command of Brig. Gen. Andrew J. Smith accompanied the battle fleet.

To secure his water flank, Porter sent a naval force under Lt. Comdr. Francis Ramsay up the Black and Ouachita rivers. In a replay of the reconnaissance expedition in May 1863, Ramsay's warships came under fire just below Harrisonburg. The Confederates concentrated their fire on the *Fort Hindman,* which took twenty-seven hits and was forced out of the fight. Ramsay transferred his command to the *Ouachita,* which was struck three times but not disabled. Eventually the Federal gunboats silenced the Confederate batteries and steamed as far north as Catahoula Shoals.

While the bulk of Banks's troops marched along the familiar ground of Bayou Teche on its way toward Alexandria, Brig. Gen. Cuvier Grover's division was carried on 13 March by boat up the Atchafalaya River to the Red River and on to Alexandria. That same day, more than two divisions belonging to Gen. William Tecumseh Sherman, who had been ordered by General in Chief Henry Halleck to cooperate with Banks, entered the Red River preceded by Porter's gunboats and landed at Simmesport, Louisiana. They forced Confederates encamped there to retreat toward Fort de Russy, about thirty miles below Alexandria on the Red River. These earthworks were the first major obstacle on the water route to Alexandria. Since the river makes a large loop north of Simmesport, by the time Porter's sailors had removed river obstacles and his fleet had reached the fort, which sits almost due west of Simmesport near Marksville, Union troops had it surrounded. Most of the Confederates in the area had already retreated, and any plans for resistance by those left behind ended when Porter's fleet approached. After a short bombardment, the three hundred Confederate defenders surrendered the position as well as eight heavy guns and two field pieces.

Three days later Porter's gunboats steamed into Alexandria just behind the retreating Confederates. Banks's troops arrived ten days later. These were exactly the same positions Porter, Banks, and Confederate Gen. Richard Taylor had held the previous May.

Once in Alexandria, Banks and Porter competed for profits and patronage. Banks, the consummate politician, hoped to send large quantities of cotton to mills starving for the product in his home state of Massachusetts, thus ensuring his power base in New England. "To his dismay, Banks discovered that the canny admiral already had his sailors scouring the nearby plantations with commandeered wagons and mules, confiscating cotton, marking the bales 'U.S.N.,' and loading them aboard the fleet's vessels for delivery for prize money to the admiralty court in Cairo, Illinois."[56] An angry Banks could not stop Porter, so he sent his own quartermaster department on a sweep into the countryside to gather as much cotton as possible, then ship it south to New Orleans.

The cotton situation was not the only thing on Banks's mind. On 12 March, Grant had been promoted to supersede Halleck as general in chief. Grant was not in favor of the Red River campaign and directed Banks to return Sherman's ten thousand men by 10 April.

The *Fort Hindman* was disabled only after taking twenty-seven hits from Confederate shore batteries. (*Cairo Public Library*)

After a week of collecting cotton and holding elections in the name of the "restored" government, Banks's troops swung out on the road toward Shreveport. The foot soldiers got a head start on the Mississippi Squadron when the *Eastport*, Porter's heaviest gunboat, grounded on the double rapids above the city. Union sailors sweated three days to get the fleet over the rapids, losing a hospital ship in the process.

Once he reached Grand Ecore on 3 April, Banks turned away from the Red River and struck out on the main stage road that followed the crest of the watershed between the Red and Sabine rivers through Pleasant Hill and Mansfield instead of following another road along the river, where his troops could continue to enjoy the support of the fleet.[57] At this opportune moment, Confederate Gen. E. Kirby Smith, commanding the Trans-Mississippi Department from his headquarters in Shreveport, ordered Taylor to halt his retreat and "make a *show* of attack in order to learn the strength of Banks' army."[58]

On 7 April the Confederates assembled near Mansfield and marched to meet Banks. At nearby Sabine Crossroads, they formed a battle line and waited for the Federals. When Banks, who had divided his troops into three corps, refused to attack, Taylor ordered his men to advance. Unknown to Taylor, he outnumbered the lead Federal corps. When the Federals began to retire, Taylor pressed his men forward. In the narrow, tree-lined road to the rear, the Federal retreat turned into a rout, which did not stop until twenty miles later when the disorganized troops reached Pleasant Hill. There all three corps combined to wait for the Confederates. The Confederate attack stalled the next day, and Taylor allowed his men to pull back.

Although Banks "won" the second contest, he had lost more than two thousand soldiers and twenty cannon. Taylor lost half that number of men. Unknown to Banks, however, Taylor's counterstroke had faltered. Still, Banks continued to backtrack toward Alexandria with Taylor's decimated command on his heels. Taylor's five thousand Confederates tried to trap Banks's twenty-five thousand Federals between the Red and Cane rivers on 23–24 April, but the odds were too great. Two days later Banks's men camped in Alexandria.

About the same time Confederates were preparing for their first attack at Sabine Crossroads, Admiral Porter detailed Lt. Comdr. Samuel Phelps to stay with the heavier gunboats at Grand Ecore as he raced with three ironclads and three wooden steamers to catch up with Banks at a planned rendezvous one hundred miles farther up the Red River. On 10 April, as the victorious Banks fell back after the battle of Pleasant Hill, Porter reached an obstruction in the river on which some bold Confederates had nailed an invitation to a Shreveport ball. Porter laughed at the audacity of his opponents, but before he could have the obstacle removed, he learned of Banks's defeat. His mood changed immediately. With no reason to advance, Porter ordered his fleet back down the Red River. Two days later, dismounted cavalry supported by artillery attacked his gunboats at Blair's Landing. The high banks of the river prohibited effective return salvos from the ships until Porter remembered a device developed by Chief Engineer Thomas Doughty of the USS *Osage:* the periscope. With this instrument, Porter was able "to survey the whole scene and to direct an accurate fire,"[59] which killed the Confederate field commander, Gen. Thomas Green.

The Confederates then tried a new tactic to stop the retreating gunboats: they diverted the flow of water from the upper Red River. By the time Porter's fleet, which had already lost one gunboat to a torpedo eight miles below Grand Ecore,[60] reached Alexandria, it was unable to pass over the rapids. If the army continued to retreat, Porter would be forced to scuttle ten ironclads. Since Banks was in overall command, he knew he would be blamed no matter what catastrophe befell the fleet, so Banks "fretted," Porter "fumed,"[61] and the river continued to fall.

The situation was saved from becoming an unparalleled disaster by thirty-eight-year-old Lt. Col. Joseph Bailey of the Fourth Wisconsin Infantry. A civil engineer before the war, Bailey proposed damming the Red River, a daunting 758 feet across at that point, to raise the water level enough to get the boats over the rapids. Porter, finding his sense of humor once again, commented, "If damning would get the fleet off, it would have

Porter's fleet passing through Bailey's dam above Alexandria *(Leslie's)*

been afloat long before."[62] But Bailey had shown his skill previously at Port Hudson when a dam he constructed across Thompson's Creek allowed two captured transports to be refloated for use by the Union army. He was given his chance.

By the time work started on Bailey's "folly" at the end of April, Taylor arrived on the scene with his badly outnumbered force. With little ammunition, he could only wait and watch, just like thousands of skeptical Union soldiers and sailors. In the meantime, Confederates below Alexandria had more luck. On 5 May, Rebel cavalry under Gen. James P. Major captured and destroyed the Federal tinclads *Signal* and *Covington* and the transport *Emma*. They also captured the transports *City Belle* and *Warner*.[63]

Back at Alexandria, the first attempt to run the rapids on 9 May freed four boats before the water fell again. Correcting his design, Bailey tried once more during the night of 12–13 May. This time, the entire fleet passed over. Bailey was immediately promoted to brigadier. Not only had he rescued a $2 million fleet, he had saved Porter's career.

Although Banks and Porter could now withdraw their respective commands, the campaign was not quite over. Southerners pushed after Banks once again. As an indication of just how intimidating foot soldiers considered gunboat protection, Confederate John Calvin Williams, writing in 1900 about his service during the Red River campaign, called the 18 May attack on Banks's army "almost under the shadow of the Federal gunboats on the Atchafalayah [*sic*]. . . . [T]he worst piece of generalship I know of during the war."[64]

Although threatened, Shreveport remained in Confederate hands throughout the war. Not until 3 June 1865 did the last Confederate iron-clad in home waters, the CSS *Missouri*, surrender to the U.S. Navy in Shreveport.[65]

If you go there . . .

Porter and Banks's dreams of capturing Shreveport in 1864 were dashed at the battle of Sabine Crossroads. The **Mansfield Louisiana State Commemorative Area,** four miles south of Mansfield on LA 175, offers a nice grassy park for those who want to learn more about the engagement. A ten-minute slide show at the interpretive center provides an overview of the entire Red River campaign. The center, which charges an admission of $2.00 per person, also displays models of the CSS *Arkansas* and the USS *Carondelet* and Civil War weapons, including an original artillery piece used by Confederate forces during the war. Of greatest interest to those desiring insight into the naval side of the Red River campaign might be the diorama that depicts the dam Bailey built near Pineville. Pieces of the original dam lie near the model.

A picnic area with grills and an interpretive trail are also available. The park is open from 9:00 A.M. until 5:00 P.M., daily except Christmas and Thanksgiving. For more information, contact: Mansfield State

The Mansfield State Commemorative Area, the point at which Banks's Red River campaign was thwarted

Commemorative Area, Route 2, Box 252, Mansfield, LA 71052 (318) 872-1474.

Farther southwest on LA 1 along the Red River sits the town of Alexandria. The Alexandria-Pineville Convention and Tourist Bureau, P.O. Box 8110, Alexandria, LA 71301 (318) 443-7049, has a brochure pinpointing the location of sites in the area associated with the Civil War. The O. K. Allen Bridge that takes Highway 165 across the Red River was built over the area where a limestone ledge caused the falls threatening Porter's fleet. In low-water stages, part of **Bailey's Dam** can be seen. According to a park employee at Mansfield State Commemorative Area, some thought has been given to preserving what is left of the wing dam in a separate park. A marker for the dam stands near the bridge. Adjacent to the dam, historical societies placed markers at the sites of **Fort Buhlow,** constructed in 1864 to repel any further invasions by Federal troops, and **Fort Randolph,** built at the same time.

Across the Red River is **Pineville.** Most of city was also destroyed during the 1864 Red River campaign, but the **Mount Olivet Church,** which served as a Union barracks during occupation, still stands on Main Street. It is open free every day.

Also in Pineville on Shamrock Street is the **National Cemetery.** Because it was the closest cemetery to Texas, many of the soldiers who fell while fighting in and around Brownsville were reinterred there from 1909 to 1911.

A bit west of Simmesport on LA 1 a marker on the south side of the highway locates the **Battle of Yellow Bayou,** the last pitched battle of Banks's ill-fated 1864 campaign. A roadside park occupies the area next to the marker.

CHAPTER 10

ARKANSAS

AFTER THE FALL of Fort Sumter, Gov. Henry Rector of Arkansas on 21 April dispatched four companies of volunteers up the Arkansas River from Little Rock to capture the federal garrison at Fort Smith. State troops had already seized the U.S. Arsenal in the capital. The regular army garrison at the fort decamped upon their approach, and the victorious armada returned downriver. Two weeks later on 6 May 1861, Arkansas formally joined the Confederate States of America.

Because of its relative isolation, Arkansas rarely served as more than a sideshow for operations in other areas. Confederates attempting to push into Missouri were stopped at Pea Ridge in northwest Arkansas in March 1862 and again at nearby Prairie Grove nine months later. In April 1864, Union troops took a turn at using Arkansas as an invasion route to the Deep South. This time the Confederates paid back the Yankees in kind, stemming Federal attempts to capture Shreveport, Louisiana, at skirmishes in southern Arkansas.

Between these land campaigns, most of the action in Arkansas focused on its waterways. After the battle at Pea Ridge, Maj. Gen. Earl Van Dorn and Gen. Sterling Price were ordered to move their forces east of the Mississippi to meet the threat posed by Grant. This created an opportunity for Brig. Gen. Samuel Ryan Curtis, commander of the Union Army of the Southwest, who wanted to strike at Little Rock, capital of Confederate Arkansas. As Curtis's army moved farther away from its base of operations in Saint Louis, however, it became more and more difficult to obtain supplies. Curtis asked for help from Secretary of War Edwin Stanton, who in turn relayed the request to Navy Secretary Gideon Welles. The job of opening a supply line was given to Flag Off. Charles Davis, who had replaced the wounded Andrew Hull Foote as commander of the Mississippi Squadron.

On 13 June 1862 Davis dispatched three gunboats from recently captured Memphis, and they met a fourth at the mouth of the White River.

Along with two transports, the fleet headed upstream to reprovision Curtis's army. About forty miles inland from the mouth of the river, Confederates had emplaced a battery at Saint Charles. The four gunboats steamed to obstructions below the fortifications and slugged it out with the defenders while the transports unloaded troops. A well-placed Confederate shell found its way into the port casemate of the *Mound City* and exploded in its steam chest, resulting in the deaths of 125 of its crew — one of the greatest single-ship losses for the Federal navy in the entire war.[1] Another gunboat towed the *Mound City* out of range, leaving only two warships to face the elated Confederates. At this moment, the colonel in command of the Union land forces signaled the gunboats to stop firing, and the army carried the enemy works without losing a single man.

The victory was a costly one for the Union forces. The deadly effects of pressurized steam could not have been made any clearer. The "howling of the wounded and the moaning of the dying" broke morale, and gunboat commanders became reluctant to proceed farther.[2] A drop in the water level made any further debate academic. Without naval support, the infantry would not advance. The fleet retraced its course back to the Mississippi, and Curtis continued his retreat eastward.

Almost a complete failure, the White River expedition did provide some minor benefits to the North. The small operation opened the river to Federal transports to within sixty miles of Little Rock, and it proved once again what cooperation between land and naval forces could accomplish.

Confederate leaders in Arkansas understood the significance of the skirmish at Saint Charles better than their counterparts. If they chose to do so, Union forces could have steamed upriver to any navigable point within Arkansas, including Little Rock. Local officials pressured Richmond to reconstitute a major command in the state to prevent such a catastrophe. Maj. Gen. Thomas C. Hindman, a former congressman from Helena, Arkansas, was given the job of protecting the trans-Mississippi. A whirling dervish, Hindman miraculously assembled an army from a population already depleted for campaigns in the East. Hindman even mined saltpeter and opened chemical laboratories to mix gunpowder. Most importantly, he provided a sense of security to the Confederate government in Little Rock. Unfortunately, he also employed draconian measures,[3] from forced conscription to seizure of cotton to strengthen his command. Complaints finally forced Richmond to replace him on 12 August 1862, but he retained a corps command. Hindman led the Confederate army that was turned back at Prairie Grove a week before Ambrose Burnside suffered the disastrous and costly repulse at Fredericksburg in the East. When Gen. William Tecumseh Sherman's December 1862 battle at

Chickasaw Bluffs met a fate similar to Burnside's, Union strategists once again looked to Arkansas to provide a morale-boosting victory for a gloomy North. Their target was the most historic point in the state: Arkansas Post.

Arkansas Post (Fort Hindman)

ALTHOUGH THE Arkansas River is navigable into Oklahoma, it offered, according to Adm. David Porter, "no inducement for any one to seek adventures in its treacherous waters."[4] Col. John W. Dunnington of the Confederate navy did not think Northern policy makers would hold that sentiment forever. To counter any potential threat posed by the Federal brown-water navy, Dunnington planned a series of defensive works at strategic sites along the state's major rivers. The task of defending the all-important Arkansas River he left for himself. Like early French and Spanish explorers and missionaries who made Arkansas Post the oldest European settlement in the lower Mississippi Valley, Dunnington chose to build his fortress on a peninsula made by a sharp bend in the Arkansas River fifty miles upriver from the Mississippi. Any positions closer to the mouth of the Arkansas were liable to flood during high water. By the end of 1862, Fort Hindman[5] and its outerworks were finished, and Brig. Gen. Thomas J. Churchill was placed in charge. On paper Churchill's assets were impressive. He commanded five thousand to six thousand men, including thirty-five artillerists from the Confederate ram *Pontchartrain* being constructed in Little Rock. Within the fort, two casemates built of oak timbers reinforced with railroad iron faced the river. In these bastions and at other points in Fort Hindman, eleven guns of various calibers threatened any attackers.

Not content simply to guard the river road to Little Rock, Churchill used the post as a base to raid Federal river traffic between Memphis and Gen. William Tecumseh Sherman's base at Milliken's Bend. Churchill's attacks presented only a small nuisance to Sherman, who was attempting late in 1862 to fight his way behind the defenses of Vicksburg along the Yazoo River. But after the capture of the unarmed transport *Blue Wing*, Union Gen. John A. McClernand, one of Sherman's corps commanders, convinced President Lincoln to let him use idle Federal troops to neutralize Arkansas Post.

On 5 January 1863, McClernand and a force of thirty-two thousand men aboard sixty steamers departed Sherman's supply depot at Milliken's Bend. Three of David Porter's ironclads and a number of tinclads served as an escort. To confuse the defenders, the fleet sailed north, past the mouth of the Arkansas into the White River, then crossed to the Arkansas via an old cut-off channel. By 9 January, a "round eyed" courier reported that "half the yankees in the west" were descending on Arkansas Post.[6] Churchill had not expected his slight stings to attract such a vengeful host, but he remained determined to hold out as long as possible.

The following day Porter closed to within four hundred yards of the fort. The Confederate works, even those fronted with iron, proved no match for the gunboats, and soon fire from the fort slackened. Porter sent the tinclad *Rattler* forward to provide enfilading fire, but the gunboat lodged on pilings placed opposite the fort by the defenders to prevent just such a move. Before Confederate gunners could destroy the vulnerable tinclad, however, a rain of shells from Porter's other gunboats silenced the fort altogether. The *Rattler* drifted back to safety, then withdrew with the rest of the fleet as night fell.

The next day Union land batteries joined the naval bombardment, and by 3:00 P.M. Confederate defenders were driven from the parapets of the main fort. Brig. Gen. Peter J. Osterhaus ordered the 120th Ohio to storm the walls, but Fort Hindman's garrison managed to hold them off. Within the next hour, all the big guns in the fortress had been knocked out, allowing Porter to send three ships upriver to cut off the Confederate retreat while the rest of the fleet continued to lob shells into the fort and rifle pits. Soon a number of white flags appeared over the Confederate positions. Porter beached some of his vessels and entered the fort with a naval landing party and some infantry. Although a few gray-clad troops held out for another hour or so, the battle was over.

The combined-forces assault on Arkansas Post *(Leslie's)*

The loss of Churchill's six thousand troops was a staggering blow to Confederate strength in Arkansas and the trans-Mississippi,[7] but McClernand's sideshow contributed little to the ultimate goal of capturing Vicksburg. Even though McClernand could claim his attack assured the safety of Grant's right flank during his forthcoming campaign by denying the Confederates continued use of Arkansas Post as a base for attacks on Union shipping, the threat from that quarter had been minimal. The most important result of the expedition up the Arkansas was psychological. The capture of Fort Hindman had an "exhilarating effect"[8] on the victorious troops who had been badly defeated only a week earlier during Sherman's disastrous attempt to overrun Chickasaw Bluffs. Furthermore, it brought some good news to the North at a time when Union troops had been unsuccessful on three or four battlefields.[9]

Grant, however, was outraged at what he called McClernand's "wild goose chase."[10] He made sure the politician-general's Army of the Mississippi ceased to exist after its mission was accomplished. Within two weeks, McClernand was relegated to a corps command once again.

Another expedition up the White River was undertaken two days after the capture of Arkansas Post. Although the first had ended poorly for the Federal gunboats, this time the Confederates evacuated the fort under construction at Saint Charles before firing a single shot and hauled off the waiting cannon on the captured steamer *Blue Wing*. Union troops regained possession of the guns at De Valls Bluff[11] about forty miles upriver on the railroad to Little Rock. After burning the depot and rolling stock, the soldiers reembarked on their transports and rejoined the army at Milliken's Bend. The White River remained open during the rest of the war except for an occasional guerrilla raid.

If you go there . . .

McClernand's attack on Arkansas Post destroyed what little was left of the original settlement, which had already been devastated in 1821 by the removal of the territorial capital to Little Rock. What men started, nature finished. By 1880, the Arkansas and its sloughs covered the last remnants of Fort Hindman. The state of Arkansas, recognizing the importance of the area, acquired the site in 1929. The 221-acre park was transferred to the federal government in 1964.

Arkansas Post National Memorial lies 2.8 miles off Highway 165 on Highway 169. Alongside the entrance road and before the visitors center, two markers explain the events of early 1863 and indicate the direction of the flooded fort. The visitors center itself is open from 8:00 A.M. to 5:00 P.M. daily except Christmas. Inside, a short video explains the history of Arkansas Post, the site of the only Revolutionary War battle in Arkansas. Exhibits feature a model of the Union naval and land attack on Fort Hindman.

A marker commemorates the battle at Arkansas Post. As with most river engagements, the site of battle is now under water.

Pamphlets describing the history of the post and the Civil War battle are available. A map indicating the locations of the important buildings in the once-thriving community is included. The visitors center also has for sale a longer work on Arkansas Post, including its role in the Civil War.

Outdoors, a replica of a portion of the Spanish fort that held off a British attack in April 1783 stands close to the visitors center. Two miles of trails lead through the old settlement and rifle pits, the only physical reminder of the fierce struggle that took place there in 1863. There are no camping or restaurant facilities in the park, but a picnic area with restrooms is available. For further information, contact: Superintendent, U.S. Park Service, Gillett, AR 72055.

Other Civil War artifacts from the area are on display at the **Arkansas Post County Museum** at the intersection of Highways 169 and 165. The museum is open March through October, Wednesday through Saturday, from 9:30 A.M. to 4:00 P.M., and Sunday from 1:00 to 4:00 P.M. During November and December, it is open Friday through Sunday. The museum, which includes several old buildings and a gift shop, is closed January and February and legal holidays. For further information, contact: Arkansas Post County Museum, P.O. Box 436, Gillett, AR 72055 (501) 548-2634.

Helena

AFTER THE FALL of Memphis in June 1862, Union sailors and soldiers continued their relentless advance down the Mississippi, occupying the strategic port of Helena, Arkansas, the following month. Situated halfway between Memphis and Vicksburg, Helena took on added importance as the deadly struggle around Vicksburg intensified. From there, a joint army-navy expedition set sail in August for the Yazoo River as part of the unsuccessful late 1862 campaign to capture Vicksburg. Besides being employed as a staging area for Federal attacks, Helena could also be utilized as a base to interdict western supplies for the beleaguered Confederate garrisons east of the river.

As the summer of 1863 approached, the situation at Vicksburg became even more desperate for the defenders as the vise around the city tightened. To relieve the pressure, Confederate Secretary of War James Seddon urged Gen. Joseph E. Johnston, nominally in charge of the western theater, to plan an attack against Helena. Johnston passed the request to Lt. Gen. Edmund Kirby Smith, commander of the Trans-Mississippi Department. On 14 June, Gen. Theophilus H. Holmes, commander of the Confederate District of Arkansas, received word in Little Rock from Brig. Gen. John S. Marmaduke that Helena had been stripped of defensive forces to assist the final Federal assault against Vicksburg. By 17 June, Holmes was conferring with Gens. Marmaduke and Sterling Price in Jacksonport, Arkansas, to thrash out the details of an attack. If all went well, the cutting of Grant's supply line at Helena would have the same effect as Maj. Gen. Earl Van Dorn's raid at Holly Springs, Mississippi, the previous December. That victory had forced Grant to abandon his first expedition against Vicksburg.

The Confederates massing to surround Helena, however, met with misfortune almost immediately. Flooded streams impeded their progress, and despite a good job of screening by Marsh Walker's cavalry, Union naval and army intelligence anticipated the attack. Rear Adm. David Porter ordered three gunboats to support Maj. Gen. Benjamin Prentiss's four-thousand-man garrison in Helena, but by 2 July only the timberclad *Tyler* was on station. Although initially skeptical about reports of an impending attack, Prentiss had extensive defenses prepared by the beginning of July. Soldiers felled trees to slow any Confederate deployment and prevent the advance of artillery support. In addition, four two-gun batteries, protected by rifle pits and abatis, were constructed to command the landward approaches.

Early on 4 July, Union pickets sent up the alarm. Because of misunderstood orders, poor coordination, and daunting geography, the first Confederate attacks met with little success. After Holmes finally made contact with General Price and straightened out the confusion, Price's two brigades were able to overrun Battery C atop Graveyard Hill in the center of the Union line. From this dominating position, the Confederates could have blasted Fort Curtis[12] protecting the town, leaving the route open for total victory. Retreating Federals had spiked the position's guns, however, and before Confederate artillery could be manhandled to the earthworks, Prentiss had restored the situation. Ordering guns from the other three batteries to concentrate their fire on Battery C, Prentiss sent a request to the *Tyler*, riding a thousand yards to the east, to open up with her 8-inch rifles.

The gunboat *Tyler* on station on the Mississippi

Union Fort Curtis at Helena, Battery C *(Library of Congress)*

The *Tyler* had been among the first of three transports converted to timberclad gunboats under the direction of Comdr. John Rodgers for use on the western rivers. Tars immediately boasted that each boat was "worth 5,000 soldiers,"[13] and no one in Helena that Independence Day would argue with the observation. Soon after the warship received Prentiss's call for help, the first of four hundred destructive shells began dropping among the Confederates, churning up the countryside and turning Graveyard Hill into an appalling reminder of its name. Estimates are that the *Tyler*'s guns alone were responsible for six hundred Confederate dead or wounded,[14] about two-thirds of the total Confederate losses. Minor Confederate gains on the left and right could neither be exploited nor make up for the carnage in the center. By 10:30 A.M. Holmes ordered a general retreat.

Prentiss's victorious troops did not look into the surrounding countryside for two days. When they finally did, scouts found only seventy-two of the most seriously wounded Confederates at a temporary hospital. Prentiss was criticized for his lack of initiative, and "much of the credit for his victory at Helena went instead to the *Tyler*, which, according to Admiral David Porter, 'saved the day [for] our little band of soldiers.'"[15]

Prentiss had played a pivotal role in saving Grant's army at an earlier battle, when the divisional defensive line he established, called the Hornet's Nest, held up the Rebel attack for several hours at Shiloh. Grant failed to recognize Prentiss's part in the victory, perhaps to protect his good friend

Brig. Gen. William Tecumseh Sherman, whose division had given way on Prentiss's right. Grant and Sherman's stars continued to rise after Shiloh, while Prentiss was denied front-line command. The criticism after Helena was the final straw. When he was passed over to command the follow-up expedition to Little Rock, Prentiss quietly resigned from the army and returned to his law practice in Illinois. The Confederate commander at Helena fared no better. "Literally sickened by his defeat,"[16] Holmes temporarily relinquished command of the District of Arkansas to Sterling Price.

All told, the Confederates suffered three crushing defeats that eighty-seventh anniversary of the Declaration of Independence. Even if Holmes's attack had been successful, it could not have offset the other disasters that befell the Confederacy that day at Gettysburg and Vicksburg.

With the capitulation of Vicksburg, which had consumed so much of the Federal efforts in the West the previous year, attention could finally be given to other operations. By August 1863, Federal gunboats once again ascended the White River, this time in search of Price's army. The naval force managed to destroy Marmaduke's pontoon bridge on a tributary and capture the only two Confederate transports on the river system, effectively cutting Confederate access to northeastern Arkansas. By September Gen. Frederick Steele's army prepared to occupy Little Rock, forcing the Confederates to burn the ironclad ram *Pontchartrain* the following month to prevent her capture. The state government moved to Washington, Arkansas, and there were no more major Confederate operations north of the Arkansas River.

If you go there . . .

Helena could have easily been washed into obscurity after the Civil War like so many other small river towns except for one thing: the town has one of only two bridges crossing the Mississippi River between Memphis and Vicksburg. Enough traffic enters and leaves the state via the bridge to maintain a modest tourist industry. Attractions include several sites related to the battle of Helena.

The first place to stop is the Arkansas Tourist Information Center on the Highway 49 bypass just south of the city. A driving-tour map that pinpoints most of the major areas of fighting is available there. Backtracking toward town, you can see **Estevan Hall** at 653 Biscoe. Although remodeled, the house was originally built in 1826 and was occupied by the U.S. Army during the Civil War. Next you will pass the site of Gen. Thomas Hindman's home on the southwest corner of Biscoe and Arkansas streets. Hindman was one of seven Confederate generals from Helena, making the town the

The earthworks at Battery D are now listed on the National Register of Historic Places.

Southern equivalent of Galena, Illinois, which boasted nine Union generals, including U. S. Grant.

Behind the house is Hindman's Hill, and if you drive up the steep climb of Arkansas Street through Prairie to Military Road, in a short distance you will come to the historical markers for **Battery D** on Crowley's Ridge.[17] Although the nearby earthworks are on private land and posted against trespassing, the host at the tourist center assured me that the property owner did not mind interested parties walking back to the well-preserved dry ditch, counterscarp, and redoubt. The rugged landscape and towering heights of the remaining earthworks provide a startling image of what the Confederates faced as they attacked 4 July 1863: "Wave after wave assaulted the steep slopes of Crowley's Ridge, to find that when they seized the heights they came under direct fire from entrenched batteries and the guns of naval vessels lying off the Helena waterfront."[18] Although in reality only one vessel added its destructive punch that day, the results were the same: naval gunfire broke up the Confederate advance. Today, the all-important Mississippi River can still be seen through the trees.

Back down on Biscoe (which becomes Columbia), turn west on York to 323 Beech. Pockmarks from shells are still visible on the parlor doors of this National Register house in which Union officers lived during the occupation. Behind the home rises Graveyard Hill and the marker for **Battery C.**

Other sites in Helena associated with the Civil War include the **Maple Hill Cemetery,** which was started in 1865 after the destruction of the existing cemetery on Graveyard Hill. Local generals Hindman and J. C.

Tappan are buried there. In 1870 hometown hero Gen. Patrick Cleburne, killed in the battle of Franklin, was reinterred in the nearby **Confederate Cemetery.**[19] A marble column stands in his memory. Also be sure to stop at the **Phillips County Library and Museum** at 623 Pecan Street. Open free of charge, Monday through Saturday, from 9:00 A.M. to 5:00 P.M., the museum has a small collection of Civil War memorabilia, including uniforms and photographs. Ask at the library desk for a copy of "The Battle of Helena," which sells for a mere fifty cents and gives a clear picture of the desperate fighting for the city.

For further information, contact: Helena Tourism Commission, City Hall, 226 Perry Street, Helena, AR 72342 (501) 338-9831.

TEXAS

MORE THAN 95 percent of the white Texas population did not own slaves, but a majority opposed emancipation. Ironically, the great landowners in Texas who utilized slave labor, like many of their counterparts throughout the South, were politically conservative and remained unionist. "They did not relish casting adrift on uncharted, radical-tossed seas."[1] If the South had truly possessed a powerful aristocracy acting as a political entity, as some have claimed, there might never have been an American Civil War.[2]

A case in point is Sam Houston, onetime president of the Republic of Texas. In 1848, Houston — a native Virginian, a former governor of Tennessee, and at that time a U.S. senator from the state of Texas — voted for the admission of Oregon as free territory. Five years later he spoke out against the Kansas-Nebraska bill and in 1859 ran for governor of Texas as an independent on a unionist platform. Supported by the propertied classes, he won the election. No doubt Houston's popularity with the electorate as a whole arose more from his status as a war hero than from an acknowledgment of his quest for peace. Nevertheless, the following year he gained enough support from southern planters to be considered as a potential presidential candidate of the Constitutional Union party. He eventually lost the nomination to John Bell of Tennessee. In the 1860 presidential election, with a southern unionist candidate supported by Houston as one of the choices, Lincoln received no votes in Texas.

Even after Lincoln's victory, Governor Houston refused to call a convention to discuss secession. Outmaneuvered by the established political machine, Houston finally agreed to a special session of the legislature, which in turn authorized an election of convention delegates. On 1 February 1861, with only 7 dissenting votes out of 174, Texas joined the Confederate States of America. Houston and a few of his supporters tried to stop the impending crisis by calling for a plebiscite, but they did not have enough influence over popular democracy. On 16 March, Houston was forced to vacate the governor's office. In the coming conflict, the conqueror of Santa Anna refused either to violate his constitutional oath by supporting the Confederacy or to raise his sword against the state he loved. Consequently, he was rejected by the people he had endeavored to serve so faithfully. Despite a late declaration of his allegiance to Texas and secession, Houston died a heartbroken man in July 1863, the month when Union victories at Vicksburg and Gettysburg doomed the Southern cause. The last words he whispered to his wife were, "Texas . . . Texas."[3]

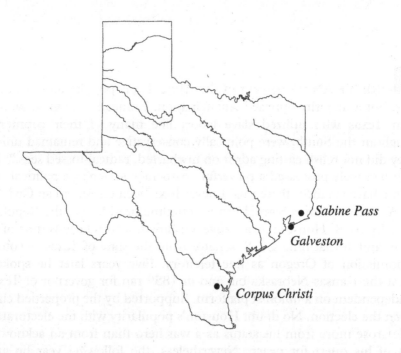

Another deeply troubled soldier on Texas soil when war clouds gathered was Robert E. Lee, a lieutenant colonel in the Second Cavalry. He met with Edmund J. Davis, a district court judge from Brownsville, in a small hotel off the Main Plaza[4] in San Antonio early in 1861 to discuss the impending constitutional crisis. Davis urged him to stand by the Union, but Lee, like Houston, could not forsake his native state.

Between sixty thousand and seventy thousand Texans, two-thirds of the state's military-age population (Houston's son included), did not share Houston and Lee's dilemma. They signed up to fight for the South.

Some of the first blood of the conflict Houston and Lee hoped to avoid was shed on Texas soil. On 1 April 1861, eleven days before the attack on

Fort Sumter, a Mexican named Ochoa hanged a county judge and issued a proclamation against the Confederacy. Cavalry sent by John "Rip" Ford caught up with Ochoa and killed twenty of his followers. The rest fled into Mexico. Ford, who had earned his nickname as an adjutant during the Mexican War by scratching "R.I.P." at the bottom of casualty lists, would eventually garner a reputation along the Rio Grande as "Texas' best-known soldier in the Civil War — in his own time, that is, not later,"[5] even though after April 1862 he held no official commission in the Confederate army.

Texas was far removed from the centers of military action in Virginia and along the Mississippi, its geography making invasions from bordering states difficult. The North tried on several occasions to gain footholds from the sea, but they all ended in defeat or met with limited success. The Texan defense of the seacoast between 1861 and 1865 proved to be one of the most brilliant unsung feats of any Confederate state during the war. Not one of the major port cities in Texas remained under Federal control at the time Lee surrendered in Virginia. True, these places suffered under a tight Federal blockade and many changed hands several times during the conflict, but perhaps that was only misplaced justice since residents along the coastal areas had voted overwhelmingly for secession.

Corpus Christi

ON 16 NOVEMBER 1862 the *New York Herald* ran a front-page headline, "The Capture of Corpus Christi, Texas," and Adm. David Farragut, writing officially, congratulated a forty-five-year-old former merchant officer for accomplishing this task. Both the headline and Farragut's praise were premature. It was true that John W. Kittredge, appointed an acting lieutenant in 1861, had orchestrated the blockade of the largest Texas port south of Galveston, but he had not been able to capture it despite a battle lasting several days between his ships and Confederate shore batteries. In fact, Farragut sent his message to Kittredge two days after the latter was a prisoner of war.

At the beginning of the Civil War, the North utilized the skills of its New England–based sailors to fill out the ranks of its navy. One such recruit was Kittredge. Familiar with the Texas coast from his days in the merchant marine, he had been given command of the *Arthur* (a bark with eighty men, one Parrott, and six 32-pounders) and assigned to patrol the Texas coast from Pass Cavallo at Matagorda Bay to Aransas Pass just north of Corpus Christi Bay. Although Kittredge's sailors captured a schooner in early 1862, the fourteen-foot draft of the *Arthur* prevented them from crossing the shallow channels that led to the intracoastal waterways along which most of the trade flowed along the Texas coast to Louisiana.

Not content to wait outside the bar for suspicious vessels, Kittredge raised the U.S. flag on Saint Joseph's Island and at the lighthouse on Harbor

Island. Strictly speaking, these forays were not part of his assignment, but Kittredge carried them out for several reasons. To begin with, supplies from the navy arrived infrequently, and Kittredge was able to acquire fresh beef and mutton for his crew during these incursions onto enemy territory. Also, he and his men picked up valuable intelligence from Union sympathizers in the area. Finally, Kittredge was ambitious, and he "proudly sought to win glory for himself."[6] Ultimately, hubris would be Kittredge's undoing. As early as 22 April 1862, local troops almost captured him on Saint Joseph's Island near Aransas Pass. During this close call, he was forced to leave behind some prisoners and two launches.

That brush with disaster did not deter him in his quest for fame. In late May 1862 the *Arthur* sailed to New Orleans and returned in early July with the shallow-draft yacht *Corypheus*.[7] Kittredge armed it with his Parrott gun and a 12-pounder howitzer and moved the yacht across the Aransas bar. His new gunboat quickly captured two sloops, which Kittredge also armed. Now he was in position to interdict intracoastal water traffic, a terrible blow to local Confederate officials who responded by ordering all shipping to remain inside the harbors. A month later, with the arrival of the steamer *Sachem*, Kittredge felt ready to attack Corpus Christi. Because of its deep draft, the *Arthur* headed back to New Orleans for supplies. Thus Kittredge would have four gunboats at his disposal, not enough to hold the city, but enough to allow the unionist mayor, Henry W. Berry, to gain control with the aid of the Union sympathizers that Kittredge knew inhabited the town in significant numbers.

To counter the threat from the sea, Confederate Col. Charles G. Lovenskiold, the city's provost marshal, sank three small schooners in the ship channel leading to Corpus Christi Bay, but on 13 August Kittredge used the *Sachem*'s steam power to remove the obstacles. Once inside the bay, he captured another vessel, which he converted to a hospital ship. Kittredge then landed at Corpus Christi under a flag of truce and demanded to be allowed to inspect Federal property in the city. Maj. Alfred M. Hobby, commander of the local forces, denied such property existed. Kittredge allowed Hobby twenty-four hours to evacuate the population before Union ships would strike. After another parley, during which the truce was extended another day, battle became unavoidable.

The twenty-six-year-old Hobby appeared to be in a hopeless situation. His command consisted of a few hundred untrained volunteers and some old cannon that might have been left behind by Zachary Taylor's army in 1846. Even if the men knew how to use the guns, which was doubtful, there was not enough powder for practice. The untrained Hobby did what he thought could be done in the intervening forty-eight hours by situating his guns in the old Kinney stockade on a bluff overlooking the bay and business district. Fortunately for the former Texas state legislator, two locals came forward to help. Felix A. Blucher, a Mexican War veteran, assisted with the two 6-pounder guns. Billy Mann, wounded at Island Number 10 and recuperating with his widowed mother, also volunteered his expertise.

Mann advised Hobby to move the two 12-pounders and the 18-pounder from their emplacements at Kinney's fort to some sand-and-shell embankments along the bay at the northern edge of the city. Mann's arguments swayed Hobby, but the latter feared there was not enough time to reposition his artillery in the old Mexican War emplacements. When the 5:00 P.M. deadline arrived and Kittredge did not attack, Hobby quietly limbered his guns and hauled them to the beach fortifications. By 2:00 A.M. the defenders had six guns situated four hundred yards from the unsuspecting Union ships.

At daybreak on 16 August, the Texans opened fire, catching the Federals completely off guard. Confederate shells hit two ships immediately, and the remaining Federal vessels were becalmed too far away to add effective counterfire. The answering salvos from the fleet were haphazard: "Thrown," according to one account, "in every conceivable direction to and within one and one-half miles about the City."[8]

The Federals eventually got the range of the Confederate works, but their shells had little effect on the sand batteries. Realizing the enemy's gunboats were not unbeatable, Confederate riflemen gained their courage and began to fire at the sailors. Mann grabbed the handmade Confederate flag stitched the day before and climbed atop the ramparts to encourage his men, warn of incoming shots, and direct outgoing rounds.

After four hours Kittredge broke off the engagement. The next day, a Sunday, the Union navy did not resume the attack, but neither side rested. Hobby's militia made use of the time by retrieving precious powder from unexploded Union projectiles among the three hundred that had been fired the previous day. Kittredge busied himself making plans. Early on the morning of 18 August, Acting Master's Mate Alfred H. Reynolds landed with thirty men and a 12-pounder rifled howitzer to attempt to take the Confederate position from the flank. A counterattack that included Confederate cavalry reserves succeeded in turning back Reynolds's force despite a heavy barrage of grapeshot from the supporting ships. With this setback for the Federals, the battle ended, and Kittredge retreated to repair his ships.

A special edition of the *Corpus Christi Ranchero* dated 19 August pronounced Corpus Christi "the Vicksburg of Texas."[9] The following day Gen. Hamilton P. Bee arrived to oversee the strengthening of the city's defenses, which gained a battery of six howitzers a week later.

Meanwhile, Kittredge continued to patrol the city's approaches, capturing the *Water Witch* on 23 August. Still determined to earn the praise he had already gained in Northern newspapers and dispatches despite his failure to capture the city, in mid-September Kittredge raided Flour Bluff, a community at the southeast corner of Corpus Christi Bay, and took several hostages. He came ashore again the next day, but this time he had pushed his luck too far. The Confederates were waiting for him. Without firing a shot, troops under Capt. James A. Ware, who had commanded the Confederate cavalry during the earlier battle, and Capt. John Ireland, a future Texas governor, captured Kittredge and his landing party. After remaining a month as a prisoner in San Antonio, the Union commander was paroled to the *Arthur.* The ship sailed for Pensacola where Kittredge reported personally to Adm. David Farragut. The *Sachem* and *Corypheus* left in December for Galveston and disaster.

The retreat of Federal forces did not end the tribulations of the local citizens. Kittredge had not forced Corpus Christi to surrender, but the city suffered because of his blockade and a severe drought. Food was so scare that when Federals landed on Mustang Island[10] against slight opposition almost a year after the departure of the *Sachem* and *Corypheus,* many of the citizens switched loyalties. The bulk of the town's defenders had been ordered to other troubled spots and those that remained were helpless to stop Federal raids. With the withdrawal of Federal forces once again in 1864, returning Confederate authorities filed indictments for treason against the collaborators. The war ended before the cases could be brought to trial.

If you go there . . .

Even though Corpus Christi played a minor role in the Civil War, the town has preserved some of the history of the era and marked the important sites of the struggle. The city's most historical attraction is **Centennial House** at 411 N. Broadway. The oldest existing structure in Corpus Christi, it was built in 1849 and served as a Confederate hospital. After the war it became an officer's mess for the federal occupation army. It is open on Wednesday afternoons, 2:00 P.M. to 5:00 P.M., for a small admission charge. Almost across the street at 401 N. Broadway, a historic marker sits on the site of the **Kinney Stockade,** where Confederate troops initially placed their artillery in August 1862. A marker at the visitors center, 1201 N. Shoreline, commemorates the spot from which the Confederates later held off the Union fleet behind sand-and-shell embankments constructed earlier by Gen. Zachary Taylor's army. A small park nearby at the corner of Twigg and Chaparral streets surrounds the area in which Taylor had drilled an artesian well adjacent to his camp. Among his troops were two other future presidents, Franklin Pierce and Ulysses Grant. Behind the park, a plaque at Buffalo and Upper N. Broadway marks the location of the developing port's original brick lighthouse. Used as a powder magazine during the Civil War, it was dismantled in 1878. Also downtown, the **Confederate Memorial,** designed by Pompeo Coppini, was erected in 1915 at Peoples and Schatzel at the Bluff, a pedestrian walkway connecting uptown and downtown. The **Confederate Memorial Fountain** was added later by the city. The **Corpus Christi Museum,** 1900 N. Chaparral, displays one of the unexploded eighty-pound shells fired by the Federal fleet. It was still live when donated. The museum is open, Tuesday through Saturday, from 10:00 A.M. to 5:00 P.M., and on Sunday from 1:00–5:00 P.M. A $2.00 admission fee is charged, but on Saturdays from 10:00 A.M. until noon, there is no charge.

Two blocks east of the museum on Chaparral Street, Heritage Park gives visitors a glimpse into a fantasy neighborhood created by moving nine of Corpus Christi's historic homes into a parklike setting. Included is the **Merriman House.** Originally situated at 801 S. Upper Broadway, the 1851 Greek Revival structure was used by Dr. Eli T. Merriman as a hospital during the Civil War. The home is open to the public, 10:00 A.M. to 2:00 P.M., Monday through Friday.

Two local cemeteries provide the final resting places for several Confederate soldiers. Inside the city at Ramirez and Waco is the **Old Bayview Cemetery.** Veterans of the War of 1812, the Texas War for Independence, and Gen. Zachary Taylor's army are also buried there. Farther outside the city on FM 666 and Old Robstown Highway lies the **Banquete Cemetery.** Its oldest stone belongs to Joseph P. Madray, a local rancher who was serving in the Confederate army when he died in 1863. Other Confederate soldiers also rest there.

Several miles up the Nueces River on FM 666 at a spot called **Santa Margarita Crossing,** a marker relates how trade came down the old Matamoros, or Cotton, Road to circumvent the Federal blockade. In the opposite direction, on State Highway 361 on the Port Aransas causeway, a marker commemorates both the importance of **Aransas Pass** to blockade running and the early successes and setbacks suffered there by Kittredge before his attack upon Corpus Christi. A map in the foyer of the **Port Aransas Civic Center,** situated just off Highway 361 near the ferry dock, explains the geographical shifts of the coastal islands and the role of the **Aransas Pass Light Station** in the Civil War. The lighthouse, which has been privately restored and is still visible straight ahead from the Station Street Pier, had been constructed in 1855. Union forces stole the lens to prevent its use and buried it in a marsh. The recovered lens is also on display in the Civic Center.

The "Port Aransas Historical Trail" brochure put out by the Boy Scouts and available at the public library next to the Civic Center suggests that the fort built on Mustang Island during the Mexican War and used by the Confederates can still be seen on a sand dune known locally as **Bunker Hill.** Since the channel has shifted south since 1875, it is doubtful that the dune served as a Civil War site.

For further information, contact: Corpus Christi Area Convention and Tourist Bureau, 1201 N. Shoreline, P.O. Box 2664, Corpus Christi, TX 78403 (512) 882-5603.

Galveston

SOON AFTER Texas seceded from the Union, on 2 March 1861 Confederate authorities in Galveston seized the Federal revenue schooner *Henry Dodge*. This early in Lincoln's administration, the U.S. Navy was not in the position, either militarily or politically, to retaliate. Besides the obvious problems encountered trying to supply a squadron so far from any Union-controlled naval base, Lincoln was still hoping for a peaceful settlement. When the war of words exploded in a brilliant flash over Fort Sumter in April, Texas would still not be considered a high priority by either Washington or Richmond. A thinly stretched Federal Navy Department concluded that the fledgling Confederates could not make much use of ports so far from what were considered the major theaters of operations along the eastern seaboard. Nevertheless, on 2 July 1861 a single Federal naval vessel, ironically named the USS *South Carolina*, took up station off the bar of Galveston Bay in a mostly symbolic attempt to enforce Lincoln's blockade.

Despite its relative unimportance, Galveston was the scene of the first actual combat involving ships of the hastily assembled blockading squadron. One of the *South Carolina*'s small boats returning from a patrol down the coast was shelled by a battery emplaced beyond the city on 3 August. At this stage in the conflict, James Alden, the ship's commander, actually expected that someone from Galveston would come forward to explain this unprovoked action. When no one approached, Alden brought his ship within range. Much to his surprise, the battery opened fire again. Alden answered in kind, killing a Portuguese man and wounding some boys. Such "acts of inhumanity unrecognized in modern warfare"[11] brought a stiff condemnation from resident foreign consuls. Alden was frustrated both by this response and his inability to prohibit enemy ships from running in and out of the port without interruption. Although almost a dozen blockade runners had been captured or destroyed since the *South Carolina* took up its duties the month before, this figure represented only a small portion of the ships entering and leaving the harbor.

Even though there was little or no threat to blockaders from the enemy during the following months, their life was not an easy one. The greatest danger faced by the sailors covering the Rio Grande outlets, Corpus Christi, Matagorda and Galveston bays, and Sabine Pass came from the lack of fresh provisions. It was only a matter of time before scurvy broke out among several crews. By the waning days of 1862, few blockaders were available beyond the vicinity of Galveston despite the fact that Adm. David G. Farragut, commander of the West Gulf Blockading Squadron, had decided, following his capture of New Orleans in April 1862, that a greater effort should be made to control enemy vessels navigating the intracoastal waterways that parallel almost the entire Texas coast.

After the destruction of the CSS *Arkansas* outside Baton Rouge, Louisiana, in August 1862, naval personnel in the lower Mississippi region felt easier about sending more ships to Texas. In September, Farragut outlined plans for the capture of Galveston and ordered Comdr. William B. Renshaw to implement them. With a fleet of four ships, Renshaw sailed into Galveston Bay on 3 October 1862 and threatened to bombard the area's defenses. The Confederates in town pulled out, and six days later Renshaw raised the Stars and Stripes over Galveston Custom House. For the most part, Galvestonians treated the Federal troops as liberators.

Hearing the news of Galveston's fall, Farragut reported to Secretary of the Navy Gideon Welles: "I am happy to inform you that Galveston, Corpus Christi, and Sabine Pass and the adjacent waters are now in our possession."[12] Farragut's report was not literally true. Corpus Christi remained firmly under Rebel control. Although the Union gunboats kept Confederate troops out of Galveston during the day, Renshaw prudently withdrew most of his small complement of men to the ships at night, leaving the city to Rebel scouts.

Galveston lies at the eastern end of a long, narrow island. During the war, a railroad line ran four miles along the island, then connected with the mainland at Virginia Point. Since he was not able to feed the city's civilians, Renshaw was reluctant to destroy the railroad bridge for humanitarian reasons. He could not have done it even if he had wanted to. Strong Confederate forces were entrenched on both sides of the bridge, and Renshaw's ships drew too much water to get close enough to bombard either the troops or the island's railroad lifeline.

Although Renshaw had managed to take Galveston without the help of the army, the lack of a large occupation force following up his success put him in an uncomfortable position. Realizing his predicament, Renshaw wrote Farragut asking for troops to hold the city and shallow-draft mortar schooners to destroy the Virginia Point fortifications. Farragut passed on the requests to Maj. Gen. Benjamin F. Butler in New Orleans. Butler indicated his willingness to accede to the navy's wishes, but no help came.

The stalemate at Galveston continued until December when word reached Renshaw through Union sympathizers that Confederate Maj. Gen. John B. Magruder was planning to recapture the city. Fearing the worst, Renshaw requested permission to abandoned his tenuous grip on Galveston. Farragut ordered him to hold. On 14 December, Maj. Gen. Nathaniel P. Banks arrived in New Orleans to supersede Butler. Hoping that a secure base at Galveston would open some of the cotton lands of East Texas to Northern mill owners clamoring for cotton, Banks decided to send reinforcements to Renshaw.[13] Within two weeks Col. Isaac S. Burrell sailed into Galveston Bay with three companies of the Forty-second Massachusetts. On Christmas Day the first 260 men of what was supposed to be an entire regiment offloaded into the city. Two shallow-draft warships arrived three days later, but Renshaw felt they were too weak to attack the railroad bridge by themselves.

The rumors concerning Magruder's impending attack proved correct. The defender of Yorktown during Gen. George McClellan's peninsula campaign had personally surveyed positions throughout Galveston Island, sometimes within sight of the Union sentries, then drawn up plans for a combined land-sea operation. The naval side of the attack consisted of two small cottonclad river steamers, each jammed with sharpshooters ready to board any ships they could reach. The land force would have the greater punch, at least on paper.

In late December 1862 Colonel Burrell visited sentry posts in the town. He suspected the train whistles and the rumbling of artillery caissons were not holiday merrymakers. The noises meant only one thing to Burrell: An attack was imminent. The colonel had wanted to billet his troops in quarters on Pelican Spit, but Renshaw insisted they occupy a building on the channel end of a four-hundred-foot city wharf. In the unlikely event that Union gunboats could not protect Burrell's position, Renshaw claimed the three companies could be rescued quickly by his steamers. Not taking any chances, Burrell ordered his men to use the wharf's planks to build breastworks on the dock itself, thereby creating fifty-foot protective gaps connected by a single-plank walkway to the island.

The moon set at 2:00 A.M. on 1 January 1863. Shortly afterward, lookouts on one of Renshaw's ships, the *Westfield,* spotted smoke coming down the bay. The anchor was raised, and the *Westfield,* which carried six guns, began to move toward the suspected enemy, only to run aground just off Pelican Spit. Although Leon Smith, commanding Magruder's sea force, retreated after being discovered, two hours later Magruder's men — about six thousand total — opened fire on both Burrell's position and Renshaw's fleet with muskets supplemented by a six-gun light battery, fourteen other field pieces, six siege guns, and an 8-inch Dahlgren mounted on a rail car. One of the volunteers manning the artillery was the governor of the Confederate Territory of Arizona, Pvt. John R. Baylor.

Burrell's men, under fire for the first time, probably did not need much encouragement when ordered to lie low behind the breastworks. Making Burrell's job a little easier, Magruder launched only one attempt to carry the Federal position during the night. Since the attackers' scaling ladders were too short, the assault was doomed, especially when the Massachusetts men proved to be determined defenders. Furthermore, gunfire from the supporting ships aimed at muzzle flashes forced Confederate artillerists to abandon their posts. The *Clifton,* the heaviest armed Union ship, was delayed from approaching the land conflict because of an unsuccessful attempt to help free the grounded *Westfield.* It was, however, able to play a role by silencing a Confederate battery situated on the east end of Galveston Island near Fort Point.

When the sun rose, Smith's two Confederate steamers once more plowed down the bay to attack the *Harriet Lane,* whose five guns had been actively engaged in the battle festering around the wharf. The Union commander, discerning the approaching enemy ships, planned to ram one, then board the other. Unfortunately, the *Lane* also grounded and was rammed, but not before sinking the *Neptune,* a cottonclad with 150 men of the Seventh Texas Cavalry on board. The one hundred sharpshooters from the second Confederate vessel, the *Bayou City* (a packet boat armed with a rifled 32-pounder in the bow) picked off the *Lane*'s captain, Comdr. Jonathan M. Wainwright,[14] and wounded her second-in-command. The *Lane,* which had served as Adm. David Porter's flagship for his mortar flotilla at New Orleans, was soon in Confederate hands. In one of many instances that brought home the divisiveness of the war, Confederate Maj. Alfred M. Lea boarded the *Lane* to find his son Edward, a Federal lieutenant, dying on the deck.[15]

When the USS *Owasco* with her four guns approached the *Lane* to ascertain what was happening, she was met by accurate rifle fire and immediately began to back down the channel past the *Clifton* and Colonel Burrell, who was signaling from the wharf for her to stop to pick up his besieged men. Immediately after the *Owasco* retreated, Smith raised a white flag on the *Lane* and sent the captain of the *Bayou City* with the *Lane*'s former acting master to request Comdr. Richard L. Law of the approaching *Clifton* to surrender. Law had no way of knowing that the *Bayou City* and *Lane* were still locked together, so Smith was effectively out of the fight. Furthermore, although only five men actually had been lost aboard the *Lane,* the acting master reported that two-thirds of the crew had been killed. With Renshaw still on the grounded *Westfield* and Wainwright, his second-in-command, dead on board the *Lane,* Law agreed to a three-hour truce during which neither side would move any ships. All this transpired without a word to Burrell on shore.

Seeing white flags on his support vessels, Burrell asked for and received a half-hour truce to communicate with the navy. His adjutant rowed out to the *Clifton* only to be told that the steamer would not move to help the stranded troops until Law returned. While the adjutant argued, the busy captain of the *Bayou City,* who had since rowed to shore, informed Burrell that the three-hour truce on the water would not extend his half-hour truce on land. His time was up. With no reasonable options, Burrell surrendered his entire command, not one of his men having been killed.

Meanwhile, Renshaw instructed Law to refuse Smith's bluff: an offer to allow all Union naval personnel to leave the bay on one ship of Renshaw's

The daring (and desperate) attack on the *Harriett Lane* in Galveston Harbor. The same attack bore the loss of the *Westfield*. *(Leslie's)*

choice. Renshaw informed Law he planned to blow up the still-grounded *Westfield* and escape with the remainder of his fleet. As Law returned to the *Clifton*, unknown to him, one final tragedy occurred to the Union forces: A premature explosion on the *Westfield* killed Renshaw and nearly twenty of his men. Although no record exists of Renshaw's orders for the disposition of Federal troops still on shore,[16] his plans for them did not matter since they were being led into captivity by the time Law reboarded his ship.

The Confederates had moved the *Lane* and the *Bayou City* to shore while Law was conferring with his commanding officer. Law, still unaware of their attached condition, regarded it as violation of the truce and immediately ordered all Union ships to leave the bay. Magruder's artillery tried to inflict some final damage, but to no avail. At the mouth of the bay, Law heard of Renshaw's death. Thinking a continuation of the blockade to be fruitless, especially if the Confederates could quickly reoutfit the *Harriet Lane*, Law returned to New Orleans.

The capture of four ships, fifteen guns, and several hundred prisoners was an impressive victory for Magruder. Even the unionist Sam Houston wrote to the Confederate general: "You deserve, sir, not only my thanks, but the thanks of every Texan."[17]

Farragut and Welles took the loss of Galveston poorly, particularly since the Confederates would be able to extract much propaganda from the victory by declaring the blockade to be broken. Law and Lt. Comdr. Henry Wilson of the *Owasco*, the only Federal ship not damaged during the battle, were both court-martialed and charged with two offenses: failing to do their

The grounded *Westfield* was destroyed to prevent its falling into Confederate hands. *(Harper's)*

utmost to recapture or destroy the *Harriet Lane* and leaving their blockading station. Nothing was said about abandoning 260 army troops.[18]

Within ten days of the debacle at Galveston, Farragut sent Capt. Henry H. Bell with the *Brooklyn* and six gunboats to recapture Galveston or at the least to prevent the *Harriet Lane* from becoming, according to Farragut, "as bad as the *Alabama*."[19] His fear proved ironic in two ways.

On 11 January 1863 Bell ordered the *Hatteras* to hail an approaching ship twenty miles south of Galveston. The ship turned out to be the *Alabama*. Raphael Semmes, her captain, had incorrectly surmised from newspapers captured just outside of Cuba that Banks was on his way to Galveston with twenty thousand troops. Semmes hoped to sneak in among the transports but found Bell's blockaders instead. He lured the curious *Hatteras* away from shore, then turned to attack the converted merchantman. The hapless *Hatteras* sank during a point-blank duel, the only Union warship to fall to a Confederate raider. In retrospect, Semmes had taken a great risk. A well-placed shot could have ended his brilliant career. Bell, for his part, decided to blockade Galveston from a distance rather than risk grounding his ships at the entrance.

The second ironic outcome of Farragut's fears revolved around the disposition of the *Lane*. She was eventually outfitted as the blockade runner *Lavinia* and escaped from Galveston one rainy night in April 1864 along with the *Alice* and *Isabel*. The latter two ships were sunk within three months trying to slip back into Galveston Bay. The *Lane* lay off Havana, Cuba, until the end of the war. She was returned to the United States in 1867, hardly an equal to the infamous raider to which Farragut compared her.

By mid-1863 a change in the political situation south of the Texas border focused Washington's attention once more on the Lone Star State. On 10 June 1863, a French army entered Mexico City. At the time Washington perceived French Emperor Napoleon III as unfriendly to U.S. interests and ordered General Banks on 24 July to invade Texas and show the flag despite the navy's desire to knock Mobile, Alabama, out of the war instead. The expectation that France might try to extend Mexico's borders into its old dominions was "lacking foundation,"[20] according to naval historian Alfred Thayer Mahan, but in this case the Federal and Confederate governments shared the same concern. A year earlier a French consul in Texas, acting in an official capacity, had written a letter to the Texas governor suggesting that Texas secede from the Confederacy. For that and other reasons, he and a French consular official in Richmond were ordered to leave the Confederacy.

Fearing that a collapse of the Confederate government in Texas could provide Texas with an excuse to declare itself an independent republic once again, Lincoln and his advisers told Banks to put his Mobile plans on hold. First, a plan to attack Sabine City failed, so another force was embarked to fight Confederates and intimidate the French. The thirty-five hundred men under the nominal command of Gen. Napoleon J. T. Dana (although Banks was along) landed on 2 November at the mouth of the Rio Grande. The river's outlet to the sea had been an ongoing political problem for the Union navy because half the waterway belonged to Mexico. Merchant ship captains hoping to evade the blockade always claimed to be sailing for Mexico. With the fall of Brownsville, Texas, on 6 November, this portal for goods into the Confederacy was theoretically closed. Its practical effect on the Southern cause was minimal, however, since very few supplies actually made the difficult trip from the tip of Texas to fighting units outside the state, especially those across the Mississippi River.

After securing the city, some of Dana's troops reembarked on transports and sailed to Mustang Island near Corpus Christi. Sailors from the escorting warship USS *Monongahela* manned a battery of two howitzers ashore as the ship shelled Confederate works. The defenders soon surrendered.[21] The task force continued to Fort Esperanza on Pass Cavallo leading into Matagorda Bay. Just a little over a month earlier a Federal fleet had smothered the fort's twenty-foot-thick walls with cannon fire and forced the defenders to spike their eight guns and retreat to Indianola on the mainland. When the fleet departed, the garrison reoccupied the two-hundred-yard-long breastworks. On 27 November, Federal forces threatened the fort a second time. They approached the position from the rear as sailors hit the beach again to work batteries in support of their attack. Once more the Confederates pulled back to Indianola.[22]

After their third easy victory of the campaign, the Union troops took to transports for the next major gulf port, Galveston. This time, however,

Banks and Dana found powerful defenses at the Brazos River[23] near the south end of West Galveston Bay, supported by the Rebel gunboat *John F. Carr.* Although the Confederate cottonclad was destroyed during a severe gale, it had made "some very good hits,"[24] enough to discourage any further advances. Since Banks concluded that his orders to show the flag were fulfilled, he did not order a major assault. By March 1864 Banks was back in New Orleans to confer with Sherman on the Red River campaign.

For the next year and a half, the Federal navy continued to tighten the blockade of Galveston Bay. Except for a few small but successful raids by sailors aboard launches, Galveston itself was not attacked. As other Southern ports fell one by one, blockade runners made for the last major harbor that was open, Galveston. The *Denbigh* shifted to Galveston after the capture of the Mobile forts and then escaped to Havana on 1 May 1865. That same month the former commander of the CSS *Albemarle,* John Maffitt, brought the blockade runner *Owl* — originally out of Wilmington, North Carolina — into Galveston Bay past sixteen Federal cruisers. To add to the insult, Maffitt steamed past them again on 9 May on his way to Havana. From there, he proceeded to Liverpool, England, evading the furious Yankees one last time.

Even though the war had ended more than a month earlier, several Confederates had not heard the news. Comdr. Matthew F. Maury, for one, sailed from England with $40,000 worth of electric torpedo equipment, determined to keep Galveston open for trade. When he heard during a stopover in Havana that Lee's army had surrendered, he chose to remain in Havana for a while. The captain of the *Denbigh,* however, decided to make another attempt at the Federal blockading fleet at Galveston. This time his luck ran out, and the ship Farragut called "too quick for us"[25] was destroyed on 24 May. Later that month, the CSS *LeCompt* was captured, the "last rebel flag on the coast afloat,"[26] according to Rear Adm. Henry Thatcher.

Finally, on 2 June 1865, Maj. Gen. E. Kirby Smith surrendered Galveston. Three days latter the U.S. flag was raised over the Galveston Custom House.

The Gulf Squadron, more a token show of force along the Texas coast than a real threat to shipping during much of the war, remained in existence for political reasons until May 1867. At that point, the French emperor finally abandoned his dream of establishing an empire in Mexico.

If you go there . . .

During the late 1960s, bulldozers rumbled in Galveston's Strand District and commenced to pulverize centuries-old warehouses. Happily for preservationists, a group of concerned citizens managed to halt the metal

monsters, and today multitudes of visitors ramble along Strand Avenue —
the former Wall Street of the West — to enjoy the nineteenth-century am-
biance.

Many of the tourists stop into the Strand District Visitors Center at
2016 Strand in the former **Hendley Row.** Those who read the historical
marker out front discover that Hendley Row is the oldest surviving commercial structure in the area. Starting in 1855, workers sank huge granite
blocks into the sandy soil of Galveston Island to support the weight of the
block-long building.

Two years after the warehouse was completed in 1859, the cupola
tower, which has since been removed, served as an observation platform for
the few Confederate troops garrisoning the port. When a union fleet captured Galveston in 1863, Federal soldiers also used the cupola for a lookout
post. During the subsequent fighting, the seventh granite pillar on the Twentieth Street side of the building was damaged. The chipped column was
never repaired. After the war, Hendley Row acted as Reconstruction headquarters.

The **Galveston County Historical Museum,** at 2219 Market, has a
bale of cotton standing next to its small but interesting Civil War section to
allow the curious to touch and understand how compacted cotton could de-
flect bullets and even cannon shot. The museum's summer hours are from
10:00 A.M. to 5:00 P.M., Monday through Saturday, and noon to 5:00 P.M.
Sunday. During the winter it closes an hour earlier. A $1.00 donation is re-
quested.

Farther down the coast, where Banks's Texas campaign began near
Brownsville, parts from two bastions of the original earthen **Fort Brown**
stand at the far end of the driving range of the Riverview Municipal Golf
Course. When the Confederates took over the six-bastioned work in 1861,
their officers were "unanimous in their disgust with it."[27] It did contribute a
miscellaneous collection of twenty-five howitzers, cannon and mortars, but
its garrison consisted of "old soldiers and deserters from the Federal Army,
with few exceptions a class of men in whom no dependence can be placed."[28]
A large stone monolith stands at the site. Its faint inscription provides details
of the fort's size. A cannon barrel sprouts a short distance from the stone
marker. A new post was built north of the old fort after the war. Before it was
abandoned in 1946, it had the distinction of being the southernmost military post in the United States. A few of the buildings from the later fort are
being renovated on Texas Southmost College.

An impressive collection of Civil War artifacts is on display at the **Historic Brownsville Museum,** situated in the restored Southern Pacific Railroad Depot on Madison Street between Sixth and Seventh streets. There is
a $2.00 admission charge to the museum, which is open Tuesday thorugh
Saturday from 10:00 A.M. to 4:30 P.M. For information, contact: Historic

Brownsville Museum, P.O. Box 4337, Brownsville, TX 78520 (512) 548-1313.

About twenty minutes toward the gulf from Brownsville via Highway 48 rises the **Port Isabel Lighthouse.** Begun in 1851, the seventy-foot-tall structure was used by both sides during the Civil War as an observation post. Today hardy visitors can climb to the top for a view of the surrounding area from 10:00–11:30 A.M. and 1:00–5:00 P.M. daily. The cost is $1.00. For information, contact: Port Isabel State Historic Park, P.O. Box 863, Port Isabel, TX 78578 (512) 943-1172.

Sabine Pass

CONFEDERATE FORCES at Sabine Pass, the outlet for the port of Beaumont, had more than a year of war to prepare for an attack. Yet when three Federal ships bombarded their batteries (called Fort Sabine) on 25 September 1862, the defenders spiked the guns, buried them, and evacuated their fortified position. An aura of invincibility[29] surrounded the Union navy after its early stunning victories along the eastern seaboard, particularly since its engagements at Port Royal, South Carolina. Confederate saltwater garrisons were not eager to challenge that reputation. Following up their victory, the next day Union forces captured Sabine City, burned Wingate's sawmill, and destroyed the railroad bridge over Taylor's Bayou on the way to Beaumont. Because the expedition had no accompanying troops, the Federals could not occupy the area, but the navy continued the blockade.

Early the next year it was the Federals' turn to be caught unprepared. On 21 January 1863 the cottonclads *Josiah Bell* and *Uncle Ben,* commanded by Confederate Maj. Oscar M. Watkins, surprised and took control of two small Union blockading ships and reopened the channel to Confederate commerce.

In March 1863 Confederate Maj. Julius Kellersberg was dispatched to Sabine Pass with thirty engineers and five hundred slaves to construct another fort. The major chose a prominent point farther into the pass than the old fort, where his guns could traverse in a 270-degree arc opposite the channel exits from the oyster reef. Kellersberg literally had to dig up the armament, sending the two 32-pounders from the old fort to Galveston to be repaired. Two 24-pounders came from Fort Grigsby, seven miles above the mouth of the Neches River. The oyster-shell-and-mud fort had been constructed in October 1862 at Grigsby's Bluff to protect Beaumont following the September Federal victory.

Comdr. Abner Read of the blockader *New London* took it upon himself to spy on Confederate activities from the abandoned eighty-foot-tall Sabine Lighthouse. His hopes of leading a surprise attack were dashed when Colonel Griffin, in charge of the troops at Sabine Pass, gained information

Two Confederate cottonclads overtake and capture the USS *Morning Light* off Sabine Pass. *(Leslie's)*

about Read's scouting party. He ordered detachments from two of his companies to hide under the lighthouse keeper's residence and wait for the Federals. The next morning, 18 April, two whaleboats carrying Read and James G. Taylor (a New York–born ship captain who fled Confederate authorities at Sabine in September 1862 and joined the Union cause[30]) landed near the lighthouse. A three-man advance guard surrendered to the Rebels, but the remainder of the crewmen tried to flee. Both Read and Taylor managed to escape but were seriously wounded. Five other Yankees died in a hail of gunfire and six more surrendered. Only one of the escaping Federals was uninjured.

By August, the Union department commander, Henry W. Halleck, made it clear he wanted "the immediate occupation of some important point in the state of Texas."[31] In the absence of Adm. David Farragut, Comdr. H. H. Bell agreed to an operation, run jointly with the army this time, to recapture the Sabine Pass fortifications. Four gunboats, under the command of the same commander who had taken the position a year earlier, Lt. Frederick Crocker, led twenty transports carrying five thousand men. They arrived early in September, but the element of surprise was lost when the master of the gunboat the *Granite City*, sent ahead to mark the channel, mistook another Federal ship for the CSS *Alabama* and fled. Lieutenant Crocker spent the night looking for *Granite City*'s signal. In the meantime, the second

The *Clifton* was disabled under Dowling's guns and eventually destroyed. *(Leslie's)*

column of attacking Federal ships crossed the bar in search of Crocker's division and inadvertently alerted the Confederate defenders. Still confident of success and desiring to move before Rebel reinforcements could arrive, Crocker took the *Clifton* and the other gunboats across the bar on 8 September and approached Fort Griffin (also known as Fort Sabine) on the Texas side of the channel.

On paper the situation seemed hopeless for the Rebels. In fact, Magruder had ordered Company F of the Texas Heavy Artillery to spike its guns and retreat, a replay of 1862. Neither of the top two Confederate commanders happened to be at the post, and Jr. Lt. Richard Dowling, along with his forty-two Irishmen, was spoiling for a fight. He ignored the orders. The Davies, as the burly Irish dockworkers were known, had "covered themselves with glory"[32] at Galveston and had no intention of withdrawing. After loading their two old 24-pounder smoothbores, two 32-pounders, and two howitzers, the Texans waited patiently under fire behind their earthworks, which had been reinforced with railroad iron and ships' timbers. The CSS *Ben* and a few other troops in the area were the only available reinforcements.

When the Union ships approached within twelve hundred yards, Dowling's artillery finally erupted. The *Sachem*, which had barely escaped Galveston during the Union's ignominious retreat at the first of the year, was not so fortunate this time. Advancing up the Louisiana side of the channel, she was holed in her steam drum and taken under tow by the *Ben*. In the Texas channel, the *Clifton*, her tiller rope shot away, drifted under the guns of Fort Griffin. In ten minutes Crocker raised a white flag. The USS *Arizona*, steaming behind the *Sachem*, picked up survivors, then backed down the channel to join the transports and troops under Maj. Gen. William B. Franklin.

The master of the *Granite City*, responsible for the loss of surprise in the first place, continued to see Confederate demons and paused on his way back across the bar to report to Franklin that a large force of Confederate field artillery was approaching to block any landing. This second figment of his imagination convinced the frustrated Franklin that he had no choice but to retreat back to New Orleans.

The Federal report following the disaster stressed the cooperation between the navy and the army. The truth, however, was that the Confederates had won a stunning victory. Without losing a cannon or a man, Dowling had killed or wounded 100 Federals, captured another 350, and taken possession of two Union ships and their thirteen cannon, increasing by one-third the size of the state's armed fleet. He became a hero throughout the South. Jefferson Davis proclaimed the battle "the Thermopylae of the Civil War," and the Confederate Congress allowed a special medal struck to commemorate the event, the only such medal to be presented to Southern soldiers during the war.[33]

Often overlooked in Civil War histories, the Confederate success had far-reaching consequences. Coupled with Braxton Bragg's victory at Chickamauga, Georgia, in mid-September, the battle at Sabine Pass was instrumental in causing the United States to lose credit overseas and the dollar to lose 5 percent of its value against gold.[34] Almost as important, the Federals made no attempt to attack the pass again during the war. That did not mean, however, that the garrison rested entirely on its laurels. Although Dowling became an army recruiter after his heroic defense and saw no further action, the men from his former post continued to win battles. On 6 May 1864, some 350 sharpshooters from Sabine Pass overwhelmed a Union landing party at Calcasieu Pass, Louisiana (the next channel east) and captured a steamer and a tinclad.[35] Farragut planned to exact some measure of revenge but postponed his efforts.

Not until 25 May 1865 was Rear Admiral Thatcher able to report that Acting Lt. Comdr. Lewis W. Pennington of the USS *Owasco* had raised the Stars and Stripes over Fort Mannahasset, six miles farther down the coast, and over Fort Griffin.

There was never a formal surrender in Texas. Some Confederate soldiers simply buried the Stars and Bars in the sands along the Rio Grande and then rode south to join in the fight between the French and the Mexicans.

The Dowling Monument at the Sabine Pass Battlefield

If you go there . . .

Sabine Pass Battleground State Historical Park lies at the end of FM 3322 just a mile and a half south of Sabine Pass, which sits fifteen miles south of Port Arthur via Highway 87. Although nothing remains of the Confederate earthworks, a large statue of a bare-breasted Dick Dowling dominates the fifty-six-acre park near the probable site of the fort. Next to the parking area, historical markers explain the battle. One plaque also tells of Kate Dorman, a widow who brought food to Dowling's men during the battle. Before the Civil War, her Catfish Hotel catered to travelers in Sabine

City and served as a temporary hospital during the conflict. Almost a century later the military turned its attention to Sabine Pass again. During World War II, a Coastal Artillery Division was stationed there to protect the oil-rich ports of Beaumont and Port Arthur. Four concrete ammunition bunkers are all that remain.

Today the park offers a boat ramp, fish-cleaning shelter, restrooms, and picnic facilities, but these can be used only during daylight hours. Nearby Sea Rim State Park offers camping with hookups. The most attractive aspect of Sabine Pass Battleground might be that it is a great place to watch ships enter and leave the Gulf of Mexico.

In **Sabine Pass** a monument to Dowling stands at the corner of Dowling and S. Gulfway (the intersection of Highway 87 and FM 3322).[36] A Dick Dowling Days celebration is sponsored annually in Sabine Pass during the Labor Day weekend or thereabouts. For further information, contact: Sabine Pass Battleground State Historical Park, c/o Park Superintendent, P.O. Box 1066, Sabine Pass, TX 77655.

Built in 1856 on the Louisiana side of the Sabine Pass channel entrance, the **Sabine Lighthouse** has six buttresses at its base that give it the appearance of a rocket. Confederates damaged its third-order Fresnel lens, but the Lighthouse Board had it repaired by the end of 1865. Decommissioned in 1952, it is no longer in use. A private citizen now owns the unique structure, which is visible from the site of Fort Griffin on clear days.[37]

EPILOGUE

ARCHER JONES, author of several excellent books on Civil War strategy, noted that during the conflict the "Union's main advantage lay in its naval supremacy." Although the U.S. Navy "failed [at] creating a blockade effective enough to keep the Confederacy from importing most of what it needed," he observed, Northern warships "gave invaluable service on the western rivers."[1] Of course the Union eventually did stop blockade running, but not by the action of blockading fleets. As the authors of *Why the South Lost the Civil War* explained, "The Union most successfully hindered Confederate blockade-running with its *army* [emphasis added] by capturing port areas and carving up the Confederacy into smaller economic units. The efficacy of the blockade off Galveston [for example] meant little after the fall of Vicksburg."[2]

Although I agree with the overall sentiment, I would suggest that it was not merely the Federal army that was responsible for neutralizing Southern ports or even carving up the Confederacy. While the U.S. Navy did not supply as much crucial support along the saltwater coasts as it did along the inland waters, the contention that Federal land forces had more to do with the collapse of the major Southern ports is not supported by the evidence. Take Mobile, Alabama, for instance. It is mentioned in *Why the South Lost the Civil War* as one of the ports that fell to pressure by land forces, but Admiral Farragut would have been surprised to hear that. Of the three significant positions that guarded the entrance to the bay and eventually fell to Union forces, Fort Powell was abandoned after an attack by U.S. gunboats unsupported by any land force, Fort Gaines was surrendered to the U.S. fleet, and the commander of Fort Morgan caved in after a bombardment by land forces *and* all the vessels in Farragut's fleet, including the reflagged *Tennessee*. Granted, the city of Mobile did not surrender at that point, partly because Farragut could not bring his deep-draft warships close enough to bombard the inner defenses. Still, the capture of the channel forts resulted in the "termination of blockade running at the port," the main objective.[3] Likewise, Fort Fisher, North Carolina, did not fall to the U.S. Navy, but the battle along the landward face remained in doubt until U.S. warships planted a line of explosives along the Rebel-controlled gun emplacements.

Jones also wrote in his 1992 book *Civil War Command and Strategy* that a Union "contingent of 800 soldiers" at Hatteras Inlet, North Carolina, "easily overcame the Confederate garrisons of the small forts guarding the inlet."[4] Truth is admittedly a slippery commodity, but the U.S. Army had little if anything to do with the capture of the Confederate earthworks at Hatteras. The defenders of Fort Clark spiked their guns and fled after a half-hour naval bombardment while the Union landing forces dried themselves and their powder along the beach. Furthermore, the Confederate commander at the second strongpoint, Fort Hatteras, refused to surrender to General Butler because the Federal army had done practically nothing during the entire fight.

Jones and his co-authors in the prize-winning *Why the South Lost the Civil War* eventually came around to admitting that Union naval power held an important key to victory:

> As long as Union armies could depend on secure, efficient water transport, they had success, dramatic in the beginning, steady and dependable later, but when they were beyond the reach of the navy and water transport, the armies encountered severe difficulties. Although naval operations in the West were as difficult as those along the Atlantic seaboard, they were far more important. Whereas the blockade had little effect on the war's outcome, naval control of the western rivers enabled Union armies to gain and maintain control of the heartland of the Confederacy. The Comte de Paris, a French observer with the Union armies, correctly noted after the war, "We shall always find . . . that whenever the Federals were supported by a river, their progress was certain and their conquest decisive." Given this causal relationship, it is clear that the Union navy delivered some important blows to Confederate power and will and provided an ingredient essential to Union success in the western theater of war.[5]

And not just the western theater. Jones et al. agreed with historian Rowena Reed who "rightly concluded that 'no Civil War campaign better demonstrated the superior advantage of water communication than the Peninsula operations.'"[6] Just by their presence, Federal warships "contributed to the dissolution of Confederate power and will,"[7] the eventual lack of which provided the "decisive deficiency in the Confederate arsenal."[8]

Because forts at Charleston, South Carolina, and a very few other places were able to repel repeated forays by the U.S. Navy, some historians have argued that during the Civil War "neither ship nor shore guns achieved a clear superiority."[9] Considering, however, the continuously smaller role coastal fortifications had and the larger role navies played in strategic thinking in the years following 1865, it would appear that military leaders in most nations assumed "sea power had prevailed."[10]

NOTES

Introduction

1. B. F. Cooling, *Forts Henry and Donelson: The Key to the Confederate Heartland* (Knoxville: University of Tennessee Press, 1987), 1.

2. W. M. Fowler Jr., *Under Two Flags: The American Navy in the Civil War* (New York: W. W. Norton & Co., 1990), 16.

3. U.S. Naval History Division, comp., *Civil War Naval Chronology: 1861–1865,* 6 vols. (Washington, D.C.: Government Printing Office, 1961–66), 1:12.

4. J. M. McPherson, *Battle Cry of Freedom* (New York: Oxford University Press, 1988), 334.

5. Ibid.

6. R. Dupuy and T. Dupuy, *The Compact History of the Civil War* (New York: Hawthorn Books, 1968), 51.

7. Confederate Com. Josiah Tattnall — famous for his excuse "blood is thicker than water" when as a neutral he reinforced the British in Chinese waters in 1859 — said of the South's chances at sea: "Long before the Southern Confederacy has a fleet that can cope with the Stars and Stripes, my bones will be white in the grave" (R. Lattimore, *Fort Pulaski* [Washington, D.C.: National Park Service, 1954], 16).

8. By 1850 cotton accounted for more than half of Britain's annual exports. On the downside, the price for cotton cloth had fallen to only a quarter of what it had been in 1800 (J. Weatherford, *Indian Givers* [New York: Crown Publishers, 1988], 44).

9. D. Donald, ed., *Why the North Won the Civil War* (Baton Rouge: Louisiana State University Press, 1969), 7.

10. Although the Confederates were the first to win a battle through the use of railroads, the first to introduce railroad ambulance cars and rail-mounted guns, and the first to launch raids against the railroads of their opponent, they could not bring themselves to impose strict controls over the various railroad managements. It was not until February 1865, when the war was lost and schemes such as the induction of slaves into the armies were first given serious consideration, that the Confederate Congress granted real powers to the government to regulate the railroads (J. Westwood, *Railways at War* [San Diego: Howell-North Books, 1981], 17, 29).

11. B. Anderson, *By Sea and by River: The Naval History of the Civil War* (New York: Da Capo Press, 1989), 12. As a kind of tribute to his services, Mallory was one of only two Confederate cabinet members to hold his position throughout the war.

12. Estimates run as high as 332 officers who shifted from the Federal to the Confederate navy (R. G. Shingleton, *John Taylor Wood: Sea Ghost of the Confederacy* [Athens: University of Georgia Press, 1979], xi).

13. Mallory wrote on 9 May 1861: "I regard the possession of an iron armored ship as a matter of the first necessity . . . inequality of numbers may be compensated by invulnerability; and thus not only does economy but naval success dictate the wisdom and expediency of fighting with iron against wood" (W. N. Still Jr., "Technology Afloat," *Civil War Times Illustrated,* November 1975, 44).

14. Fowler, *Under Two Flags,* 42.

15. R. M. McMurry, *Two Great Rebel Armies* (Chapel Hill: University of North Carolina Press, 1989), 153.

16. Ibid., 154. McMurry's observation is not original. The famous military strategist B. H. Liddell Hart wrote in the early 1950s, "the close proximity of the rival capitals [has] caused a disproportionate attention to be concentrated upon the eastern theatre of war. It was in the west that the decisive blows were struck. The capture of Vicksburg and Port Hudson in July 1863 was the real turning point of the war" (*Strategy* [New York: Frederick A. Praeger, 1964], 154). Speaking at the beginning of the following decade, Pulitzer Prize-winner Bruce Catton stated, "the real decision was not reached in Virginia; it was reached in the Mississippi Valley. The final doom of the Confederacy was written in the West rather than in the East" (B. Catton, "Glory Road Began in the West," *Civil War Times,* July 1960, 4).

17. R. Beringer et al., *Why the South Lost the Civil War* (Athens: University of Georgia Press, 1986), 4.

18. McMurry, *Two Great Rebel Armies*, 15.

19. J. Fiske, *The Mississippi Valley in the Civil War* (Boston: Houghton Mifflin Co., 1900), 193. "From January 1863 until the river became too low for navigation in June, the navy [in all, six or eight light-draft 'tinclad' steamboats] convoyed 400 steamboats and 150 barges on the Cumberland to Nashville without the loss of a single ship" (Beringer, *Why the South Lost the Civil War*, 190).

20. McMurry, *Two Great Rebel Armies*, 61.

21. Beringer, *Why the South Lost the Civil War*, 4.

22. Anderson, *By Sea and by River*, 6.

23. Almost a century after the Civil War, the navy again found itself unprepared for river warfare, this time in Vietnam. Similar to the Southern states, Vietnam provided sailors with "hot, humid, and tedious work performed aboard improvised vessels." To battle the Viet Cong, the United States implemented a policy "consciously drawn from the Civil War experience on the Mississippi River. The Civil War also at least marginally inspired the Mobile Riverine Force's heaviest armed assault vessels, the so-called monitors, which replicated the configuration and silhouette of the double-turreted Union monitors. The use of the Civil War as a point of reference for naval warfare suggests how irrelevant the navy's twentieth-century blue-water experience had become by the mid 1960s" (K. Hagan, *This People's Navy* [New York: Free Press, 1991], 371–73).

24. Anderson, *By Sea and by River*, 9.

25. W. Trotter, *Ironclads and Columbiads* (Winston-Salem: John F. Blair, 1989), 29.

26. Still, "Technology Afloat," 8.

27. "Of an estimated 2,742 attempts to slip through the blockade during the war, some 2,525 runners — 92 percent — got through, a clear demonstration of the steam engine's potential for changing warfare at sea" (Hagan, *This People's Navy*, 164).

28. Still, "Technology Afloat," 8.

29. Fowler, *Under Two Flags*, 59.

30. Anderson, *By Sea and by River*, 16. By the end of the war the Union navy had amassed 670 ships served by 60,000 seamen (Dupuy, *The Compact History of the Civil War*, 52).

31. Navy Department, *Civil War Naval Chronology*, 2:101.

32. Beringer, *Why the South Lost the Civil War*, 186.

33. Fowler, *Under Two Flags*, 77.

34. Rear Adm. J. Hayes, "Fleet Against Fort," in *Civil War Ordnance — I* (Washington, D.C.: American Ordnance Association, 1960–61), 28. Adm. Samuel F. du Pont wrote after receiving word of Lee's 1863 invasion of the North, "If the rebels now raiding in Pennsylvania knew it, they would destroy the Reading Railroad and cut off every squadron from its coal, which would be virtually destroying them. We are now living from hand to mouth for want of it" (Still, "Technology Afloat," 9).

35. Hayes, "Fleet Against Fort," 28.

36. Beringer, *Why the South Lost the Civil War*, 4.

37. To be fair, the problems with a mobile defense were many, as Philip Shiman points out in *Fort Branch and the Defense of the Roanoke Valley, 1862–1865* (N.p.p.: Fort Branch Battlefield Commission, 1990). To begin with, the South lacked reliable mobility. Southern railroads sometimes performed miracles, but it was not wise to count on them too heavily. Furthermore, planters — many of whom owned farms along waterways — threatened not to waste time with crops that could be seized easily by marauding Yankee gunboats. So although Richmond politicians had little choice but to sacrifice much of the coastline in the face of the North's overwhelming naval advantage, political pressure forced the Confederacy to adopt a cordon defense of the interior. Well-sited earthworks along each major waterway, it was hoped, would accomplish three things: (1) delay invaders until reinforcements arrived, (2) give nearby landowners the sense that their interests were being watched over, and (3) tie up as few troops as possible.

38. A. Tapert, ed., *The Brothers' War* (New York: Vintage Books, 1989), 167.

39. E. Lewis, *Seacoast Fortifications of the United States* (Annapolis, Md.: Leeward Publications, 1979), 4.

40. For a discussion of the debate on naval construction in the early 1800s and its relationship to foreign affairs and the American Civil War, see Hagan, *This People's Navy*, 25.

41. Lewis, *Seacoast Fortifications*, 43.

42. F. G. Hill, *Roads, Rails and Waterways* (Norman: University of Oklahoma Press, 1957), 153.

43. B. Montgomery, *A History of Warfare* (New York: World Publishing Co., 1968), 440.

44. Fowler, *Under Two Flags*, 89.

45. Still, "Technology Afloat," 45.

46. Ibid. The difference between a smoothbore cannon firing a spherical shell and a rifled cannon

firing a cylindrical shot is roughly analogous to a quarterback trying to achieve accuracy by throwing a football or a basketball.

47. The U.S. Army's Abrams tank utilizes a 120mm smoothbore rifle to fire fin-stabilized ordnance.

48. C. Gray, *The Leverage of Sea Power* (New York: Free Press, 1992), 174.

Chapter 1 • Virginia

1. C. Degler, "There Was Another South," in *The Civil War*, ed. S. W. Sears (New York: American Heritage Press, 1991), 37.

2. Ibid.

3. Sen. John Crittenden of Kentucky proposed ending the secession crisis in 1861 by reinstating the 36°30′ line between slave and free territories, either in existence or later acquired. The Republicans rejected the legislation on the grounds that it amounted to just short of a declaration of war against Mexico and Central and South America. The amendment suggested by the peace conference would apply the 36°30′ line only to present territory and require a majority vote of all senators to establish any new territories. Once again, territorial issues would be decided by which section of the country held the most votes in the senate, the same situation that had led, in general, to the present deadlock.

4. J. M. McPherson, *Battle Cry of Freedom* (New York: Oxford University Press, 1988), 273.

5. Ibid., 278.

6. A. Cromie, *A Tour Guide to the Civil War*, 3d ed. (Nashville: Rutledge Hill Press, 1990), 279.

7. J. Robertson Jr., *Civil War Sites in Virginia* (Charlottesville: University Press of Virginia, 1991), viii.

8. D. Porter, *Naval History of the Civil War* (Secaucus, N.J.: Castle, 1984), 40.

9. S. W. Sears, *George B. McClellan: The Young Napoleon* (New York: Ticknor & Fields, 1988), 130.

10. R. Shingleton, "Raider's Blow Stinging," *America's Civil War*, April 1990, 44.

11. I. Musicant, "The Fires of Norfolk," *American Heritage*, March 1990, 58.

12. G. F. Amadon, *Rise of the Ironclads* (Missoula, Mont.: Pictorial Histories Publishing Co., 1988), 16. During the ship's last voyage under the Stars and Stripes, Alban C. Stimers served as chief engineer and Ashton Ramsay was his assistant. Later, Stimers became engineer in chief of the USS *Monitor*. Ramsey held the same position on the CSS *Virginia*, the former *Merrimack*.

13. Musicant, "The Fires of Norfolk," 59.

14. Amadon (*Rise of the Ironclads*, 18) speculates that by doing so, McCauley was trying to buy time for the navy yard. McCauley may have thought that if the *Merrimack* sailed, the Rebels would attack the yard before reinforcements could arrive or the ordnance be destroyed.

15. Originally called Fortress Monroe, the defensive structure at Old Point Comfort became Fort Monroe in 1832 at the order of the secretary of war. Strictly speaking, a fortress surrounds a city, and although Fort Monroe covers sixty-three acres, it never enclosed a town. The U.S. Post Office was slower than the army to recognize the fact and kept the name Fortress Monroe until 1941 (The Casemate Museum, *Is It a Fort or a Fortress?* Tales of Old Fort Monroe, no. 5 [Fort Monroe, Va.: The Casemate Museum, 1970]).

16. The name comes from the granite leavings, called rip rap, used to create the artificial island upon which the fort was being built.

17. W. C. Davis, *Duel Between the First Ironclads* (Baton Rouge: Louisiana State University Press, 1975), 78.

18. Jones carries the Welsh idiom *ap* meaning "son of."

19. Davis, *Duel Between the First Ironclads*, 92.

20. Ibid., 101.

21. Amadon, *Rise of the Ironclads*, 42. David Porter wrote that Buchanan's orders were "certainly most inhuman, since the crew of the 'Congress' were not responsible for the act of the troops on shore" (*Naval History of the Civil War*, 125).

22. Wood's grandfather was Zachary Taylor, and Jefferson Davis was an uncle by marriage. Wood had served on the *Cumberland* in 1853, and his father, Maj. Robert Crooke Wood, remained loyal to the Union, serving with distinction in the Federal medical service.

23. This was the second time the *Minnesota* had a close call in Hampton Roads. On 9 October 1861 a Confederate two-man submarine closed on the Union flagship. Mistaking a grappling line for an anchor chain, the submersible surfaced too quickly to attach a torpedo. A Federal guard boat sounded an alarm, but the submarine managed to resubmerge and make its escape. In April 1864 a

Confederate torpedo boat snaked one hundred miles down the James and exploded a torpedo against the hull of the *Minnesota*, which sprung some frames and planking but did not sink (The Casemate Museum, *Fort Monroe in the Civil War*, Tales of Old Fort Monroe, no. 6 [Fort Monroe, Va.: The Casemate Museum, 1970]).

24. P. Rouse Jr., *Endless Harbor: The Story of Newport News* (Newport News: n.p., 1969), 21.

25. W. N. Still Jr., *Iron Afloat: The Story of the Confederate Armorclads* (Columbia: University of South Carolina Press, 1985), 39.

26. S. Harris, "Lion's Tail Touched," *Great Battles*, July 1992, 50.

27. R. Dupuy and T. Dupuy, *The Compact History of the Civil War* (New York: Hawthorn Books, 1968), 129.

28. Still, *Iron Afloat*, 40.

29. R. Shingleton, *John Taylor Wood: Sea Ghost of the Confederacy* (Athens: University of Georgia Press, 1979), 48.

30. E. K. Reid, "The Legend, History, and Archaeology of Fort Boykin in Virginia," *The Chesopiean*, October–December 1970, 123.

31. F. E. Lutz, *The Prince George-Hopewell Story* (Richmond: William Byrd Press, 1957), 164.

32. B. Anderson, *By Sea and by River: The Naval History of the Civil War* (New York: Da Capo Press, 1989), 82.

33. Sears, *McClellan*, 218.

34. Navy Department, *Civil War Naval Chronology*, 2:74.

35. Ibid., 2:75.

36. Ibid., 2:81.

37. Sears, *McClellan*, 224.

38. R. Reed, *Combined Operations in the Civil War* (Lincoln: University of Nebraska Press, 1993), 181.

39. Lutz, *The Prince George-Hopewell Story*, 165.

40. J. Coski, *The Army of the Potomac at Berkeley Plantation* (N.p.p.: n.p., 1989), 24.

41. What has been billed with only slight exaggeration as "the first carrier task force" appeared off Fort Powhatan soon after to ensure, I presume, that the position would not be used again by Confederates. The Union balloon barge *George Washington Parke Custis* was assigned to the force of gunboats to observe the effects of a naval bombardment, but the results of the action are not known (R. D. Layman, *Before the Aircraft Carrier* [Annapolis: Naval Institute Press, 1989], 116).

42. Still, *Iron Afloat*, 170.

43. Ibid., 171.

44. T. Savas, "Last Clash of the Ironclads: The Bungled Affair at Trent's Reach," *Civil War*, February 1989, 18.

45. Ibid., 22.

46. Navy Department, *Civil War Naval Chronology*, 5:78.

47. M. Knepler, "Fort Norfolk a Link to Our Past," *Norfolk Compass*, 24–25 July 1991, 7.

48. Coski, *Army of the Potomac*, 32.

Chapter 2 • North Carolina

1. R. Beringer et al., *Why the South Lost the Civil War* (Athens: University of Georgia Press, 1986), 70.

2. J. Barrett, *North Carolina As a Civil War Battleground: 1861–1865* (Raleigh: North Carolina Department of Cultural Resources, 1987), 5. The origin of the term *Tar Heel* is obscure. Stories date back to the Revolutionary War and several are associated with the Civil War. However it took hold, the name stuck.

3. W. Trotter, *Ironclads and Columbiads* (Winston-Salem: John F. Blair, 1989), 10.

4. Barrett, *North Carolina As a Civil War Battleground*, 7.

5. J. Bowen, *Battlefields of the Civil War* (Secaucus, N.J.: Chartwell Books, 1986), 77.

6. Trotter, *Ironclads and Columbiads*, 16.

7. Ibid., 26.

8. J. Merrill, *The Rebel Shore* (Boston: Little, Brown and Co., 1957), 17.

9. Barrett, *North Carolina As a Civil War Battleground*, 17.

10. Trotter, *Ironclads and Columbiads*, 23.

11. Ibid., 34. Stringham was imitating "tactics used in the Allied bombardment of Odessa during the Crimean War" (R. Reed, *Combined Operations in the Civil War* [Lincoln: University of Nebraska Press, 1993], 13).

12. M. Shier, "Hatteras Inlet: The First Revenge," *Civil War Times Illustrated*, November 1978, 10.

13. Ibid., 44.

14. Merrill, *The Rebel Shore*, 3.

15. U.S. Naval History Division, comp., *Civil War Naval Chronology: 1861–1865*, 6 vols. (Washington, D.C.: Government Printing Office, 1961–66), 1:24.

16. R. A. Sauers, "Laurels for Burnside," *Blue & Gray Magazine*, May 1988, 9.

17. Barrett, *North Carolina As a Civil War Battleground*, 26.

18. E. Thomas, "The Lost Confederates of Roanoke," *Civil War Times Illustrated*, May 1976, 13.

19. Sauers, "Laurels for Burnside," 20. Both Butler's and Foster's replies took place before Ulysses Grant's more famous quotation at Fort Donelson in Tennessee.

20. Trotter, *Ironclads and Columbiads*, 93.

21. Sauers, "Laurels for Burnside," 50.

22. P. Branch Jr., *The Siege of Fort Macon* (Morehead City, N.C.: Herald Printing Co., 1988), 37.

23. Sauers, "Laurels for Burnside," 124.

24. Ibid., 125.

25. Barrett, *North Carolina As a Civil War Battleground*, 44.

26. P. Shiman, *Fort Branch and the Defense of the Roanoke Valley, 1862–1865* (N.p.p.: Fort Branch Battlefield Commission, 1990), 9.

27. Ibid., 26.

28. Ibid., 57.

29. Trotter, *Ironclads and Columbiads*, 224.

30. Ibid., 229.

31. W. Durrill, *War of Another Kind: A Southern Community in the Great Rebellion* (New York: Oxford University Press, 1990), 197.

32. T. Gibbons, *Warships and Naval Battles of the Civil War* (New York: Gallery Books, 1989), 107.

33. Navy Department, *Civil War Naval Chronology*, 4:45.

34. R. Roberts, *Encyclopedia of Historic Forts* (New York: MacMillan Publishing Co., 1988), 614.

35. "The Fort Fisher Story," photocopied booklet available at Fort Fisher Museum, 1.

36. Ibid. The original Malakoff Tower held off the combined land and naval forces of Great Britain and France during the Crimean War.

37. R. Gragg, *Confederate Goliath: The Battle of Fort Fisher* (New York: HarperCollins, 1991), 11.

38. One is on display at the Washington Navy Yard in Washington, D.C.

39. Gragg, *Confederate Goliath*, 27.

40. H. Turner, "Rocked in the Cradle of Consternation," *Civil War Chronicles*, Spring 1993, 25.

41. Butler's idea to use jets of water to blast down enemy earthworks proved workable during the 1973 war in the Middle East.

42. Trotter, *Ironclads and Columbiads*, 352.

43. W. Lamb, "The Confederates Repulse an Attack on Fort Fisher," in *The Blue and the Gray*, ed. H. S. Commanger (Indianapolis: Bobbs-Merrill Co., 1950), 839.

44. Lamb's pet 150-pounder Armstrong rifle is on display at the U.S. Military Academy at West Point.

45. Trotter, *Ironclads and Columbiads*, 362.

46. D. Porter, *Naval History of the Civil War* (Secaucus, N.J.: Castle, 1984), 697.

47. Lamb, "The Confederates Repulse an Attack on Fort Fisher," 840.

48. Trotter, *Ironclads and Columbiads*, 368.

49. Gragg, *Confederate Goliath*, 74.

50. Turner, "Rocked in the Cradle of Consternation," 31.

51. Lamb, "The Confederates Repulse an Attack on Fort Fisher," 841.

52. Trotter, *Ironclads and Columbiads*, 385.

53. Porter, *Naval History of the Civil War*, 701.

54. Gragg, *Confederate Goliath*, 99.

55. Ibid., 109.

56. Ibid., 131.

57. Ibid., 149.

58. Ibid., 151.

59. Ibid., 166.

60. R. Watson, "Yankees Were Landing Below Us," *Civil War Times Illustrated*, April 1976, 16.

61. Gragg, *Confederate Goliath*, 235.

62. Ibid., 240.

63. "Ft. Fisher Variance Denied in Carolina Political SNAFU," *The Confederate Naval Historical Society Newsletter,* October 1992, 1.

Chapter 3 • South Carolina

1. L. Wright, *South Carolina* (New York: W. W. Norton & Co., 1976), 16.
2. Two years later Congressman Lawrence Keitt of South Carolina attempted a similar maneuver on Galusha Grow, a Pennsylvania Republican (R. Sewell, *A House Divided* [Baltimore: Johns Hopkins University Press, 1988], 67).
3. Wright, *South Carolina,* 168.
4. B. Collins, *The Origins of America's Civil War* (New York: Holmes & Meier, 1981), 50.
5. University professor R. H. Sewell, for example, points out in his book *A House Divided,* 88, it was, not secession, but preservation of the plantation system that was of paramount importance to the planter class, "and time would show that many [planters] would pursue this goal even when it clashed with the maintenance of Confederate independence."
6. Wright, *South Carolina,* 164.
7. Ibid., 155, 179.
8. G. Spieler, "Fort in St. Helena Named for Gen. Frémont," *The Beaufort Gazette,* 12 August 1986, 5A. Poinsett also gave his name to the poinsettia.
9. W. A. Swanberg, *First Blood* (New York: Charles Scribner's Sons, 1957), 31.
10. Wright, *South Carolina,* 171.
11. R. Beringer, *Why the South Lost the Civil War* (Athens: University of Georgia Press, 1986), 70.
12. Swanberg, *First Blood,* 8.
13. J. M. McPherson, *Battle Cry of Freedom* (New York: Oxford University Press, 1988), 237.
14. Wright, *South Carolina,* 154.
15. McPherson, *Battle Cry of Freedom,* 234.
16. Ibid., 237. For a broader discussion of the degree to which people of substance in the South supported the Union, see C. Degler, "There Was Another South," in *The Civil War,* ed. S. W. Sears (New York: American Heritage Press, 1991).
17. That total represents the largest percentage of manpower from any state in the Confederacy (Wright, *South Carolina,* 176).
18. R. Gragg, *Civil War Quiz and Fact Book* (New York: Harper & Row, 1985), 123.
19. B. Anderson, *By Sea and by River: The Naval History of the Civil War* (New York: Da Capo Press, 1989), 51.
20. As it turned out, the rail line was not cut and Savannah held out until Sherman marched to the sea and gave Lincoln the city as a Christmas present in 1864 (W. Rose, *Rehearsal for Reconstruction: The Port Royal Experiment* [New York: Vintage Books, 1964], 5).
21. Ibid., 6.
22. D. Ammen, *The Atlantic Coast* (New York: Blue and the Gray Press, n.d.), 17. Ammen commanded the steam gunboat USS *Seneca* during the attack on Port Royal.
23. E. M. Burton, *The Siege of Charleston, 1861–1865* (Columbia: University of South Carolina Press, 1987), 68.
24. W. M. Fowler Jr., *Under Two Flags* (New York: W. W. Norton & Co., 1990), 72.
25. Burton, *The Siege of Charleston,* 68.
26. Ammen, *The Atlantic Coast,* 15.
27. As early as September, William Elliott warned his sons to remove the family's slaves from Hilton Head because he feared a Federal attack on Port Royal (Rose, *Rehearsal for Reconstruction,* 5).
28. Burton, *The Siege of Charleston,* 67.
29. D. Porter, *Naval History of the Civil War* (Secaucus, N.J.: Castle, 1984), 57.
30. Anderson, *By Sea and by River,* 57.
31. Porter, *Naval History of the Civil War,* 73.
32. A. B. Feuer, "The 'Circle of Fire' at Port Royal," *Civil War,* vol. 16, 32. One young slave who thought he was hearing thunder remembered his mother telling him, "Son . . . dat ain't no t'under, dat Yankee come to gib you Freedom" (Rose, *Rehearsal for Reconstruction,* 12).
33. For comparison, the *Wabash* fired 880 rounds; the *Susquehanna* more than 750 (Burton, *The Siege of Charleston,* 72). A total of more than 3,500 shells had pounded the Confederate forts during the five-hour confrontation (Feuer, "'Circle of Fire' at Port Royal," 32). Of further interest, according to G. Spieler, "Beaufort's Forts: Symbols of Early Settlement," *The Beaufort Gazette,* 6 July 1972 (photocopy), Mrs. Drayton knew her two sons were firing at each other that day. The abandoned Confederate fort on Otter Island guarding Saint Helena Sound, just north of Port Royal, was renamed Fort Percival Drayton after its occupation by Union troops.

34. Burton, *The Siege of Charleston,* 73.

35. Ibid., 74.

36. Ammen, *The Atlantic Coast,* 32.

37. Anderson, *By Sea and by River,* 59.

38. Porter, *Naval History of the Civil War,* 62.

39. Anderson, *By Sea and by River,* 58.

40. J. Merrill, *Du Pont: The Making of an Admiral* (New York: Dodd, Mead & Co., 1986), 268.

41. Ibid., 269, 270.

42. Anderson, *By Sea and by River,* 60. Ammen suggests that the loss of the lighter-draft vessels in the early November storms and a lack of ammunition for the guns of the smaller navy vessels prevented a more aggressive movement into the interior (*The Atlantic Coast,* 33). Still, the navy managed to occupy the abandoned post on Otter Island, called Fort Heyward, that controlled Saint Helena Sound, the next anchorage north of Port Royal.

43. U.S. Naval History Division, comp., *Civil War Naval Chronology: 1861–1865,* 6 vols. (Washington, D.C.: Government Printing Office, 1961–66), 2:5.

44. M. Soper, "Mystery Forts Display Slated at Hilton Head," *News and Courier,* 4 April 1965 (photocopy).

45. R. Bailey, "Nature Conservancy Buys Island with Civil War Fort," *Civil War News,* November 1993, 51.

46. W. Robinson in his book, *American Forts: Architectural Form and Function* (Urbana: University of Illinois Press, 1977), 74, stated that Castle Williams, situated on the western extremity of Governor's Island in New York Harbor, was the "first work in America fully casemated for artillery."

47. Swanberg, *First Blood,* 6.

48. Ibid., 20. Floyd's act was not illegal since South Carolina was entitled to its share of surplus government property, but under the circumstances his action could not be called wise. Later, during the war, Floyd cited his unpopularity within the North due to his actions immediately prior to the Civil War as an excuse to escape from Fort Donelson after the decision was made to surrender the garrison to Grant in February 1862.

49. On 15 May 1861, Anderson was promoted to brigadier general and within two weeks was given command of the newly created Military Department of Kentucky. Out of respect for the neutrality of Anderson's native state, department headquarters were located in Cincinnati, Ohio. Due to "nervous prostration" brought on by his ordeal in Charleston, he turned over his duties after three months to his second-in-command, William Tecumseh Sherman (B. McGinty, "Robert Anderson: Reluctant Hero," *Civil War Times Illustrated,* May–June 1992, 46).

50. Another distinguished person attached to Fort Moultrie's history was Edgar Allan Poe, who soldiered there in the 1830s. The innovative writer used Sullivan's Island as the setting for "The Gold Bug."

51. Swanberg, *First Blood,* 34.

52. Ibid., 43. It is interesting to note that although Doubleday's use of mines could be considered the first adoption of the new weapon during the Civil War, the North would constantly condemn the South for mine warfare. Adm. David D. Porter, for instance, called the utilization of mines at Port Royal by the Confederates "an unworthy attempt at revenge" (*Naval History of the Civil War,* 59).

53. Swanberg, *First Blood,* 105.

54. A. Wilcox and W. Ripley, *The Civil War at Charleston* (Charleston: Post-Courier, 1989), 4.

55. Swanberg, *First Blood,* 50.

56. Buchanan changed his mind about the relief expedition and tried to stop the *Star,* but it was too late. He then dispatched Capt. David Farragut and the USS *Brooklyn,* a heavily armed screw steamer, to assist the unarmed ship, but Farragut was ordered to remain outside the bar (Swanberg, *First Blood,* 145).

57. Ibid., 148.

58. "The National Troubles," *New York Times,* 4 January 1861, 1, in *Civil War Front Pages,* ed. J. Wagman (New York: Fairfax Press, 1989).

59. Swanberg, *First Blood,* 280.

60. Ibid., 286.

61. Ibid.

62. Shortly after returning to New York with the Sumter garrison, Meade resigned his commission in the U.S. Army and joined the forces of his native state. Three months later he died of disease while stationed in Richmond (Burton, *The Siege of Charleston,* 60–61).

63. McPherson, *Battle Cry of Freedom,* 273.

64. Burton, *The Siege of Charleston,* 44. Four years later, Ruffin shot himself "after penning a last page of vitriol: '. . . I here repeat . . . my unmitigated hatred to Yankee rule . . . and the perfidious, malignant and vile Yankee race'" (Swanberg, *First Blood,* 329).

65. Burton, *The Siege of Charleston*, 49.

66. Swanberg, *First Blood*, 322.

67. "Great National Tragedy," *Philadelphia Inquirer*, 15 April 1861, 1, in Wagman, *Civil War Front Pages*.

68. Burton, *The Siege of Charleston*, 87.

69. Wilcox and Ripley, *The Civil War at Charleston*, 27.

70. Burton, *The Siege of Charleston*, 89.

71. Ibid., 103.

72. Ibid., 110.

73. Ibid., 124.

74. Wilcox and Ripley, *The Civil War at Charleston*, 42.

75. H. Nash Jr., "Ironclads at Charleston," *Civil War Times*, January 1960, 1. No method of correcting a compass in an iron ship was known at that time.

76. W. Ripley, *The Battery* (Charleston: Post-Courier Booklet, 1989), 50.

77. B. Pohanka, "Carnival of Death," *America's Civil War*, September 1991, 33.

78. G. Ward, "Some Fought for Freedom, Some for Glory," *New York Times Book Review*, 17 November 1991, 36.

79. Pohanka, "Carnival of Death," 34.

80. Burton, *The Siege of Charleston*, 173.

81. Ibid., 176.

82. F. Lord, "The 'Swamp Angel,'" *Civil War Times Illustrated*, December 1962, 36.

83. Burton, *The Siege of Charleston*, 179–80.

84. Ripley, *The Battery*, 45.

85. Burton, *The Siege of Charleston*, 204.

86. Ibid., 207.

87. Wilcox and Ripley, *The Civil War at Charleston*, 70.

88. J. Thomson, interviewed by the author, Charleston, S.C., 15 August 1990.

89. Burton, *The Siege of Charleston*, 286.

90. W. Keith, "Fort Johnson," *Civil War Times Illustrated*, November 1975, 32–39.

91. This had been Birney's second foul-up. On 25 May 1864 he had led an attempt to cut the Charleston and Savannah Railroad. As the side-wheeler *Boston*, one of the transports carrying troops and horses for the expedition, snaked through the tidal Ashepoo River toward the railroad bridge at the Ashepoo ferry, it grounded at 11:00 P.M. The next morning Confederate artillery arrived, and the cautious Birney ordered the transport burned to avoid capture, thus ending Federal efforts to penetrate Southern defenses in the area. Divers pinpointed the wreck on 2 June 1979 and took from it more than seven thousand artifacts (H. Tower Jr., "Salvaging the 'Boston,'" *Sea Classics*, July 1985, 61).

92. Burton, *The Siege of Charleston*, 298.

93. During World War II, five one-hundred-foot telescopic steel ladders were installed on DUKWs for the assault against Normandy (G. Pawle, *Secret Weapons of World War II* [New York: Ballantine Books, 1968], 312).

94. Burton, *The Siege of Charleston*, 300.

95. Anderson, *By Sea and by River* (New York: Da Capo Press, 1962), 175.

96. Although Sherman pushed his bummers toward Columbia and not Charleston, in early May he finally managed to pay the city a visit, his first since his tour of duty at Fort Moultrie many years earlier. He wrote: "Any one who is not satisfied with war should go and see Charleston, and he will pray louder and deeper than ever that the country may in the long future be spared any more war" (Burton, *The Siege of Charleston*, 324).

97. Ibid., 318.

98. U.S. Department of the Interior, National Park Service, *Fort Sumter: Anvil of War* (Washington, D.C.: Government Printing Office, 1984), 51.

99. W. C. Davis in his book *Battle at Bull Run* (Baton Rouge: Louisiana State University Press, 1977), 197, speculates about whether or not Bee's comment was meant to be a compliment: "Major Thomas Rhett, of Jackson's staff, claimed ever after that a few hours [after the alleged incident took place] Bee painfully detailed to him his anger that, while he and [Col. Francis S.] Bartow were being mauled by the Federals, Jackson stood on the hill — like a stone wall?— instead of coming to their aid, and that the destruction of his command was largely the fault of the Virginian." Since Jackson's men were lying behind a hill and not standing at all, this interpretation seems to make at least some sense.

100. W. Rogers Jr., *The History of Georgetown County, South Carolina* (Spartanburg, S.C.: Reprint Co., 1990), 411.

101. Ammen, *The Atlantic Coast*, 66. He writes that the operation took place in May, but several other sources suggest it occurred in June.

102. J. Fitch, "Georgetown and the Civil War" (unpublished paper), 5. Other records suggest the Union raiders made it twenty miles past Georgetown on the Black River before turning back, but Fitch's account makes more sense in light of the fact that soon after Prentiss's initial visit to Georgetown, Richmond's policy toward the district changed. On 25 March Gen. John Pemberton, who had followed Lee as supervisor of South Atlantic coastal defenses in the area, ordered troops protecting Winyah Bay to reinforce Charleston. On 2 August, just a few days after Prentiss reached Georgetown, Pemberton ordered fortifications constructed at Mayrants Bluff.

103. The gunboat *Pee Dee* was burned 18 February 1865 to avoid capture (T. Gibbons, *Warships and Naval Battles of the Civil War* [New York: Gallery Books, 1989], 174).

104. Rogers, *History of Georgetown County*, 414.

105. Navy Department, *Civil War Naval Chronology*, 5:54.

106. Fitch, "Georgetown and the Civil War," 2.

Chapter 4 • Georgia

1. Atlanta was not the capital of the state during the Civil War. Milledgeville held that distinction from 1804–68.

2. B. Hull, *St. Simons: Enchanted Island* (Atlanta: Cherokee Publishing Co., 1980), 73.

3. D. Ammen, *The Atlantic Coast* (New York: Jack Brussel, n.d.), 58.

4. Locals insist it was Katie Green, the widow of Nathanael, who as hostess to Eli Whitney showed him her cotton gin.

5. J. Mitchell, "Convincing Test for Rifled Cannon," *Military History*, June 1987, 12.

6. R. Lattimore, *Fort Pulaski* (Washington, D.C.: National Park Service, 1954), 14.

7. He would not live to see that illusion of invincibility shattered. In late May he took his infantry north; two months later he was killed while leading a charge on Federal batteries at Manassas.

8. Lee apparently did not make it clear to those affected that the order to evacuate the islands came from Confederate Secretary of War Judah P. Benjamin, who sent on 18 February 1862 the following directive: "Withdraw all forces from the islands in your department to the mainland" (M. Burton, *The Siege of Charleston, 1861–1865* [Columbia: University of South Carolina Press, 1987], 80).

9. Lattimore, *Fort Pulaski*, 28.

10. Q. Gillmore, *The Siege and Reduction of Fort Pulaski* (Gettysburg, Pa.: Thomas Publications, 1988), 34.

11. Lattimore, *Fort Pulaski*, 35–36.

12. Maj. John B. Gallie, the first commander of Fort McAllister, was decapitated by a shell fragment.

13. D. Porter, *Naval History of the Civil War* (Secaucus, N.J.: Castle, 1984), 371.

14. K. Bennett, "Gun Platforms at Sea," *Military History*, August 1992, 28.

15. B. Emerson, "CSS Atlanta," *Scale Ship Modeler*, October 1991, 43.

16. In his excellent work on Sherman's march through Georgia, J. Miles suggests that on 11 December Union troops tried to burn the railroad bridge over the Savannah River but were foiled by Confederates on the South Carolina shore supported by a "large gun mounted on a rail car" (*To the Sea* [Nashville: Rutledge Hill Press, 1989], 220).

17. R. Durham, "Savannah: Mr. Lincoln's Christmas Present," *Blue & Gray Magazine*, February 1991, 43.

18. At this point, Sherman was in a barge being rowed to Fort McAllister after meeting with Gen. John Foster at Hilton Head and then running aground on his return trip (Miles, *To the Sea*, 222).

19. Durham, "Savannah," 48.

20. As late as 1903, two 15-inch Rodman guns of the Civil War period were still in use here (*Fort Screven [1897–1945]* [N.p.p.: Tybee Island Association, 1988], 16).

21. E. Coulter, *Wormsloe: Two Centuries of a Georgia Family* (Athens: University of Georgia Press, 1955), 233.

Chapter 5 • Florida

1. *Gossypium barbadense*, the tropical American cotton called Sea Island, could grow a strand up to two and a half inches long, compared to half an inch or so for Old World cotton (J. Weatherford, *Indian Givers* [New York: Fawcett Columbine, 1988], 42, 44).

2. M. Derr, *Some Kind of Paradise* (New York: William Morrow and Co., 1989), 296.

3. Ibid., 300.

4. During the war, 160 craft were captured in Florida waters attempting to evade the Northern blockade (ibid., 303).

5. Some books and maps spell the name McRae, but according to one account the post was named after Col. William McRee, U.S. Army Engineers (D. Davis et al., *Fort Barrancas 1875* [Pensacola: Pensacola Historical Society, 1988], 16).

6. T. J. Hunsaker, "Cannon Manned by Rival Nations," *Military History,* August 1988, 52. These shots preceded by some six hours the *Star of the West* episode at Charleston, South Carolina.

7. B. Anderson, *By Sea and by River: The Naval History of the Civil War* (New York: Da Capo Press, 1989), 20.

8. Z. H. Burns, *Confederate Forts* (Natchez, Miss.: Southern Historical Publications, 1977), 29.

9. Anderson, *By Sea and by River,* 22.

10. Although historians disagree about the effect the *Powhatan* would have had on the situation at Fort Sumter, it is doubtful the ship could have done anything more than watch the surrender. Still, Lincoln pleaded ignorance and Seward apologized to Welles.

11. V. Parks et al., *Pensacola in the Civil War* (Pensacola: Pensacola Historical Society, 1983), 17, suggest Anderson had already decided to retreat as darkness approached.

12. A. Jones, *Civil War Command and Strategy: The Process of Victory and Defeat* (New York: Free Press, 1992), 51.

13. T. Muir Jr. and D. Ogden, *The Fort Pickens Story* (Pensacola: Pensacola Historical Society, 1989), 10.

14. Parks, *Pensacola in the Civil War,* 20.

15. J. Coleman and I. Coleman, *Guardians on the Gulf: Pensacola Fortifications, 1698–1980* (Pensacola: Pensacola Historical Society, 1982), 55.

16. A. Bergeron Jr., *Confederate Mobile* (Jackson: University Press of Mississippi, 1991), 151.

17. R. Gragg, *Civil War Quiz and Fact Book* (New York: Harper & Row, 1985), 135.

18. R. Gragg, *Confederate Goliath* (New York: HarperCollins, 1991), 11.

19. R. Reed, *Combined Operations in the Civil War* (Lincoln: University of Nebraska Press, 1993), 16–17.

20. Bergeron, *Confederate Mobile,* 53.

21. S. R. Wise, *Lifeline of the Confederacy: Blockade Running During the Civil War* (Columbia: University of South Carolina Press, 1988), 3.

22. "Fort Gadsden State Historic Site," Florida Department of Natural Resources brochure.

23. U.S. Naval History Division, comp., *Civil War Naval Chronology: 1861–1865,* 6 vols. (Washington, D.C.: Government Printing Office, 1961–66), 2:42.

24. A. Gerrell, "The History of the Fort at St. Marks, Florida, During the Civil War" (unpublished manuscript), 4.

25. R. McMurry, "The Presidents' [*sic*] Tenth and the Battle of Olustee," *Civil War Times Illustrated,* January 1978, 16.

26. Gerrell, "History of the Fort at St. Marks," 6.

27. McMurry, "Battle of Olustee," 17.

28. On 23 August 1864 the Federals lost 28 killed, 5 wounded, and 188 captured at Gainesville, Florida, making it the second bloodiest battle on Florida soil, but more men were engaged at Santa Rosa Island, Natural Bridge, and Olustee.

29. *A History of Cedar Key* (Cedar Key: Cedar Key Beacon, 1990), 17.

30. S. Proctor, "Saltmaking Along Florida's Gulf Coast: Profitable but Vulnerable CW Business," *Civil War Times Illustrated,* November 1962, 46.

31. Ibid.

32. Ibid., 48.

33. There was a Camp Ward situated across the Wakulla River from the fort. This Confederate camp may have accidentally lent its name to the fort on some Union maps (Gerrell, "History of the Fort at St. Marks," i).

34. C. G. Jameson, *East Martello Tower* (Key West: Key West Art and Historical Society, 1985), 6.

35. U.S. Naval History Division, comp., *Civil War Naval Chronology: 1861–1865,* 6 vols. (Washington, D.C.: Government Printing Office, 1961–66), 1:2.

36. C. Cox, *A Key West Companion* (New York: St. Martin's Press, 1983), 61.

37. Navy Department, *Civil War Naval Chronology,* 4:92.

38. "The span of time during which [Martello towers] were built was considerable: three-quarters of a century lay between the construction of the first two towers in South Africa in 1796 and the termination of the uncompleted work on the last two at Key West in the United States [in 1873]" (S. Sutcliffe, *Martello Towers* [Cranbury, N.J.: Fairleigh Dickinson University Press, 1973], 16).

39. A. Manucy, *A Handbook for Fort Jefferson History,* May 1942, 6.

40. "Fort Jefferson, Monstrous Creation in the Gulf Off Key West, Predates Alcatraz As Island Prison," *Miami Herald,* 30 September 1934, 15.

41. J. M. Merrill, *Du Pont: The Making of an Admiral* (New York: Dodd, Mead & Co., 1986), 275.

42. D. Ammen, *The Atlantic Coast* (New York: Jack Brussel, n.d.), 52.

43. Ibid., 53.

44. Merrill, *Du Pont,* 275.

45. T. Graham, "The Home Front: Civil War Times in St. Augustine," in *Civil War Times in St. Augustine,* ed. J. Fretwell (Saint Augustine: Saint Augustine Historical Society, 1986), 25.

46. Ammen, *The Atlantic Coast,* 56.

47. G. Buker, "St. Augustine and the Union Blockade," in *Civil War Times in St. Augustine,* ed. J. Fretwell (Saint Augustine: Saint Augustine Historical Society, 1986), 4.

48. J. Ward, *Old Hickory's Town: An Illustrated History of Jacksonville* (Jacksonville: Florida Publishing Co., 1982), 141.

49. Merrill, *Du Pont,* 277.

50. R. Mann, "War on Yellow Bluff" (an unpublished paper relying on a "popular story" about Confederate artillery removed from Saint Johns Bluff to Yellow Bluff. These guns may have engaged the *Uncas*).

51. Ward, *Old Hickory's Town,* 144.

52. Mann, "War on Yellow Bluff," 1.

Chapter 6 • Alabama

1. Even so, Alabama's planters were far from reactionary. In 1819, "Alabama's planter elite drew up the most liberal state constitution of that time" (B. Collins, *The Origins of America's Civil War* [New York: Holmes & Meier, 1981], 47).

2. V. Van der Veer Hamilton, *Alabama* (New York: W. W. Norton & Co., 1977), 30.

3. Ibid., 26.

4. C. E. Macartney, *Mr. Lincoln's Admirals* (New York: Funk & Wagnalls Co., 1956), 23.

5. A. T. Mahan, *Admiral Farragut* (New York: Haskell House, 1968), 240.

6. A. T. Mahan, *The Gulf and Inland Waters* (New York: Charles Scribner's Sons, 1883), 221, states that the plating came from rolling mills in Atlanta.

7. A. Bergeron Jr., *Confederate Mobile* (Jackson: University Press of Mississippi, 1991), 4.

8. B. Anderson, *By Sea and by River: The Naval History of the Civil War* (New York: Da Capo Press, 1989), 234.

9. The steam frigate *Niagara* had appeared off Mobile Bay the first week in May, but her patrol area consisted of the entire eastern Gulf Coast and she did not always stand off Mobile.

10. Bergeron, *Confederate Mobile,* 125.

11. W. M. Fowler Jr., *Under Two Flags: The American Navy in the Civil War* (New York: W. W. Norton & Co., 1990), 233.

12. A. T. Mahan, *The Gulf and Inland Waters,* 222.

13. Anderson, *By Sea and by River,* 238.

14. Fowler, *Under Two Flags,* 237.

15. U.S. Naval History Division, comp., *Civil War Naval Chronology: 1861–1865,* 6 vols. (Washington, D.C.: Government Printing Office, 1961–66), 4:63. Farragut used somewhat stronger language regarding the placement of torpedoes in a letter to Secretary of the Navy Welles: "I have always deemed it unworthy of a chivalrous nation" (ibid., 6:65).

16. Mahan, *The Gulf and Inland Waters,* 231.

17. Macartney, *Mr. Lincoln's Admirals,* 67.

18. By the end of the campaign, torpedoes in Mobile Bay accounted for the sinking of ten Federal ships (Bergeron, *Confederate Mobile,* 70).

19. Macartney, *Mr. Lincoln's Admirals,* 68; Anderson, *By Sea and by River,* 242. As the fleet neared Fort Morgan, Farragut was standing in the port-side shrouds. Captain Drayton had even ordered a quartermaster to secure Farragut with a "bridle" to prevent the admiral from being knocked into the water by a cannonball striking the flagship. That Farragut could have shouted across the *Hartford*'s poop deck and the deck of *Brooklyn*'s consort, the *Octorara,* to Alden on the *Brooklyn* or hear a warning shouted from the *Brooklyn* is highly unlikely. Macartney (*Mr. Lincoln's Admirals,* 68) writes, "I have been unable to find any confirmation of the alleged shout of Farragut as he was passing the *Brooklyn* and was told that torpedoes were ahead. Lieutenant John C. Kinney, the army officer who passed Farragut's signals to the *Brooklyn* comments that while the admiral may have said it, it is doubtful if he shouted it to the *Brooklyn,* for 'there was never a moment when the din of battle would not

have drowned any attempt at conversation between the two ships.'" In the Navy Department's *Civil War Naval Chronology*, 4:95, "Flag Lieutenant John C. Watson *later* [emphasis added] recalled that Farragut's exact words were: 'Damn the torpedoes! Full speed ahead, Drayton! Hard astarboard; ring four bells! Eight bells! Sixteen bells!'" Steering gears were rigged so that moving the tiller to starboard moved the ship to port.

20. D. Porter, *Naval History of the Civil War* (Secaucus, N.J.: Castle, 1984), 593.

21. Mahan, *The Gulf and Inland Waters*, 236.

22. D. Wegner, "The Black Leech of Mobile," *Sea Classics*, January 1971, 17. Mahan speculated in his book *Admiral Farragut* what Buchanan might have accomplished had he been more bold at the outset of the battle instead of later and steamed into the Union fleet as it passed Fort Morgan in formation. If he had sunk the flagship then, the outcome of the action certainly would have been affected. Likewise, after the Union fleet had entered the bay, it might have been more productive for Buchanan to engage in a distant duel rather than a close-quarters brawl. The blue-water fleet could not maneuver very widely in the shallow bay because of the draft of its ships. While long-range fire would not bother the *Tennessee*, any hits scored on the wooden ships would be telling. Farragut still controlled three lethal shallow-draft ironclads, but it remained for Buchanan to test if they had the speed to trap him.

23. Although blockade duty seemed like "living death," when Lt. George Perkins found that Farragut planned to enter Mobile Bay, he gave up his passage on a steamer north to volunteer as commander of the *Chickasaw*. After the war, the old ironclad was converted to a railroad transfer, plying the waters between New Orleans and Gouldsboro, Louisiana, until 1941. Her hulk remained afloat until the end of World War II (ibid., 15, 17).

24. R. Hays and R. Farrelly Jr., *Fort Gaines Under Two Flags and the Battle of Mobile Bay* (Dauphin Island: Island Printing & Publishing, 1990), 7.

25. Bergeron, *Confederate Mobile*, 146.

26. Farragut continued to perform naval duties the remainder of the war, inactive as they were, and in 1866 became a full admiral. The next three years he was feted by admirers on both sides of the Atlantic before dying 14 August 1869 at Portsmouth Navy Yard, New Hampshire.

27. Bergeron, *Confederate Mobile*, 175.

28. After the war the *Osage* was sold along with the *Tennessee* and *Nashville* at a public auction (T. Gibbons, *Warships and Naval Battles of the Civil War* [New York: Gallery Books, 1989], 57).

29. When the Confederates abandoned Battery McIntosh, they left behind some goats, thus giving rise to the name Goat Island. Either the goats managed to get to the mainland or alligators got them.

Chapter 7 · Mississippi

1. J. R. Skates, *Mississippi* (New York: W. W. Norton & Co., 1979), 103. Given this attitude, it is not surprising Mississippi became the second state to secede, right behind South Carolina.

2. R. Beringer et al., *Why the South Lost the Civil War* (Athens: University of Georgia Press, 1986), 69.

3. "In 1860, three-fourths of all Southern families owned no slaves" (R. Sewell, *A House Divided* [Baltimore: Johns Hopkins University Press, 1988], 6).

4. Skates, *Mississippi*, 108.

5. D. Martin, *The Vicksburg Campaign* (New York: Gallery Books, 1990), 117.

6. Z. H. Burns, *Confederate Forts* (Natchez, Miss.: Southern Historical Publications, 1977), 40.

7. P. Robbins, "When the Rebels Lost Ship Island," *Civil War Times Illustrated*, January 1979, 42.

8. Ibid., 43.

9. Maj. Gen. Mansfield Lovell, commander of the troops at New Orleans, called the buildup at Ship Island "a harmless menace" (P. M. Chaitin, *The Coastal War* [Alexandria, Va.: Time-Life Books, 1984], 61).

10. R. P. Weinert, "The Neglected Key to the Gulf Coast," *Journal of Mississippi History*, November 1969, 14–15.

11. Maj. Martin L. Smith of the Confederate Corps of Engineers for one (Robbins, "When the Rebels Lost Ship Island," 44).

12. B. F. Cooling, *Forts Henry and Donelson: The Key to the Confederate Heartland* (Knoxville: University of Tennessee Press, 1987), 4.

13. It would be the United States that would "first interrupt the free navigation on the Mississippi River." On 8 May 1861, the "head of customs at Louisville, Kentucky, was ordered to prevent shipment of arms, ammunition, and provisions to the seceded states" (J. Winters, *The Civil War in Louisiana* [Baton Rouge: Louisiana State University Press, 1991], 45).

14. J. Korn, *War on the Mississippi: Grant's Vicksburg Campaign* (Alexandria, Va.: Time-Life Books, 1985), 17; Martin, *The Vicksburg Campaign*, 7, 10.

15. Korn, *War on the Mississippi*, 19.

16. "The Civil War in America," *Illustrated London News*, 19 July 1862, 84.

17. "Roll calls revealed that from 30 to 60 percent of the crews were on the sick list, while Williams' troops were reduced from 3,200 to only 800 fit for duty" (D. F. Bastian, *Opening of the Mississippi during the Civil War*, 6).

18. Gillespie, "Legendary Wake of Terror," 24. For a more detailed discussion of the battle, see W. N. Still Jr., *Iron Afloat* (Columbia: University of South Carolina Press, 1988).

19. The Navy Department may have already decided to send Farragut downriver toward the gulf.

20. U.S. Naval History Division, comp., *Civil War Naval Chronology: 1861–1865*, 6 vols. (Washington, D.C.: Government Printing Office, 1961–66), 2:83.

21. R. Huffstot, "The Brief, Glorious Career of the CSS Arkansas," *Civil War Times Illustrated*, July 1968, 27.

22. For Sherman's own discussion of the attack, see W. T. Sherman, "Vicksburg by New Years," *Civil War Times Illustrated*, January 1978, 44–48.

23. "Delegates to Visit Fort Pemberton Site," *Greenwood Commonwealth*, 21 October 1933.

24. W. M. Fowler Jr., *Under Two Flags: The American Navy in the Civil War* (New York: W. W. Norton & Co., 1990), 211.

25. For a descriptive discussion of Porter's setback, see J. Milligan, "Expedition into the Bayous," *Civil War Times Illustrated*, January 1977, 12–21.

26. D. Porter, *Naval History of the Civil War* (Secaucus, N.J.: Castle, 1984), 299.

27. Ibid.

28. Fowler, *Under Two Flags*, 217.

29. Sometimes spelled Haines's Bluff.

30. J. M. McPherson, *Battle Cry of Freedom* (New York: Oxford University Press, 1988), 647.

31. Fowler, *Under Two Flags*, 219.

32. For a discussion, see Martin, *The Vicksburg Campaign*, 147–48.

33. Porter, *Naval History of the Civil War*, 321; Navy Department, *Civil War Naval Chronology*, 3:84, 85.

34. D. F. Kemp, "Gunboat War at Vicksburg," *Civil War Chronicles*, Summer 1993, 31.

35. K. T. Urquhart, ed., *Vicksburg: Southern City under Siege* (New Orleans: Historic New Orleans Collection, 1987), 27.

36. Navy Department, *Civil War Naval Chronology*, 3:91; this account misidentifies the spot as Milliken's Bend, *Mississippi*.

37. According to S. Walesby and T. Roscoe, *Navy: History and Tradition* (Washington, D.C.: n.p., 1959), Porter had his sailors fly kites over Confederate positions in Vicksburg that dropped leaflets saying, "Think of one small biscuit." I could not find any other books that mentioned this propaganda ploy.

38. M. F. Perry, *Infernal Machines: The Story of Confederate Submarine and Mine Warfare* (Baton Rouge: Louisiana State University Press, 1985), 45.

39. M. S. Hendrix, *The Legend of Longwood* (Natchez: Maxwell Printing Corp., 1972), n.p.

40. There seems to be some question as to whether the mines that doomed the ship were electrically activated or not. While most historians suggest they were, Perry argues in his book that they were not galvanic torpedoes but were set off by fuses attached to friction primers (Perry, *Infernal Machines*, 33).

41. E. Bearss, *Hardluck Ironclad: The Sinking and Salvage of the Cairo* (Baton Rouge: Louisiana State University Press, 1980), 101.

42. Porter, *Naval History of the Civil War*, 285.

43. A natural cutoff was formed across DeSoto Peninsula in 1876, changing the course of the river and leaving Vicksburg about three miles from its banks (Bastian, *Opening of the Mississippi During the Civil War*, 8).

Chapter 8 · Tennessee

1. T. L. Connelly, *Civil War Tennessee* (Knoxville: University of Tennessee Press, 1986), 13.

2. The Virginia army at Manassas used gunpowder from the Cumberland River mills (ibid., 15).

3. R. M. McMurry, *Two Great Rebel Armies* (Chapel Hill: University of North Carolina Press, 1989), 142.

4. Connelly, *Civil War Tennessee*, 18.

5. B. F. Cooling, *Forts Henry and Donelson: The Key to the Confederate Heartland* (Knoxville: University of Tennessee Press, 1987), 13–14.

6. Ibid., xiv

7. Polk and Brig. Gen. Lloyd Tilghman were reportedly on the outskirts of Paducah on a reconnaissance mission preparatory to occupation of the city when Grant made his move (R. Dupuy and T. Dupuy, *The Compact History of the Civil War* [New York: Hawthorn Books, 1968], 62).

8. Cooling, *Forts Henry and Donelson*, 29.

9. Ibid., 42.

10. J. D. Hill, *Sea Dogs of the Sixties* (New York: A. S. Barnes & Co., 1961), 166; Dupuy, *The Compact History of the Civil War*, 64, also cites "evidence of fraud and corruption" among Frémont's subordinates.

11. The person who first proposed an attack toward Fort Henry is unclear. More than likely, a number of individuals played major or minor roles in formulating the initial concept.

12. Although Fort Heiman is positioned slightly south of Fort Henry, it is actually in Kentucky due to the way the state borders run in the twin rivers region.

13. Cooling, *Forts Henry and Donelson*, 57.

14. Connelly, *Civil War Tennessee*, 24.

15. E. Bearss, *The Fall of Fort Henry Tennessee* (Dover, Tenn.: Eastern National Park and Monument Association, 1989), 26.

16. Meeting Foote aboard his flagship, Tilghman is reported to have said, "I am glad to surrender to so gallant an officer." Foote replied, "You are perfectly right, sir, in surrendering, but you should have blown my boat out of the water before I would have surrendered, to you" (ibid., 28).

17. Cooling, *Forts Henry and Donelson*, 128–29.

18. Ibid., 128.

19. Ibid., 158.

20. Ibid., 160.

21. E. Bearss's well-researched *Unconditional Surrender: The Fall of Fort Donelson* (Dover, Tenn.: Eastern National Park and Monument Association, 1991), 35, makes no mention of any argument between Union officers at the Dover Hotel and states only that Wallace was breakfasting with his old friend Buckner when Dove arrived, asked some questions, and departed. Wallace told an aide later that he was "highly suspicious of the navy's designs . . . that the navy seemed to be . . . looking for swords."

22. Grant may have stated he would accept nothing but unconditional surrender, but Buckner did not believe he would be so unchivalrous. It turned out that Buckner was correct, at least in assuming the Union commander would eventually grant more generous terms.

23. B. Anderson, *By Sea and by River: The Naval History of the Civil War* (New York: Da Capo Press, 1989), 99.

24. Ibid., 99.

25. Cooling, *Forts Henry and Donelson*, 227.

26. E. F. Williams III, *Fustest with the Mostest* (Memphis: Historical Hiking Trails, 1973), 5.

27. W. R. Brooksher and D. K. Snider, "Devil on the River," *Civil War Times Illustrated*, August 1976, 12. The map accompanying the article incorrectly places Fort Heiman and Paris Landing south of Big Sandy River. A map in Williams, *Fustest with the Mostest*, 27, is more accurate.

28. Brooksher and Snider, "Devil on the River," 18, write that he placed the batteries "on" the island, but that would not make any sense. A map in the Navy Department's *Civil War Naval Chronology: 1861–1865*, 6 vols. (Washington, D.C.: Government Printing Office, 1961–66), 4:130, shows the Rebel guns on the west side of the river, the same side from which Forrest later attacked Johnsonville.

29. Much of the destruction was caused by Federal guards worried about the depot falling into Confederate hands. They thought Forrest may have intended to cross the river and bring away some of the supplies (Navy Department, *Civil War Naval Chronology*, 4:130).

30. Brooksher and Snider, "Devil on the River," 19.

31. E. Johnson, *A History of Henry County Tennessee* (N.p.p.: n.p., 1958), 1:85–86.

32. "The Siege of New Madrid," photocopy from New Madrid Historical Museum.

33. Anderson, *By Sea and by River*, 103.

34. "The Fight at Island Number 10," *New York Herald*, 23 March 1862, in *Civil War Front Pages*, ed. J. Wagman (New York: Fairfax Press, 1989). According to R. D. Layman, *Before the Aircraft Carrier* (Annapolis: Naval Institute Press, 1989), 116, this was a historic first-use of "Aerial guidance of naval gunfire."

35. A. T. Mahan, *The Gulf and Inland Waters* (New York: Charles Scribner's Sons, 1883), 36. Navy Department, *Civil War Naval Chronology*, 6:235, suggests the *Winchester* was scuttled to avoid capture. Its intentional sinking could have been for both reasons.

36. W. M. Fowler Jr., *Under Two Flags: The American Navy in the Civil War* (New York: W. W. Norton & Co., 1990), 173.

37. Foote expected to return after a short hiatus. That was not to be the case. After convalescing, Foote was given a desk job in Washington. In the spring of 1863, Welles asked him to take command of the squadron off Charleston, South Carolina. He never made it. On 26 June, Foote died in his room at the Astor Hotel in New York City.

38. Williams, *Confederate Victories at Fort Pillow*, 41. The *Christian Recorder*, commenting on the "sickening" massacre at Fort Pillow, placed part of the blame on the U.S. Congress: "While [legislators] have professed to regard every man wearing the U.S. uniform, as being equal in theory, they have acted towards the black soldiers, in such a way, as to convince the Confederate government that they, themselves, do not regard the black soldiers as equal to the white. The rebels have taken advantage of this equivocation, to commit just such horrible butchery as that at Fort Pillow" (J. M. McPherson, *The Negro's Civil War* [New York: Pantheon Books, 1965], 221). Whether or not the blood of Forrest's men ran particularly hot because their opponents were black, traitorous Tennesseans, bushwhackers, or all three cannot now or ever be surmised. The crux of the case in a legalistic sense depends upon whether or not the fleeing soldiers took their weapons with them. Exactly a year before the attack, in April 1863, the U.S. Army adopted an order signed by Lincoln in one of the first attempts to codify an international law of war. General Order 100 — known as the Lieber Instructions after its German-American author, Francis Lieber — stated in part that whether or not an enemy is armed is crucial in deciding whether to attack (see "Attacks on Retreating Iraqis Follow the Rules," [Minneapolis] *Star Tribune*, 27 February 1991, 14A). Forrest argued that the large number of weapons found below the bluffs proved that the retreating Federal forces had been armed. Whatever the case, the high Federal death toll tarnished a solid victory for Forrest, a judgment one can understand only if it is assumed there is some kind of underlying morality in war. As Forrest himself observed: "War means fighting and fighting means killing" (R. Mitchell, *Civil War Soldiers* [New York: Simon & Schuster, 1988], 54). Certainly Forrest's behavior after the war only added fuel to the fire of controversy. In 1867, Forrest — the former millionaire who had earned his money as a slave trader and ended the Civil War as a "beggar"—accepted the position of grand wizard in the newly reestablished Ku Klux Klan. In an interview, Forrest claimed that the Klan was "directed not so much against blacks but against carpet-baggers and scalawags." Within two years, Grand Wizard Forrest realized that his so-called honorable and patriotic organization had become intractable, and he "wanted no further part of it." In late January 1869, he issued General Order Number 1, the only directive to ever come from Imperial Headquarters, calling for the official disbandment of the Klan. At first glance, his action appears noble, but he may have done it just to "disassociate" Imperial Headquarters from responsibility for the acts of the rank and file, which were becoming more and more reprehensible (W. Wade, *The Fiery Cross: The Ku Klux Klan in America* [New York: Simon and Schuster, 1987], 40–41, 51, 59).

39. D. Martin, *The Vicksburg Campaign* (New York: Gallery Books, 1990), 147. Had Grant lost the battle, his drinking problems, which were much more than just rumors, would have undoubtedly led to his dismissal.

40. Navy Department, *Civil War Naval Chronology*, 2:45.

41. J. Fiske, *The Mississippi Valley in the Civil War* (Boston: Houghton Mifflin Co., 1900), 87.

42. Navy Department, *Civil War Naval Chronology*, 2:45.

43. William Micajah Barrow, "The Civil War Diary of William Micajah Barrow," ed. E. A. Davis. Photocopy in possession of Margaret Pullen.

44. Navy Department, *Civil War Naval Chronology*, 2:45.

45. B. Kitchens, *Gunboats and Cavalry: A History of Eastport, Mississippi* (Florence, Ala.: Thornwood Book Publishers, 1985), 89.

46. Ibid., 90.

47. Ibid.

48. R. Reed, *Combined Operations in the Civil War* (Lincoln: University of Nebraska Press, 1993), 206.

49. R. Fowler, "Capture of New Orleans," *Civil War Times*, May 1960, 5.

Chapter 9 • Louisiana

1. J. Winters, *The Civil War in Louisiana* (Baton Rouge: Louisiana State University Press, 1991), 7.

2. Ibid., 34. Perhaps as a token of appreciation, no further restrictive legislation was passed on a statewide basis against free blacks in the state during the duration of the war.

3. W. M. Fowler Jr., *Under Two Flags: The American Navy in the Civil War* (New York: W. W. Norton & Co., 1990), 57.

4. B. Anderson, *By Sea and by River: The Naval History of the Civil War* (New York: Da Capo Press, 1989), 16.

5. Fowler, *Under Two Flags,* 58.

6. In April 1862, for example, the Confederate Navy Department ordered the unfinished ironclad *Louisiana* upriver. Only the protests of the local commander kept the ship at New Orleans (Winters, *The Civil War in Louisiana,* 81). Even after Farragut brought his fleet over the bar into the Mississippi, the Southern high command discounted the threat. On 9 April, Flag Off. George Hollins, C.S.N., telegraphed Confederate Secretary of the Navy Stephen Mallory from Fort Pillow, Tennessee, for authority to bring his fleet downriver to support New Orleans. Mallory, "convinced that the serious threat to New Orleans would come from Flag Officer [Andrew Hull] Foote's force in the upper river rather than from Farragut's fleet below, denied Hollins' request" (U.S. Naval History Division, comp., *Civil War Naval Chronology: 1861–1865,* 6 vols. [Washington, D.C.: Government Printing Office, 1961–66], 2:47).

7. Forts Jackson and Saint Philip on the Mississippi River, Forts Pike and Macomb at the outlets for Lake Ponchartrain, and Fort Livingston at the mouth of Barataria Bay. A sixth position, Battery Bienvenu, guarded Saint Bernard Parish east of New Orleans. Construction began in late 1826 on an "earthen fort intended for twenty 24- and/or 32-pounders with two 13-inch mortars" (R. Roberts, *Encyclopedia of Historic Forts* [New York: MacMillan Publishing Co., 1988], 331).

8. J. Fiske, *The Mississippi Valley in the Civil War* (Boston: Houghton Mifflin Co., 1900), 114.

9. P. M. Chaitin, *The Coastal War* (Alexandria, Va.: Time-Life Books, 1984), 61.

10. J. Winters, *The Civil War in Louisiana,* 18.

11. Butler, "a scheming politician from Massachusetts," had also commanded the land force during the Hatteras Inlet expedition in August 1861. The success of the operation there, which had little to do with Butler, nonetheless made up for "a reputation that had been damaged by his recent mishandling of troops in Virginia" (Fowler, *Under Two Flags,* 61).

12. A. T. Mahan, *The Gulf and Inland Waters* (New York: Charles Scribner's Sons, 1883), 63. This was probably one of the ships stationed on the eastern bank of the river. The rest of this small group was withdrawn.

13. Ibid., 121.

14. Chaitin, *The Coastal War,* 66.

15. Fiske, *The Mississippi Valley in the Civil War,* 116.

16. Chaitin, *The Coastal War,* 67.

17. C. E. Macartney, *Mr. Lincoln's Admirals* (New York: Funk & Wagnalls, 1956), 48.

18. Mahan, *The Gulf and Inland Waters,* 79.

19. Winters, *The Civil War in Louisiana,* 84. Lovell was criticized for not withdrawing this force to the city once the fleet had bypassed it. Since the camp lacked wagons or teams, it is hard to imagine how the guns could have been saved (R. Fowler, "Capture of New Orleans," *Civil War Times,* May 1960, 7).

20. Chaitin, *The Coastal War,* 74.

21. One Confederate prisoner from the fort claimed a recruiting officer got him drunk: "that was the last he recollected for three days when he found himself in the forts" (R. Mitchell, *Civil War Soldiers* [New York: Simon & Schuster, 1988], 41).

22. Fowler, *Under Two Flags,* 127.

23. J. A. Greene, *The Defense of New Orleans, 1718–1900* (Denver: National Park Service, 1982), 258.

24. Ibid., 261.

25. Roberts, *Encyclopedia of Historic Forts,* 331.

26. A. Bergeron, "Six Original Guns Remain in Bayou Near New Orleans, La.," *The Artilleryman* (Winter 1993): 8.

27. Williams, West Point Class of 1837, had served as aide-de-camp to Gen. Winfield Scott in the Mexican War.

28. Louisiana Department of Tourism, "The Old State Capitol" (brochure) (New Orleans: Louisiana Department of Tourism, n.d.).

29. Buchanan's brother, Franklin, as commander of the CSS *Virginia* (*Merrimack*) had sunk Thomas's former ship, the USS *Congress,* at Hampton Roads the previous March.

30. On 14 February, the USS *Queen of the West,* under orders to disrupt traffic on the Red River, had grounded under the guns of a fort on the Red River fifteen miles up from the mouth of the Black River (probably Fort de Russy) and been captured after taking several hits. Exactly two months later, the reflagged ship was engaged by Federal gunboats as it came to Taylor's aid in Grand Lake and was sunk, thus ensuring that Grover's flanking operation would not be thwarted (D. Porter, *Naval History of the Civil War* [Secaucus, N.J.: Castle, 1984], 297; H. Gosnell, *Guns on the Western Waters* [Baton Rouge: Louisiana State University Press, 1993], 201–2).

31. On 4 September 1863, a Federal column under Gen. C. C. Crocker found the post evacuated (R. Roberts, *Encyclopedia of Historic Forts,* 330).

32. "In losing Brashear City we lose command of the admirable inland system of water communication that has served the Union cause so well in Louisiana. The loss of material of war in the loss of Brashear City proves to be considerable. Berwick's Bay was commanded by about twenty-five of the best cannon we had in the Southwest, all of which fell into the enemy's hands" ("Affairs in Louisiana," *New York Times,* 6 July 1863, 4).

33. Porter, *Naval History of the Civil War,* 350.

34. A. Josephy Jr., *The Civil War in the American West* (New York: Alfred A. Knopf, 1991), 176.

35. Porter, *The Naval History of the Civil War,* 263.

36. L. L. Hewitt, *Port Hudson: Confederate Bastion on the Mississippi* (Baton Rouge: Louisiana State University Press, 1987), 21.

37. Ibid., 31.

38. J. Wukovits, "Decks Covered with Blood," *America's Civil War,* March 1992, 42.

39. Hewitt, *Port Hudson,* 77.

40. After Port Hudson, however, Farragut sent the young man home to his wife: "I am too devoted a father to have my son with me in troubles of this kind. The anxieties of a father should not be added to those of a commander" (Macartney, *Mr. Lincoln's Admirals,* 61).

41. Hewitt, *Port Hudson,* 85–86. Cummings died four days later.

42. The Congressional Medal of Honor originated during the Civil War as an incentive to citizens and soldiers. The first medals were awarded 25 March 1863 to six of the men from Andrews Raiders, the group that stole the locomotive General in April 1862. A total of 1,527 medals were passed out during the Civil War, almost four times the number presented during World War II. In 1916 a board began to review medals awarded up to that point and 911 names were stricken from the list, a "majority of these were from a single Civil War regiment — the 27th Maine Volunteer Infantry — who had received the Medal as an inducement to sign up for an additional tour of duty" (D. Cooke, *For Conspicuous Gallantry . . .* [Maplewood, N.J.: C. S. Hammond & Co., 1966], 11). The board also disqualified Mary Walker, a Civil War surgeon who was the only woman ever granted the privilege. Her award was reinstated in 1977.

43. Wukovits claims in his article that it was one of the ship's own cannonballs being heated as an incendiary that slipped free from handlers and caused the fire.

44. Gardner may have believed the Federals would never attack. Lincoln's Emancipation Proclamation, which took effect at the beginning of 1863, had caused a morale problem within the Union rank and file. Federal deserters from Baton Rouge being held in Port Hudson said in March 1863 that the Union army was divided and demoralized because of "the negro question" and "that the Yankees will not fight" (R. Mitchell, *Civil War Soldiers* [New York: Simon & Schuster, 1988], 42).

45. Macartney, *Mr. Lincoln's Admirals,* 62.

46. Hewitt, *Port Hudson,* 158.

47. Ibid., 163.

48. E. Cunningham, "The Story of Port Hudson," in *Battle of Baton Rouge, 1862* (N.p.p.: Committee for the Preservation of the Port Hudson Battlefield, n.d.).

49. Banks paroled the enlisted men among his numerous prisoners but held the officers. The Confederate government ordered all enlisted men paroled at both Vicksburg and Port Hudson to report to various reorganization points by 15 September for return to active duty. The North declared this violated the rules of prisoner exchange to which both sides had earlier agreed. In any case, many of the men in Gardner's army did not show up again in formal military records (R. Miller, *The Train Robbing Bunch* [College Station, Tex.: Creative Publishing Co., 1983], 33–34).

50. Cunningham, "The Story of Port Hudson."

51. J. M. McPherson, *Battle Cry of Freedom* (New York: Oxford University Press, 1988), 638.

52. J. Minton, "Civil War Buff Wants to Spread the Word about Port Hudson," *Sunday Advocate* [Baton Rouge], 29 April 1990, 4B.

53. Interviewed by the author, Port Hudson State Commemorative Area, Zachary, La., 6 May 1990.

54. The Port Hudson Campaign Committee purchased an additional 256 acres in February 1993. To learn more about helping to preserve Port Hudson and other Civil War sites, contact: Civil War Battlefield Campaign, 1800 North Kent Street, Suite 1120, Arlington, VA 22209 (703) 525-6300.

55. Official report of Lt. Comdr. James P. Foster, U.S. Navy, to Rear Adm. David D. Porter, 23 January 1864, as cited in "'Dixie' Brethren Decorate Yankee Grave in Louisiana," *The Royal Arch Mason,* June 1949.

56. A. Josephy Jr., *The Civil War in the American West,* 196.

57. Some Civil War-era maps indicate a road running along the Red River all the way to Shreveport, e.g., a map of the Red River campaign prepared in 1864, shown in Johnson, "The Red River Campaign," 164–65. Other maps of the period do not. It is difficult to imagine that Banks would want to leave his naval escort if he had a choice. Josephy, *The Civil War in the American West,* 198, suggests

that Banks simply did not do an adequate job of scouting and never learned of the alternate route along the Red River. Banks may also have left the river to gather more cotton without naval interference.

58. J. C. Williams, "A Rebel Remembers the Red River Campaign," *Civil War Times Illustrated,* January 1979, 28.

59. Navy Department, *Civil War Naval Chronology,* 4:41.

60. The boat lost was the *Eastport*. It had been captured from Confederate forces in February 1862 after Union gunboats pounded Fort Henry on the Tennessee River into submission. No one on the warship even knew it had struck a mine until water was discovered in the hold. Other vessels brought extra pumps, but the falling river threatened any attempts to save the gunboat. On 26 April 1864 the ironclad was set afire to prevent capture (T. Gibbons, *Warships and Naval Battles of the Civil War* [New York: Gallery Books, 1989], 14).

61. E. G. Longacre, "Rescue on Red River," *Civil War Times Illustrated,* October 1975, 8.

62. Ibid., 9.

63. R. Gragg, *Civil War Quiz and Fact Book* (New York: Harper & Row, 1985), 136.

64. Williams, "A Rebel Remembers the Red River Campaign," 29.

65. Gragg, *Civil War Quiz and Fact Book,* 143.

Chapter 10 • Arkansas

1. W. M. Fowler Jr., *Under Two Flags: The American Navy in the Civil War* (New York: W. W. Norton & Co., 1990), 185. Porter suggests that the death toll was so high because Confederates fired at Union sailors who had jumped overboard to avoid being scalded to death (D. Porter, *The Naval History of the Civil War* [Secaucus, N.J.: Castle Books, 1984], 173–74).

2. Fowler, *Under Two Flags,* 184–85.

3. H. S. Ashmore, *Arkansas: A History* (New York: W. W. Norton & Co., 1978), 83.

4. Porter, *Naval History of the Civil War,* 293.

5. Also known as Post of Arkansas.

6. R. Coleman, *The Arkansas Post Story* (Sante Fe, N.M.: Southwest Cultural Resources Center, 1987), 107.

7. One case in point: Col. Robert R. Garland and his troops from Camp McCulloch near Victoria, Texas, had just received their regimental flag from the ladies of Victoria when it was captured during the battle (C. D. Spurlin, "Camp Henry E. McCulloch," *The Handbook of Victoria County,* 14).

8. Porter, *Naval History of the Civil War,* 293.

9. U.S. Naval History Division, comp., *Civil War Naval Chronology: 1861–1865,* 6 vols. (Washington, D.C.: Government Printing Office, 1961–66), 3:8.

10. Coleman, *Arkansas Post Story,* 116.

11. Porter calls it Duvall's Bluff.

12. Named after Maj. Gen. Samuel A. Curtis, U.S.A., the victor at Pea Ridge.

13. B. F. Cooling, *Forts Henry and Donelson: The Key to the Confederate Heartland* (Knoxville: University of Tennessee Press, 1987), 23.

14. E. T. Crisler Jr., *The Battle of Helena* (Phillips County Historical Society, 1983), 21.

15. S. R. Davis, "Death Takes No Holiday," *America's Civil War,* May 1993, 74.

16. A. Castel, "Theophilus Holmes — Pallbearer of the Confederacy," *Civil War Times Illustrated,* July 1977, 16.

17. Batteries A and B have recently been placed in the National Register of Historic Places. Batteries C and D were already in the register.

18. H. Ashmore, *Arkansas: A History* (New York: W. W. Norton & Co., 1978), 84–85.

19. Cleburne was one of the South's most gifted yet controversial general officers. He became the first major figure to propose recruiting slaves for the Confederacy. In fact, by the end of 1863 he suggested emancipating all slaves as an incentive. He even persuaded other officers to sign a petition advocating his plan. The authorities in the Army of Tennessee and at Richmond "suppressed the petition and ordered Cleburne's silence" (R. Mitchell, *Civil War Soldiers* [New York: Simon & Schuster, 1988], 191).

Chapter 11 • Texas

1. T. R. Fehrenbach, *Lone Star* (New York: Collier, 1968), 329.

2. For a discussion of Northerners' perceptions of the Southern aristocracy's supposed role in the war, see R. Mitchell, *Civil War Soldiers* (New York: Simon & Schuster, 1988), 32–33.

3. A. Josephy Jr., *The Civil War in the American West* (New York: Alfred A. Knopf, 1991), 28.

4. The Menger Hotel in San Antonio, the oldest continually operating major hotel in the United States, claims Robert E. Lee as one of its patrons. Since it was built in 1859 and attracted many important guests, Lee may have gone there in 1861, but since the site of the meeting was on the Main Plaza and the Menger fronts Alamo Plaza, it was probably not the site of this particular meeting.

5. Fehrenbach, *Lone Star,* 377.

6. N. C. Delaney, "Corpus Christi — The Vicksburg of Texas," *Civil War Times Illustrated,* July 1977, 6.

7. Captured 13 May 1862 at Bayou Bonfouca, Louisiana (U.S. Naval History Division, comp., *Civil War Naval Chronology: 1861–1865,* 6 vols. [Washington, D.C.: Government Printing Office, 1961–66], 2:63).

8. Delaney, "Corpus Christi," 44.

9. Ibid., 46.

10. The Union troops landed on the south end of the island and marched toward the small Confederate fort on the north end guarding Aransas Pass. The USS *Monongahela* stood in close to shore and fired five rounds at the lighthouse, then switched attention to the fort. After fifteen rounds, a white flag went up as eighty-nine Rebels surrendered (F. R. Holland Jr., *The Aransas Pass Light Station: A History* [Corpus Christi: n.p., 1976], 47).

11. W. M. Fowler Jr., *Under Two Flags: The American Navy in the Civil War* (New York: W. W. Norton & Co., 1990), 98. Gary Cartwright points out in *Galveston* (New York: Atheneum, 1991), 100, that — according to a log kept by a twenty-four-hour watch on top of the Hendley Building — the first shots exchanged in Galveston occurred on 6 August between the USS *Dent* and the south battery at the foot of Twentieth Street. Two days later the south battery opened on the USS *South Carolina.* Once the firing started, "Men, women, and children ran to the beach, too excited to consider the danger."

12. Navy Department, *Civil War Naval Chronology,* 2:101.

13. Josephy, *The Civil War in the American West,* 165.

14. Grandfather of the commander of Corregidor in World War II of the same name.

15. K. Burns, *The Civil War* (Beverly Hills: Pacific Arts Video Publishing, 1990); Cartwright, *Galveston,* 106. Robert Morris Franklin, an eyewitness to the events of 1 January 1863, delivered a speech on the battle that was subsequently published. It lists under "killed" a Lt. Comdr. Edward Lee, but a publisher's notation states that the correct spelling is Lea (R. M. Franklin, *Battle of Galveston* [Galveston: San Luis Press, 1975], 11).

16. H. C. Westwood, "The Battle of Galveston," *Proceedings,* January 1983, 56.

17. Josephy, *The Civil War in the American West,* 167.

18. Wilson, as a subordinate commander, was exonerated two months later. Law was suspended for three years but was back on duty before the end of the war, reaching a captaincy in 1877.

19. Westwood, "The Battle of Galveston," 56.

20. A. T. Mahan, *The Gulf and Inland Waters* (New York: Charles Scribner's Sons, 1883), 185.

21. Navy Department, *Civil War Naval Chronology,* 3:156.

22. Early in the war, many Union regulars on frontier garrison duty had marched to Indianola where they waited for ships to carry them north. Col. Earl Van Dorn, in command of the Department of Texas, seized the Union vessel *Star of the West* at Indianola on 19 April 1861 and arrested several hundred Federal soldiers. Earlier that year in January, the *Star* had been fired upon as it attempted to relieve Fort Sumter. On 4 May, the *Star* was commissioned as a receiving ship of the Confederate navy at New Orleans (Navy Department, *Civil War Naval Chronology,* 1:12).

23. According to W. G. McAlexander, chairman of the Brazoria County Historical Committee, the "actual line of defense in case of attack by Banks was to be the San Bernard River, which is west of the Brazos. There were camps of cavalry, infantry, and artillery stretched from the coast on up into Wharton County. It was from these camps that John Magruder launched his successful attack to recapture Galveston. The Brazos was protected by Fort Quintana and Fort Velasco at the mouth of the river. Upstream was the Brazos Dam Battery . . . built by slaves in 1862. It is interesting to note that part of the cannons captured at Sabine Pass were moved and used at Fort Velasco" (McAlexander to Page, 20 January 1991).

24. Navy Department, *Civil War Naval Chronology,* 3:168

25. Ibid., 5:100.

26. Ibid., 5:111.

27. H. M. Hart, *Old Forts of the Southwest* (New York: Bonanza Books, 1964), 37.

28. Ibid.

29. J. M. McPherson, *Battle Cry of Freedom* (New York: Oxford University Press, 1988), 371.

30. W. T. Block, "The Civil War Comes to Jefferson County Texas," *Blue & Gray Magazine,* September 1986, 14. Taylor's family remained in Texas throughout the war and one of his sons served in the Confederate army.

31. Ibid., 18.

32. E. Niderost, "Personality," *America's Civil War*, May 1988, 62.

33. Niderost, "Personality," 66.

34. Fehrenbach, *Lone Star*, 370.

35. Navy Department, *Civil War Naval Chronology*, 4:57.

36. The thriving antebellum community of Sabine City, or simply Sabine, has disappeared. The current town of Sabine Pass stands near the same location.

37. F. Holland Jr., *Great American Lighthouses* (Washington, D.C.: Preservation Press, 1989), 207.

Epilogue

1. A. Jones, *Civil War Command and Strategy* (New York: Free Press, 1992), 9–10.

2. R. Beringer et al., *Why the South Lost the Civil War* (Athens: University of Georgia Press, 1986), 63.

3. A. Bergeron Jr., *Confederate Mobile* (Jackson: University Press of Mississippi, 1991), 151.

4. Jones, *Civil War Command and Strategy*, 140.

5. Beringer, *Why the South Lost the Civil War*, 192.

6. Ibid., 152.

7. Ibid., 198.

8. Ibid., 64.

9. W. T. Adams, "The Ship-Shore Duel," in *Civil War Ordnance — I* (Washington, D.C.: American Ordnance Association, 1960–61), 20.

10. J. Hayes, "Fleet against Fort" in *Civil War Ordnance — I* (Washington, D.C.: American Ordnance Association, 1960–61), 28.

WORKS CITED

Amadon, George F. *Rise of the Ironclads*. Missoula, Mont.: Pictorial Histories Publishing Co., 1988.

Ammen, Daniel. *The Atlantic Coast*. New York: Jack Brussel, n.d.

Anderson, Bern. *By Sea and by River: The Naval History of the Civil War*. New York: Da Capo Press, 1989.

Anthis, Judith, and Richard M. McMurry. "The Confederate Balloon Corps." *Blue & Gray Magazine*, August 1991, 20–24.

Ashmore, Harry S. *Arkansas: A History*. New York: W. W. Norton & Co., 1978.

Barrett, John Gilchrist. *North Carolina As a Civil War Battleground: 1861–1865*. Raleigh: North Carolina Department of Cultural Resources, 1987.

Bastian, David F. *Opening of the Mississippi During the Civil War*. N.p.p.: n.p., n.d.

Bearss, Edwin C. *The Fall of Fort Henry Tennessee*. Dover, Tenn.: Eastern National Park and Monument Association, 1989.

———. *Hardluck Ironclad: The Sinking and Salvage of the Cairo*. Baton Rouge: Louisiana State University Press, 1980.

Bennett, Keith W. "Gun Platforms at Sea." *Military History*, August 1992, 26–32.

Bergeron, Arthur W., Jr. *Confederate Mobile*. Jackson: University Press of Mississippi, 1991.

———. "Six Original Guns Remain in Bayou Near New Orleans, La." *The Artilleryman* (Winter 1993): 8.

Beringer, Richard et al. *Why the South Lost the Civil War*. Athens: University of Georgia Press, 1986.

Block, W. T. "The Civil War Comes to Jefferson County Texas." *Blue & Gray Magazine*, September 1986, 10–18.

Bowen, John. *Battlefields of the Civil War*. Secaucus, N.J.: Chartwell Books, 1986.

Branch, Paul, Jr. *The Siege of Fort Macon*. Morehead City, N.C.: Herald Printing Co., 1988.

Burns, Zed H. *Confederate Forts*. Natchez, Miss.: Southern Historical Publications, 1977.

Burton, E. Milby. *The Siege of Charleston, 1861–1865*. Columbia: University of South Carolina Press, 1987.

Cartwright, Gary. *Galveston*. New York: Atheneum, 1991.

The Casemate Museum. *Fort Monroe in the Civil War*. Tales of Old Fort Monroe, no. 6. Fort Monroe, Va.: The Casemate Museum, 1970.

———. *Is It a Fort or a Fortress?"* Tales of Old Fort Monroe, no. 5. Fort Monroe, Va.: The Casemate Museum, 1970.

Castel, Albert. "Theophilus Holmes — Pallbearer of the Confederacy." *Civil War Times Illustrated*, July 1977, 10–17.

Catton, Bruce. "Glory Road Began in the West." *Civil War Times*, July 1960, 4–5ff.

Chaitin, Peter M. *The Coastal War*. Alexandria, Va.: Time-Life Books, 1984.

Coleman, James C., and Irene S. Coleman. *Guardians on the Gulf: Pensacola Fortifications, 1698–1980.* Pensacola: Pensacola Historical Society, 1982.

Coleman, Roger E. *The Arkansas Post Story.* Sante Fe, N.M.: Southwest Cultural Resources Center, 1987.

Collins, Bruce. *The Origins of America's Civil War.* New York: Holmes & Meier, 1981.

Connelly, Thomas L. *Civil War Tennessee.* Knoxville: University of Tennessee Press, 1984.

Connor, Michael. "A Forgotten Fort at the End of Nowhere." *New York Times,* 20 November 1988, 16.

Cooke, Donald E. *For Conspicuous Gallantry.* Maplewood, N.J.: C. S. Hammond & Co., 1964.

Cooling, Benjamin Franklin. *Forts Henry and Donelson: The Key to the Confederate Heartland.* Knoxville: University of Tennessee Press, 1987.

———. "Forts Henry and Donelson: Union Victory on the Twin Rivers." *Blue & Gray Magazine,* February 1992, 10–20ff.

Coulter, Ellis Merton. *Wormsloe: Two Centuries of a Georgia Family.* Athens: University of Georgia Press, 1955.

Coski, John M. *The Army of the Potomac at Berkeley Plantation.* N.p.p.: n.p., 1989.

Cox, Christopher. *A Key West Companion.* New York: St. Martin's Press, 1983.

Crisler, E. T., Jr. *Battle of Helena.* N.p.p.: Phillips County Historical Society, 1983.

Cromie, Alice. *A Tour Guide to the Civil War.* 4th ed. Nashville: Rutledge Hill Press, 1993.

Cunningham, Edward. *Battle of Baton Rouge, 1862.* N.p.p.: Committee for Preservation of the Port Hudson Battlefield, n.d.

Davis, D. Douglass et al. *Fort Barrancas 1875.* Pensacola: Pensacola Historical Society, 1988.

Davis, Steven R. "Death Takes No Holiday." *America's Civil War,* May 1993, 22–28ff.

Davis, William C. *Battle at Bull Run.* Baton Rouge: Louisiana State University Press, 1977.

———. *Duel Between the First Ironclads.* Baton Rouge: Louisiana State University Press, 1975.

Degler, Carl N. "There Was Another South." In *The Civil War.* Edited by Stephen W. Sears. New York: American Heritage Press, 1991.

Delaney, Norman C. "Corpus Christi — The Vicksburg of Texas." *Civil War Times Illustrated,* July 1977, 4–9ff.

Derr, Mark. *Some Kind of Paradise.* New York: William Morrow and Co., 1989.

Dobbs, John F. *From Bunker Hill to Manila Bay.* New York: n.p., 1906.

Donald, David, ed. *Why the North Won the Civil War.* Baton Rouge: Louisiana State University Press, 1969.

Dupuy, R. Ernest, and Trevor N. Dupuy. *The Compact History of the Civil War.* New York: Hawthorn Books, 1968.

Durham, Roger S. "Savannah: Mr. Lincoln's Christmas Present." *Blue & Gray Magazine,* February 1991, 8–18ff.

Durrill, Wayne K. *War of Another Kind: A Southern Community in the Great Rebellion.* New York: Oxford University Press, 1990.

Emerson, Bill. "CSS Atlanta." *Scale Ship Modeler,* October 1991, 38–44.

Fehrenbach, T. R. *Lone Star.* New York: Collier Books, 1968.

Feuer, A. B. "The 'Circle of Fire' at Port Royal." *Civil War* 16 (February 1989): 25–32.

Fiske, John. *The Mississippi Valley in the Civil War.* Boston: Houghton Mifflin Co., 1900.

Fowler, Robert H. "Capture of New Orleans." *Civil War Times,* May 1960, 4–7.

Fowler, William M., Jr. *Under Two Flags: The American Navy in the Civil War.* New York: W. W. Norton & Co., 1990.

Freehling, William W. *Prelude to the Civil War.* New York: Harper & Row, 1968.

Fretwell, J., ed. *Civil War Times in St. Augustine.* Saint Augustine: Saint Augustine Historical Society, 1986.

Gerrell, Allen. "The History of the Fort at St. Marks, Florida, during the Civil War." Unpublished paper.

Gibbons, Tony. *Warships and Naval Battles of the Civil War.* New York: Gallery Books, 1989.

Gillmore, Quincy A. *The Siege and Reduction of Fort Pulaski.* Gettysburg, Pa.: Thomas Publications, 1988.

Gosnell, H. Allen. *Guns on the Western Waters: The Story of River Gunboats in the Civil War.* Baton Rouge: Louisiana State University Press, 1993.

Gragg, Rod. *Civil War Quiz and Fact Book.* New York: Harper & Row, 1985.

———. *The Illustrated Confederate Reader.* New York: Harper Perennial, 1991.

Gray, Colin. *The Leverage of Sea Power.* New York: Free Press, 1992.

Greene, Jerome A. *The Defense of New Orleans, 1718–1900.* Denver: National Park Service, 1982.

Hagan, Kenneth J. *This People's Navy: The Making of American Sea Power.* New York: Free Press, 1991.

Hart, B. H. Liddell. *Strategy.* New York: Frederick A. Praeger, 1964.

Harris, Shawn Curtis. "Lion's Tail Touched." *Great Battles,* July 1992, 50–56.

Hays, Robert D., and Richard L. Farrelly, Jr. *Fort Gaines under Two Flags and the Battle of Mobile Bay.* Dauphin Island: Islander Printing & Publishing, 1990.

Hewitt, Lawrence Lee. *Port Hudson: Confederate Bastion on the Mississippi.* Baton Rouge: Louisiana University Press, 1987.

Hill, Forest G. *Roads, Rails and Waterways.* Norman: University of Oklahoma Press, 1957.

Hill, Jim Dan. *Sea Dogs of the Sixties.* New York: A. S. Barnes & Co., 1961.

Holland, F. R., Jr. *The Aransas Pass Light Station: A History.* Corpus Christi, 1976.

Huffstot, Robert S. "The Brief, Glorious Career of the CSS Arkansas." *Civil War Times Illustrated,* July 1968, 20–27.

Hunsaker, Trevor Jay. "Cannon Manned by Rival Nations." *Military History,* August 1988, 50–53.

Johnson, E. McLeod. *A History of Henry County Tennessee.* Vol. 1. N.p.p.: n.p., 1958.

Jones, Archer. *Civil War Command and Strategy: The Process of Victory and Defeat.* New York: Free Press, 1992.

Josephy, Alvin M., Jr. *The Civil War in the American West.* New York: Alfred A. Knopf, 1991.

Kantor, MacKinlay. *If the South Had Won the Civil War.* New York: Bantam Books, 1965.

Keith, Willis J. "Fort Johnson." *Civil War Times Illustrated,* November 1975, 32–39.

Kemp, Daniel F. "Gunboat War at Vicksburg." *Civil War Chronicles,* Summer 1993, 26–32.

Kennedy, Frances H., ed. *The Civil War Battlefield Guide.* Boston: Houghton Mifflin Co., 1990.

Kitchens, Ben Earl. *Gunboats and Cavalry: A History of Eastport, Mississippi.* Florence, Ala.: Thornwood Book Publishers, 1985.

Korn, Jerry. *War on the Mississippi: Grant's Vicksburg Campaign.* Alexandria, Va.: Time-Life Books, 1985.

Lamb, William. "The Confederates Repulse an Attack on Fort Fisher." In *The Blue and the Gray.* Edited by Henry Steele Commanger. Indianapolis: Bobbs-Merrill Co., 1950.

Lattimore, Ralston B. *Fort Pulaski.* Washington, D.C.: National Park Service, 1954.

Layman, R. D. *Before the Aircraft Carrier.* Annapolis: Naval Institute Press, 1989.

Lewis, Emanuel Raymond. *Seacoast Fortifications of the United States.* Annapolis, Md.: Leeward Publications, 1979.

Longacre, Edward G. "Rescue on the Red River." *Civil War Times Illustrated,* October 1975, 4–9ff.

Lord, Francis A. "The 'Swamp Angel.'" *Civil War Times Illustrated,* December 1962, 36–37.

Macartney, Clarence Edward. *Mr. Lincoln's Admirals.* New York: Funk & Wagnalls Co., 1965.

Mahan, Alfred Thayer. *Admiral Farragut.* New York: Haskell House, 1968.

———. *The Gulf and Inland Waters.* New York: Charles Scribner's Sons, 1883.

Mann, Robert W. "War on Yellow Bluff." Unpublished paper.

Martin, David. *The Vicksburg Campaign.* New York: Gallery Books, 1990.

McGinty, Brian. "Robert Anderson: Reluctant Hero." *Civil War Times Illustrated,* May–June 1992, 44–47ff.

McMurry, Richard M. "The Presidents' [sic] Tenth and the Battle of Olustee." *Civil War Times Illustrated*, January 1978, 12–24.

———. *Two Great Rebel Armies*. Chapel Hill: University of North Carolina Press, 1989.

McPherson, James M. *Battle Cry of Freedom*. New York: Oxford University Press, 1988.

———. *The Negro's Civil War*. New York: Pantheon Books, 1965.

Merrill, James. *Du Pont: The Making of an Admiral*. New York: Dodd, Mead & Co., 1986.

———. *The Rebel Shore*. Boston: Little, Brown and Co., 1957.

Miers, Earl S. *The Web of Victory: Grant at Vicksburg*. Baton Rouge: Louisiana State University Press, 1984.

Miles, Jim. *To the Sea*. Nashville: Rutledge Hill Press, 1989.

Milligan, John. "Expedition into the Bayous." *Civil War Times Illustrated*, January 1977, 12–21.

———. *Gunboats Down the Mississippi*. Annapolis: United States Naval Institute, 1965.

Mitchell, John A. "Convincing Test for Rifled Cannon." *Military History*, June 1987, 12–16.

Mitchell, Reid. *Civil War Soldiers*. New York: Simon & Schuster, 1988.

Monaghan, Jay. *Civil War on the Western Border, 1854–1865*. Lincoln: University of Nebraska Press, 1984.

Montgomery, Bernard. *A History of Warfare*. New York: World Publishing Co., 1968.

Muir, Thomas, Jr., and David P. Ogden. *The Fort Pickens Story*. Pensacola: Pensacola Historical Society, 1989.

Musicant, Ivan. "The Fires of Norfolk." *American Heritage*, March 1990, 56–65.

Nash, Howard P., Jr. "Ironclads at Charleston." *Civil War Times*, January 1960, 1ff.

———. *A Naval History of the Civil War*. New York: A. S. Barnes and Co., 1972.

Niderost, Eric. "Personality," *America's Civil War*, May 1988, 8ff.

Perry, Milton F. *Infernal Machines: The Story of Confederate Submarine and Mine Warfare*. Baton Rouge: Louisiana State University Press, 1985.

Piston, William Garrett. *Lee's Tarnished Lieutenant*. Athens: University of Georgia Press, 1987.

Pohanka, Brian C. "Carnival of Death." *America's Civil War*, September 1991, 30–36.

Porter, David D. *Naval History of the Civil War*. Secaucus, N.J.: Castle, 1984.

Proctor, Samuel. "Saltmaking Along Florida's Gulf Coast: Profitable but Vulnerable CW Business." *Civil War Times Illustrated*, November 1962, 46–48.

Quarles, Benjamin. *The Negro in the Civil War*. New York: Da Capo Press, 1989.

Raphael, Morris. *The Battle of Bayou Country*. Detroit: Harlo Press, 1984.

Reed, Rowena. *Combined Operations in the Civil War*. Lincoln: University of Nebraska Press, 1993.

Ripley, Warren. *The Battery*. Charleston: Post-Courier Booklet, 1989.

Robbins, Peggy. "When the Rebels Lost Ship Island." *Civil War Times Illustrated*, January 1979, 4–9ff.

Roberts, Robert B. *Encyclopedia of Historic Forts*. New York: Macmillan, 1988.

Robertson, James I., Jr. *Civil War Sites in Virginia*. Charlottesville: University Press of Virginia, 1991.

Robinson, Willard B. *American Forts: Architectural Form and Function*. Urbana: University of Illinois Press, 1977.

Rogers, George, C., Jr. *The History of Georgetown County, South Carolina*. Spartanburg, S.C.: Reprint Co., 1990.

Rose, Willie Lee. *Rehearsal for Reconstruction: The Port Royal Experiment*. New York: Vintage Books, 1964.

Rouse, Parke, Jr. *Endless Harbor: The Story of Newport News*. Newport News: n.p., 1969.

Sauers, Richard A. "Laurels for Burnside." *Blue & Gray Magazine*, May 1988, 8–20ff.

Savas, Theodore P. "Last Clash of the Ironclads: The Bungled Affair at Trent's Reach." *Civil War* 16:15–22.

Sears, Stephen W. *George B. McClellan: The Young Napoleon*. New York: Ticknor & Fields, 1988.

Selfridge, Thomas O., Jr. *What Finer Tradition*. Columbia: University of South Carolina Press, 1987.

Sewell, Richard H. *A House Divided.* Baltimore: Johns Hopkins University Press, 1988.

Shier, Maynard J. "Hatteras Inlet: The First Revenge." *Civil War Times Illustrated,* November 1978, 4–11ff.

Shiman, Philip. *Fort Branch and the Defense of the Roanoke Valley, 1862–1865.* N.p.p.: Fort Branch Battlefield Commission, 1990.

Shingleton, Royce. *John Taylor Wood: Sea Ghost of the Confederacy.* Athens: University of Georgia Press, 1979.

———. "Raider's Blow Stinging." *America's Civil War,* April 1990, 38–44.

Skates, John Ray. *Mississippi.* New York: W. W. Norton & Co., 1979.

Spedale, William A. *Battle of Baton Rouge: 1862.* Baton Rouge: Land and Land Publishing Division, 1985.

Stern, Philip van Doren. *The Confederate Navy: A Pictorial History.* New York: Da Capo Press, 1992.

Still, William N. "Confederate Behemoth: The CSS *Louisiana.*" *Civil War Times Illustrated,* November 1977, 20–25.

———. *Iron Afloat: The Story of the Confederate Armorclads.* Columbia: University of South Carolina Press, 1985.

———. "Porter . . . Is the Best Man." *Civil War Times Illustrated,* May 1977, 4–9ff.

———. *Savannah Squadron.* Savannah: Coastal Heritage Press, 1989.

———. "Technology Afloat." *Civil War Times Illustrated,* November 1975, 4–9ff.

Suhr, Robert Collins. "Street Fight in Baton Rouge." *America's Civil War,* November 1990, 42–48.

Sutcliffe, Sheila. *Martello Towers.* Cranbury, N.J.: Fairleigh Dickinson University Press, 1973.

Swanberg, W. A. *First Blood.* New York: Charles Scribner's Sons, 1957.

Swanson, Betsy. *Historic Jefferson Parish.* Gretna, La.: Pelican Publishing Co., 1975.

Tapert, Annette, ed. *The Brothers' War.* New York: Vintage Books, 1989.

Thomas, Emory. "'Damn the Torpedoes . . .': The Battle for Mobile Bay." *Civil War Times Illustrated,* April 1977, 4–10ff.

———. "The Lost Confederates of Roanoke." *Civil War Times Illustrated,* May 1976, 10–17.

———. *Travels to the Hallowed Ground.* Columbia: University of South Carolina Press, 1987.

Tower, Howard B., Jr. "Salvaging the 'Boston.'" *Sea Classics,* July 1985, 58–61.

Trotter, William R. *Ironclads and Columbiads.* Winston-Salem: John F. Blair, 1989.

Trudeau, Noah Andre. "Fields Without Honor: Two Affairs in Tennessee." *Civil War Times Illustrated,* July–August 1992, 42–49ff.

Turner, Henry M. "Rocked in the Cradle of Consternation." *Civil War Chronicles,* Spring 1993, 24–35.

Urquhart, Kenneth Trist, ed. *Vicksburg: Southern City Under Siege.* New Orleans: Historic New Orleans Collection, 1987.

U.S. Department of the Interior, National Park Service. *Fort Sumter: Anvil of War.* Washington, D.C.: Government Printing Office, 1984.

U.S. Naval History Division, comp. *Civil War Naval Chronology: 1861–1865.* 6 vols. Washington, D.C.: Government Printing Office, 1961–66.

Vanderbloom, Gretchen. *Texas Parks Guide.* N.p.p.: Affordable Adventures, 1988.

Van der Veer Hamilton, Virginia. *Alabama.* New York: W. W. Norton & Co., 1977.

Wade, Wyn Craig. *The Fiery Cross: The Ku Klux Klan in America.* New York: Simon and Schuster, 1987.

Wagman, John, ed. *Civil War Front Pages.* New York: Fairfax Press, 1989.

Walesby, Stokes, and Theodore Roscoe. *Navy: History and Tradition.* Washington, D.C.: n.p., 1959.

Ward, James Robertson. *Old Hickory's Town: An Illustrated History of Jacksonville.* Jacksonville: Florida Publishing Co., 1982.

Watson, Robert. "Yankees Were Landing below Us." *Civil War Times Illustrated,* April 1976, 12–21.

Weatherford, Jack. *Indian Givers.* New York: Crown Publishers, 1988.

Wegner, Dana M. "The Black Leech of Mobile." *Sea Classics,* January 1971, 12–17ff.

———. "The Port Royal Working Parties." *Civil War Times Illustrated,* December 1976, 22–31.

Weinert, Richard P. "The Neglected Key to the Gulf Coast." *Journal of Mississippi History,* November 1969, 14–15.

Westwood, Howard C. "The Battle of Galveston." *Proceedings,* January 1983, 49–56.

Westwood, John. *Railways at War.* San Diego: Howell-North Books, 1981.

Wilcox, Arthur M., and Warren Ripley. *The Civil War at Charleston.* Charleston: Post-Courier Booklet, 1989.

Williams, Edward F., III. *Confederate Victories at Fort Pillow.* Memphis: Nathan Bedford Forrest Trail Committee, 1984.

———. *Fustest with the Mostest.* Memphis: Historical Hiking Trails, 1973.

Williams, John Calvin. "A Rebel Remembers the Red River Campaign." *Civil War Times Illustrated,* January 1979, 20–31.

Wilson, John. "Commands." *America's Civil War,* May 1988, 12–16.

Winters, John. *The Civil War in Louisiana.* Baton Rouge: Louisiana State University Press, 1991.

Wise, Stephen R. *Lifeline of the Confederacy: Blockade Running during the Civil War.* Columbia: University of South Carolina Press, 1988.

Wright, Louis B. *South Carolina.* New York: W. W. Norton & Co., 1976.

Wukovits, John F. "Decks Covered with Blood." *America's Civil War,* March 1992, 41–45.

INDEX